T0267392

PROGRAMMABLE
LOGIC CONTROLLERS

PROGRAMMABLE LOGIC CONTROLLERS
A PRACTICAL APPROACH TO IEC 61131-3 USING CODESYS

Dag H. Hanssen
Institute of Engineering and Safety, University of Tromsø, Norway

Translated by
Dan Lufkin

This edition first published 2015
© 2015 John Wiley & Sons, Ltd

Registered Office
John Wiley & Sons, Ltd, The Atrium, Southern Gate, Chichester, West Sussex, PO19 8SQ, United Kingdom

For details of our global editorial offices, for customer services and for information about how to apply for permission to reuse the copyright material in this book please see our website at www.wiley.com.

The right of the author to be identified as the author of this work has been asserted in accordance with the Copyright, Designs and Patents Act 1988.

Wiley also publishes its books in a variety of electronic formats. Some content that appears in print may not be available in electronic books.

Designations used by companies to distinguish their products are often claimed as trademarks. All brand names and product names used in this book are trade names, service marks, trademarks or registered trademarks of their respective owners. The publisher is not associated with any product or vendor mentioned in this book.

Limit of Liability/Disclaimer of Warranty: While the publisher and author have used their best efforts in preparing this book, they make no representations or warranties with respect to the accuracy or completeness of the contents of this book and specifically disclaim any implied warranties of merchantability or fitness for a particular purpose. It is sold on the understanding that the publisher is not engaged in rendering professional services and neither the publisher nor the author shall be liable for damages arising herefrom. If professional advice or other expert assistance is required, the services of a competent professional should be sought.

Authorised Translation from the Norwegian language edition published by Akademika forlag, Programmerbare Logiske Styringer – basert på IEC 61131-3, 4. Utgave. This translation has been published with the financial support of NORLA.

Library of Congress Cataloging-in-Publication Data

Hanssen, Dag Håkon, author.
    Programmable Logic Controllers: A Practical Approach to IEC 61131-3 using CODESYS / Dag Hakon Hanssen.
        pages cm
    Includes bibliographical references and index.
    ISBN 978-1-118-94924-5 (pbk.)
1. Sequence controllers, Programmable.   2. Programmable logic devices.   I. Title.
    TJ223.P76H36 2015
    621.39′5–dc23
                                                          2015018742

A catalogue record for this book is available from the British Library.

Set in 10/12pt Times by SPi Global, Pondicherry, India

1   2015

Contents

Programmable Logic Controllers
A Practical Approach to IEC 61131-3 Using CODESYS

First edition

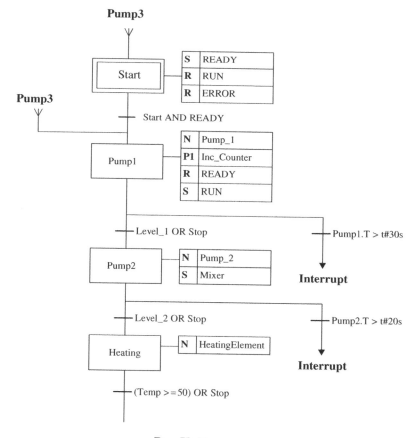

Dag H. Hanssen

Preface

As long as there have been competing producers of PLCs on the market, there have been different programming languages from one PLC brand to another. Even though the same languages, beginning with Instruction Lists (IL) and Ladder diagram (LD), have been used by most of the producers, all of them added their own "dialects" to the languages. When physical programming terminals replaced software-based programming tools, the differences between languages of the various producers escalated. Several programming languages also saw the light of day. This development was the natural result of the attempt by the producers to make themselves stand out among increasing competition by developing the most user-friendly languages and tools.

When the IEC[1] 61131-3 standard came out in 1993, the situation started to improve. This standard was the result of the work that had been ongoing for several years in which the best from the various languages and dialects from different producers was assembled into a single document. This is not a rigid standard in the sense that the producers *must* follow all requirements and specifications, but more a set of guidelines that the producers could choose to follow to a certain extent. Today, most of the equipment producers have come to realize the advantages of organizing themselves in accordance with the standard. All of the major producers of PLCs, such as Telemecanique, Wago, Mitsubishi, Klockner Moeller, Allen-Bradley, Omron, Siemens, and so on, have therefore, to a greater or lesser extent, adapted their programming tools to IEC 61131-3.

This book covers close to 100% of the specifications and guidelines that are given in Standard (International Electrotechnical Commission, 2013).[2] The book will therefore be interested to everyone who works with, or wants to learn about programming PLCs, no matter which PLC brand they use.

---

[1] IEC—International Electrotechnical Commission. This edition of the book was updated in conformity with the 3rd edition of IEC 61131-3, issued February 2013.
[2] The Standard IEC 61131-3 is introduced in Chapter 5.

The book does not assume any previous knowledge of programming.
Comments and suggestions for contents will be gratefully received.
The book is divided into five main parts:

- Part 1: Hardware   Chapters 1–3
- Part 2: Methodic   Chapter 4
- Part 3: IEC 61131-3   Chapters 5–8
- Part 4: Programming   Chapters 9–13
- Part 5: Implementation   Chapters 14–15

Chapter 1 contains a brief history and a short description of the design and operation of PLCs in general. Chapters 2 and 3 give a basic introduction to digital and analog signals and equipment for detection, measurement, and manipulation of discrete and continuous quantities.

Chapter 4 focuses on methods for planning and design of structurally efficient programs. It also provides an introduction into Boolean algebra. Chapters 5 and 6 introduce the IEC standard elements such as literals, keywords, data types, variables, and addressing. Chapters 7 and 8 cover standardized functions and functional blocks.

Chapters 9 to 13 deal with programming: Chapter 9 covers programming with LD. Chapter 10 covers functional block diagrams (FBD). Chapter 11 covers the structured text (ST) language. The last language covered in the book is actually not a programming language as such, but rather a tool for structuring program code. This is called a Sequential Function Chart (SFC) and is described in Chapter 12.

Chapter 13 contains some larger practical programming examples.

The last two chapters in the book cover programming tools. Here, I have chosen to focus on CODESYS. There are several reasons for this; first, CODESYS follows the standard almost 100%. Furthermore, CODESYS is a hardware-independent programming tool that is currently used by well over 250 hardware suppliers. Finally yet importantly, the program can be downloaded free and it contains a simulator. Most of the program code in the book was written and tested with this tool.

I would like to thank the following persons and companies:

- Associate Professor Tormod Drengstig, University of Stavanger, for much good feedback, suggestions for improvements, and the contribution of several examples
- Assistant Professor Inge Vivås, Bergen University College, for giving his permission to reuse some problems (Section 4.6.4 and Problems 4.10 and 10.5)
- Assistant Professor Veslemøy Tyssø, Oslo and Akershus University College of Applied Science, for having read an earlier edition of the book and having provided expert contributions
- Colleagues and management at the University of Tromsø, Department of Engineering and Safety, for the support and patience
- Schneider Electric for granting me permission to use material from their "Automation Solution Guide" when writing about sensors in Chapter 2

Dag H. Hanssen

Part One

Hardware

1

About PLCs

The programmable logic controller (PLC) has its origin in relay-based control systems, also called hard-wired logic.[1]

Before PLCs became common in industry, all automatic control was handled by circuits composed of relays,[2] switches, clocks and counters, etc (Figure 1.1). Such controls required a lot of wiring and usually filled large cabinets full of electromagnetic relays. Electricians had to assemble controls or use a prepared relay wiring diagram. The relay wiring diagrams showed how all the switches, sensors, motors, valves, relays, etc. were connected. Such relay wiring diagrams are the forerunners for the ladder diagram (LD) programming language, which is still a common programming language used in programming PLCs.

There were many disadvantages with these mechanical controls. In addition to taking up a lot of room, they demand time and labor to implement them and to make any changes in such equipment. A relay control usually consists of hundreds of relays connected together with wires running in every direction. If the logical function needs to be changed or expanded, the entire physical unit must be rewired, something that is obviously expensive in terms of working time. Since the relays are electromechanical devices, they also had a limited service life, something that led to frequent operational interruptions with subsequent disruption.

There also was no way of testing before the control was wired up. Testing therefore had to take place by running the unit. If there was a small failure in the schematic diagram or if an electrician had connected a wire wrong, this could result in dramatic events.

---

[1] Originally, the designation PC—Programmable Controller—was used. This naturally caused some confusion when Personal Computer became a well-known concept.
[2] A relay is an electromechanical component that functions like an electrical switch. A weak current (so-called control current) activates the switch so that a stronger current can be switched on or off.

Programmable Logic Controllers: A Practical Approach to IEC 61131-3 Using CODESYS, First Edition. Dag H. Hanssen.
© 2015 John Wiley & Sons, Ltd. Published 2015 by John Wiley & Sons, Ltd.

Figure 1.1   Example of a relay and a timer (mounted on a connector board)

1.1   History

The first PLC came into commercial production when General Motors was looking for a replacement for relay controls. Increased competition and expanded demands on the part of customers meant a demand for higher efficiency, and the natural step was to design a software-based system that could replace the relays. The requirement was that the new system should be able to:

- Compete on price with traditional relay controls
- Be flexible
- Withstand a harsh environment
- Be modular with respect to the number of inputs and outputs[3]
- Be easy to program and reprogram

Several corporations started work on providing a solution to the problem. Bedford Associates, Inc. from Bedford, Massachusetts, suggested something they called a "modular digital controller" (MODICON). MODICON 084[4] was the first PLC that went into commercial production. The key to its success was probably the programming language, LD, which was based on the relay diagrams that electricians were familiar with. Today there is no question about the use of programmable controls; the question is rather what type to use.

The first PLCs were relatively simple in the sense that their function was to replace relay logic and nothing else. Gradually, the capabilities improved more and more and functions such as counters and time delays were added. The next step in development was analog input/output and arithmetic functions such as comparators and adders.

With the development of semiconductor technology and integrated circuits, programmable controls became widely used in industry. Particularly when microprocessors came on the market in the beginning of the 1970s, development proceeded at a rapid pace.

---

[3] This means that it must be possible to increase the number of inputs and outputs by inserting extra modules/boards/blocks. In order to offer cheaper hardware, there are also many PLCs that are not modular.

[4] 084 indicates that it was the 84th project for the company. After that, the corporation established a new company, (MODICON), which focused on producing PLCs.

The PLCs of today come with development tools in the form of software with every imaginable ready-to-use function. Examples are program codes for managing communications as well as processing functions such as proportional integrator/derivative regulators, servo controls, axial control, etc. In other words, there is the same pace of development as with the PC (Figures 1.2, 1.3, and 1.4).

The communications side also experienced rapid development. Demand grew quickly for PLCs that could talk to one another and that could be placed away from the actual production lines. Around 1973 Modicon developed a communications protocol that they called Modbus. This made it possible to set up communications between PLCs, and the PLCs could therefore be located away from production. Modicon's Modbus also provided for management of analog signals. As there became more and more manufacturers of PLCs and

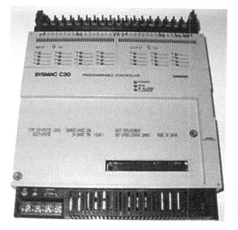

Figure 1.2   Omron Sysmac C20—Nonmodular PLC with digital I/O and programming terminal

Figure 1.3   PLCs from Telemecanique come in different sizes

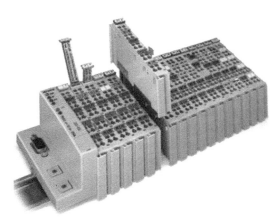

Figure 1.4   Newer generation PLC from Wago with Profibus coupler and I/O

associated equipment, there also developed more proprietary[5] and nonproprietary communications protocols. The lack of standardization, together with continual technological
development, meant that PLC communication became a nightmare of incompatible protocols and various physical networks. Even today, there are problems, although manufacturers
now offer solutions for communications over a selection of known and standardized
protocols.

Several programming languages also came into use. Earlier LD, as we mentioned, was
synonymous with PLC programming. *Instruction List* (IL) was also an early language that had
many similarities with the assembly language that used for programming microprocessors.
Later the graphical language *Sequential Function Chart* (SFC) was added. This was specially
developed for implementation of sequential controls.

1.1.1   More Recent Developments

All of the aforementioned languages were incorporated into the international standard
IEC 61131-3 (International Electrotechnical Commission, 2013). The standard also
defines the *function block diagram* (FBD) graphic language and the *structured text* (ST)
language. FBD has a symbol palette that is based on recognized symbols and functions
from digital technology. ST is a high-level language that provides associations with Pascal
and C.

Before the IEC 61131-3 standard appeared, and for many years thereafter, there were
relatively large differences between PLCs from various manufacturers. This was particularly
true of capabilities for selection of programming language and how the language that was
implemented in the PLCs was designed. Recently, to the delight of users, manufacturers began

---

[5] A proprietary protocol is owned by the manufacturer who developed it. The source code is not freely accessible.
A non-proprietary protocol is either a standard protocol or an open protocol that is distributed by many manufacturers
who make equipment for communication over such a protocol.

to follow IEC 61131-3 to a greater and greater extent. This made it easier to go from one brand of PLC to another as well as making it easier, to a certain extent, for customers to know what they were getting.

There are also a number of "software-based PLCs" on the market. As the name indicates, this software is designed to control processes directly from a PC. The challenge has been to build systems that are sufficiently reliable and robust. Industry is generally critical of such solutions, mostly based on experience with many a computer crash.

Another amphibious solution is the possibility of buying a circuit board for a computer onto which the program code can be loaded. The board is made so that it is capable of carrying on with the job independently even if the computer should crash.

In recent years, manufacturers have devoted considerable resources to developing solutions for connecting instruments and actuators into a network. Such a communication bus is called a *fieldbus*, referring to the fact that there is communication between field instruments, in other words, instruments below the process level. Other standards and *de facto*[6] standards are also on the market.

Work on an IEC standard for the fieldbus started as early as 1984/1985. The requirement was naturally that the standard should be an open fieldbus solution for industrial automation. It should include units such as motor controls, decentralized I/O, and PLCs, in addition to the distributed control systems (DCS) and field instruments used in the processing industry. The goal was also that the standard should cover all pertinent areas such as building automation, process automation, and general industrial automation.

It was not until the end of 1999 that those involved came to an agreement. The result was that a total of eight (partially dissimilar) systems were incorporated into a standard called *IEC 61158*. In other words, this was not an open solution. Even though manufacturers and suppliers argued that it was good for users to have plenty of choices, this unity did not make things much easier for engineers and others working on automation.

Several of the major manufacturers currently offer integrated solutions with I/O modules for all of the major fieldbus standards where a controller (PLC) or a gateway manages communication among the various standards simultaneously.

Another trend is that manufacturers of hardware and communication solutions offer more equipment for wireless communication (Ethernet). What is new here is that these also include individual sensors and individual instruments. In this way, it is possible to implement wireless systems right out to the sensor level.

1.2 Structure

As we said, there are a great many types of PLCs on the market. Hundreds of suppliers include PLCs of various sizes in their stock. The smallest PLCs have relatively small memory capacity and calculating capability and usually limited or no capability for expansion of the number of I/Os. The largest have processor power equivalent to powerful computers,

---

[6] *De facto* is a Latin expression that means "actually" or "in reality." De facto is the opposite of *de jure,* which means "according to law." If something is *de facto,* it means something that is generally recognized. A de facto standard is thus a standard that is so widely used that that everyone follows it as though it were an authorized standard. (*Source:* Wikipedia.)

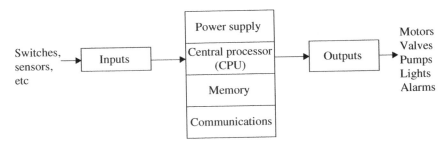

Figure 1.5   Block schematic representation of a PLC

have a large number of I/Os, and handle multitasking.[7] Such PLCs usually have a supervisory function (master) in an industrial data network where smaller PLC types can be incorporated as slaves.

If we make a simplification, we can say that a PLC functions in the same way that a computer does. Schematically, we can break a PLC down into six major units as shown in Figure 1.5.

The main parts thus consist of a central processing unit (CPU), memory, power supply, circuit modules to receive and transmit data (I/O units), and communications modules. We can perhaps also add displays/indicator lights since most of the PLCs incorporate LEDs that indicate the state of the PLC and/or the digital I/Os. Some also have displays that can furnish other information. In order for us to understand how a PLC operates and functions, it is necessary to look a little closer at the main components.

The main units are connected together with wires or copper strips called buses. All communications between the main parts of the PLC take place via these buses. A bus is a collection of a number of wires, for instance, eight, where information is transferred in binary form (one bit per wire in parallel). Typically, a PLC will have four buses: address bus, data bus, control bus, and system bus:

1. The data bus is used for transfer of data between the CPU, memory, and I/O.
2. The address bus is used to transfer the memory addresses from which data will be fetched or to which data will be sent. An address can indicate, for instance, a location down to a word in a particular register. A 16-line address bus can thus transfer $2^{16} = 65\,536$ different addresses.
3. The control bus is used for synchronizing and controlling traffic circuits.
4. The system bus is used for I/O communication.

Central Processing Unit
This is the brain of the PLC. Here are performed all of the instructions and calculations, and it controls the flow of information and how the program operates. Normally the CPU is a part of the physical block and contains the memory, communications ports, status indicator lights, and sometimes the power supply.

---

[7] Can run several parallel program sessions simultaneously.

Memory

The size of the memory varies from one brand of PLC to another, but the memory can often be expanded by installing an extra memory card, for instance an SD card. A PLC will commonly have the following memory units:

- Read-only memory (ROM) for permanent storage of operating system and system data. Since the information stored in a ROM cannot be deleted, an erasable programmable ROM (EPROM) is used for this purpose. In this way, it is possible to update a PLC operating system.
- Random access memory (RAM) for storage of programs. This is because a RAM is very fast. Since the information in a RAM cannot be maintained without current, PLCs have a battery so that the program code will not be lost in the event of a power failure. Some PLCs also have the capability of program storage in an EPROM. RAMs are also used when the program code is running. This is used, for instance, for I/O values and the states of timers and counters.
- Some PLCs offer the capability of inserting extra memory.

Figure 1.6 shows a typical memory board for a PLC that has an EPROM for a backup copy of the program.

Communications Unit

This unit incorporates one or more protocols for handling communications. All PLCs have a connection for a programming cable and often for an operator panel, printer, or network. Various physical standards are used, for both the programming port and for the ports for connections to other equipment. Current PLCs are usually programmed from an ordinary PC with a programming tool developed for that particular type of PLC.

It is not always necessary to have a direct connection between the PLC and the PC in order to transfer the program code to the PLC. However, it is currently the most common approach—at least for smaller systems. Sometimes, the programming can be performed via a network consisting of several PLCs and other equipment or via Ethernet. Some PLCs also have a built-in web server.

The development of instrumentation buses has enabled PLC manufacturers to supply built-in, or modular, solutions for communications via a large number of various protocols. Examples of such are the AS-i bus, PROFIBUS, Modbus, and CANbus.

ROM	Operating system
	Data
Built-in RAM	Program
	Constants
FLASH EPROM	User program backup

Figure 1.6 Typical memory board

Current developments are toward expanded use of Ethernet as a protocol for high-speed communications. Most manufacturers are offering solutions for this.

Power Supply

All PLCs must be connected to a power supply. Usually the power supply is an interchangeable module, but some smaller PLCs have the power supply as an integrated part of the processor and communications module. Even though the electronics in the PLC operate at 5 V, it is impractical to use this as an operating voltage. Most manufacturers therefore provide power supplies in several versions: 220 V AC, 120 V AC, and 24 V DC. If there is no access to power-line voltage, a variant with 24 V DC can be the solution. Usually there is access to 24 V out in the facility since this voltage level is standard for most sensors and transmitters. The advantage of being able to use a power supply that connects to the power line is that there is often a 24 V output on the unit that can be used for powering sensors.

It is practical to have the power supply as a replaceable module. Then the PLC can be used in other physical locations in processing where there is not access to the same voltage level.

1.2.1   Inputs and Outputs

This is the contact between a PLC and the outside world. In a modular PLC, all inputs and outputs take place in blocks or modules that are designed to receive various types of signals and to transmit signals in various formats. There are input blocks for digital signals, analog signals, thermal elements and thermocouples, encoders, etc. There are also output blocks for digital and analog signals as well as blocks for special purposes.

Every input and output has a unique address that can be utilized in the program code. The I/O modules take care of electric isolation to protect the PLC and often have built-in functions for signal processing. This means that input and output signals can be connected directly without needing to use any extra electronic circuitry.

Chapter 2 deals with digital signals, sensors, and actuators, in Chapter 3 the theme is analog signals, and standard signal formats. On the next few pages, there follows only a general introduction to the inputs and outputs of a PLC.

Figure 1.7 on the next page shows a sketch of a process section that is controlled by a PLC. Various signal cables are drawn in the figure for the sake of illustration.

The process is equipped with three pressure transmitters and one flow transmitter. These constitute the input signals to the PLC in the figure.

Based on these measurements, among others, the PLC is programmed to control two pumps. The signals to the pumps thus constitute the output signals from the PLC.

The figure also shows an example of how a PLC rack can be assembled. From left to right, we see the following:

- The controller itself (CPU, memory, status lights, etc.) with built-in Ethernet (the unit in this case also has a built-in web server).
- A power supply (can supply sensors and other small equipment).
- I/O-modules (digital outputs, tele-modules, analog inputs and outputs).
- End modules that terminate the internal communications bus.

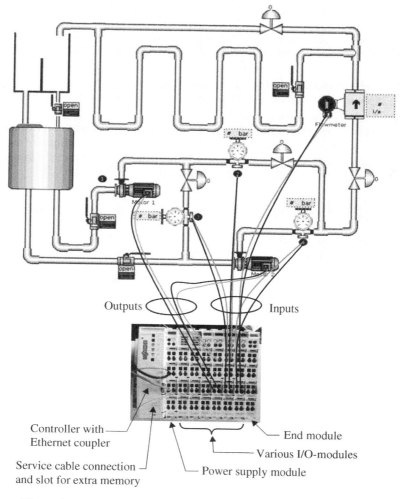

Outputs   Inputs

Controller with —————
Ethernet coupler   ———— End module

Service cable connection ┘   ———— Various I/O-modules
and slot for extra memory   ———— Power supply module

Figure 1.7   Illustration of a process section that is controlled by a PLC

1.2.1.1   Inputs

Digital input signals generally have a potential of 24 V DC, while the internal voltage in the
PLC is 5 V. In order to protect the electronics in the PLC, the input modules generally use
optical couplers (optical isolators). An optical coupler consists primarily of a light-emitting
diode (LED) and a phototransistor.[8] Figure 1.8 illustrates the principle.

The diode and the transistor are electronically separated, but light can pass between them.
When the signal at the input clamping circuit is logically high, the LED will emit an (infrared)

---

[8] A phototransistor is a type of bipolar transistor with transparent encapsulation. When the base–collector junction is
sufficiently illuminated, the junction is biased and the transistor becomes conductive.

light. This light then triggers the transistor and results in a logically high signal in the electronic circuits in the module, where the potential is 5V.

The gap between the LED and the phototransistor separates the external circuit from the internal electronics in the module. The internal electronics are thereby protected so that even though the PLC operates at 5V internally, it is possible to use voltage levels at the input from 5 up to 230V.

How much current an individual input can handle depends upon the engineering specifications of the input module in question. However, it is seldom that this is significant because most sensors have a low operating current.

Analog signals are fed into a PLC via analog-to-digital (A/D) converters. Converters are built into the analog input modules/cards. An analog signal is thus continually sampled and converted into binary values. Although in principle this requires only 1 bit for a low state input, often 16 bits are used to store values to an analog input.

1.2.1.2 Outputs

Standard digital output modules are often found in three different main types:

1. Relay outputs
2. Transistor outputs
3. Triac outputs

Relay Outputs
This type of output has the advantage that it can handle heavy loads and can be connected to both DC and AC loads at different voltages. When the CPU sets an output logically high, the associated output relay in the module in question closes and the external circuit to which the load is connected is completed (see Figure 1.9). The relay makes it possible for weak currents in the

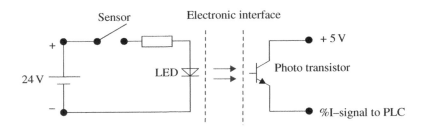

Figure 1.8   Principle of an optical coupler

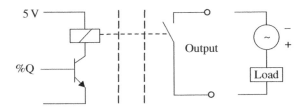

Figure 1.9   Principle of a relay output

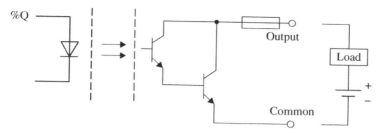

Figure 1.10 Principle of a transistor output

PLC to activate loads in which currents up to several Amperes can pass. In addition, the relay provides isolation between the PLC and external circuits.

Transistor Outputs

Compared to transistor outputs, relay outputs are relatively slow. Another advantage that makes transistor outputs popular is that they are cheaper than relay output modules. As the name indicates, such modules use transistors to complete the external circuits. It is this electronic switching that makes such modules significantly faster than relay modules, which switch with mechanical relays.[9] The disadvantage of transistor outputs is that, unless one uses an additional external relay, they can only be used for switching DC. They also cannot handle wrong polarity and are particularly sensitive to overload. Fuses with built-in electronics are therefore used in order to protect these outputs. Optical couplers are also used for electrical isolation (see Figure 1.10).

The operation of the circuit in the figure is as follows: When the output address is set logically high by the program, the phototransistor conducts. This triggers the next transistor and this completes the external circuit. Series connection of transistors (often called *Darlington* circuits) is used to increase the current capacity of the output stage.

You can read more about relay and transistor outputs in Section 2.7.3.

Triac Outputs

Triac outputs are not very common. They are used in situations that require fast switching of AC. Such outputs are also extremely sensitive to overcurrent and are protected with fuses.

1.3   PLC Operation

As discussed earlier, a PLC operates, in principle, in the same way as a PC. This means that a PLC must be programmed in order for it to perform its tasks. For a PLC, this usually means controlling and monitoring a *process*. This somewhat diffuse concept is used as a generalized word to describe a limited physical environment:

- A process can for instance be a room in a building with heating ovens, light, and ventilation. Then it can be the task of the PLC to control physical quantities such as temperature, CO_2 content, and humidity in the space.

---

[9] So-called solid-state relays are now available which switch electronically. I do not know to what extent these will be adopted by manufacturers in production of output modules with relay outputs.

- A process can also consist of a conveyor belt with goods, sensors, pneumatic pistons, and a labeling machine. The task of a PLC would then typically be to control labeling of goods, count goods, sort them, and group them.

The word *state* is often used to describe the various operating modes of a process. What states a process has depends on the nature of the process (process type). A process can have, for instance, the following states: *Fill tank—agitate—heat—Drain*.

The word *state* can also be used more specifically, for instance, for a temperature that has reached a certain value.

It is also the nature of the process that dictates what sensors and actuators are needed. Physical quantities that must be sensed can be distance, proximity, level, pressure, temperature, flow, velocity, rpm, etc. When the sensors that sense the physical quantities are connected to a PLC input module, the PLC has all of the information that is required in order to control and monitor the process. What is missing then are *actuators* and a *user program*.

- The function of actuators is to operate upon and change the states of the process. The type of process therefore determines what activators are required. These can be pumps, valves, switches, or motors.
- The user program employs available information from sensors, internally stored data, and the state of outputs to make decisions and calculate new output signals to the actuators.

Software
In almost all cases, there exist dedicated data tools for development of programs. Users can sit in the office and work on program code until they are sure that it is going to function in the PLC. Many of these programming tools have built-in functions for error detection and simulation, something that makes the job significantly simpler. When the user has finished programming, the PLC can be connected to the PC via a dedicated programming cable, and the program can be transferred from the PC to the PLC. When this has been done, the PC can be disconnected and the PLC is ready to perform its control tasks.

1.3.1   Process Knowledge

Before a PLC can be programmed, it is necessary to have good knowledge about the process (the part of the facility) that the PLC is going to control. Good understanding of the process is important in order to obtain good results, and sometimes it is necessary in order to get the control to function at all. This can be a time-consuming part of the job and often implies access to the understanding that operating personnel are familiar with. Remember that no one knows a process better than the people do whose daily job it is to make it work. Having said this, remember that operating personnel often have strong opinions about the process and how it should function and be controlled and that this is not necessarily the optimum way of doing things. It can be difficult to think in a new direction and to see other possibilities when things have been done in the same way for a long time.

Try to obtain available documentation such as engineering data, wiring diagrams, reporting forms, troubleshooting guides, maintenance SOPs, and the like.

I/O-Lists

An I/O-list is a basic part of choosing the correct PLC and the right accessories. The I/O list must therefore contain an overview of all of the required input and output signals. It is natural to group these by type, such as digital and analog. The analog can be further grouped according to standard signal formats, such as 4–20 mA, 0–10 V, type of temperature sensor, etc. Sometimes, the special signal formats impose extra requirements on hardware.

The digital signals can also be grouped. For instance, there are counter inputs and integral counter modules that measure pulses with higher frequencies than a normal digital input can tackle. An example of such a rapidly changing signal is a signal from an *encoder*,[10] which is a type of equipment that can be used for counting rpm and positional control.

Should the input blocks be of the *sink* or *source*[11] type? The type of actuator affects the selection of the proper type of output blocks: Should you use relay outputs or transistor outputs? How should the various actuators be supplied?

In addition to the flow of the process, desired performance and requirement for sensors, actuators, and I/O modules, it is also necessary to evaluate other aspects in and around the operation:

• Safety of personnel
• Any danger of fire or explosion
• Provision of alarms

Safety

This is a comprehensive theme that I am only going to touch on here. There are naturally laws and regulations concerning safety and I merely refer to those. At a minimum, you can try to describe what should happen in the event of a power failure, communications breakdown, activation of stops and emergency stops, etc.

Safety for humans and animals is something that must be taken <u>extremely</u> seriously. For instance, if a person is caught in a drive mechanism, then the actuator in question must be deactivated and an alarm sounded, at a minimum. In a power failure, you must decide whether the control should start again from where it stopped when the power failure happened, or whether it should be started anew. The same is true of a communications breakdown. There should be built-in monitoring of communications between the PLC and the HMI/SCADA[12]/operator panel so that the control is not cut off from manual override.

Almost all process facilities will also have one or more emergency stops, motor monitors, and the like. How to handle such events must also be described for later programming.

This also applies to switching over between automatic and manual control in a regulator, even though this is not so critical. This is often a natural portion of the process control.

---

[10] See Section 2.4.5.
[11] See Section 2.5.1 on page 48.
[12] Human–Machine Interface/Supervisory Control And Data Acquisition.

Provision of Alarms

Even though it is important to provide alarms in order to indicate when something has happened, it often turns out that an operator is drowning in alarms. Make a careful evaluation of which signals need to be specially monitored, what breakdowns must be handled by the PLC, and what the human–machine interface should handle, for instance.

The provision of alarms and safety will be significant considerations in how the program is organized (split up and grouped into critical and less-critical sections of programming).

Programming Situations

In order to simplify the programming, even at this stage it can be useful to formulate something about the flow in the process. It is easy to identify the flow when processes proceed from one state to the next in a particular order (e.g., filling—heating—agitating—draining).

Sometimes, several things happen simultaneously, or in parallel, and sometimes manual activities or process-controlled events decide what should be the next step in the sequence. It is often good to describe these sequences in words and/or by the use of a flow chart, state diagram, or the like. Which signals and events affect the transition from one step to the next in sequence? How should the various steps be performed? Which actuators should be activated and when should they be activated?

Sometimes, the process to be controlled is of such a nature that the transition from one state to another does not follow a predetermined pattern, but rather proceeds in a more random pattern. Such systems are referred to as *combinatoric* (despite the fact that the output states may well be a function of time as well). For such systems, it may be advantageous to use a slightly different procedure to develop the algorithms for control. There are methods that can be used to determine these algorithms in a systematic way and one of these will be described in Chapter 4.

1.3.2   Standard Operations

A process is in continual change. Even though the process has approached a stationary state, for instance, the fluid level in the tank has reached 80%, there will be disturbances in the form of pressure-drop in tubing, changed withdrawal of fluid and the like, that require that the PLC continually monitor the state of the input signals and correct the output signals. All PLCs in normal operation[13] therefore perform the same four operations[14] in a repeating cycle (Figure 1.11):

1. Internal processing
2. Read inputs
3. Program execution
4. Update outputs

---

[13] By this we mean a PLC that is in RUN mode. Other typical modes are *programming, stop, error,* and *diagnostic* (troubleshooting).

[14] This is a somewhat broad-brush treatment since the CPU is performing minor operations in addition to those mentioned. For instance, the CPU checks to what extent any of the inputs or outputs are forced to particular states by the user (the programmer). In addition, communications tasks are performed as mentioned under *Internal processing*.

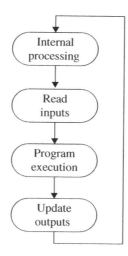

Figure 1.11   Operations that are performed in RUN mode

Internal Processing

A PLC always checks its own state before it performs user-related operations. If a response from hardware such as I/O or communications modules is lacking, the PLC gives notice of this by setting one or more *flags*. A flag is an internal Boolean address that can be checked by the user and/or an associated display or indicator light that gives a notification to the operator of an error state. For serious errors, normal operation is interrupted and the system goes over into an error state. Errors on individual inputs and individual outputs are also reported by setting flags. An example is when a system measures 0 current at an input configured for standard 4–20 mA signal or when an output is overloaded.

Software-related events that are performed in the internal operation are updating clocks, changing modes between run, stop, and program and setting *watchdog*[15] times to zero, among others.

Read Inputs

In this operation, input status is copied over to memory. How long this takes depends on the number of input modules and the number of inputs at each module that is in use. Analog inputs take significantly longer to read since this involves digitization of the analog values. In order not to reduce the update frequency of outputs, the PLC does not wait for new values to be available, but rather continues with the next operation in the cycle. This means that even though the physical values change continually, the same measured value can be used many times before an updated value is accessible in the memory.

Why copy the values to memory instead of reading the values where they are used in the program code? There are two reasons for this. First, it is quicker to read in all the values in the

---

[15] These are timers that the system uses to prevent the performance of an operation lasting longer than a determined maximum time. If the system is not ready to execute the user program within a half second, for instance, it may be that the program does not come out of a while-loop or the like. This results in an error state.

same operation. More importantly, this avoids possible problems when the same input address is used at several places in the program code. If the state of the input changes during the course of program execution, this can have serious consequences for the result of the program. A minor disadvantage of having the input values read simultaneously is that the system overlooks input pulses of a duration shorter than the total scan time (cycle time). See Section 1.3.2.

Program Execution

Execution of the program code takes place primarily in the order in which the code is written by the user. Smaller programs can be written in a coherent block of code, but larger programs require a different structuring of the code. The IEC 61131-3 standard defines guidelines for assignment of *priority*. Interruption routines and supervisory routines are assigned a higher priority than the main program. Activation of emergency stops is a common event that should cause interruption in the execution of the main program. Other reasons for changing the sequence of execution are conditional jumps or calls of subroutines, functions, and function blocks.

During the course of program execution, internal variables and output addresses are updated in the memory. The physical change in output values, however, is not changed until the final operation.

Update Outputs

In this last operation in the cycle, the output memory is read so that the state and values of the digital and analog outputs are updated. Later on in the book, we will see that the fact that the outputs are not updated until after the program code has been executed can be significant for how the program code is designed.

Note that a PLC in stop mode continues to perform in internal processing and read the inputs. The outputs are either set to a user-defined state/value (fallback) or maintained in their final state.

1.3.3   Cyclic, Freewheeling, or Event-Controlled Execution

The four operations described earlier are repeated continually, as discussed. Each cycle of operations is called a *scan,* and the time it takes the system to perform a scan is called the *scan time* or the *cycle time*. This is proportional to the size of the program, memory capacity, and type of processor. Usually this amounts to milliseconds and the cycle is repeated several times per second.

The effective scan time can vary from one scan to the next. In a scan, a new event may have suddenly appeared, one that activates a different part of the program code. In most types of PLCs, however, it is possible to configure where and how often a new scan is performed. Control of the manner in which the program is executed is achieved by associating the program to a *task.*[16] The three common modes in which a task is executed are as follows:

1. Cyclic
2. Freewheeling
3. Event-controlled

---

[16] The concept of *task* will be further described in Section 5.3.

Cyclic execution is based on having a fixed interval between the start of each scan. This interval must naturally be set long enough so that the execution of a single scan does not exceed the interval time. Such a control of execution speed can conveniently be used in the program code for counting and timing, for instance. A program block that includes a regulator is an example of code that should (must) be executed at fixed intervals.

With *freewheeling* execution, a new scan begins as soon as the previous one has completed. Because the code can contain many event-controlled events, the scan time can vary somewhat from one scan to the next. This is the fastest way of running a program.

Event-controlled execution is based on having the task (with associated program) be executed only if a (Boolean) condition is fulfilled. This can be useful in a program that normally is not to be performed and that is to be triggered by a particular event. An example of such a program could be emergency stop routines, startup routines and other extraordinary events.

One can also control how often the CPU scans a particular program unit by assigning a *priority* to the task(s). Tasks with higher priority will be monitored and scanned more often. Such tasks will typically contain important program units that manage critical events such as emergency stops or alarms.

Such control of executing and prioritizing program code makes it possible to build up multiapplications and/or a hierarchic structure of program units.

1.4   Test Problems

Problem 1.1
(a) What type of control was replaced by the PLC?
(b) What advantages are achieved by the use of a PLC?
(c) Name some differences between a newer PLC and the PLC from the 1970s.
(d) Most PLCs have a battery. Why do you think they have one?
(e) What is a CPU?
(f) Select a random PLC from a randomly selected manufacturer and do an Internet search for the various modules for the PLC. Make a list of at least 15 different modules that can be installed in the rack for the selected PLC.

Problem 1.2
(a) Name some advantages and disadvantages of transistor outputs and relay outputs.
(b) What is the purpose of an optical coupler and what two basic components does it contain?
(c) List the operations that a PLC performs during the course of a scan.
(d) What is the reason that a PLC checks the status of all inputs before each scan before the program code is executed and not during execution?
(e) What are cyclic execution and freewheeling execution?

2

Digital Signals and Digital Inputs and Outputs

Chapter Contents

- Switches:
  Buttons, limit switches, safety devices, magnetic switches
- Detectors—Logical sensors:
  Inductive sensors, capacitive sensors, photocells, ultrasound sensors, rotation sensors (encoders) RFID
- Connecting logical sensors:
  Two- and three-wire sensors, various sensor outputs, positive and negative logic (sink and source, NPN, and PNP), standard input types
- Digital outputs and actuators:
  Relays, contactors, solenoids, magnetic valves, connectors

2.1 Introduction

This chapter begins with an orientation on logical input and output equipment such as various sensors and transmitters and actuators. There is a huge number of available input and output devices on the market. Only a number of classic devices will be presented here. We therefore advise the reader to investigate what possibilities are on the market in order to choose equipment that is best suited to the task at hand.

The chapter also discusses connecting (discrete) input and output equipment to a programmable logic controller (PLC).

A digital (or logical) sensor usually comes equipped with a transmitter with standard 24 V output and is therefore well adapted to PLCs. What is most important about connections is polarity and common reference potential.

Programmable Logic Controllers: A Practical Approach to IEC 61131-3 Using CODESYS, First Edition. Dag H. Hanssen.
© 2015 John Wiley & Sons, Ltd. Published 2015 by John Wiley & Sons, Ltd.

In order for a PLC to be able to read the values at the inputs and transmit values at the outputs, the PLC must be *configured*. This is done with the aid of a software tool that is associated with the PLC type in question. Configuration of PLC blocks and modules is not the theme of this chapter, but we will review some properties that are typical for digital input and output modules.

There are also many input and output devices that are designed for connection to various fieldbuses, Ethernet, and other more specialized communications protocols. Physical principles and areas of application are nevertheless the same.

2.2 Terminology

Here we will attempt to define a number of concepts that are essential in our discussion of signals and sensors. In an academic context, it is important to utilize a terminology that is unambiguous and which preferably originates from concise definitions. However, this is not always the most reasonable approach in a practical context. Here one must keep in mind the goal of the usage of the terminology. In most situations, it is more important to be able to understand and make oneself understood than to use concepts that are perhaps more correct. The terminology that is presented here is therefore a mixture of definitions and "*de facto* concepts" (concepts that are widely used among manufacturers, suppliers and users, but which are not standardized).

Here we shall study the concepts of *discrete, digital, logical, binary, Boolean, sensor, transducers,* and *transmitter.*

2.2.1 Discrete, Digital, Logical, and Binary

There are signals all around us in one form or another. We can divide signals into two general classes: namely *continuous* (analog) and *discrete*.

A discrete signal is a signal that is defined only at particular moments in time.

Typically, such a signal originates from sampling of an analog signal. A discrete signal will then consist of a sequence of quantities called *samples* that are uniformly separated in time (see Figure 2.1). We call the separation in time between each sample the sampling period, and the inverse of this is the sampling frequency.

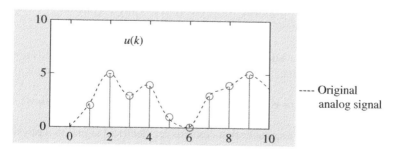

Figure 2.1 Illustration of a discrete signal

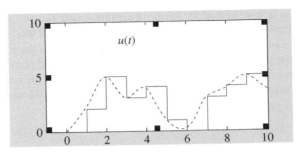

Figure 2.2   Digital signal

A digital signal is a discrete signal that can assume only a limited set of values.

A digital signal typically originates from *quantifying* a discrete signal (see Figure 2.2). What happens in quantification is that each discrete value is rounded off to the nearest permissible digital value. In practice, it is a number of possible powers of 2, for instance, 2^8 (256) or 2^{16} (64 536). This is connected with how many bits are used to represent the values in a PC or a PLC, for instance. You can read more about sampling and quantifying in Section 3.2. A *binary* signal is a special variant of the digital signal that has *only* two permissible values. We like to call these values (logically) "low" and "high" values. Electrically, these values can be represented by 0 and 5 V or 0 and 24 V, for instance. It is also common to use the word *state*. A variable (quantity) that can assume only two possible values is called a *logical* or *Boolean* quantity.

In the binary number system, the figures 1 and 0 are used to show the state of the logical quantity and in mathematics the concept of TRUE/FALSE is used.

In the context of programming, it is perhaps most common to use this latter form even though many compilers accept the use of 1 and 0 as well.

2.2.2   Sensors, Transducers, and Transmitters

As mentioned in the introductory section, there are many words and concepts in circulation that refer to the same things. Normally this is not a problem because everyone in the industry knows that this is the case. Nevertheless, sometimes misunderstandings can occur, and therefore it is reasonable to try to clarify some concepts.

The following definitions originate from the IEEE[1] 1451.2 (Institute of Electrical and Electronics Engineers, 1997):

- *Transducer*: A transducer is a device that converts energy from one form to another.
- *Sensor*: A sensor is a transducer that converts a physical, biological, or chemical quantity to an electrical signal.
- *Smart sensor*: A smart sensor is a transducer that offers functions beyond those offered by a regular sensor.
- *Actuator*: An actuator is a transducer that converts an electrical signal to a physical motion.

---

[1] IEEE—Institute of Electrical and Electronics Engineers.

As we see, the word "transducer" is a very general concept that can be used for a number of different devices. Some examples of transducers are as follows:

- Electric motor: Electrical energy to mechanical energy
- Switch: Mechanical to electrical energy
- Microphone: Acoustical to electric energy
- Loudspeaker: Electrical to acoustic energy
- LED: Electrical energy to light

Some people will perhaps react to the use of the word "sensor" and say that the signal from a sensor does not necessarily have to be electrical. A somewhat more generous definition of a sensor could be:

A sensor is a unit that reacts to a change in a physical quantity and generates a signal that can be measured or interpreted.

The problem is that all of these concepts can be used interchangeably, both in literature and in catalogs, manuals and specifications from manufacturers and distributors. Some use the first definition, that a sensor is a complete unit that reacts to a change in the physical quantity and converts this change to an electrical signal. Nowadays, this is not completely correct because the electrical signal from a commercial sensor is usually linearized, filtered, and standardized (e.g., to 4–20 mA).

Others use the word *transmitter* (e.g., level transmitter) for a complete unit, while others use the concepts sensor + transmitter as illustrated in Figure 2.3. This terminology is extremely common. In particular, this is true of temperature sensors such as thermocouples and resistance temperature detectors (e.g., PT100). For such sensors, there are transmitters that can be ordered separately. An example of the structure of a sensor i shown in Figure 2.4.

Even though it is perhaps not entirely correct, in this book we will (generally) use the word sensor for a complete unit that outputs a standardized electrical signal (Figure 2.5).

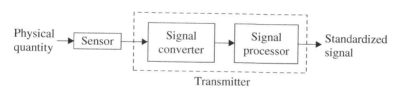

Figure 2.3   Common terminology

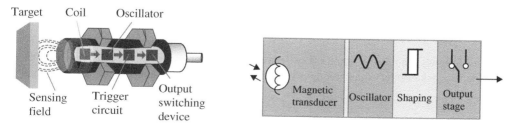

Figure 2.4   Illustration of sensor with built-in converter (Pepperl+Fuchs.)

Figure 2.5   The terminology that will be used in this book

There will also be a distinction between sensors that provide a binary signal, that is, they have two output states and sensors that produce an analog (continuous) signal.

This latter will be referred to only as a sensor, while the former will be referred to as a *logical, discrete,* or *digital sensor/detector/transducer:*

A discrete sensor/detector/transducer is a unit that reacts when a change in a physical quantity exceeds a certain threshold or limit and which closes or opens an electrical contact via an electronic output stage.

2.3   Switches

By *switch,* we mean here a mechanical unit where a contact closes when the switch is operated or activated. Switches are used in this context mostly for various starting and stopping functions or to detect when something has come into a predetermined position.

Switches come in many varieties depending upon the application. There can be flip-flop switches, start/stop switches, toggling[2] switches (a push-button that switches between off and on when operated), spring-loaded pushbuttons, emergency stop switches, limit switches, safety devices, etc. Even though design, application, and size vary, what switches have in common is that they have two states (on or off, closed or open, activated or not activated, etc.).

Figure 2.6 shows some variants of what we can call manual switches.

2.3.1   Limit Switches

Another group of switches includes limit switches. Such switches are placed so that they are activated when a moving part comes into a predetermined position, and often this position is the end of a motion. This gives them the name of limit switches or end-stop switches.

In contrast to the switches shown in Figure 2.6, limit switches are activated automatically by a mechanical motion. Examples might be a piston that comes into a certain position or an item on a conveyor belt that passes a certain point. Figure 2.7 shows some versions of limit switches. Most are spring-loaded to protect the switches. Some have wheels placed on the part that comes into contact with the moving equipment, while others only have a pin, rod, or the like as a contact point.

2.3.2   Safety Devices

Figure 2.8 shows examples of some safety devices that function as switches. Such devices are used to reduce the risk of injury to operating personnel and for stopping machinery quickly and simply.

---

[2] Not to be confused with a *toggle switch*, a switch, usually small, single-pole and single-throw that is operated by a short, round lever that moves through a small arc.

Figure 2.6 Various switches (Reproduced with permission from Schneider Electric)

Figure 2.7 Limit switches in many variants (Telemecanique) (Reproduced with permission from Schneider Electric)

Figure 2.8a shows a *light barrier*. These are most often used to break the power to moving machinery if something or someone interrupts a beam of light. (This is actually not a switch as it is been defined here, but rather a type of discrete (photoelectric) sensor. Read more about photocells on page 36.)

Figure 2.8b shows a *cord-pull switch*. Inside the unit, there is a cord stored on a spring-loaded wheel. This cord can be extended and fastened, for instance, along the length of a machine and then the wheel locked. When the cord-pull is locked any tension on the cord will immediately interrupt the current and the machine will stop.

Figure 2.8c shows a *two-hand switch* panel, where two buttons must be pushed simultaneously in order to start a machine, for instance, a press or a plate cutter. This keeps the operator from having a free hand that could get into the press.

2.3.3 Magnetic Switches

A *magnetic switch* is a general designation for electromagnetic switches where electrical energy is transformed into mechanical motion. These are often called *solenoid switches*. Sometimes, the concept of magnetic switch is used for a type of switch called a *reed switch*, and we are going to do that here. This type of magnetic switch typically consists of two overlapping springy strips of material containing iron, encapsulated in glass or plastic. The contacts can be of the normally open (NO) or normally closed (NC) type.

In the normally open type of magnetic switch, the two strips do not contact each other in the initial condition (see Figure 2.9). If the switch is in the presence of a magnetic field from a permanent magnet or a solenoid coil that comes close enough (typically 1 mm), the strips will become magnetized and press against each other. This closes the contacts. A normally closed variant works in the opposite way.

The switches can be purchased as independent components, or incorporated into unit together with a relay ready for use for various voltage levels and current loads. Since the

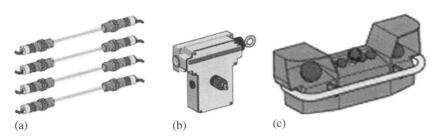

(a)   (b)   (c)

Figure 2.8   Some safety devices (Reproduced with permission from Schneider Electric)

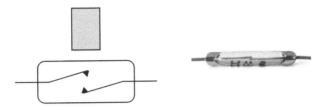

Figure 2.9   Principle of operation and an example of a reed switch

contact surfaces are encapsulated in a hermetically sealed container, the contacts are not subject to corrosion. Encapsulation of the contact points also means that the switches are well suited for use in areas where there is danger of explosion.

Magnetic switches are used for many purposes. One example is burglar alarms where they are placed on the frames of windows and doors. When a window is opened, the contacts in the switch open and the alarm goes off.

2.4   Logical Sensors

The other main group of units is the *logical sensor*. Another common name is *detector*. Logical sensors function in principle as follows:

When a physical quantity changes beyond a defined limit, the sensor's output goes logically high or low. In contrast to switches, which are activated mechanically, sensors are activated electronically because of a change in a physical quantity. The physical quantity can be distance, fluid level, temperature, etc. Logical sensors are used for detection of process states but provide only information on whether a state is true or false. An example of such a sensor is a thermostat that is used to connect or disconnect the power supply to a heating oven. As examples of industrial logical sensors, we can name inductive and capacitive proximity detectors, ultrasonic detectors, and photocells.

Applications cover a wide spectrum, but the following requirements frequently appear:

- Monitoring the presence or absence of an object.
- Determining the angular or linear position of an object
- Monitoring the motion of objects or obstacles to objects
- Determining the presence (or level) of a gas or liquid
- Counting

In order to meet these requirements, many different physical principles and combinations are used:

- Mechanical, such as pressure or force (electromechanical limit switches)
- Electromagnetic field (inductive proximity detectors)
- Illumination or light reflection (for photocells)
- Capacitance (capacitive proximity detectors)
- Acoustic (ultrasonic sensors)
- Fluid pressure (pressure switches)

Sensors can also have various types of output stages. Some sensors have an output that is an electromagnetic switch, but most of them have an output unit that is a transistor circuit (e.g., transistor–transistor logic or TTL). Most sensors used in PLC applications are standardized at 24 V for all applications.

However, there is nothing obligatory in having 24 V represent logical 1 (high state of sensor output) and 0 V represent logical 0 (low state of sensor output). In Europe, this is most common and is called *positive logic*. Sensors with *PNP output* function in this way.

If the voltage that represents logical 1 is *lower* than the voltage that represents logical 0, it is called *negative logic*. Sensors with *NPN outputs* function in this way. It is important to keep this in mind when ordering sensors since the two output types cannot always be used simultaneously on the same input module. This subject will be thoroughly reviewed in Section 2.5.1.

Note that several of the sensor types that are presented here are based on physical phenomena that can also be measured continuously. For instance, there are ultrasound-level meters and ultrasound-level detectors. The former type provides an analog signal that is proportional to the fluid level in a tank, for instance, while the latter type (the level detector) is discrete and the output shifts between off and on when the fluid surface is below or above a certain level. Many of these sensors could just as well be presented in Chapter 3.

2.4.1 Inductive Sensors

Inductive sensors or *inductive proximity detectors* utilize a physical principle that means that they can function for detection of objects containing iron. Together with capacitive proximity detectors (see Section 2.4.2) and photocells, they are one of the fundamental components used in industrial automation.

They are also contact-free, that is, they do not make contact with the objects that they detect. In this way, there is no mechanical wear taking place. This means that such sensors have a long service life and require little or no service.

The sensors consist, in principle, of a coil that has wire wound around an iron core. The coil is connected to a capacitor and together these two form an oscillator. This oscillator sets up a high-frequency (typically 100 kHz to 1 MHz) alternating electromagnetic field in the core and in the vicinity of the sensor surface. When one end of the core comes close to a metallic object, the total AC resistance (the reluctance) decreases because this is much lower for iron than for air. This change in turn leads to an increase in current in the sensor's circuits, which then activates an electronic switch (see Figure 2.10).

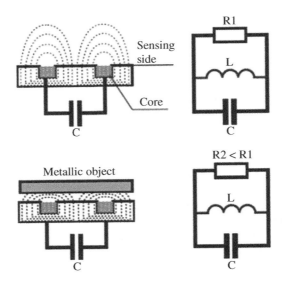

Figure 2.10 Inductive detector—principle (Reproduced with permission from Schneider Electric)

Figure 2.11 Inductive sensors (Reproduced with permission from Schneider Electric)

Figure 2.11 shows some inductive sensors of various designs. Practical detection distances between sensor and object varies from a few millimeters to a few centimeters. There are also analog designs: sensors that give an analog signal that are proportional to the distance from the object. These can be used to measure both linear and rotational movements and distances but have the same limitations with respect to the distance to the object.

Figure 2.12 shows a couple of applications of inductive proximity detectors. In the example of the left, one detector is used to detect the presence of a food can, while another checks that there is a cover on the can. In the example on the right, an inductive detector is used to sense the RPM or the position depending upon whether the PLC measures the time between the pulses or counts the number of pulses.

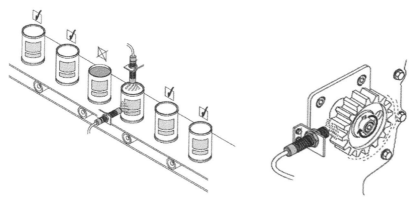

Figure 2.12   Examples of use of inductive sensors (Reproduced with permission from FESTO)

2.4.2   Capacitive Sensors

Capacitive proximity detectors can, in contrast to inductive ones, be used to detect all types of objects and not metallic objects alone. Examples can be water, glass, plastic, wood, metal, etc. The physical principle utilized is the same as that of a plate capacitor: the shorter the distance between the plates, the greater the area of the plates or the higher the permittivity in the dielectric yields higher capacitance. This is expressed by the formula

$$C = \frac{\varepsilon_0 \cdot \varepsilon_r \cdot A}{d}$$

A is the area of the plates, d is the separation between the plates, ε_0 is the permittivity of air, and ε_r is the relative permittivity (relative to air).

An oscillating electric field is used to detect this change in capacitance by generating a current. When the field changes beyond a certain limit, the sensors output (relay or transistor output) is activated.

Capacitive sensors come in two main versions. The most common type can detect any object regardless of material. In this type, both plates are built into the sensor (see Figure 2.13). Since the plates have a given area and the distance between them is fixed, the capacitance can be changed only by a change in the permittivity. Without any object by the sensor, the dielectric consists only of air and the relative permittivity is equal to 1. With an object in its place next to the sensor, the relative permittivity increases and the capacitance increases.

The other main type can detect *conductive* objects such as metal or water and also functions at a greater distance. This can take place even when the object is behind an insulating material. An example of such an application is detection of a fluid level in a plastic tank. This main type has one plate built into the sensor while a fastening bracket, a machine cover or the like, to which the sensor is attached, constitutes the ground electrode.

An illustration of the principle for this type is shown in Figure 2.14. The illustration at the left in the figure shows the electric field without an object nearby, while the illustration on the right shows the field when a metallic object is in the vicinity.

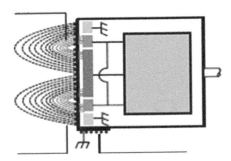

Figure 2.13 Principle of capacitive sensors with built-in ground electrode (Reproduced with permission from Schneider Electric)

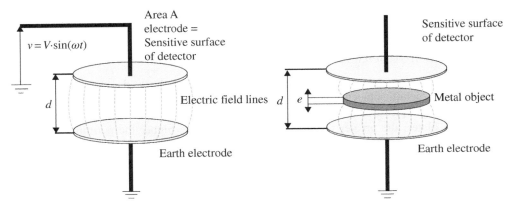

Figure 2.14 Principle of a capacitive sensor for conductive materials (Reproduced with permission from Schneider Electric)

The property that is utilized here is a change in the effective separation between the plates. This can be formulated as follows:

$$C = \frac{\varepsilon_0 \cdot \varepsilon_r \cdot A}{d - e}$$

where e is the thickness of the metallic object.

Figure 2.15 shows some capacitive sensors of various sizes; the sensing distance varies from 2 to 15 mm.

2.4.3 Photocells

Photocells, or photoelectric detectors as they are also called, contain an emitter that sends out light and a photodetector that detects incoming light. Light that is emitted from the light-emitting diode is usually infrared. This wavelength is chosen to reduce the problem of photodetectors becoming confused by other illumination.

Figure 2.15 Examples of capacitive proximity detectors (Reproduced with permission from Schneider Electric)

There are also photocells that operate on other wavelengths in order to be able to distinguish objects of different colors. Such photocells are called color sensors.

Photocells are found in three major versions: *Transmitting, reflecting,* and *retroreflecting.* The difference between versions is the placement of the photodetector and the ability of the object to be detected to reflect light.

- The *transmitting* type is based on transmitter and receiver in separate units that are placed on either side of the object that is to be detected. When an object comes between the units, the light beam is prevented from reaching the photodetector. This is illustrated in Figure 2.16a. The advantage of this type is that the detection distance can be great (several tens of meters, depending upon the lens of the transmitter), even though it may be very difficult to install a transmitter and receiver in line when the separation gets up to 10 m or more. The difficulty is that there are two units, both of which require a power supply.
- In the *reflecting* type, the photodetector is built into the same unit as the emitter. If the object is of such a nature that it can reflect the light, the photodetector will record when the object passes (Figure 2.16b). Both the shape and the color of the object are significant in how well this functions, along with color of whatever lies behind the object. For a given separation, a white object can be simpler to detect than a gray or black object. If the background has a lighter color than the object, this can make detection nearly impossible.
- If the object is not suitable for reflected light, a reflective surface can be installed on the side opposite. In this case the photodetector will receive light until an object interrupts the beam (Figure 2.16c). This variant is called *retro-reflecting*. The detection difference can be very large here as well; possibly up to 20 m. The use of this type can be difficult if the object has a smooth or reflective surface such as a window or a polished metallic object. Then the sensor can mistake the object for the reflective surface.

There are also special variants of the retroreflecting type that utilize polarized light. The transmitted light is polarized (vertically) by means of a linear polarizing filter. The reflective surface changes the polarization in portions of the light such that it is returned as horizontally polarized light. The object, however, does not change the polarization. In this way the detector can distinguish between light reflected from the object and light reflected from the reflective surface.

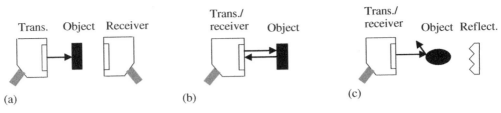

Figure 2.16   (a) Transmitting type, (b) reflecting type, (c) retroreflecting type

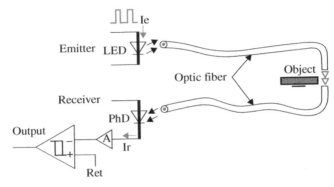

Figure 2.17   Optical fiber combined with photocells (Reproduced with permission from Schneider Electric)

It is also possible to combine photocells with optical fibers. In such equipment, a fiber cable is placed between the transmitter and the detection region between the detection region and the receiver (see Figure 2.17). This arrangement can be used if:

- The object to be detected is very small (millimeter size),
- The photocell must be located away from the detection region,
- The detection region is in an explosives area or the temperature is high.

The advantage of photocells is that they are very versatile and can be used for detection of objects at distances ranging from a few millimeters to several tens of meters.

If the detection distance is small, one should evaluate the use of a capacitive or inductive sensor because these are significantly cheaper. A disadvantage of photocells is that they stop working if they become contaminated since the detection principle is based upon light.

Figure 2.18 shows photocells in various versions.

Another type of optical sensor is the *laser sensor*. These differ from photocells in that the light that is transmitted is a laser light (from a laser diode). Such sensors are used in cases where there is a requirement for a high degree of precision because the resolution can be as good as a few microns.

The analog versions can also be used to undertake extremely accurate measurements. The digital versions are used more in quality inspection.

Figure 2.18 Photocells (Pepperl + Fuchs)

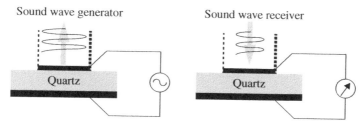

Sound wave generator

Sound wave receiver

Quartz

Quartz

Figure 2.19 Principle of an ultrasonic sensor (Reproduced with permission from Schneider Electric)

2.4.4 Ultrasonic Sensors

An ultrasonic sensor functions in a way similar to that of the photocell of the reflecting type. The difference is that the unit transmits sound pulses instead of light. The frequency of the sound is above the range of hearing for people (>20 kHz), up in the so-called ultrasonic region. The sound waves are generated by means of an electroacoustic transducer (piezoelectric element). The applied electric energy (AC) is transformed into mechanical vibrations in the form of sound waves (see Figure 2.19).

The sensor is based upon the echo principle. When an object passes the sensor, emitted pulses are reflected and these are picked up by the sensor's built-in receiver unit. It is also possible to use the principle for an analog variant of the sensor. Here the time between the transmission of the pulse and its reception is calculated by a built-in electronic circuit. This time is proportional to the distance to the object (e.g., to the fluid level in a tank).

The velocity of sound in air at 20° C is approximately 340 m/s, so at a distance of 1 m, for instance, to the object it takes about 3 ms for a sound pulse to be transmitted, reflected, and recorded at the receiver.

Ultrasound sensors are typically used for distances less than or equal to 1 m, but there are versions that can sense over longer distances (<10 m). An advantage of ultrasound is that the sensor can detect all objects, no matter what the color or shape.

Just like photocells, ultrasonic sensors are also used in three configurations: reflecting, retroreflecting, and transmitting.

2.4.5 Rotating Sensors (Encoders)

Encoders are used for positioning, rpm control, and speed control.

A widely used principle for encoders is to utilize light. An optical encoder consists in principle of one or more sets of light emitting diodes and photodetectors (phototransistors) and a disk. The disc, which is attached to the shaft of an encoder and physically fixed to a machine or motor that is to be monitored, has small holes evenly distributed around the disc. When light from the emitting diode passes through the holes in the rotating disk, light pulses are detected by the photodetector. Either these pulses of light can be counted in order to measure an angular displacement or the pulse frequency can be used as a measure of the rotational speed (see Figure 2.21).

The resolution of an encoder is determined by the number of holes that the rotating disk has. The disc that is illustrated in Figure 2.21 has 12 holes. This gives a resolution of $360°/12 = 30°$. With 60 holes in the disc, the resolution becomes $6°$. By using more light sensors and placing holes in several rows, one can obtain a resolution of fractions of a degree.

The resolution can also be improved (double for the same rows of holes) by detecting both the rising and falling flanks of the received light pulses. In other words, by detecting when a hole on the disc *arrives* at the photocell and when the hole *leaves* the photocell.

It is important to distinguish between the resolution in the number of degrees and the physical accuracy of the machine motion that the encoder is to monitor. If the encoder is

Figure 2.20   Ultrasonic sensors (Reproduced with permission from Schneider Electric)

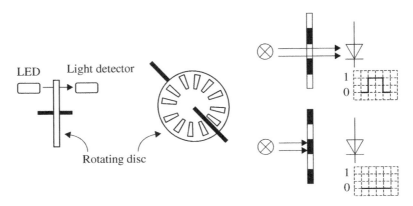

Figure 2.21   Principle of encoder with one row of holes

mounted on a converter mechanism to measure a linear motion, for instance, with the purpose of cutting a workpiece into suitable lengths, the physical accuracy can be calculated as follows:

$$\frac{\text{Linear movement per revolution}}{360} \times \text{Accuracy in degrees}$$

Encoders come in two main versions: incremental and absolute.

With an *incremental encoder*, the PLC must count the pulses transmitted by the encoder (relative to a starting time or a starting position) in order to obtain the angle or the position. The number of pulse trains they transmit varies. The simplest can have just one row of holes and therefore one pulse train.

Figure 2.22 shows a common variant with three pulses that are sent out on separate outputs (channels). The signals are designated A, B, and 0. The pulse trains on channels A and B are phase-shifted 90° relative to each other. This makes it possible to determine in *which direction* it is rotating. If we receive a rising flank for A before B, the rotation is clockwise, and the reverse if B comes first. On channel 0, there is only one single pulse that is used to record the number of revolutions that the encoder makes.

An *absolute encoder* reports that the actual angle or position in the form of a binary signal. The number of bits is equal to the number of rows of hole tracks. Figure 2.23 shows the principle of an absolute encoder that has three hole tracks. The number of positions that can be distinguished from one another is in this case $2^3 = 8$, which gives a resolution of $360°/8 = 45°$.

It is common to design the discs so that the holes form a sequence with *Gray coding*. Only one bit changes from one sector to the next in this code. The disc below is coded in such a way.

Figure 2.24 shows the bit pattern from a Gray-coded disc with five hole tracks. This gives $2^5 = 32$ sectors and equally many combinations of bits. (Only the first 16 combinations are shown in the figure.)

Absolute encoders have two additional advantages over incremental encoders:

1. Position reading from an absolute encoder is not affected by a power failure. When the power comes back, an absolute encoder will continue to indicate the correct position.
2. The use of an absolute encoder is more secure with respect to interference. Noise can certainly affect/change the signals from the encoder, but as soon as the noise stops/decreases, the signal from the encoder returns to normal.

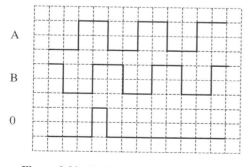

Figure 2.22 Pulse train on channels A, B, and 0 for an incremental encoder

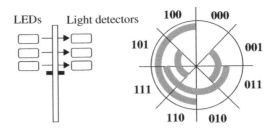

Figure 2.23   Principle of an absolute encoder

Value →	0	1	2	3	4	5	6	7	8	9	10	11	12	13	14	15	
Bit 1	0	1	1	0	0	1	1	0	0	1	1	0	0	1	1	0	*LSB*
Bit 2	0	0	1	1	1	1	0	0	0	0	1	1	1	1	0	0	
Bit 3	0	0	0	0	1	1	1	1	1	1	1	1	0	0	0	0	
Bit 4	0	0	0	0	0	0	0	0	1	1	1	1	1	1	1	1	
Bit 5	0	0	0	0	0	0	0	0	0	0	0	0	0	0	0	0	*MSB*

Figure 2.24   Bit pattern reading a Gray-coded disk with five hole tracks

Example 2.1

An encoder with a resolution of (at least) 3° is to be designed. How many holes must the rotating disk have if it is an incremental type with one row of holes?

   Answer: In order to obtain a resolution of 3° with only one row of holes, the number of holes must be equal to 360/3 = 120.

Example 2.2

We want the same resolution here, that is, at least 3°, but with an absolute encoder:

   Answer: Many more holes will be needed here. The reason is that an absolute encoder reports actual angular positions. The number of sectors with holes must be equal to 120 in order to obtain the proper resolution ($3 \times 120 = 360$), but each sector must be differentiated from the others by means of a unique combination of bits. In order to differentiate among 120 different positions, we must use at least 7 bits ($2^7 = 128$). This implies that the rotating disk must contain seven rows of holes (by using 7 pairs of LEDs and phototransistors). Each angular position can then be identified by reading these 7 bits so that a particular position can be represented by, for instance, the binary number 1010101.

   The minimum number of holes is therefore $7 \times 120 = 840$.

2.4.5.1   Other Encoders

A different and simpler principle that can be utilized to measure position or angular motion is a sensor based upon a *potentiometer* (Figure 2.25). When the shaft rotates, the resistance in the potentiometer and voltage drop across it (current through it) changes proportionately.

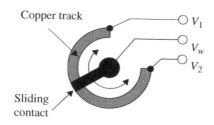

Figure 2.25 Angular measurement based on a potentiometer

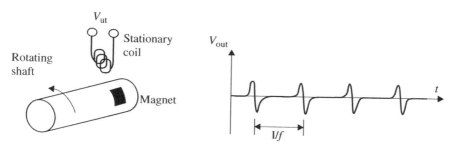

Figure 2.26 Tachometer based on induction

Potentiometers are popular because they are very inexpensive and require only a simple electrical circuit to convert motion to a (standard) electrical signal.

A *tachometer* is a variant of an encoder. They are specially designed to measure the speed of rotating axes. A common approach is to mount a magnet on the rotating shaft. When the shaft rotates, the magnet passes a stationary coil in which a current is induced when the magnet passes by. In this way, the sensor can record a pulse for each revolution. The time between each pulse then gives a measure of the speed (Figure 2.26). This type of equipment is relatively cheap. There are also versions in which the output is an analog signal where voltage or current is proportional to speed.

There are also tachometers that utilize other principles; some use inductive proximity detectors where the rotating disk is covered with metallic areas.

2.4.6 Other Detection Principles and Sensors

The sensors and measurement principles that are described earlier are all related to detection of the presence of something or the measurement of motion, position or speed. What they all have in common is that they come in discrete versions, that is, versions that transmit a discrete signal. The list of sensors could certainly be much longer but, as we mentioned before, we must limit our priorities of subjects. Particularly, pressure switches (and vacuum switches) such as *pressostats* should perhaps be presented in this group.

Among the modern types of equipment, we could also mention radio frequency identification (RFID) and cameras (television cameras). This is equipment and technology that actually falls entirely outside the group of logical sensors, but which is being applied in more and more areas, and it is therefore proper to mention it.

RFID

RFID was developed for applications where there is a need to obtain more information about and keep track of objects or individuals. Applications could, for instance be tracking, admission control, inventory (logistics), or sorting. Identification is achieved by providing each object or individual with an electronic tag that contains an antenna, an identification code, memory, and a little logic (see Figure 2.27).

The information stored in the memory of a tag can be read out by (or written to) a *reader* without there being any physical contact with the tag. This takes place by means of electromagnetic waves in the radio frequency region generated by the RFID reader. When the tag comes close to the reader, several things happen (see Figure 2.28):

- The tag receives energy from the reader by means of an electromagnetic field inducing a voltage across the antenna in the tag.
- The reader modulates the amplitude of the radiated field in order to generate read or write commands to the tag's integrated circuit.
- The tag responds to the reader by modulating its own power absorption. Electronics in the reader sense the information and transform it to a digital signal.

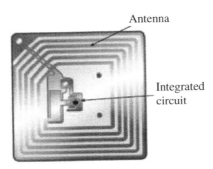

Figure 2.27   Contents of an electronic tag (Reproduced with permission from Schneider Electric)

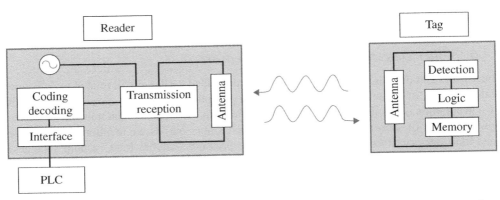

Figure 2.28   RFID system with tag and reader connected to a PLC (Reproduced with permission from Schneider Electric)

The built-in logic in the tag acts as a connection between the antenna and the memory. Tags can be obtained with various degrees of complexity and are ordered for the application in which they will be used. The simplest utilize only modulation for sending the ID code, but the more advanced models can consist of a microcontroller with encryption algorithms, for instance, for increased security (payment cards).

If there is a requirement to update and store information in the tag, they are obtainable with various amounts of memory, ranging from a few bites to several kilobytes. The cheapest tags cannot be written to (ROM based), but the most expensive are based on EEPROMs or a type of ferroelectric RAM; in contrast to ordinary RAM, this is not dependent upon a built-in battery source.

The physical embodiment (and encapsulation) of the tags is also different. The cheapest and simplest are protected only by a thin layer of plastic and the tags can be glued to objects as though they were adhesive labels. For rougher industrial environments there is, normally a requirement for better encapsulation and the possibility of fastening the tags in a more secure way. Figure 2.29 shows tags of various designs.

2.5   Connection of Logical Sensors

Before we see how logical sensors can be connected to PLC input modules, blocks or cards, we should first look briefly at the various types of sensors output stages that are available.

Many sensors have traditionally been produced in both two-wire and three-wire variants even though three wires are decidedly the most common. A three-wire sensor has, as the name indicates, three connections: one for connecting to 0 V, one for connecting to +24 V and one connector that is the connection to the output of the sensor. (See for instance the sensor in Figure 2.34.) The advantage of three-wire sensors is that they can be made in various versions depending upon whether one wants a sensor output that turns a voltage off and on or a current off and on. The following types of outputs are available:

- Simple switching output (24 V on/off)
- Relay output (for AC)
- TTL (5 V)
- NPN/PNP (turns current on/off)

The first and the second types are simple to connect because the sensor output permits the passage of current through the sensor output in both directions. One therefore does not need to worry about whether the PLC input block is properly configured as would be required for sensors with NPN or PNP output.

Sensors with TTL output use 0 and 5 V to indicate low and high state (normally open). They can therefore not be connected to standard 24 V discrete input blocks. Special blocks must be used.

NPN/PNP output is most common in standard industrial sensors. Many sensors of this type will carry current levels up to a few amperes and can therefore be used for direct switching of smaller loads.

Figure 2.30 illustrates how logical sensors and switches can be connected to a discrete input module. As we see, the three-wire sensor is provided with its own connectors. When the sensor

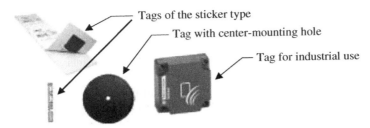

Figure 2.29 Tags of various types (Telemecanique) (Reproduced with permission from Schneider Electric)

is activated the state of the sensor changes and the PLC input in question changes state. This switch is simpler because it does not need its own power supply. When the switch is activated, the circuit is closed and the input changes state.

This happens because there is a connection between the other input contacts and the connector marked COM. The designation COM is short for *common*. Most often, there is one common point for all of the discrete inputs, but the inputs can also be divided into groups of 4 and 4, for instance, with each group having its COM point. The idea here is to make the input blocks more flexible with respect to the use of sensors with different types of output. See Section 2.5.1 for more about this.

Two-Wire Sensors

A two-wire sensor does not have its own contacts for connection to the power supply but receives its power because the sensor is connected to a closed circuit all the time. This assumes that the input blocks that are used will permit a small current in the circuit whether or not the sensors are

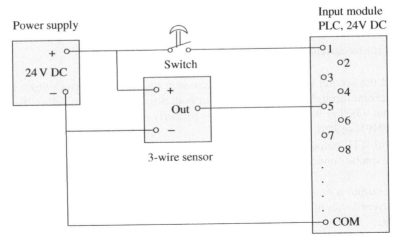

Figure 2.30 Switch connected to input one- and three-wire sensor connected to input 5

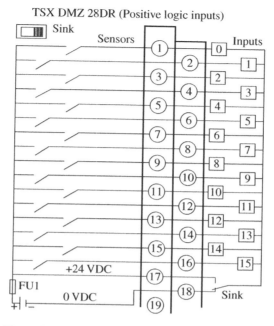

Figure 2.31 Connecting sensors to a discrete module

active. When the sensors are not active, this current is small. When the sensor is activated, the current increases. This increase in current is registered by the input block and the address to the input in question changes state. The advantage of such sensors is the saving in cabling.

Two-wire sensors are connected in the same way that one would connect a switch.

Figure 2.31 shows an illustration of connecting sensors/switches to a 24 V DC discrete block (type TSX DMZ 28DR from Telemecanique). Both two-wire and three-wire sensors can be used. The sensors that are used should obviously be 24 V standard to avoid relays or other electronics between the sensors and the block. Sensors with lower operating voltage can be used since the limit for setting and input high is often lower than 24 V.[3]

2.5.1 Sink/Source

When sensors with output types NPN and PNP are being connected, it is important to get the polarity right. The polarity depends upon how the input module and sensor are designed. There are two possibilities:

1. Positive logic (sink or drain)
2. Negative logic (source)

---

[3] For example, the limit for guaranteeing setting a discrete input high is 11 V for the TMX DMZ 28DR block from Telemecanique. The limit for being sure that an input is set logically low on this module is a maximum of 5 V. Voltages above this value *can* set or maintain the input high (Schneider Electric, 2002 and 2004).

A general description of these two forms of logic is as follows:

1. *Positive logic:* The voltage that represents logical 1 (true) has a more positive value than the voltage that represents logical 0 (false).
2. *Negative logic:* The voltage that represents logical 0 is more positive than the voltage that represents logical 1.

The difference between these is the direction that the current flows: Out of the sensor output and into the PLC input (sink-connected PLC input), or out of the PLC input and into the sensor output (source-connected PLC input). This latter may sound a little foolish, but it is just a question of where one connects to +24 V and where one connects to 0 V.

This is especially confusing because the concepts of sink and source are used with reference to both the sensors and the PLC inputs as well as to transistor output modules (see Section 2.7.3). The reason that the designations sink and source refer to the direction of the current: the sink should remind us of a drain, a place where a current flows toward. The source is the place where the current originates. Since the current either must flow from the sensor to the input module or from the input module to the sensor we can say the following:

- *Sink-connected PLC inputs* (Figure 2.32): The sensors are connected to the source and the direction of the current is out of the sensor and into the PLC input. All switches and two-wire sensors must be connected to +24 V and the common point (COM) on the input block is connected to 0 V. This configuration is the most common. When a sensor or switch is activated, a contact is closed from +24 V to the input. This sets the value in the associated input address to logically high.
- *Source-connected PLC inputs* (Figure 2.33): The sensor is now sink-connected and the direction of current is from the PLC inputs. This connection requires that all switches and sensors are connected to 0 V and the common points on the input block (COM) are connected to +24 V. When a sensor is activated, we get a closed circuit and the input address in question changes state.

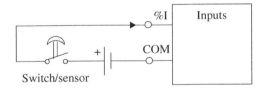

Figure 2.32   Sink-connected input module

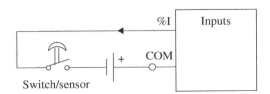

Figure 2.33   Source-connected input module

2.5.2 Selecting a Sensor with the Proper Type of Output

It is not always possible to mix positive and negative logic in the same input module, so it is important to know the difference. This applies especially when sensors are being ordered. Many input modules can be configured to either sink or source and on some modules <u>groups</u> of inputs and outputs can be configured differently. Whether we select one or the other depends upon the sensors and signal sources that are being used:

* *NPN output:* The direction of current is into the sensor's output. This therefore requires a source-connected PLC input.
* *PNP output:* The direction of current is out of the sensor's output. This therefore requires a sink-connected PLC input.

Generally, sensors with NPN output are most common in equipment produced in the United States, while PNP output is the most common for sensors produced in Europe. Many sensors, however, can be configured to the desired format by switching a small switch, for instance. This is the case for the sensors in Example 2.3.

Example 2.3

Figures 2.34 and 2.35 show the schematic wiring for a photocell from the manufacturer OMRON, configured with NPN output and PNP output, respectively. There is a switch in the middle of each illustration that is used to change between the two choices. The boxes marked "Load" will in this context be one of the PLC's discrete inputs even though sensors with a NPN/PNP outputs can switch minor loads directly, as we mentioned previously.

NPN output: Here we see that the direction of the current is *inward* at the sensor output (pin 4) and COM at the PLC input block must then be connected to +24V: the output from the sensor is naturally connected to the PLC input (%I). We then have a *source-connected* PLC input.
PNP output: The output from the sensor is (naturally enough) still connected to the PLC input (%I). The direction of the current is *outward from the sensor output* and *inward* at the PLC input. The COM terminal on the PLC input module here must be connected to 0V and the PLC input is *sink-connected*.

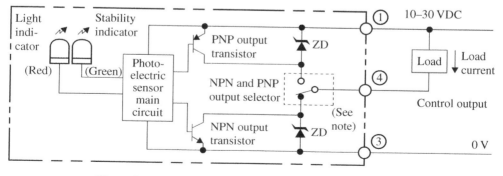

Figure 2.34 NPN output requires source-connected PLC input

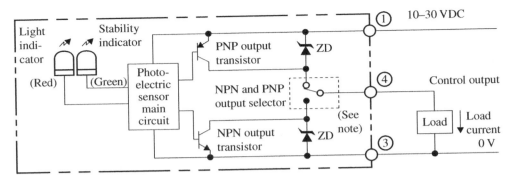

Figure 2.35   PNP output requires sink-connected PLC input

Summary

As we have seen, it can be very confusing with all of the concepts of sink, source, NPN, PNP, positive logic and negative logic. Here is a summary:

- A sensor with NPN output should be connected in the following way: The output signal from the sensor is connected to the input in question on the PLC block, while +24 V is connected to COM on the input block. We say that the sensor is sink-connected and that the PLC input is source-connected. With reference to the PLC, this is called negative logic.
- A sensor with PNP output should be connected in a similar way with the difference that 0 V is connected to COM on the input block. Here the sensor is source-connected and the PLC input is sink-connected. This is called positive logic and is the most common.

2.6   Properties of Discrete Inputs

One would think that a discrete input could not have so many different properties because switches and discrete sensors have only two states. But some care must be taken in the selection and configuration of input modules, and therefore it can be helpful to group the input types. The configurations that can be made vary and depend upon what capabilities the manufacturer has implemented.

Normal Input

This is the standard preset configuration for a discrete input and can be used in most instances. Typically, a discrete sensor or switch can be active for a certain time before the input is able to detect that. How long this standard time is varies among the various types of PLCs and input modules. Usually it is a few milliseconds.

Such a short delay is often desirable because it keeps the inputs from changing state because of voltage ripple. Both physical switches and electromagnetic switches in sensors can quickly change before a proper contact closes.

Filter Input

These are configurable inputs in which a delay time can be specified before the input changes state. The reason for this being called a filter input is that the input ignores changes of state with a duration shorter than the specified time. Shorter signal changes are thus filtered out of the module. A normal input is thus a filtered input. The reason for configurable filter times is to make it possible to record rapid signal changes and to prevent input addresses from changing state when the discrete signal has a longer ripple. Sometimes for practical reasons, it is also desirable to have a certain delay between the activation of a sensor and the setting of an input.

Latching Inputs

All PLCs have a so-called holding function (Set/Rest) available in the programming language they use. These are used to hold values high or low after the criterion for high/low is no longer present. Holding (locking) in a connection with discrete input blocks is something entirely different. Such inputs are called latching inputs, high-speed inputs, or pulse-catcher inputs.

Discrete inputs of this type are used in situations where the change of state that one wishes to register has a shorter duration than the scan time of the PLC. In such cases, the change in input would not be registered by the program.

Interrupt

Interrupt is used in order to break off the normal program sequence and immediately execute an interrupt routine. Such interrupt routines are also called *events*.

In some discrete input modules, it is possible to configure one or more inputs so that when the input is activated the main program is immediately interrupted so that an interrupt routine can be performed. Such interrupt routines can be used in connection with safety, for instance, one example could be the activation of an emergency stop so that the program shuts down the facility. With a less serious interrupt, the unit can easily be programmed so that the main program continues as it was before the interrupt took place.

Counter Input

Some modules have inputs that can be configured as counter inputs. Such inputs are used for connecting sensors that send out a train of pulses, for instance, an incremental encoder. The TSX DMZ 28DR module has two such inputs and can count pulses with a speed up to 500 Hz.

2.7 Discrete Actuators

Actuators are the designation for all of the output hardware that is used to control and manipulate process states. Such equipment can be valves, motors, pumps, pistons, etc. As is the case with discrete sensors, there are also a large number of types of discrete (logical) actuators. The general designation of *discrete* in this context means that they have two states and that it is natural for them to be controlled directly from discrete PLC outputs. The group of discrete actuators will therefore include (among others):

- Relays and contactors
- Solenoids
- Magnetic valves
- Resistive loads, lights, and alarms
- (Stepping motors)

Now it is obvious that there are many more actuators and control outputs that are discrete. Examples of these are used to turn off and on motors, wipers, pistons, heating elements, etc. Generally these types of actuators require much higher currents (or voltages) than normal to drive them directly from a discrete output module. In such cases, relays or contactors are used to switch the actuators. Along with these are a large group of pneumatic and hydraulic cylinders and valves. These are controlled by opening and closing valves for air and hydraulic fluid. It is therefore sufficient in this context to study magnetic valves that can be used for this purpose. Pneumatic and hydraulic equipment are therefore not treated in this textbook.

2.7.1 Relays and Contactors

These are far the most common types of discrete actuators since they can be used for switching on and off all other types of discrete actuators. The purpose of relays and contactors are to permit a small current to switch a larger current. A relay consists of two magnetic iron components: an iron core in the coil, a movable armature and a spring (see Figure 2.36). The spring is used to hold the armature away from the core when there is no current in the coil. The armature is connected to a movable contact. When current flows in the coil, the resulting magnetic field pulls the armature against the coil and the electric contacts are closed or opened.

An electromagnetic relay is susceptible to mechanical wear, both because of movable parts and because of contact corrosion as a result of arcing. This can be avoided by using *solid-state*

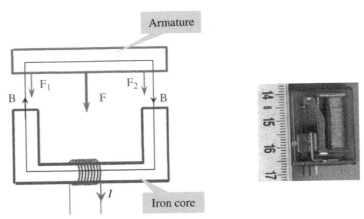

Figure 2.36   Principle of a relay and example of a small relay (Reproduced with permission from Leif L. Hansen)

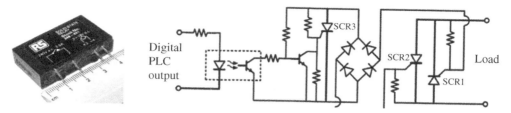

Figure 2.37 Solid-state relay with electronic schematic

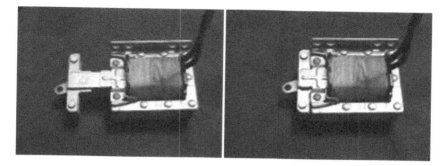

Figure 2.38 A solenoid in deactivated and activated position

relays (SSRs) (Figure 2.37). These are electronic relays (switches) that consist of a transistor/thyristor circuit. Optical couplers are used to protect the input side of the relay.

There are currently commercial versions of SSR that can handle over 1000 A.

Relay Outputs and Contactors

Activation of the current in the relay coil can be a result of a discrete PLC output going logically high, but it is also common to use discrete output blocks where relays are incorporated into the block itself. Such relays can handle a few amperes of current load and in many cases this is sufficient to drive loads directly. If not, the outputs may be used to switch a *contactor* that, in turn, turns loads off and on.

A contactor is, in principle, merely a relay that tolerates higher power. One example of the use of contactors is a so-called motor starter. A motor starter also has built-in overload protection, a so-called motor guard. The motor guard is a type of heat-controlled relay where a coil heats up a bimetal that in turn releases a spring that controls some extra contacts.

2.7.2 Solenoids and Magnetic Valves

A *solenoid*[4] is simply a coil with a movable core called an armature. The coil is obviously there to produce a magnetic field. Figure 2.38 illustrates the construction and function of a

---

[4] Solenoid is a concept that is used in many different contexts in electromagnetism. What we have described here is properly a *solenoid switch*. Originally the word describes what we now call a coil: wire wound around a metallic object.

Figure 2.39   A solenoid for industrial applications

Figure 2.40   Example of magnetic valve (GSR Ventiltechnik GmbH & Co.)

solenoid. Normally the armature is held outside the coil by a spring (see Figure 2.39). When current flows through the coil, for instance, when a PLC output goes logically high, the armature is drawn in to the center of the coil. In other words, a solenoid is a device that converts an electric signal to a (short) mechanical motion.

It can obviously be made with a reverse function so that the armature normally lies within the coil and is pushed out when the coil carries current.

There are many different types of solenoids. Some have a holding function where permanent magnets hold the armature in one or both end positions even when the coil is no longer carrying current. This is a solution that can be applied where a holding function must tolerate a power outage or, for instance, in battery-powered applications in order to save current. A solenoid can also be provided with an extra coil to give more power in both directions or to provide double power in one direction. A common application of a solenoid is for door locks (a button is placed on the inside that must be pressed in order to open the door). Another variant is the so-called pull-in for a starter motor in an automobile. When the ignition key is turned, the starter motor and the pull-in receive current. The pull-in engages the pinion gear on the shaft of the starting motor into contact with the flywheel.

Magnetic Valves

A *magnetic valve* (solenoid valve) is a solenoid where the mechanical motion opens and closes a valve. These are often used in pneumatic and hydraulic systems and are often used to turn on and turn off the flow of a liquid. A valve can have several inputs and outputs. A three-way valve can, for example, be used to switch an incoming flow of air between two different outlets.

A very common application of pneumatic magnetic valves is the control of cylinders and linear actuators. Magnetic valves provide quick and secure switching, are reliable in operation and require very little service.

In an ordinary family home, they are found on dishwashers, washing machines, and in the form of safety valves even though the dimensions of these are small compared with those used in industry.

2.7.3   Transistor Outputs versus Relay Outputs

All of the types of discrete actuators discussed above can be connected directly to discrete output modules. As described at the end of Chapter 1, the two most common types of discrete output are transistor outputs and relay outputs. It is important to understand the principal differences between these two types.

Transistor Outputs

Transistor outputs for PLCs are made for switching DC, typically 24 V. They are primarily used for resistive or inductive loads or lights. They can of course also switch other types of loads by using an external relay, for instance. Another important difference compared to relay outputs is that transistor outputs can provide only a very limited amount of current.

Similar to discrete input modules, transistor output modules come in two varieties: sink-connected or, more common, source-connected. Some modules are made so that they receive 24 V power supply through an internal bus that connects together the various modules in the PLC rack.

A source-connected variant of such a module functions in such a way that when the output address is set high, the voltage is switched from 0 to +24 V at the output to which the load is connected. The other side of the load is always connected to 0 V. In order to obtain a closed circuit, it is important that the 0 V point is the same for the load and the module.

See Figures 2.41 and 2.42, which show the principle for connecting a load (actuator) to either a source-coupled or a sink-coupled variant of a transistor output.

Note: If you have not included an external relay, the attached load will be supplied directly from the module. You must therefore read the documentation to find out how much the output can be loaded (i.e., how much current it can provide).

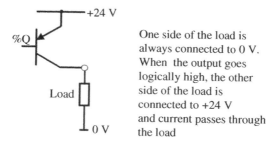

One side of the load is always connected to 0 V. When the output goes logically high, the other side of the load is connected to +24 V and current passes through the load

Figure 2.41   Source-connected transistor output

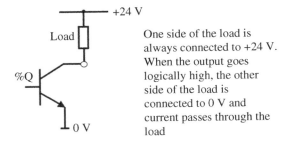

One side of the load is
always connected to +24 V.
When the output goes
logically high, the other
side of the load is
connected to 0 V and
current passes through the
load

Figure 2.42   Sink-connected transistor output

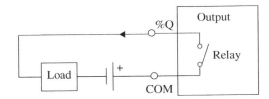

Figure 2.43   Connection of load to relay output

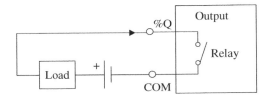

Figure 2.44   Connection of load to relay output—opposite polarity

Relay Outputs

Relay outputs are more flexible because they can also be used to activate or deactivate (switch)
connected loads having different voltages as well as AC. This means that it is also not important which way the current flows in the associated external circuit or which polarity is used.

Figures 2.43 and 2.44 show the connection of a load (actuator) where the operating voltage
of the load is connected with opposite polarity in the two figures. This is possible because a
relay output is simply a switch that can be connected to the module when the associated output
address is set high, so which way the current is flowing is not critical. Note that the COM point
is connected to opposite polarities in the two figures.

Also note that you will be able to hear a clicking sound in the module when a relay output
switches state.

2.8   Test Problems

Problem 2.1
(a) Discuss the differences between analog, discrete, digital, and binary signals.
(b) What is a transducer?

(c) What is the difference between a detector and a sensor (in the PLC context)? Name some typical applications of sensors.

(d) What is the practical difference between inductive and capacitive sensors?

(e) What is the difference between photocells of the transmitting and the reflecting types?

(f) Discuss how an <u>incremental</u> encoder can be designed if the encoder is to have a resolution of better than 1°.

(g) Discuss how an <u>absolute</u> encoder can be designed if the encoder is to have a resolution of better than 1°. How many holes must the rotating disk have in that case?

(h) What is a tachometer?

(i) What is a solenoid? Name three types of equipment where solenoids are used.

Problem 2.2

(a) What is required in order to connect a two-wire sensor to an input module?

(b) What is a source-connected PLC input? What type of output must the sensors have in order to connect them to a source-connected input?

(c) Draw a sketch that shows how a three-wire sensor (PNP type) can be connected to a discrete input.

(d) Draw a sketch that shows how a 220V light bulb can be connected to a relay output.

(e) What properties can discrete inputs have?

3

Analog Signals and Analog I/O

> **Chapter Contents**
> - Analog versus discrete signals:
>   Sampling, quantification, coding
> - Analog "sensors":
>   Sensors, standard transmitters, measurement transformation, RTD elements, thermocouples
> - Connection of analog equipment:
>   Management of measured data, filtering, calibration, loss, compensation, grounding, cabling
> - Properties of analog input modules:
>   Resolution, updating speed, linearity, and so on
> - Analog output modules and their properties:
>   D/A-conversion, standard signal formats

3.1 Introduction

In the previous chapters, we discussed discrete, digital, and binary signals. Here, we will concentrate on analog signals. We begin with a definition:

> An analog signal is a signal with an amplitude that varies continuously with time (time-continuous) and within a given amplitude range.

In other words: An analog signal is defined for every instant of time within a given interval. A signal can be continuous in time but not in amplitude and is therefore, strictly speaking, not an analog signal, but we usually call it an analog signal anyway.

Programmable Logic Controllers: A Practical Approach to IEC 61131-3 Using CODESYS, First Edition. Dag H. Hanssen.
© 2015 John Wiley & Sons, Ltd. Published 2015 by John Wiley & Sons, Ltd.

Both discrete and analog signals can be represented as a unique function of frequencies that are called the signal's frequency spectrum. This is then a description of the frequency content of the signal. Filtering is a process where the frequency spectrum is modified, converted, or manipulated to satisfy a given or desired specification. This can involve amplification or suppression of a particular frequency range (selected frequency components) or removal or isolation of a particular frequency component. The uses of filters are many, but usually, the goal is to reduce signal contamination by removing noise that has been added during transmission of signals or disturbances that are the result of inaccuracies in measurements.

In this chapter, we will give a brief introduction to the processing of analog signals. We will look at various standard formats for signals in process engineering, how analog signals are converted to discrete (digital) signals, and vice versa in the PLC. We will also look briefly at the processing of discrete and analog signals, considerations involved in cabling, and a bit about connecting analog equipment.

3.2   Digitalization of Analog Signals

Most signals that are processed are analog to begin with (by nature). But the power and flexibility of computers, microprocessors, PLCs, and other digital equipment have made it necessary and vital to digitalize analog signals and process the digital signals in various ways.

A typical signal-processing system can be illustrated as shown in Figure 3.1.

The first operation (input filtering) reduces measurement noise and limits the frequency content of the signal for digitization. In operation number two, the actual conversion of the analog signal to a discrete signal takes place. This happens in a so-called *analog-to-digital converter* (A/D converter). Operation number three refers to what happens within the digital equipment (PLC, PC, etc.), while the last two stages cover conversion of the digital result to an analog output signal.

Analog signals can be read into the PLC via analog input modules (input blocks). Such modules come in many variants, but all have built-in filters. The first two steps in Figure 3.1 are built into such modules.

3.2.1   Filtering

All measurement signals will contain electrical noise. This is noise that typically appears in the form of high-frequency oscillations around the measurement signal itself. See Figure 3.2.

Such measurement noise is often the result of disturbances from other electronic equipment, for example, from the power supply or from operational equipment such as motors and pumps. Of course, measurement noise can also be a result of changes in the physical process variable that is being measured. An example of this is measuring the level of a fluid surface when the surface is disturbed (has ripples).

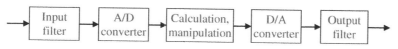

Figure 3.1   Typical operations in a signal-processing system: digitizing, processing, and reconstruction

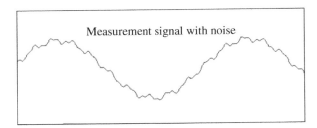

Figure 3.2   Example of measurement signal that contains noise

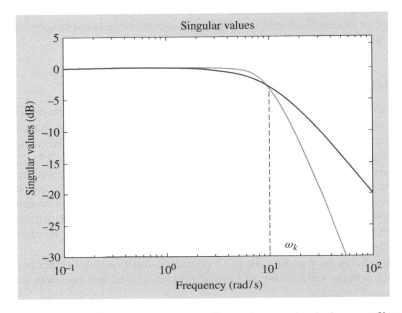

Figure 3.3   The frequency response to a first- and a second-order low-pass filter

Regardless of the cause, it is necessary to filter the signal in order to remove or reduce the noise. If the measurement noise has a frequency content that corresponds to the natural changes in the measurement signal, we have a major problem, and then it is not possible to filter it out. The simplest is then to try to remove the cause of the noise (see Section 3.5.1 on cabling).

As mentioned, the energy of the noise generally is in a higher range on the frequency scale than the energy in the signal. In this way, the noise can be removed or reduced by the use of a *low-pass filter*. To put it simply, a low-pass filter works by allowing all energy that lies below a certain frequency (the *cutoff frequency* of the filter) to pass through the filter unhindered, while energy above the cutoff frequency is reduced in strength.

Figure 3.3 shows the frequency response to a first-order and a second-order low-pass filter. A first-order filter is usually sufficient in most situations (higher orders give steeper filters). The cutoff frequency (ω_k) is most often defined as the frequency for which the damping is -3 dB.

The most common situation in the PLC context is that such a filter function is built into the analog input module in the form of hardware or software. The programmer can often configure the input to have a filter function and specify at which frequency the filter effect is to begin. How these values are stated varies between PLCs from individual manufacturers. Some utilize the filter's *response time*, $T_r = 1/\omega_k = 1/2\pi f_k$, while others operate with the concept of a *filter coefficient*, α. This coefficient indicates the filter effect of a first-ordered digital filter. Higher filter coefficients provide more filter effect (lower cutoff frequency).

3.2.2   A/D Conversion

Analog-to-digital converters are, as indicated, the unit that is used in order to digitize analog signals. In order to avoid using an A/D converter for each individual analog input signal, normally there is a multiplexer that routes one signal at a time into the A/D converter. Typically, there will also be an interface that contains a so-called "sample and hold" circuit.

A/D conversion can also include several other steps such as are shown in Figure 3.4. These steps are:

1. Sampling at fixed time intervals (sampling period *T*).
2. Use of a "sample and hold" circuit for quantifying and coding.
3. *Quantifying*. Here, each sample value is rounded off to the "nearest level possible."
4. *Coding*. Here, each quantified value is converted to a binary code. When the samples are quantified and coded, the signal is usually referred to as a digital signal.

Sampling

When an analog signal is sampled, this takes place at a certain speed called the sampling frequency. The concept of *sampling period* is often used or just plain sampling time. This is the time interval between each sample, *T*. Other notations that are common are Δt or T_s. The relationship between sampling frequency and sampling period is given by $f = 1/T$. If, for instance, we have a sampling period of $T = 0.1$ seconds, the sampling frequency $1/T = 10$ Hz, in other words, 10 sampling points every second. Sampling thus occurs at fixed intervals of time between samples as shown in Figure 3.5.

The discrete signal can be written as a sequence (arithmetic series) of all values (the numbers). Let us call this series $y(k)$, where the argument k indicates the sample number or, expressed another way, where in the sequence the value occurs. See Figure 3.6.

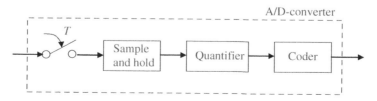

Figure 3.4   Principle for A/D conversion

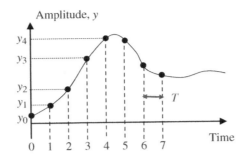

Figure 3.5   Illustration of sampling

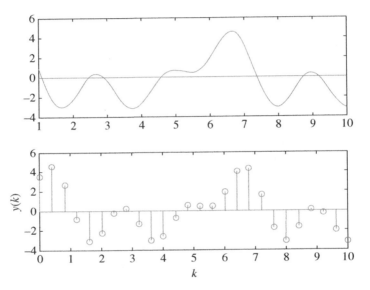

Figure 3.6   Original analog signal and the discrete signal $y(k)$

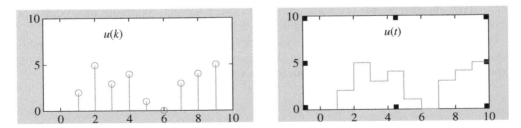

Figure 3.7   The signal before and after the "sample and hold" circuit

Sample and Hold

This said functional circuit is used to maintain the amplitude constant until the next sample arrives. This is done to permit the A/D converter to process the complete sample, that is, to both quantify and code. An illustration of the operation of a "sample and hold" function is shown in Figure 3.7.

Quantification

All digital systems (PCs, microcontrollers, PLCs, etc.) use a certain number of bits to represent and store a value. This means that the discrete sampled values are rounded off to the nearest possible level. How big this roundoff is depends on the number of bits used in the quantification. More bits give better resolution.

Example 3.1

In order to illustrate the effect of quantification, we take a (rather unrealistic) example with a three-bit quantifier. This means that the digital system has three bits available for a binary representation of each value. This makes the following quantified levels possible:

$$000,001,010,011,100,101,110, \text{ and } 111.$$

Let us assume that a signal that varies in the range 0–10V is to be digitized. The binary code 000 will then represent 0V and 111 will represent 10V (Figure 3.8).
After sampling, we will have (approximately) the following series of values:

$$y(k) = 1.8, 3.9, 5.3, 6.6, 7.3, 9.1, 5.8,...$$

These values must now be coded so that each value receives the binary code that is closest to the original value. Refer again to the figure and find that the series will have the following digital codes:

$$y(k) = 001, 011, 100, 100, 101, 110, 100,...$$

We see that even though the discrete samples can be quite different in value, they may have the same digital code. In this example, the value 5.3 and of the value 6.6 will both be represented by the binary number 100. This is what we call *quantification error*. It is easy to calculate what the maximum distortion introduced by this error will be. This number will then describe how good a resolution we have in our sampling process.

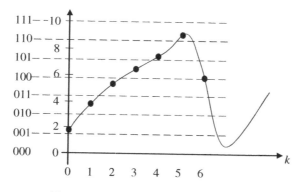

Figure 3.8   Example of quantification

With three bits, we have $2^3 = 8$ possible levels. This gives $8 - 1 = 7$ different intervals within which the individual sample can lie. Since the analog signal range is 0–10V, the difference (in volts) between each quantification level will be equal to $10 / 7 = 1.43\,V$. We get the maximum error when the sample lies between two levels, so the maximum error here is equal to $0.71\,V$.

A general formula for quantification error can be written as

$$\text{Error} = \frac{y_{max} - y_{min}}{2 \cdot \left(2^n - 1\right)}$$

where y_{max} and y_{min} represent the limits for the analog (electrical) signal range and n is the number of bits used in the quantification.

Example 3.2

An analog signal has an electrical value range from 4 to 20 mA. The signal is sampled and quantified with an 8-bit A/D converter. As a result of around half, the greatest error we can get will then be

$$\frac{y_{max} - y_{min}}{2 \cdot \left(2^n - 1\right)} = \frac{20 - 4}{2 \cdot \left(2^8 - 1\right)} = \frac{16}{2 \cdot \left(256 - 1\right)} = 0.0314\,mA$$

3.3   Analog Instrumentation

Instrumentation is actually a term that is too inclusive to be reasonably treated in full in a textbook on PLC programming. In the previous chapters, we discussed some logical sensors and the physical principles upon which their functions are based. This was done out of necessity so that the reader could recognize the most important sensor types.

Sensors/transmitters for measurement of quantities such as pressure, flow, temperature, and so on are dealt with in the specialty of instrumentation engineering which is a type of background knowledge that most of the people who work with PLCs have. Nevertheless, I have chosen to describe temperature sensors in this chapter because some type of temperature sensor (for instance, the PT100) can often be connected directly into some analog input modules.

Instead of a comprehensive introduction into the various principles of measurement, I have chosen to write about the different signal formats that are standard in traditional instrumentation, both for signals from the sensors and signals to actuators. Except for sensors and actuators that are designed for direct connection to field buses and the like, there are hardly any pieces of equipment that are not adapted to one or more of the ordinary signal formats.

3.3.1   About Sensors

As defined in the previous chapters, we will use the concept of *sensor* to refer to a unit that measures a physical quantity and converts this to a standard electrical signal.

There exist multitudes of analog sensors to measure all conceivable physical quantities. In the typical process industry, the most common quantities are temperature, pressure, flow, and level, but sensors for measuring things like humidity, oxygen, pH, distance/position, RPM, CO_2, etc. are also off-the-shelf merchandise.

Here, we will not go into detail about the various sensors that are obtainable; rather, we will be content to discuss two things: sensors/transmitters that output a standard electrical measurement signal and temperature sensors (thermocouples, resistance temperature detector (RTD), and thermistors). Temperature sensors can be purchased without extra electronics in the form of transmitters. They will then be sensors that do not output a standard electrical measurement signal. Thermocouples output a small voltage (thermovoltage) and RTDs and thermistors function so that the resistance in the sensor changes as a function of temperature. In accordance with the definition in Section 2.2, these are not temperature-sensitive sensors, but rather *transducers*. Many analog input modules for PLCs have built-in functions that permit temperature sensors to be connected directly to the modules nevertheless. If you want measurement signals in standard format, for example, because you have an input module that requires that, transmitters for temperature sensors can be purchased separately.

3.3.2 Standard Signal Formats

There are naturally many examples of current equipment that can be connected to various bus systems such as PROFIBUS, AS-i bus, CANbus, or Modbus, and the use of such bus systems increases continually. Nevertheless, it is perhaps still most common for sensors to be adapted to one or more of the electrical standards:

- 4–20 mA
- 1–5 V
- 0–10 V
- 0–5 V
- 0–20 mA

The reason for this standardization is obvious because it should be as simple as possible to connect a measurement signal to a PLC, for instance. When instrumentation buses (field buses) are used, standard transmitters are often used because these can be connected to the bus via other equipment.

The standard formats listed can also be collected in fewer categories because 0–20 mA corresponds to 0–5 V and 4–20 mA corresponds to 1–5 V, respectively. This conversion is obtained by sending current signals through a resistance of $250\,\Omega$.

3.3.3 On the 4–20 mA Standard

Of the electrical standards listed, 4–20 mA is decidedly the most common. There are several reasons for this:

1. A voltage signal is more susceptible to electromagnetic noise than a current signal.
2. When a measurement signal is in the form of the current signal, the measurement signal can be sent over a longer distance without loss (assuming that the sender can maintain

current strength). When we transmit voltage signals, conduction losses will always give a drop in voltage that can be significant for accuracy.

3. A lower limit of 4 mA is better than 0 mA because it is possible to monitor for a loss in the measurement signal.

Item 1

A voltage signal is more subject to noise than a current signal because electromagnetic noise can result in an added potential in the measurement signal via induction. Such errors can also be the result of potential differences in grounding. See Section 3.5.1.

Item 2

This is the most important reason for preferring current signals. Conductor loss is unavoidable but can be reduced to acceptable limits by using the proper cable. This is because voltage loss is a natural result of conduct or resistance. The recommended minimum cross section of twisted-pair cable for transmission of analog measurement signals is $0.28\,\text{mm}^2$. Such a cable has a typical conducting resistance of approximately $6.4\,\Omega$ per 100 m (per wire). The significance of conduct or resistance depends upon the input resistance at the unit (for instance, an analog input module) to which the signal is connected.

When we transmit a current signal, conduction losses is not a problem. This is a natural result of the fact that the current that moves from one terminal at the source must necessarily come back to the other terminal. *Note*: This naturally assumes that the current source can provide the current when the resistance increases.

Item 3

Assume that you have a level measurement device that is calibrated to output 0 mA at zero level and 20 mA at the level of 5 m. If the PLC registers 0 mA, this will be interpreted as a level of 0 m (which it could be), but 0 mA could also be the result of a break in the signal cable or a damaged level transmitter. This is the reason that a lower limit of 4 mA is to be preferred.

Example 3.3

A temperature transmitter has a measurement range from −30 to 70°C. The measurement signal is a current signal between 4 and 20 mA. There is a linear relationship between the temperature and the output measurement signal. At what temperature *t* is the measurement signal equal to 14.8 mA?

For the sake of neatness, we will make a sketch of the problem statement:

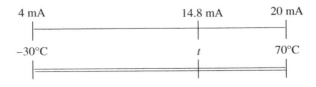

So how to find t? From the figure, we see that

$$\frac{\left(t-\left(-30°C\right)\right)}{\left(70°C-\left(-30°C\right)\right)} = \frac{14.8-4}{20-4} \Leftrightarrow \frac{t+30°C}{100°C} = \frac{10.8}{16} \Leftrightarrow$$

$$t = \frac{10.8}{16} \cdot 100°C - 30°C = \underline{\underline{37.5°C}}$$

3.3.4   Some Other Properties of Sensors

Among the kinds of errors from the sensor, we can distinguish between dynamic errors and static errors.

For *dynamic* errors, we can simply say that they result from the fact that it takes a certain amount of time for the sensor to output a stable electric signal after the physical variable being measured has changed. We usually talk about the *response time* of a sensor. A thermocouple is an example of a slow transducer where the response time can be significant if fast updates are required.

A *static* error is a stationary error which is a departure from the expected value *after* a sensor has stabilized. There can be many causes for a static failure: The natural tolerance stated by the manufacturer, calibration error, poor resolution, hysteresis and dead zone (often a result of where), improper application, etc.

It can often be difficult to determine whether a signal is outputting an erroneous signal. Sometimes it is necessary to compare the measurement with another reliable measurement.

Many sensors are equipped with adjustment screws to *calibrate* the sensor (transmitter). This adjusts the relationship between the physical signal and the electrical measured value, and this can reduce or remove static error. Because it is extremely important that the measured signal be as correct as possible, calibration should be done at fixed intervals, for instance, once per year.

3.4   Temperature Sensors

There are many different physical relationships that can be utilized for measuring temperature. Here, we will briefly review the three most important types of sensors used in industry:

- Thermocouples
- RTD (PT100 et al.)
- Thermistors

Among other types, we can mention *radiation pyrometers*. These can be used in situations where it is physically impossible or difficult to come into direct contact with the media in question.

3.4.1   Thermocouple

A thermocouple is based on the phenomenon that when two wires of different metal are connected, a voltage arises at the point of contact.[1] The size of this *thermal voltage* varies with temperature, and by measuring this, the temperature at the point of contact can be determined. In Figure 3.9, point A is the measurement point, and point B is called the reference point or the *cold* point.

---

[1] Thomas Seebek, 1821.

Point **A**, T_A Point **B**, T_B

Figure 3.9   Principle of the thermocouple

Table 3.1   Characteristics of the three types of thermocouple

Type	α (μV/°C)	Temperature range (°C)	Metal (alloy)
J	50	0–750	Iron/Constantan
K	39	−200 to 1250	Chromel/Alumel
T	38	−200 to 350	Copper/Constantan

The most important property of a thermocouple, aside from the temperature range for which it is designed, is the sensitivity, α, of the unit given in μV/°C.

There are (at least) 10 types of standardized thermocouples. Each of the types has its own characteristics. Three of the most common are the types J, K, and T, and the properties of these are shown in Table 3.1.

Other less common types are designated B, E, L, N, R, S, and U.

Thermocouples are simple, cheap, and relatively robust. Since they generate the voltage themselves, they do not require any operating voltage. They can be used without encapsulation (or with only modest encapsulation), and they therefore react relatively rapidly to temperature changes.

The greatest disadvantage is that the thermal voltage is extremely low, so that in practice, it must be amplified in order to avoid interference with measurements by weak noise signals. The sensitivity is typically about 1°C.

Thermocouples come with two wires of different types but with guaranteed properties. These wires are relatively expensive. When a thermocouple is to be used over a distance greater than specified for the attached cable, one can by so-called compensation cables. These are made of different types of metals and are therefore more reasonable. If the recommended type of compensation cable is used, there will not be any loss in the measured thermal voltage.

3.4.2   PT100/NI1000

All metals have the property that their electrical resistance rises with temperature. The type of temperature sensor based on this principle is generally designated as an RTD. Most often platinum (Pt) is used for low-temperature sensors that utilize this characteristic. Nickel is used to a certain extent because nickel is cheaper than platinum, but sensors of nickel are less accurate.

The most common unit is called a PT100 where PT stands for platinum and 100 stands for the resistance of 100 Ω at 0°C. At −200°C, the resistance is 18.53 Ω; at 100°C, the resistance is 138.5 Ω; and at +850°C, the resistance is approximately 390.38 Ω.

Even though the change in resistance with temperature is not exactly linear, we can use the following approximate relationship between temperature $T(°C)$ and resistance $R(\Omega)$ with acceptable accuracy in the temperature range 0–100°C:

$$R = 100 + 3.85 * T$$

A widely used RTD made of nickel is NI1000. There is also a variant called PT1000 that is used to some extent.

RTD units come in many designs and are usually calibrated by the manufacturer for various temperature ranges. This is very important if you are going to measure a narrow temperature range. A typical PT100 can be used in the temperature range −200 to 850°C, and this is a clear indication that there will be not much variation in the output signal if the unit is going to be used between 0 and 30°C.

The PT100 unit is relatively cheap and standardized. In industrial applications, however, it demands solid encapsulation, and the unit therefore reacts to temperature change somewhat more slowly than a thermocouple. However, the accuracy is somewhat better.

Figure 3.10 shows what a PT100 unit with encapsulation (industrial model) looks like. The picture at the right shows an example of the connection point inside the metal cover. The PT100 is often delivered with a transmitter with signal conversion placed within the watertight metal cover. The signal will then typically be the standard 4–20 mA.

Figure 3.11 shows an example of a simple PT100 sensor. In the background, there is a ruler to show that the sensor itself can be very small (here about 2×2 mm).

Figure 3.10   An industrial model of the PT100

Figure 3.11   Simple sensor—PT100 (thin-film RTD)

3.4.3 Thermistors

A thermistor, like an RTD, is also based on the change in resistance with a change in temperature, but the thermistor is made of a semiconductor material. Most thermistors have a resistance that decreases with increasing temperature. This is designated as negative temperature coefficient (NTC), but there are also *PTC* versions. Compared to a PT100 unit, thermistors are more accurate (about 10 times as sensitive), but they are also very nonlinear.

They therefore require comprehensive calibration with the associated conversion. Thermistors can be made very small and then react quickly to changes in temperature. The price increases along with the requirement for accuracy.

3.5 Connection

As mentioned previously, there are many types of analog input modules that can be ordered from various PLC manufacturers. The cheapest modules can be connected only to measurement signals that conform to the usual standard 4–20 mA/1–5 V and 0–10 V. There are also modules for direct connection of thermocouples and RTDs such as the PT100. Here, we will look at some of the aspects about connecting sensors that has an analog output.

3.5.1 About Noise, Loss, and Cabling

In nearly all industrial instrumentation, there is a common problem with noise having a negative effect on measured signals. Two main types of noise are radio-frequency noise and electromagnetic interference (EMI). The sources of such noise can be AC and DC motors, mobile and stationary radios, and other equipment that communicates via radio, TV, walkie-talkie, static discharges, large contactors and relays, other heavy-duty equipment, transformers, fluorescent tubes, etc.; the result of such noise can sometimes be negligible, but occasionally, there are severe consequences for operation of the facility.

Measurement signals that operate at low signal strength are particularly susceptible to noise; these include signals generated by temperature sensors such as RTD (ohms) or thermocouples (mV).

The greater the separation between sensors and modules, the more noise is typically captured since the cables themselves can act as antennas for radio-frequency noise or induced currents from EMI sources.

An effective way of reducing the noise problem is to use transmitters such that the measurement signal comes in the form of high-level signals (for instance, 4–20 mA). The signals can then be transmitted over considerable distances. If you're going to select transmitters that are going to be used in areas that are strongly subject to noise, it can therefore be beneficial to check the specifications applying to protection against such noise.

A concept that is closely associated with EMI is electromagnetic compatibility (EMC). The following definition of EMC is taken from Kurt-Even Kristensen/Petter Brækken:

> The ability of a facility, piece of equipment or system to function satisfactorily in its electromagnetic environment without encountering unacceptable electromagnetic disturbance from something in this environment.

In other words, EMC for equipment or a system is that the equipment or system:

- Does not interfere with other equipment or systems that may be located in the same environment
- Are not susceptible to interference from other equipment or systems
- Do not interfere with themselves

Of greatest importance in connection with analog measurements is to attempt to reduce potential noise in the signals. It is also important to be careful to balance any potential differences. It is therefore recommended that one pay attention to the following:

- Types of cables and conductors
- Cable shielding and grounding
- Placement

Type of Cable

In order to reduce the effects of noise, shielded twisted-pair cable should be (must be) used. The conductor resistance may also be significant for transmission of a measurement signal over greater distances. This particularly applies to transmission of voltage signals and in connecting thermistors, and RTD is in two-wire and three-wire connections.[2] Fortunately, input modules for analog signals have high input impedance.[3] This prevents even long measuring cables from having a significant voltage drop across the cable. See Example 3.4.

As is well known, the resistance of the conductor can be calculated from the following relationship:

$$R = \frac{\rho \cdot L}{A} \left(\rho = \text{resistivity}, L = \text{length}, A = \text{cross section} \right)$$

For copper, $\rho = 17.9\,\Omega \cdot \text{mm}^2/\text{km} = 0.0179\,\Omega \cdot \text{mm}^2/\text{m}$.

In other words, a copper wire with a cross section of $1\,\text{mm}^2$ will have a conductive resistance equal to $1.79\,\Omega/100\,\text{m}$. A wire with a cross section of $1\,\text{mm}^2$ is a relatively heavy wire to measure such signals. The recommended minimum thickness is a cross section of $0.28\,\text{mm}^2$. A conductor with this cross section has a conductive resistance of approximately $6.4\,\Omega/100\,\text{m}$.

Example 3.4

A 200-m paired cable with a cross section of $0.28\,\text{mm}^2$ is used to transmit a 0–10 V measurement signal to an analog input that has an impedance of 1 MΩ. How big will the maximum voltage drop across the cable be?

Since there are two wires in the cable, the total resistance will be

$$2 \cdot \frac{0.0179 \cdot 200}{0.28} = 25.6\,\Omega$$

---

[2] See Section 3.5.3, Connection of the PT100.
[3] Schneider Electric specifies the input impedance for its TSX AEZ414 module to be about 10 MΩ when the module is provided with operating voltage.

The current through the cable will then have a maximum value of

$$\frac{10V}{\left(1\cdot10^6+25.6\right)\Omega}\approx10\,\mu A$$

Voltage drop across the cable is then

$$10\cdot10^{-6}\cdot25.6=0.26\,mV$$

As the example shows, the loss over a cable with this cross section is small, even at a relatively long distance. Since the measurement signal was originally 10V, we will then measure about 9.9997V. This is so insignificant a loss that the equipment will scarcely be able to measure it in practice.

Cable Shielding and Grounding

Cables that will be used to carry analog measured values must be shielded in order to reduce the effects of noise. The shielding of the cable must be connected to ground at one end in order to keep it from functioning as a *ground loop*, where the current through the shielding itself can lead to noise in the signal. (For high-frequency signals, the shielding should be grounded in both ends.)

For modules with unisolated channels, the use of sensors and preactuators that are not referenced to ground are recommended. Otherwise, all sensors should be referenced to the same point at which the modules are connected to ground. See Figure 3.12.

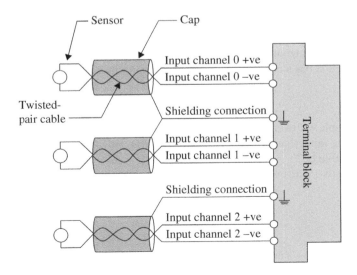

Figure 3.12   Connecting sensors

Cable Placement

Conductors that transfers signal of the same type with the same reference potential to ground can be grouped together. Discrete I/O cables (especially from relay outputs) should be placed as far away from the analog cables as possible. The same is true for power supply cabling.

3.5.2 Connecting Sensors

As Figure 3.12 shows, all electric measurement signals that are in standard format (for instance, 1–5 V, 0–10 V, or 4–20 mA) can be connected directly to the connectors at the analog input modules. When suitable cables are used, there can also be a considerable distance between the transmitter and the module. See also Example 3.4 on page 65.

Some modules are adapted to one or more standard electrical measurement ranges, but still others can be configured for the individual inputs. The module in Figure 3.13 is a configurable module that can handle several different types of signal. If one wants to connect to a measurement signal that arrives as a standard current signal (0–20 mA/ 4–20 mA), one must attach a resistance (shunt resistance) of 250 Ω in parallel across the input terminals in question.[4] (This figure shows such a shunt resistor connected across terminals 7 and 8.)

This works because the module has high input impedance. In this way, the current signal that the sensor sets up will pass through the resistor and become a voltage drop across it (4 mA * 250 Ω = 1 V and 20 mA * 250 Ω = 5 V). The figure also shows that the module can have the thermocouple connected directly, without the use of the transmitter.

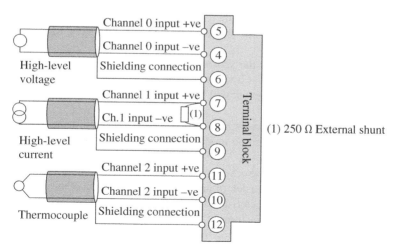

Figure 3.13 Example of various connections to the TSX AEZ 414 module

---

[4] Some manufacturers offer such multirange modules with their own connectors for current signals so that the user does not need to provide these. There is then a built-in shunt resistor in the module.

One Sensor: Several Inputs

Occasionally, one would like to connect to the signal from one and the same sensor to several analog input modules. This is possible but one should make sure that the sensor can maintain all of its properties at a higher loading.

If the transmitter at the sensor provides a voltage signal, the inputs may be connected in parallel. The total resistance will therefore decrease (to one-half for two equivalent modules), and normally, the transmitter will not have any problem maintaining the proper output voltage.

If the transmitter provides a current signal, the input module must be wired in series and then the total resistance in the circuit will increase. Then you must check that the transmitter will be able to maintain the current. The maximum possible distance between sensor or transmitter and input modules will naturally be reduced as well.

3.5.3   Connection of a PT100 (RTD)

Many analog input modules are designed to connect directly to temperature sensors such as thermocouples and RTDs, without needing to use transmitters to convert the measurement signal to an electrical signal. Such modules are apt to be expensive, but one saves money in not having to buy the transmitters.

RTD elements are actually only temperature-dependent resistances. In order to be able to measure the signals from RTDs, the module must therefore convert a change in resistance to drop in voltage. This is easily accomplished in having such modules have a built-in current supply that sets up a constant current through the sensor. When the resistance in the sensor changes with temperature, the voltage drop across the sensor will also change as the temperature changes.

If the input module has only one current connector[5] and several RTD elements are to be connected to the module, all of these must be connected in series. The current source is designed for this, but one must also be aware that if there is a failure in one of the sensors or in the supply cable, the signal from all the sensors that are connected in the loop will be lost.

Note: Under no circumstances may the sensors be connected in parallel! This will naturally mean that each sensor receives only a fraction of the current from the current source and the measurement results from all the sensors will be misleading.

The built-in current source generates a relatively small current to keep the sensors from being heated up by the current.[6] In some modules, the current is sent out as pulses to further reduce the heating effect.

Suppliers of modules guarantee correct operation up to a given maximum resistance (cable + sensor).[7] This total resistance therefore determines the maximum length of the connecting cables. It is also necessary to know the characteristics of both the connecting cables, and the maximum total resistance is given by the manufacturer of the analog module.

Now, we will study three ways of connecting an RTD: two-wire, three-wire, and four-wire connections.

[5] This is the case for the TSXAEZ414 module from Telemecanique.
[6] For the AEZ 414 module, the manufacturer gives this current at 1.437 mA.
[7] For the 750–464 module from Wago, this current is stated as less than 350 µA.

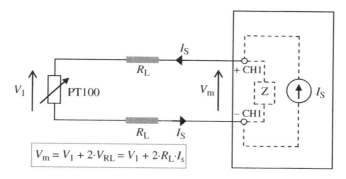

Figure 3.14 PT100 connected in two-wire connection

3.5.3.1 RTD in Two-Wire Connection

In connecting an RTD in a two-wire connection, the current is connected from the source in the module directly into the input terminals where the cables from the sensor are also connected. See Figure 3.14. Here, the module's internal current source is illustrated by the symbols +Is and −Is. Z represents the input impedance. Because of the high input impedance, in practice, the entire current passes through the sensor. The module will then measure the resulting voltage drop.

The major disadvantage of such a connection is that the measured values will not be correct (the error is directly proportional to the distance between the sensor and the module, something that is naturally due to the resistance in the conductors (marked R_L in the figure). The voltage drop V_2 measured by the module is greater than the voltage drop V_1 across the sensor because of the voltage drops in the conductors. The advantage of the two-wire connection is that it requires only half as much wire as a four-wire connection.

Example 3.5 Calculation of Cable Loss for a P100 in a Two-Wire Connection

Assume that a two-wire PT100 sensor is located 50 m from the PLC and connected via a copper cable with a conductor cross section of 1 mm². Assume that we know that the temperature at the sensor is 75°C. What temperature can be read at the input module?

Answer: The cable resistance can be easily calculated as $R = 0.0179 \cdot 50 \cdot 2/1 = 1.8\,\Omega$.

This resistance will therefore be in addition to the resistance of the PT100 unit. If we use the approximation that one degree of temperature increase corresponds to a $0.39\,\Omega$ increase in resistance, the cable loss will be interpreted as an addition to the temperature of $1.8/0.39 = 4.6°C$. The temperature that will be read by the PLC will therefore be approximately 79.6°C instead of 75°C for an error of a full 6% (4.6/75 * 100%).

However, the voltage drop across the measurement cable can be compensated for. It is possible to configure the modules by subtracting a constant quantity (*bias*) from the measurement. The magnitude of this compensating voltage can be simply determined by multiplying the current from the module by the total conductor resistance.

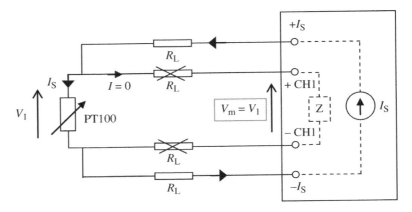

Figure 3.15   PT100 connected in a four-wire connection

3.5.3.2   RTD in Four-Wire Connection

In connecting an RTD in a four-wire connection, the current is sent from the module source through its own conductors right out to the sensor. See Figure 3.15.

Since the inputs have (relatively) high impedance, no significant current will flow through the connector cables. In the figure, this is illustrated by having the symbols for conductor resistance crossed out (the resistance, naturally, has not gone away). *At any rate, the voltage drop across the input terminals will thereby be equal to the voltage drop across the sensor* ($V_m = V_1$).

It is for this reason that this is the connection that provides the highest accuracy without compensation. However, the four-wire connection needs twice as much cable as the two-wire connection.

Figure 3.16 shows a connection diagram for how several RTDs can be connected to the same module. We see that the source current I_S from the module goes through all of the sensors and back into the module. The three signal inputs to the module are marked ±CH1, ±CH2, and ±CH3. Since the conductor resistance in the signal conductors is not significant, I have chosen to illustrate this in the figures; the sketch also shows that one can save a little cabling because –CH1 and +CH2 are the same point, electrically speaking. The same is true of –CH2 and +CH3.

3.5.3.3   RTD in Three-Wire Connection

This is a variation on the two previous connections. Here, we are using a separate conductor to carry a constant current out to the unit while the return passes through one of the measurement conductors. This cuts the error in half relative to the two-wire connection. See Figure 3.17.

Another advantage of the configuration in Figure 3.17 is that *the module can compensate automatically for measurement errors due to conductor resistance.*[8] This is possible because the module can register the voltage drop V_{Loss} shown in the figure.

Given that this requires three conductors of the same type and length out to the unit, the magnitude of the voltage drop V_{Loss} is identical to the voltage drop across the measurement

---

[8] This is done in the 750–464 module from Wago.

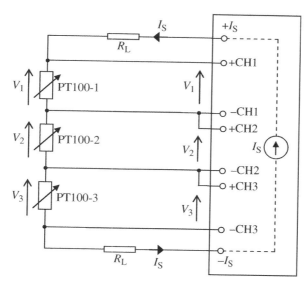

Figure 3.16   Three PT100 sensors connected to the same module

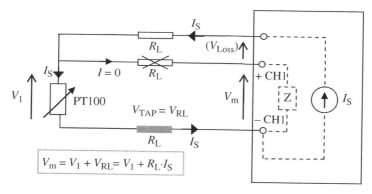

Figure 3.17   PT100 connected in a three-wire connection. (*Note*: Modern modules designed for three-wire measurement can compensate automatically for the conductor loss.)

conductors that constitute the measurement error. Firmware[9] in the module can then easily compensate for the error by subtracting the value of V_{Loss} from the measured value, and the measurement ends up being correct.

This is not possible in a two-wire connection simply because there is not another measurement point other than the two where the voltage drop across the (sensor + cable) is measured.

---

[9] Firmware is the designation for programming that is permanently stored in electronic equipment, generally in ROM or flash memory.

3.5.4   Connecting Thermocouples

Thermocouples such as types B, J, K, and so forth provide output signals in the form of a voltage. This voltage is very low and also depends on the temperature in the connecting terminals.

The simplest and cheapest way of connecting a thermocouple is just to connect the wires to the desired input terminals (naturally, assuming that the module is designed to be connected to a thermocouple). Cold-point compensation is then performed within the module since the temperature inside the module is reasonably constant and is used as a reference temperature for the unit. This measurement setup can be affected by changes in the PLC temperature. However, the recommended implementation is for cold-point compensation to be done by the module with the help of a reference-temperature measurement. This is normally done with a built-in PT100 or a thermistor.

Note that it is not recommended to obtain measurement data from one and the same thermocouple by the help of several modules. In theory, since the measurement signal is in the form of voltage, one would think that the signal from a thermocouple could be connected to several modules. In practice, this cannot be done because it does not furnish effective cold-point compensation.

3.6   Properties of Analog Input Modules

Every PLC distributor can usually offer several different analog input modules, completely depending upon your requirements. If you are going to select the proper modules, there are often many aspects that should be taken into consideration before the selection, perhaps the most important are:

- Electrical (and physical) measurement ranges
- Requirement for accuracy (resolution)
- Number of input signals
- Requirement for speed (updating speed of the module)
- How the signals are physically connected to the module
- Requirements for use in explosive environments

Other criteria that can come into question are:

- *Tolerance (physical)*: How much physical abuse such as dust, temperature, etc. will the module tolerate? How much will the individual inputs tolerate?
- *Linearity*: Is the module linear across the entire range of measurement?
- *Calibration/Adjustment*: For instance, can you add a bias the measurement to compensate for a poorly installed sensor or transmitter or to compensate for a voltage drop over long cabling hauls? This last comes into question when one uses a PT100 two-wire connection.
- Filtering possibilities.

3.6.1   Measurement Ranges and Digitizing: Resolution

Like a PC, a PLC can work only with digital quantities. It is therefore necessary to convert analog measurement signals to digital quantities. This transformation takes place in the input block's own built-in A/D converter.

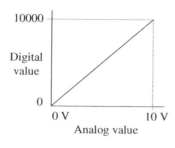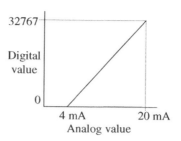

Figure 3.18 Conversion from analog signal to whole-number value

Which format (binary, BCD, HEX, etc.) will represent the signal values varies for the different brands of PLC. Even though the individual modules and blocks themselves sample the analog signals with 16-bit resolution, for instance, the effective resolution normally is not correspondingly high. This is because the manufacturers generally have chosen to use whole-number values to represent the analog signals. This makes it simpler from both the engineering and the programming point of view to manage the analog quantities. Usually, 16 bits are used to represent the corresponding binary value.

For instance, an analog signal connected to PLC of the Omron C200H will be represented as a binary number corresponding to values between 0 and 4000. In the TSX series from Telemecanique, an analog signal will be converted to a decimal value between 0 and 10000 by default.

Wago uses a standard 16-bit representation. Since one bit is used for a sign, a bipolar electrical quantity is represented by numbers between $-2^{16} = -32768$ and $2^{16} - 1 = 32767$ (one combination represents the value 0).

There is of course a linear relationship as shown in the graphical presentation in Figure 3.18.

Example 3.6

A temperature transmitter is calibrated to provide an electrical signal between 4 and 20 mA for temperatures between −20 and 50°C. In the PLC, the measured value is stored as an integer between 0 and 10000. A temperature of +20°C will therefore appear in the PLC as the number

$$\frac{10000}{50-(-20)} \cdot \left(20-(-20)\right) = \frac{10000}{70} \cdot 40 \approx 5714$$

The exact number according to this calculation is 5714.2857, but rounding off to the nearest integer gives a small error. How great the error can be is easy to calculate:

$$\text{Maximum error}: \frac{50-(-20)}{2 \cdot (10000-0)} = 0.0035°C$$

If we had not divided by 2 here, the answer from calculation would be equal to the interval (in °C) between two integers. We have the maximum error when the measurement falls between two integers, for instance, 2546.5, which would then be rounded off to the number 2647.

3.6.2   Important Properties and Parameters

In this section, we will consider some of the properties of analog input modules that are interesting in a practical context. These can be:

- Update time
- Linearization
- Overshoot
- Alignment
- Calibration
- Filters

Update Time

For an analog input, it is interesting to know the time it takes for the value of the measured signal to become available for the user program. This depends upon the following:

- The response time of the sensor (for instance, temperature sensors are relatively slow).
- The update time of the analog module. Here, there is usually a certain delay as the result of filtering.
- The cycle time of the user program (scan time).

It is important to be clear about the performance of an analog module with respect to speed. In most cases, the module in question will be sufficiently fast, but if the PLC is also being used as a PID-controller, for instance, this can be too slow for some processes, the alternative is to procure a faster module or to use an external PID-controller and possibly adjust the setting point of the controller from the PLC.

   With respect to the speed of analog modules, we distinguish between the scan time for a single channel (input) and the scan time for the module as a whole (cycle time). However, the scan time for the cycle is always the same, even if some of the channels are not being used.

Example 3.7

The AEZ 414 module from Telemecanique has these published scan times:

Per channel: 104 ms
Cycle time: 520 ms

Linearization

All modules that can be directly connected to thermistors, for instance, must be able to perform a linearization of the measured signal. This is because there is a nonlinear connection between temperature change and resistance change and the measured voltage is not a linear function of temperature either.

Overshoot

No matter what measurement ranges selected for channel input, the module will register any overshoot. The module checks whether the measurement lies within the measurement range, that is, between the lower and upper range limits. Overshoot is generally monitored by setting a flag (a Boolean address associated with the channel in question.

Alignment

It is often possible to adjust a desired measured value by adding a constant positive or negative *bias* to the measurement. It may be desirable in those instances to know that a measured signal is erroneous because it is either too low or too high. The reason for this error can be an incorrectly calibrated sensor or a conductor loss that one wishes to compensate for. This latter is the case when using a PT100, for instance, in a two-wire connection.

Calibration

In some modules, it is possible to perform the calibration of the module itself. This can come into question when the module does not measure correctly on one of the channels, for example. Such a calibration is normally not to be recommended.

Filters

All analog input modules are equipped with low-pass filters for filtering measurement signals. The reason for using a low-pass filter is that the physical quantities often change relatively smoothly in comparison to noise (which also is typically higher in frequency). The cutoff frequency of the filter can normally be adjusted.

3.7   Analog Output Modules and Standard Signal Formats

Many of the same properties that apply to input modules also apply to output modules as well. Typical equipment that can be controlled by analog signals are valve position, frequency-controlled pumps and motors, and controller (set point).

The most common standards are 0–10 V, ±10 V, 4–20 mA, and 0–20 mA, but there are also modules that use other formats.

For voltage outputs, there are limitations on how much current a module can provide. Actuators connected to outputs must therefore have an input resistance that is greater than the minimum limit published for the module in question. Otherwise, the module will not be able to maintain the output voltage.

If a module is short-circuited, the output voltage will naturally enough be equal to 0 V, but the outputs are normally protected by optical couplers to handle this.

In order to be able to control actuators with standard current signals, modules have a built-in current source. The actuators must therefore have a resistance that exceeds a defined minimum limit. This limit is also specified in the data sheets for the modules in question.

For all PLCs, it is also possible to specify what is to be sent out from an output if the PLC stops or is set in to stop mode. This applies to digital outputs as well. Either the output value is set to its lower limit, for instance, 0 V or 4 mA (FALSE for digital outputs), or the output will maintain the last value transmitted.

We will close the chapter with an example of an analog output module and its specifications.

Example 3.8

The AEZ414 module from Telemecanique has four outputs for 0–10 V/±10 V. The response time of the module is 400 μs, which is very fast compared to an analog input module. The module uses 11 bits (+sign) in its D/A converter, which gives a resolution of $10/(2^{11} - 1) = 5$ mV. (Typical error according to the datasheet, however, is 0.45% corresponding to 45 mV.)

Maximum load of the outputs is 5 mA, which corresponds to actuators having an input resistance not less than 2 kΩ. The module has permanent short-circuit protection.

3.8   Test Problems

Problem 3.1
(a) What are the major differences between a thermistor and an RTD?
(b) An analog input module uses 12-bit A/D conversion. What is the largest possible round-off error that can occur as a result of quantifying if the signal to be digitized lies in the range −10 V to +10 V?
(c) Assume that a PT100 sensor is located 40 m from the PLC. The sensor is connected to an input module on the PLC via a copper cable with a conductor cross section of 0.25 mm². The temperature at the sensor is 50°C. What temperature can be read at the input module if the sensor is connected to a two-wire connection? (The resistivity of copper is 0.0179 Ω·mm²/m.)

Problem 3.2
A temperature sensor provides an analog signal between 4 and 20 mA for temperatures between 10 and 80°C. The temperature sensor is connected to an analog input that has the address %IW3. Assume that the PLC converts the current signal to a whole-number value between 0 and 32 000. At what temperature is the content of the address %IW3 equal to 12 000?

Problem 3.3
The table below shows data for three analog quantities that are connected to a PLC.

Symbol name	Inputs	Physical range	Electrical range	Internal representation
Temp	%IW3.0	−50 to 200 (°C)	4–20 mA	0–32 767
Pressure	%IW3.1	0–5 (bar)	1–5 V	0–32 767
Level	%IW3.2	0–150 (cm)	0–20 mA	0–32 767

(a) As the table shows, three active transmitters are used, all of which have different electrical measurement ranges. Briefly state which of the three standard measurement ranges is preferable, where there is a choice, and say why.

(b) During a run, the value in address %IW3.0 is about 9600. What electrical measurement value corresponds to this and what is the temperature (in degrees)?

(c) It is suspected that there is an error in the level sensor and/or the level transmitter such that the measured error is perhaps outside the defined acceptable limit of 5%. A manual reading is therefore made and it appears that the level is approximately 90 cm. By using a multimeter, the current at the level transmitter is read at 13 mA. Is this within the acceptable error limits, or should something be done?

Problem 3.4

A small PT100 element (symbolized by a variable resistance) is installed at the end of a relatively long cable. Two of the wires, green and green/white, are connected to one end of the unit, while the two others, red and red/white, are connected to the other end of the sensor. Schematic:

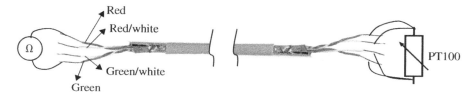

In the problems below, you can use the approximation that $0.385\ \Omega$ corresponds to $1°C$.

(a) Assume that you use a multimeter and measure the resistance between the red and green wires as illustrated in the figure above. You measure $113\ \Omega$. Then you measure the resistance of the PT100 unit itself (at the other end of the cable) and read $110.8\ \Omega$.
  1. How much is the resistance in one of the wires in the cable?
  2. What is the temperature where the PT100 unit is located?

(b) Assume that you connect the cable as a two-wire connection (where you use only the red and green wires) to an RTD module on the PLC. How great a measurement error do you get as a result of the conduct resistance in the cable?

(c) Assume that you again connect the cable as a two-wire connection but that you connect green and green/white in parallel to one connector and red and red/white in parallel to the other connector. What temperature will you read now?

(d) What, if anything, can be done to remove the measurement error attributable to loss in the cable?

Part Two
Methodic

4

Structured Design

There are 10 kinds of people in the world:
Those who understand binary numbers and those who do not.
(Unknown)

4.1 Introduction

Many of the fundamental operations and signal-processing routines performed by a PLC require that the programmer have a fundamental knowledge of and understanding of binary numbers, logical (Boolean) quantities, and Boolean algebra. We can use logical functional expressions to describe instructions and actions and use Boolean algebra to simplify these for implementation. For more advanced programmers, there are also techniques and systematic presentations that can be used in order to structure both the tasks that the PLC is to solve and the operational mode of the program itself. This chapter is intended to cover the necessary knowledge concerning these subjects.

Programmable Logic Controllers: A Practical Approach to IEC 61131-3 Using CODESYS, First Edition. Dag H. Hanssen.
© 2015 John Wiley & Sons, Ltd. Published 2015 by John Wiley & Sons, Ltd.

The chapter therefore begins with a short introduction to digital techniques. We will look at number systems such as the binary number system and the hexadecimal number system as well as conversions between these.

4.2   Number Systems

A basic knowledge of different number systems and conversions among these systems is necessary in connection with programming PLCs. Which format the values and numbers are stored in and processed in varies between different PLCs, but most of them use one or more standard formats. These formats can be binary numbers (BCD coded), hexadecimal, and octal, in addition to decimal members. Here, we will discuss the formats that are used most frequently.

4.2.1   The Decimal Number Systems

A brief presentation of the decimal number system is useful to facilitate understanding of the structure of the other number systems. The decimal number system or the 10-base system, as it is also called, operates with the number 10 as the *base number*. Fundamentally, this means that this number system uses 10 different numerals to write all numbers. Furthermore, the base number is the factor between positions of the numerals.

Example 4.1

As is well known, a decimal number can be split up as shown below:

$$3647 = 3 \cdot 10^3 + 6 \cdot 10^2 + 4 \cdot 10^1 + 7 \cdot 10^0 = 3000 + 600 + 40 + 7$$

As we see, each different numeral has a defined *weight* depending upon its placement in the number:

3647

Number of thousands ⊢   ⊣ Number of units

Number of hundreds ⊢   ⊣ Number of 10's

4.2.2   The Binary Number System

All digital equipment such as computers is based on *binary* numbers. These are numbers that are built up out of only two different numerals, namely, 0 and 1. In digital equipment, the numeral 0 is represented by a voltage of 0 V, while the numeral 1 is represented by a voltage of 5 V.

The word *binary* comes from the fact that each numeral has two states. All binary numbers can be expressed by means of only the two numerals 0 and 1. The binary number system is also called the 2-base system. The base number in that number system is therefore 2.

Example 4.2

Any random binary number can be split up as shown below:

$$11010101 = 1 \cdot 2^7 + 1 \cdot 2^6 + 0 \cdot 2^5 + 1 \cdot 2^4 + 0 \cdot 2^3 + 1 \cdot 2^2 + 0 \cdot 2^1 + 1 \cdot 2^0$$
$$= 1 \cdot 128 + 1 \cdot 64 + 0 \cdot 32 + 1 \cdot 16 + 0 \cdot 8 + 1 \cdot 4 + 0 \cdot 2 + 1 \cdot 1$$
$$= 128 + 64 + 0 + 16 + 0 + 4 + 0 + 1 = 213 \,(\text{decimal})$$

Here, each numeral has a particular *weight* depending upon its placement in the number:

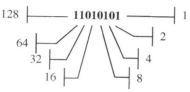

There is a factor of 2 (the base number) between each position in the number.

(Perhaps now you understand the quotation on the first page of this chapter?)

In the digital world, we call each of the 1s and 0s a *bit*. The bit that has the highest weight (value) is designated the most significant bit (MSB). The bit that has the lowest weight is designated the least significant bit (LSB). A group of eight bits, such as in the example above, is called a *byte* while a group of 16 bits is called a *word*.

4.2.3 The Hexadecimal Number System

Numbers that originally are in binary form are often displayed and transmitted in another form, namely, as *hexadecimal* numbers. The hexadecimal number system is also used in PLCs and has the base number of 16. This means that there are 16 different symbols that are used in this number system. These are

$$0,1,2,3,4,5,6,7,8,9,\mathbf{A},\mathbf{B},\mathbf{C},\mathbf{D},\mathbf{E},\mathbf{F}$$

As we see, the letters A through F are used instead of the numbers 10–15.

Example 4.3

$$E3C8 = 14 \cdot 16^3 + 3 \cdot 16^2 + 12 \cdot 16^1 + 8 \cdot 16^0 = 58312 \,(\text{decimal})$$

Again, the numeral has a *weight* depending upon its position in the number:

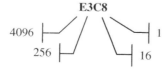

There is a factor of 16 (the base number) between each position in the number.

Table 4.1 Examples of decimal, binary, and hexadecimal numbers

Decimal	Binary	Hexadecimal
0	0000	0
1	0001	1
2	0010	2
3	0011	3
4	0100	4
5	0101	5
6	0110	6
7	0111	7
8	1000	8
9	1001	9
10	1010	A
11	1011	B
12	1100	C
13	1101	D
14	1110	E
15	1111	F

The hexadecimal number system is often used to represent binary numbers because the numbers can be expressed much more compactly. For example, a four-place hexadecimal number corresponds to a binary number of 16 bits (a word).

Table 4.1 contains the numbers from 0 to 15 in decimal, binary, and hexadecimal form.

The binary number 1111, which is 15 in decimal and F in hexadecimal, is the largest number that can be expressed with four bits. The standard register size[1] in most PLCs is therefore 16 bits. The largest number that we can store in a register address is 1111 1111 1111 1111 which corresponds to FFFF in hexadecimal.

The corresponding decimal number is

$$FFFF = 15 \cdot 16^3 + 15 \cdot 16^2 + 15 \cdot 16^1 + 15 \cdot 16^0 = 65535$$

If bipolar values, that is, values that could be either positive or negative, are to be stored, the MSB is used as a sign bit. In that case, values between -2^{15} and $2^{15} - 1$, that is, between $-32\,768$ and $32\,767$,[2] can be stored by using 16 bits.

As mentioned previously, sometimes hexadecimal numbers are used as an alternative to the binary form when values are to be shown on the display/screen or when values are to be transmitted. That is to say that a 16-bit number is divided into groups of four numerals. Each of the groups is represented by a symbol between 0 and F. Example:

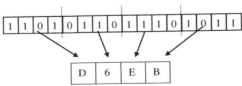

---

[1] A register is a storage location where numbers can be stored in binary form.
[2] The reason that the largest possible value is "merely" $2^{15} - 1 = 32\,767$ is that one of the bit combinations, namely, where all 16 bits are equal to 0 is used to represent only the number 0.

4.2.4   Binary-Coded Decimal Numbers

Numbers in binary-coded decimal (BCD) form are not so different from numbers in binary form. The difference is that for each numeral (0 through 9) in the decimal number is represented by four bits. This means that the numbers 0–9 are precisely like the numbers 0–9 in binary form. If we study a four-bit number, however, we have six bit combinations that are not valid in BCD form. These are the combinations for the hexadecimal numbers A–F (decimal 10–15). Table 4.2 shows the BCD code.

Example 4.4

The decimal number 6923 will be stored in BCD form as 0110 1001 0010 0011. Note that this is entirely different from the binary notation. In binary form, the same number would be represented as 0001 1011 0000 1011 (try the conversion yourself) while the hexadecimal number would be 1B0B.

What are the consequences of this? First, it limits how large a number we can operate within 16-bit registers. The largest number in BCD form would then be 9999. However, the advantage is that in calculation operations with larger integers, the content of two adjacent addresses, each address holding a four-digit number, can be considered as a single number, that is, an eight-place number. For example, we can then perform the multiplication 99999999 * 99999999. The result of this operation is $9.99 * 10^{15}$, and the result will occupy four addresses or 64 bits. In most cases, such large numbers will be more than sufficient.

Summary

All digital equipment such as a PLC performs calculations and stores values in binary form. However, it is not particularly user-friendly to work with and read binary numbers. Therefore, most digital equipment operates with several different number systems where one of them is, of course, the decimal number system. All PLCs of recent vintage use the decimal number system in the user interface.

Some older PLC models, for example, the OMRON 200H, use BCD numbers.

Table 4.2   Binary-coded decimal numbers

Decimal number	BCD code
0	0000
1	0001
2	0010
3	0011
4	0100
5	0101
6	0110
7	0111
8	1000
9	1001

A number in a PLC can be in binary form and perhaps will be displayed in hexadecimal form. Knowledge about number systems can be useful when we perform calculations in a PLC or when we process analog signals. The next chapter will touch on some of these problems.

4.2.5 Conversion between Number Systems

Binary to Decimal

Example 4.2 showed how one can convert a binary number to a decimal number. It is necessary only to add up all of the weights of all of the 1s in the number.

Example 4.5

$$0101101 = 0\cdot2^6 + 1\cdot2^5 + 0\cdot2^4 + 1\cdot2^3 + 1\cdot2^2 + 0\cdot2^1 + 1\cdot2^0 = 32+8+4+1 = 45$$

It is naturally also possible to write numbers with a *decimal point* in binary form as shown in the next example. Notice how the numbers after the decimal point are weighted. The base number is, naturally enough, still 2, but the exponent that indicates the position is negative.

Example 4.6

$$11010.101 = 2^4 + 2^3 + 2^1 + 2^{-1} + 2^{-3} = 16+8+2+0.5+0.125 = 26.625$$

Decimal to Binary

In order to convert from decimal numbers to binary numbers, you must divide (either do it in your head or with a calculator).

The procedure is to divide the decimal number by 2 repeatedly. If the division yields an integer, the remainder is 0. If the division does not yield an integer, the remainder is 1. This remainder (0 or 1) becomes the LSB in the binary number and is written down. Then one continues to deal with the result from the previous division until the number is reduced to nothing (zero).

The last remainder from the last division becomes the MSB in the resulting binary number. Therefore, we have to switch around and read the number from bottom to top.

Example 4.7

54/2	=> Answer: 110110	94/2	=> Answer: 1011110
27 + 0		47 + 0	
13 + 1		23 + 1	
6 + 1		11 + 1	
3 + 0		5 + 1	
1 + 1		2 + 1	
0 + 1		1 + 0	
		0 + 1	

Hexadecimal to Binary and Vice Versa

Hexadecimal numbers can be converted to binary numbers simply by converting each individual numeral to a four-bit binary number.

Example 4.8

$$6DA7 = 0110\ 1101\ 1010\ 0111$$

$$6 \quad D \quad A \quad 7$$

The largest hexadecimal number is, as mentioned previously, FFFF, which corresponds to 16 1s.

From Binary and Hexadecimal to BCD

To convert numbers from binary and hexadecimal form to BCD, it is simplest to proceed via the decimal form.

Example 4.9

$$6DA7 = 6 \cdot 16^3 + 13 \cdot 16^2 + 10 \cdot 16^1 + 7 \cdot 16^0$$
$$= 28071_{10} = 0010\ 1000\ 0000\ 0111\ 0001_{BCD}$$

4.3 Digital Logic

In order to be able to program PLCs more efficiently and to reduce the risk of ambiguous program algorithms, it is an advantage to master digital logic. Most often, outputs and internal variables are controlled by a combination of states of other variables and input signals. A little example could be to start a pump when a start switch is activated but only if the level in the tank is lower than a certain value.

In this section, we will therefore present the basic logical functions and how calculations can be performed in a computer or PLC based on *Boolean* algebra.

There are three basic logical functions: AND, OR, and NOT. In addition, there is a function frequently used called *Exclusive Or* (XOR) along with combinations of AND, OR, and NOT.

These basic functions are shown below along with their symbols,[3] functional expressions, and functional tables (truth tables). The symbols are used in drawing and designing digital circuits and in the graphical programming language in the FBD[4] standard.

The functional expressions are used when the algorithms for combinatorial controls are to be described with text. The functional tables, or truth tables as they are also called, describe the structure of the logical functions. For AND and OR, the operation is also illustrated with simple circuit diagrams consisting of a switch, a lamp, and a battery. In the following, functions are presented with two inputs but there can often be three or more.

---

[3] There exists an alternative set of symbols that are also in common use. Both sets of symbols appear in the IEEE 91—1984 standard.

[4] FBD—Function Block Diagram.

Figure 4.1 Integrated circuit (IC)

```
1A   [ 1      14 ]  V_CC
1Y   [ 2      13 ]  6A
2A   [ 3      12 ]  6Y
2Y   [ 4      11 ]  5A
3A   [ 5      10 ]  5Y
3Y   [ 6       9 ]  4A
GND  [ 7       8 ]  4Y
```

Figure 4.2 Pin configuration for SN7408N

All of these basic logical functions are found as electronic components in the form of integrated circuits (ICs). These can be used to construct simple controls when there is no need to be able to modify them in the future.[5] Each IC can contain several ports of the same type. How many depends upon how many inputs each port has (Figures 4.1 and 4.2).

AND

As the name indicates, AND functions in such a way that the output from the function is logically high (a 1) when both (all) inputs are logically high. Otherwise, the output is logically low (0). The functional expression reads thus: *F equals A and B*. The expression could also be read as $F = A$ AND B, but it is common to use the times sign instead of AND.

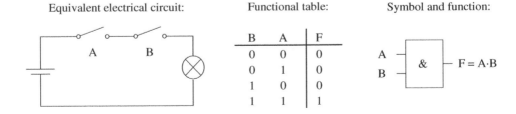

Equivalent electrical circuit: Functional table: Symbol and function:

B	A	F
0	0	0
0	1	0
1	0	0
1	1	1

$F = A \cdot B$

---

[5] *Note*: It is currently more common to use microcontrollers, and this type of integrated circuit has more or less become obsolete.

The circuit illustrates the mode of operation: The lamp (F) lights if both switch A <u>and</u> switch B are closed.

OR

The output of an OR is logically high when one or more of the inputs are logically high. The functional expression reads thus: *F equals A **or** B*. Note the use of the plus sign in the functional expression.

Equivalent electrical circuit: Functional table: Symbol and expression:

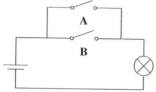

B	A	F
0	0	0
0	1	1
1	0	1
1	1	1

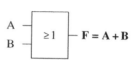

$F = A + B$

NOT

This is an inverter. The output variable state is the inversion (opposite) of the state of the input variable. We read: *F equals **not** A*. Note the use of the inversion sign $\div$

Symbol and functional expression: Functional table:

$F = \overline{A}$

A	F
0	1
1	0

NAND

NAND is a combination of NOT and AND. The output from such a function is the inverse of the output from an AND. This means that the output is logically low when all inputs are logically high. Otherwise, the output is logically high.

Symbol and functional expression: Functional table:

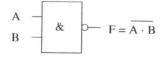

$F = \overline{A \cdot B}$

B	A	F
0	0	1
0	1	1
1	0	1
1	1	0

NOR

A combination of NOT and OR. As the functional expression shows, the output variable is equal to the inverse of the output from an OR.

Symbol and functional expression: Functional table:

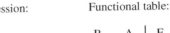

B	A	F
0	0	1
0	1	0
1	0	0
1	1	0

XOR

This is a special variant of OR that is called XOR. In contrast to an ordinary OR, the output here is logically high when only one of the inputs is logically high.

Symbol and functional expression: Functional table:

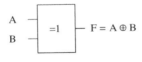

B	A	F
0	0	0
0	1	1
1	1	0
1	1	0

With these basic building blocks, one can construct many useful (and useless) circuits such as those shown in the following examples. Note that there are many types of ready-made digital circuits on the market: from the simple types that are presented here to advanced circuits such as arithmetic units, memory circuits, converters, and microprocessors. It is entirely practical to build anything at all based on so-called off-the-shelf components. For larger hardware-based controls, such as those for a washing machine, for example, it is more usual to employ programmable circuits (EPROM, PAL, etc.) or microprocessors.

Example 4.10

The circuit in Figure 4.3 is an adder that adds two single-bit numbers. The result of the addition appears as the two bits F1 and F2, where F1 is the LSB. In order to understand the operation of the circuit, it is easiest to set up a function table for the circuit (the last column shows the sum in decimal form):

B	A	F2	F1	Decimal
0	0	0	0	$0+0=0$
0	1	0	1	$0+1=1$
1	0	0	1	$1+0=1$
1	1	1	0	$1+1=2$

In this example, the circuit was given beforehand, something that unfortunately seldom happens in practice. Most often, one takes the desired function or operation as a starting point and then designs the circuit or codes from that.

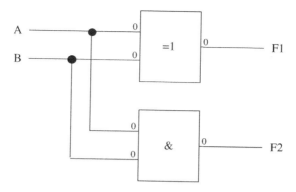

Figure 4.3   One-bit adder

Example 4.11

In a chemical processing facility, liquid chemicals are used in production. The chemicals are stored in three different buffer tanks. A level sensor located in each tank gives a logical high signal when the level in the tank in question falls below a lower limit. We will design a digital circuit that provides a logical high alarm signal when the level in *at least two of the tanks* gets too low.

If we call the three level sensors A, B, and C and the alarm signal from the circuit is F, we can set up a functional table for the circuit:

A	B	C	F
0	0	0	0
0	0	1	0
0	1	0	0
0	1	1	1
1	0	0	0
1	0	1	1
1	1	0	1
1	1	1	1

It is actually not necessary to set up such a table for this simple problem, but it can be nice for the sake of an overview. One possible implementation of a circuit for this control is shown in Figure 4.4. In the following section, we will see how this is developed.

4.4   Boolean Design

4.4.1   *Logical Functional Expressions*

Logical functions are expressions that describe the behavior or the desired mode of operation of the combinatorial circuit. Such logical expressions can also be useful to describe control algorithms for instructions and actions in a PLC program.

Functional expressions arise either directly from a descriptive problem statement or as a result of processing and simplification by means of Boolean algebra (Section 4.4.2). Functional expressions describe for what combinations of input variables the output in question should be logically high.

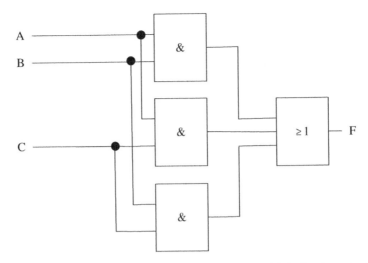

Figure 4.4   Implementation of circuit (possible FBD code) for level monitoring

Example 4.12

For the circuit in Example 4.11, it is a good idea to minimize the expression by thinking through a little logic. Based on the description of the operation of the control, we can analyze the problem as follows:

If two of the tanks have too low a level, that is, if for example signals A and B are logically high, the alarm should go off (F should be logically high).

Furthermore, we can say that because the alarm should go off no matter which two tanks have a low level, it is unimportant whether the third tank has a low level or not. This means that the last condition that should result in an alarm, the fact that all three level sensors are giving signals (A and B and C) can be neglected. The other conditions also cover this.

Accordingly, we can set up the following functional expression for the alarm output F:

$$F = A \cdot B + A \cdot C + B \cdot C \qquad (4.1)$$

(We read this: F equals A and B *or* A and C *or* B and C.)

Note that the expression for an active alarm in the example above is actually a minimized (simplified) functional expression. If we had taken the output point in the functional table alone, that is, without thinking practically about the process, we would have set up the following functional expression:

$$F = \overline{A} \cdot B \cdot C + A \cdot \overline{B} \cdot C + A \cdot B \cdot \overline{C} + A \cdot B \cdot C \qquad (4.2)$$

This method of expressing functions is called Sum of Products (SOP). If you compare the expression with the table in Example 4.11, you will see that for each combination of input signals where F is logically high, we can write an AND expression for the combination. After that, we just add up (OR operation) all the expressions.

We see from the functional expression for this that there is a proper description of F where F equals 1 when (A is 0) AND (B is 1) AND (C is 1) OR (A is 1) AND (B is 0) AND (C is 1), etc.

The functional expression in (4.2) and the simplified functional expression in (4.1) are actually completely identical in the sense that they describe the same logical function. The difference shows up only when we are going to implement the function in the form of a digital circuit or a program code. This tells you right away that it is the minimized expression that we will prefer.

Now, it is not always easy to undertake such a minimization based on only an understanding of the process or on practical evaluations. Often, there is a requirement for a more methodical and mathematical approach. Such a minimization can in many cases be made simply based on knowledge of simple logical algebra, or Boolean algebra, as it is also called. This is discussed in the next section, but before we go on to that, we will study one more example:

Example 4.13

When you have a completed simplified functional expression,[6] it is easy to design the actual circuits or to program code in FBD. Assume that we have

$$F = A \cdot \bar{B} + \overline{\bar{A} \cdot C}$$

The circuit or FBD code for this function is then as shown in Figure 4.5.

4.4.2 Boolean Algebra

A logical variable, signal, or quantity can assume two values or states. Various designations are used in different contexts:

- 1 or 0
- Logical high or logical low (or just high or low)
- 5 V/0 V (or possibly 24 V/0 V)
- TRUE/FALSE

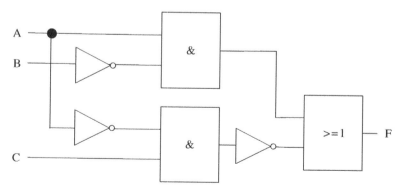

Figure 4.5   Implementation of functional expression

---

[6] Now the actual expression in this example can be reduced more. Try it for yourself after having gone through the next section.

In the PLC context, the words *discrete quantity* or *digital quantity* are often used, but the designation *Boolean* variable or signal is also common. The branch of mathematics that deals with Boolean quantities is called Boolean algebra.

In the following, we will briefly study the basic rules of Boolean algebra and show how these can be used to minimize logical expressions.

Boolean Rules

The following rules are based on one or two variables, but the rules naturally apply generally, that is, for an undetermined number of variables and for cases where the members are not single variables but rather the products or sums of variables.

We begin with Boolean addition: Consider A is a Boolean variable that can have the values 0 or 1. Based upon our newly acquired knowledge of an OR operation, we can set up the following rules (compare these with functional tables for an OR port):

$$A + 0 = A$$
$$A + 1 = 1$$
$$A + \overline{A} = 1$$
$$A + A = A$$

An explanation of the rules above:

- If one of the signals is 1, the result is 1 in any case.
- If other signals are 0, the result depends upon the value of signal A.
- If A is 0, then $\overline{A}$ must be 1.
- $A + A = A$ (because $1 + 1 = 1$ and $0 + 0 = 0$).

Correspondingly, we can start from the operation of an AND port and set up

$$A \cdot 0 = 0$$
$$A \cdot 1 = A$$
$$A \cdot \overline{A} = 0$$
$$A \cdot A = A$$

In addition to these fundamental equations, there are the usual rules of calculation that you have learned in mathematics, such as calculating with parentheses and that the order of factors is irrelevant.

Example 4.14

In Example 4.12, we arrived at a logical function for when an alarm should become active by means of thinking practically. The expression was actually a simplified version of the following functional expression:

$$F = \overline{A}BC + A\overline{B}C + AB\overline{C} + ABC$$

Now, we will find the simplified expression by using Boolean algebra:

$$F = \bar{A}BC + A\bar{B}C + AB\bar{C} + ABC$$
$$= \bar{A}BC + A\bar{B}C + AB\bar{C} + ABC + ABC + ABC$$
$$= BC(\bar{A} + A) + AC(\bar{B} + B) + AB(\bar{C} + C)$$
$$= BC \times 1 + AC \times 1 + AB \times 1$$
$$= BC + AC + AB = \underline{AB + AC + BC}$$

Here is a minimization obtained by reverse use of the rule $\mathbf{A + A = A}$. In this way, the term ABC can be written three times. The purpose of this is to utilize the fact that the term ABC has two signals in common with each of the three other terms. Normally, we would not write down all of the terms several times since this takes time and space, but just use this fact in this simplification, namely, that terms can be used several times.

De Morgan's Theorem

Another rule that is very useful is the so-called De Morgan's theorem. This rule is used to convert expressions that contain negations.

The most practical way to describe this theorem is mathematically:

$$\overline{A \cdot B} = \bar{A} + \bar{B} \quad \text{and} \quad \overline{A + B} = \bar{A} \cdot \bar{B}$$

These relationships can be easily demonstrated by setting up a functional table. (Try it yourself!) The theorem is useful and can also be used for larger expressions where the terms consist of groups of variables, such as those shown in the next example.

Example 4.15

Here, we would use Boolean algebra to reduce the functional expression:

$$Y = \overline{A\bar{B} + C} \cdot (\bar{A}C + B)$$

As we see, the expression contains three variables or signals: A, B, and C. In order to be able to reduce this expression, it is necessary to split it up. Use De Morgan's theorem to split the negations in the first half of the expression:

$$Y = \overline{A\bar{B} + C} \cdot (\bar{A}C + B)$$
$$= \overline{A\bar{B}} \times \bar{C} \cdot (\bar{A}C + B)$$
$$= (\bar{A} + \bar{\bar{B}}) \cdot \bar{C} \cdot (\bar{A}C + B)$$
$$= (\bar{A} + B) \cdot \bar{C} \cdot (\bar{A}C + B)$$

De Morgan's theorem is used once again in the next step in conversion, and in the last operation, we use the fact that $\overline{\overline{B}} = B$.

The remaining operations in the simplification of this expression are

$$
\begin{aligned}
Y &= \left(\overline{A} + B\right) \cdot \overline{C} \cdot \left(\overline{A}C + B\right) \\
&= \left(\overline{A} + B\right) \cdot \left(\overline{A}C\overline{C} + B\overline{C}\right) \\
&= \left(\overline{A} + B\right) \cdot \left(0 + B\overline{C}\right) = \left(\overline{A} + B\right) \cdot B\overline{C} \\
&= \left(\overline{A}B + BB\right) \cdot \overline{C} \\
&= \left(\overline{A}B + B\right) \cdot \overline{C} \\
&= \left(\overline{A} + 1\right) \cdot B\overline{C} \\
&= \underline{\underline{B\overline{C}}}
\end{aligned}
$$

As we see, this expression can be reduced significantly. Note also that the signal A disap-
peared during the simplification. This means that the value of A did not have any significance
for the resulting output Y. The next example gives a comparable result.

Example 4.16

$$
\begin{aligned}
F &= \left(\overline{A} + B\right) \cdot B \\
&= \overline{A}B + BB \\
&= \overline{A}B + B \\
&= \left(\overline{A} + 1\right) \cdot B \\
&= 1 \cdot B = \underline{\underline{B}}
\end{aligned}
$$

It is not obvious that the expression $\left(\overline{A} + B\right) \cdot B$ above can be reduced to B. However, this is
the type of expression that appears relatively often, though in different variations. A practical
evaluation of the expression makes it possible to see this clearly. Here, there is an AND operation where B is one of the factors. If B is 0, the answer is 0. If B is 1, the expression in
parentheses equals 1 and the answer is 1. In any case, $F = B$.

In the examples above, we have utilized some simplifications and shown how some relationships can be useful in adding to the list of rules that deal with reduction:

$$
\begin{aligned}
\overline{\overline{A}} &= A \\
(A + B)A &= A \\
A + AB &= A \\
A + \overline{A}B &= A + B
\end{aligned}
$$

(Also applies with $\overline{A}$ instead of the A's or $\overline{B}$ instead of B)
   (Variant of the foregoing)

You can certainly check this for yourself (for instance, by using De Morgan's)! Finally, we will take another small example:

Example 4.17

$$F = (A + \bar{B}) \cdot (A + C\bar{D})$$
$$= AA + AC\bar{D} + \bar{B}A + \bar{B}C\bar{D}$$
$$= A(1 + C\bar{D} + \bar{B}) + \bar{B}C\bar{D}$$
$$= \underline{\underline{A + \bar{B}C\bar{D}}}$$

4.5   Sequential Design

This section deals with planning, structuring, and presenting processes or production procedures that have a sequential structure. We will review various graphical representations and if we construct and use them methodically, they can be of considerable help when we later write program code.

When a process is to be controlled and the events (actions) will take place in a particular order, we have a sequential process. In order to express this in a somewhat more sophisticated way:

A system that has the property that the output signals from the control depend only upon the instantaneous value of the input signals is called a *combinatorial* system. If the output signals also depend upon what phase or state (in time) the process takes place, we have a *sequential* system.

This and the next section deal with techniques and schematic representations that can be helpful in working out the algorithms for a sequential process.

The goal of the chapter is not to come up with ready-made solutions simply to be implemented, since this can be done in various ways.[7] Even though it is the programming of the PLC that is the focus of this book, the PLC is only one of several possible types of hardware that we could select to implement these solutions. Other possibilities are microprocessors or a PC with an I/O card.

The solution that one selects for a given control problem will depend upon many factors: Access to equipment, costs, complexity of the facility that is to be controlled, the environment in which the control is to be located, physical size, time factors, and whether or not it is important to be able to modify the control at a later time. However, there is one thing that is common to all of these implementations. The preliminary work must be done in order that the control itself can be wired up or programmed. Among other things, we will learn to set up flowcharts. Such charts can constitute a central part of the documentation of controls.

4.5.1   Flowchart

It is not only a good habit to draw up a flowchart (or the like) for the process flow or the functioning of the program; it is often entirely necessary in the planning phase or as documentation for the process flow. (As a basis for program code, I prefer to use the *state diagram*; see Section 4.6.2).

---

[7] Implementation of some of the examples here in the form of PLC code will come in subsequent chapters.

Many different software packages can be useful in drawing charts and diagrams. One of them is *Microsoft Visio*, but you will certainly find suitable open-source software that can also be used.

A flowchart can be drawn in various ways, depending upon what is to be illustrated and what set of symbols is used. The symbols in Table 4.3 is a selection taken from among many flowchart symbols in use.

Table 4.3 Overview of recommended symbols for use in flowcharts

Symbols for use in flowcharts		
	Termination	Start or end of a sequence/program part (this is also a state in the process)
	Sequence step	This represents states in the process where a task or a set of instructions is performed
	Selection/test	Usually a logical test is performed here, which has two possible outcomes: yes or no. If the result is yes, the process flow continues to the next state. If the outcome is no, it is understood that the current condition is maintained
	Flow	The flow direction from a step to the next
	Jump	Is used when the chart continues to another place on the page or to another page
		x—Identification number (jump number)
		y—Page number, if applicable
		Note that x is numbered successively. For example, the numbering does **not** start again on the new page
	Target of jump	Used for the target of a jump
		x—Identification number (target number)
		y—Page number, if applicable
		Target number = associated jump number
	Comment	Can be used next to a step for information
	Subroutine	Used in the master flowchart to refer to a macro sequence, program part, or subroutine. **Name** can be the title of a macro, for instance, "Washing process." **X** can be a page number
	Manual operation	Can be used to note that there must be performed a manual user-controlled operation such as filling a magazine
	Display	Communication with operator panel/HMI

Example 4.18   A Simple Flowchart

Let us look at a little everyday example that illustrates how a flowchart can be used in many contexts. Assume that you are thinking about how to spend the day: Go fishing or play video games? This can be illustrated as in Figure 4.6.

4.5.2   Example: Flowchart for Mixing Process

Figure 4.7 shows a process that is part of an industry known and loved by many.[8]
In this process, water is mixed with sugar and fermented barley in a predetermined ratio. The mixing process should proceed as follows:

- Assume that the tank is empty at the start. When the start button (Start) is pressed, magnetic valve MV1 opens so that water runs into the tank.
- When the level reaches sensor LT2, the water supply is closed and the motor for the conveyor belt starts at the same time that the agitator (Stir) starts.
- When the level reaches transmitter LT3, the motor stops and the magnetic valve MV2 at the outlet opens (the agitator will continue to run).
- When the level falls below LT2, the agitator is also stopped.
- When the level then falls below LT1, valve MV2 is closed. The sequence can be initiated again by pushing the start button.

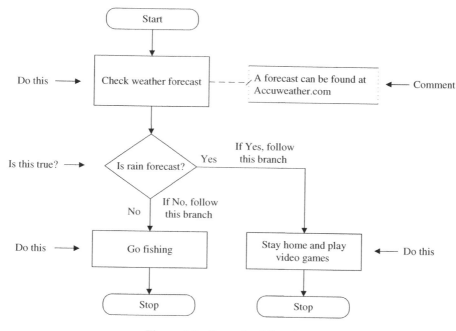

Figure 4.6   Example of flowchart

---

[8] Perhaps relatively more so in certain parts of the country…

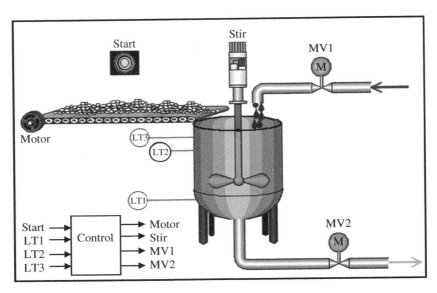

Figure 4.7   Mixing process

Before you start to draw the flowchart, you should do some preliminary work as discussed in Section 1.3.1. What is important here is to think through the entire sequence, especially how many steps the sequence should be divided in.

Generally, this is an approximate evaluation even though it **could** be the result of finding out how many times there will be a change in the output signals.

If there are several *alternative* paths through the sequence (several branches), and only one branch should be selected, you have what we can call an OR-branch. Then the transition to either branch will have its own conditions. It is important that these conditions be *unique* so that the sequence cannot proceed along more than one branch.

If the sequence **should** continue along several parallel branches *simultaneously*, then you have what we can call an AND-branch (simultaneous branch).

From the description of how this process is to be controlled, we will see that there are no branches in the sequence. One possible flowchart for the control of this process is shown in Figure 4.8.

A couple of things in the flowchart above are worthwhile mentioning. The first is the *formulation* of actions (events, instructions). An action that should be active in only one sequence step should be formulated as "Valve MV1 open." This indicates that the action ends when the sequence continues to the next step.

An action that should remain active through several steps, on the other hand, is formulated like such as "Start agitator," for example. Then there must be a corresponding "Stop agitator" somewhere else in the chart. In principle, there is nothing to prohibit formulating the first action as "Open valve MV1," but then we would have to write "Close valve MV1" in the very next step. Such formulations are significant if the program code is going to be developed directly from the flowchart.

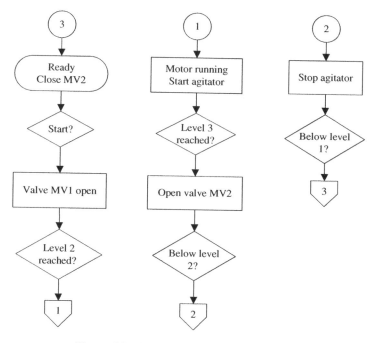

Figure 4.8   Flowchart for the mixing process

Also, note the usage and numbering of *references*. Here, the sequence is deliberately split up to illustrate that. The numbering functions in this way:

The jump down to the left in the flowchart is marked jump number 1. Target number 2 up to the right belongs together with jump number 2. When the flowchart is limited to one page or just a few pages, it is not necessary to indicate page numbers.

4.5.3   Example: Flowchart for an Automated Packaging Line

Figure 4.9 shows an illustration of a packaging line. The facility consists of two single-working cylinders (1 and 2) that go into plus position when the valves Y1 and Y2 receive a high signal (24 V). When Y1 and Y2 are set low (0 V), the cylinders will go back into minus position.

Each cylinder has two built-in sensors, A0/A1 and B0/B1, respectively, that detect when the pistons are in the plus position (that is, when it is extended) and when the pistons are in minus position.

Furthermore, there is a gripping mechanism at the end of each piston. These close and hold the products when they receive a high signal (Y3 and Y4) from the control unit. When the grips are closed, the sensors D1 and D2 send a high signal.

Two sensors, C1 and C2, detect when the cartons are in position at the magazines.

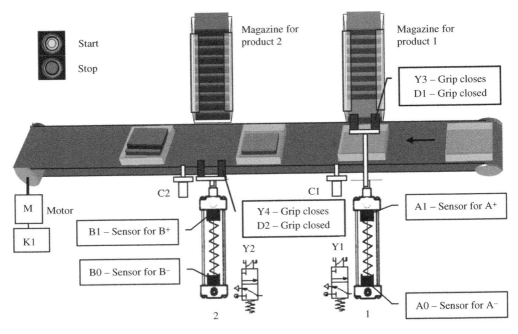

Figure 4.9   Automated packaging line

The facility shall function as follows:

- When the start button is pressed, the conveyor belt starts.
- When a carton has come into position at magazine 1, the following takes place (in chronological order): The belt stops, piston 1 extends, the grip closes around the product, the piston returns, the grip opens, and the belt starts. An identical operation takes place at magazine 2.
- When 10 cartons have been filled with product 1 and product 2, both the conveyor belt and the pistons stop so that the magazines can be refilled. The system is then started again with the start button.
- If the stop switch is activated, the conveyor belt stops as soon as the active piston has finished handling the product in question.

If we were to draw up a flowchart for the sequence in *normal operation*,[9] it would probably look like the one shown in Figure 4.10 on the next two pages.

It is unnecessary to write "Yes" and "No" after questions since it is understood that the sequence continues downward if the result of the test is TRUE. In the same way, it is understood that the sequence remains in its current state (the state prior to testing) if the result of the next test is FALSE.

---

[9] Normal operation means operating without interruption as a result of emergency stops or power failure.

Note that in the flowchart, "internal" actions and instructions are not described in the steps or in a step of their own. Such instructions can be, for instance, incrementing a counter or activating a time delay. You can consider such things in the flowchart, but it is not necessary since the flowchart is meant only as an aid in the planning phase or to illustrate the flow of the process in documentation.

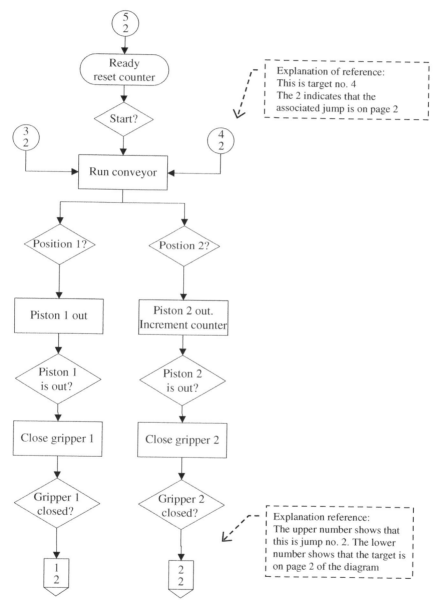

Figure 4.10   Flowchart for automatic packaging line

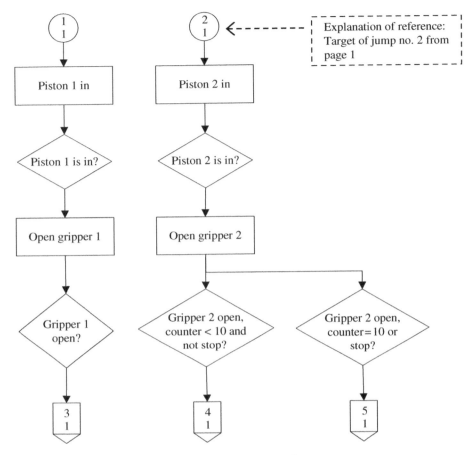

Figure 4.10   (Continued)

It is better that the individual steps in the chart are related to physical events in the sequences of the process and not to programming behavior. It is also not always necessary to consider such events during the planning phase.

You can also make a choice as to what extent you will use easily understood words and sentences in steps and questions (so-called pseudocode) or use something that more closely resembles variables and programming code. The first choice is entirely okay in the planning stage, but the latter is better for "transforming" the flowchart in to code or for documentation of the program code. In the next section, which deals with state diagrams, I have usually chosen to use code and variables.

As mentioned, when the flowchart is being translated to code, it is an advantage to use proper formulations. There is an important difference between "run belt" and "start belt" when the flowchart is converted to program code. "Run belt" indicates that the belt should run only during that particular step, while "start belt" implies that the belt starts at that step and eventually must be stopped in a later step in the sequence.

One thing that becomes obvious in the flowchart in Figure 4.10 is that the flow of the sequence is divided into two branches with identical operations, only for two different cylinders. It is therefore tempting to utilize this similarity in developing a program based on the flowchart. This would result in using less code than implementing it directly.

When we later are learning about programming languages, we will, among other things, tackle a couple of these examples and implement the code for controlling the processes. Then this preliminary work in drawing a flowchart will really prove its value. Particularly, if we use SFC (see Chapter 12), the transition from flowchart to code will be easy.

Example 4.19   Wash Operation

A bottling plant has a juice tank that is used in soft drink production. This tank is washed after each batch. The wash operation functions as follows:

- When a starting switch is activated, the tank is filled with water by holding a valve open until the tank is full (level sensor gives logical high signal).
- Then the water is heated with the help of a heating element.
- When the water has reached a temperature of 95°C, the heating is stopped and an agitator starts.
- The agitator runs for 5 minutes.
- Then the tank is drained by holding a bottom valve open until the tank is empty (another level sensor switches to logical low signal).
- The entire operation is repeated three times. After that, the program awaits a new signal to start.

From the description of what should happen physically during the sequence, we can identify the following five states:

- *Ready*
- *Filling*
- *Heating*
- *Stirring*
- *Draining*

The figure at the right shows a possible flowchart for the sequence. The chart is partially prepared for later implementation with regard to state names and conditions.

(A counter may be incremented in one of the examples every time filling starts)

4.5.3.1   Top–Down Design

Using the flowchart as we have studied it here is called *top–down design*. The flowchart is used to describe the primary changes in state that occur over time. The way to proceed is always first to identify the main states in the process. This is itself a good task since there is often a natural flow in the sequential process. It is also usual that individual main states can be divided up into smaller portions. Such a main state can be called a *macro-step*.

Some development tools utilize macro-steps as an extra functionality in SFC. Others implement them by having a normal step call up another program (that also can be developed in

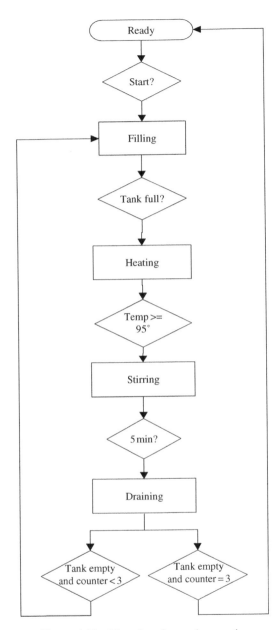

Figure 4.11   Flowchart for wash operation

SFC). Every macro-step, at any rate, can consist of several ordinary steps so that they constitute their own small sequences within the main sequence. Figure 4.12 shows a sketch of the
principle of using macro-steps.

Macro-steps are provisionally not defined in SFC in the IEC 61131-3 standard. It is nevertheless easy to structure program code so that it makes use of such macro-steps.

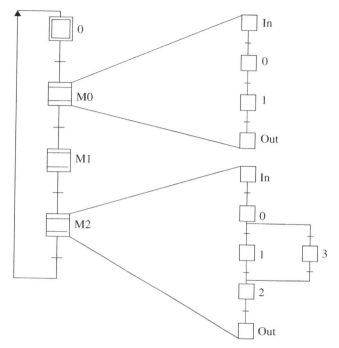

Figure 4.12   Illustration of the use of macro-steps

In fact, this is one of the many advantages of the standard in that code can easily be broken up into smaller units, each of which can be programmed in any one of the five defined languages in the standard.

4.5.4   Sequence Diagrams

The design of a flowchart, and possibly a state diagram, is an extremely useful preliminary task before you throw yourself into the programming itself. Personally, I think that it should be an obligatory part of the work of a programmer. What we are now going to study is not equally applicable, but I still think that we should illuminate the subject.

Sequence diagrams are, in the PLC context, considered more of a curiosity. This is because such diagrams do not lend themselves to more than just a few variables and signals or to cases in which the sequence contains branches. I would still like to focus on this in the book because I believe that it can contribute to increased understanding of things such as:

- Boolean conditions and combinations that can, and cannot, occur
- How to avoid ambiguities in the code
- The importance of detecting signal changes and not merely signal states
- When Boolean actions should be stored[10] (by using Set/Reset)

---

[10] One often activates an action (for instance, starts a pump) in one phase of a process and then deactivates it at a later time. This is different from an action that is to remain active as long as a given condition is present.

If you are going to implement a less complex control with the help of hardware (ICs and other components), sequence diagrams can also be useful.

4.5.4.1   Construction of Sequence Diagrams

The purpose of a sequence diagram is to show the state of all Boolean signals in the control unit for a defined sequential operation. This means that we have to draw the sequence of all input and output signals (I/O signals) for the control unit, plus any internal signals within the control, for instance, signals to and from counters and time delays.

We could draw such diagrams by drawing up the digital signal formats for each signal, but since a sequence diagram only shows the state of Boolean quantities and signals, it is sufficient to distinguish between when a signal has a high value and a low value. In order to make the sequence diagram more legible, it is therefore best to mark only when signals have a logical high value, since the absence of a marking indicates that the signal has a logically low value.

We indicate a logical high value by using a horizontal mark.

We must also indicate when a signal goes high and when the signal goes low by using a short vertical mark. Figure 4.13 shows the principle, compared to drawing both logical high and logical low values for signals A, B, and C.

We see from the diagram that we obtain a better overview and a more compact portrayal of the signal sequences by only taking into account logical high values.

The lines marked 1, 2, 3, etc. in Figure 4.13 can be called *action lines* or *event lines*.[11] In general, each action line will mark activation and deactivation of one or more events or a change in the value of the signal that is involved in the conditions at a control unit. It is extremely important that we be consistent with this so that we never allow a change in condition to appear between two action lines. More on this later.

From the time perspective, the separation between action lines has **no** significance. We use the same separation between all action lines no matter whether an operation takes 45 minutes (for instance heating a liquid in a tank) or takes one second (for instance, the movement of a piston).

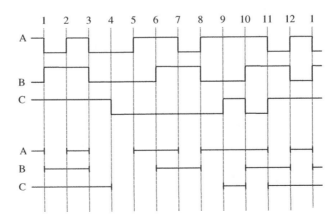

Figure 4.13   Examples of sequence diagrams

---

[11] See Lien (1995).

If we want to include the time perspective in order to improve oversight, we can do that by writing a comment in the sequence diagram, for instance in the upper corner of the time interval in question (between two lines).

The diagram in Figure 4.13 also shows that a change occurs at each action line, where one or more signals changes state. After 12 changes, the same pattern repeats, and this is indicated by placing the numeral 1 at the action line that is like the first one. It is a fact that sequential systems have repeating sequences. This comes out clearly in the diagram with numbering the events.

Signals that have a logical high value when the system starts up are marked by drawing horizontal lines on the left side of the diagram without any vertical mark at the beginning.

The following is important when working up a sequence diagram: *Only one discrete <u>input</u> signal or Boolean condition should change state at each action line.* Even if two signals change nearly simultaneously, this should be marked on two adjacent lines. If you are unsure about the sequence of such events, the choice that you make should be one that is based upon knowledge of the process that is to be controlled.

However, many output signals and actions can change at the same action line. The reason for this is that actions are logical functions of the system's input signals and internal variables and several actions can be triggered simultaneously by changes in state, for instance, an input signal.

Example 4.20   Sequence Diagram for a Double-Acting Cylinder

Assume that we use two limit switches (see Section 2.3) to get feedback on when a piston has come into position. See Figure 4.14. Then we have a total of four signals: Two for the cylinders that control the air supply in the positive direction (A$^+$) and the minus direction (A$^-$) and a signal from each of the limit switches (SA$^+$ and SA$^-$).

In order that we always have power on the piston, we must be sure that there is compressed air in one of the directions all the time. Therefore, either A$^+$ or A$^-$ will have a high value at any time.

Assume that the piston, after a start switch has been activated, will make one out–in motion. The sequence diagram is then as shown in Figure 4.14.

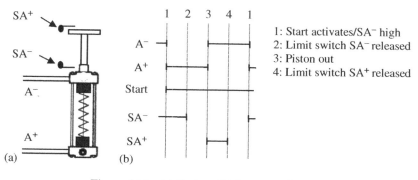

Figure 4.14   (a) System, (b) Sequence diagram

Example 4.21

Assume that we have two double-acting pneumatic pistons. We want the sequence where the first piston A goes out. Then piston B makes an in–out motion before piston A finally returns. Assume further that each of the pistons receives two logical signals from the control unit, one to control the piston in the plus direction and one to control the piston in the minus direction. We call these signals A+, A−, B+, and B−.

As in the previous example, there are two limit switches installed on each cylinder so that we know when it has come completely out (plus position) and completely back (minus position). These signals, which we can call SA+, SA−, SB+, and SB−, constitute the input signals to the control unit or PLC.

Figure 4.15 shows the sequence diagram. In order to best display what is happening, a so-called *motion diagram* has also been drawn at the top of the diagram. This clearly shows the desired motions of the two pistons A and B.

Assume that the initial state is when both the piston A and piston B are in the minus position. This is to say that the limit switches SA− and SB− both emit a high signal.

Some comments on the sequence diagram:

The limit switches will not be released immediately when the pistons begin their return motion. Even though this occurs a fraction of a second later, this should be noted on new action lines in the diagram.

These are double-action cylinders that should always be supplied with compressed air in one or the other direction. So, for instance, the A+ and A− signals should never be high simultaneously. We can then concentrate in the program on the conditions that are to be added to drive the piston in one direction. The inverse condition will drive the piston in the other direction.

4.5.5 Example: Sequence Diagram for the Mixing Process

Figure 4.7 dealt with a mixing process for which we designed a flowchart. In order to structure the problem and visualize the signals involved, we will draw a sequence diagram. As mentioned

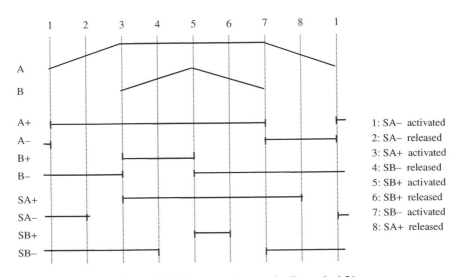

Figure 4.15 Sequence diagram for Example 4.21

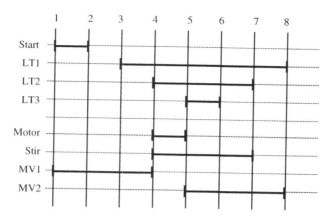

Figure 4.16 Sequence diagram for the mixing process

previously, it is not necessary to write a program to control the process, but we want to have a good mental image of the signal changes during the sequence. The sequence diagram is as shown in Figure 4.16.

Here, the signal from the start button is drawn as a short-duration signal, even though it is not sure that the operator would release the button right away.[12] Also note that the input signals and output signals are collected into separate groups because this generally provides a better overview.

The rule that only one input signal or internal variable should change state at any individual action line is naturally respected. This is extremely important because the diagram furnishes the basis for the program code.

4.5.5.1 Concerning Analog Signals and Internal Signals

Most often, there will also be analog signals in a control system. Examples of analog signals can be obtained from a valve, input signals from a temperature or pressure transducer, control signals from a frequency-controlled pump, etc. We cannot illustrate analog signals in a sequence diagram, but we can perform comparisons of analog signals such as testing whether a measurement exceeds a given value. The result from such a comparison can be represented by a Boolean signal. For example, we can compare a measured temperature with a desired value. We can then mark in the diagram when the temperature is equal to or greater than the desired value.

All the Boolean variables that appear in the diagram do not necessarily need to be related to external signals. Internal signals in the PLC such as the output Q from a timer (time delay) or a counter can also be represented in the diagram. We then use the name of the counter or time delay, followed by .Q, for instance Count.Q or Ten_sec.Q.

We close this subject with an example that contains both the time delay and the result from a comparison.

---

[12] In Chapter 9, we will write a code for this process in the Ladder programming language, and there, we eliminate the significance of how long the button is held in.

4.5.6   Example: Batch Process

Figure 4.17 shows a process section in which two chemicals, A and B, are mixed together. **S1**, **S2**, and **S3** are level switches of the NC (normally closed) type that change state when the fluid reaches the level in question. **Ts** is a temperature sensor. The facility also has a starting button, **Start** and a stopping button, **Stop1**.

The facility is to function as follows:

- At the signal to start, valve A opens.
- At level S2, valve A closes, the heating element is turned on, the agitator starts, and valve B opens.
- At level S3, valve B closes.
- When 85°C is reached, a timer is activated. 30 seconds after, the heating is turned off and valve C is opened.
- Below level S2, the agitator stops.
- Below level S1, valve C closes and valve A opens again.
- The sequence is repeated until Stop1 is pressed.

The sequence diagram in Figure 4.18 is drawn based upon the following assumptions, evaluations, and choices:

- Assume that the tank is empty at the start. Note that the level switch is NC type so that it gives a logical high signal when it is not activated.

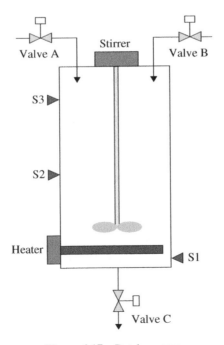

Figure 4.17   Batch process

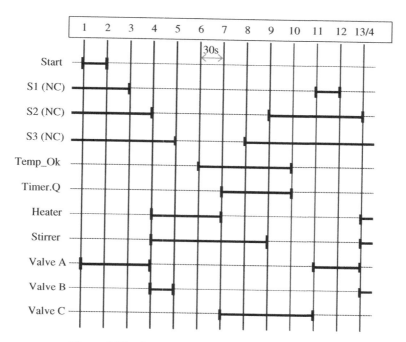

Figure 4.18   Sequence diagram for the batch process

- An ON time delay is activated when the desired temperature is reached (Temp_Ok). After 30 seconds, the time delay output Timer.Q goes high. Note the time comment between action lines 6 and 7.
- The facility completes an ongoing sequence before any eventual stop. In the program code, we must then store the event "Stop pressed" and check this at the end of the current sequence. However, it is impractical to draw alternative outcomes in the sequence diagram so the Stop cannot be illustrated.
- After the heating element (Heater) has turned off, we do not know when the temperature will fall below the desired temperature again. Here, it is assumed that this happens after the fluid level has dropped to below level 2.

4.6   State-Based Design

We have seen that flowcharts and sequence diagrams can be used in the planning and development stage for illustrating a problem schematically. Later, and based on such diagrams, we will develop structural program codes for sequential systems.

Even though making useful flow diagrams, sequence diagrams, and state diagrams, which we soon shall study, is associated with a certain amount of work, this effort is quickly compensated for by faster development of the program code. In other words, the total development time is shorter if one expends a little time in planning the program structure. Most probably, the number of errors in the code that have to be detected and corrected will also be smaller.

The use of flowcharts is not limited to systems that have a markedly sequential nature, but they are not as well suited when there are multiple paths from any one state. In some cases, the system that is to be controlled can be described with a set of unique and distinct states without there being any dominant sequential process in the system. In such cases, it may be more practical to use *state diagrams*.

State diagrams are typically used to describe states in the development of *finite-state machines*. By definition, this is a "machine[13]" that is always in one of a specified number of unique states and where transitions to other states are based upon instantaneous states along with combinatorial functions of input signals and internal variables. Which state comes next, in other words, is a result of user-controlled events (for instance, pressing a button) and/or the result of internal calculations.

There are two variants of finite-state machines: the *Moore* model and the *Mealy* model. The Moore model—which is more widespread and which is the one we will use—is based on the idea that actions that are to be performed are associated with states. In other words, changes of output signal are dependent only upon the state that is active at any given time. In a Mealy machine, the output signals are directly dependent upon the input signals as well.

4.6.1   Why Use State Diagrams?

A widespread use of the state diagram technique is in the development of user interfaces. A user interface is normally based upon various user choices resulting in the activation of various program segments, where each segment is a state in a state diagram. The execution of the program segment can lead to another program segment or to anticipation of a new user-controlled event.

However, here, we will focus on the use of state diagrams as a design technique for later development of program code for controlling processes. In the chapter on sequential design, we saw that process flow could be split up into a set of defined states and that the transition from one state to another depends upon the values of one or more signals or variables. Both of these conditions will appear clearly in a state diagram.

In addition to state diagrams being useful to develop concrete algorithms for control, the technique can also be used to plan code structure and applications. As complexity increases, so does the need for structured techniques for planning and design. Everyone who works in software development knows the concept of the state diagram, which is an important part of Unified Modeling Language (UML). UML is a modeling and requirement specification language for software development.

4.6.2   State Diagrams

The state diagram is therefore used to illustrate states, to show how states follow one another, and to show which conditions must be satisfied in order for a system to go from one state to another. These conditions are called *transitions*. It is also common to have state names reflect something about the actions that will be performed in the individual states. In other words, the

---

[13] The concept of *machine* is somewhat misleading these days, but it had its origin in digital techniques in which free-standing machines—based on hardware assembled from digital components—were developed with this technique. Nowadays the technique is used for development of program codes and algorithms.

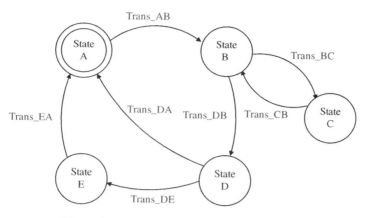

Figure 4.19   Example of a generic state diagram

state diagram gives the same information as a flow diagram, except that a state diagram is faster to draw up, more compact, and also more usable for nonsequential systems.

The initial state, which is marked here with double outlines, is the state in which the system starts when power is turned on (placed in RUN). Often, this will be an idle state where no actions are performed (perhaps with the exception of initiating or resetting variables). The control (the finite-state machine, PLC program, etc.) remains in this state and waits for a start signal from an operator, for instance.

What the other states describe and contain depends upon the process that the diagram is made for. These can be actions that are being performed, such as starting a pump or opening the valve. It can also be *nothing*, with the understanding that the system is merely waiting for a certain time or for a signal from a sensor, for example.

The transitions will be logical expressions where input signals can be involved, probably in combination with internal variables. In the completed program code, only the transition conditions that come *directly after* the active step are tested. Related to the diagram in Figure 4.19, this means, for instance, that it is not significant when the transition Trans_DA is satisfied as long as the system does not find itself in state D.

Example 4.22   Conveyor Belt

Figure 4.20 shows a state diagram for control of the conveyor belt in a packaging facility. The facility is to operate as follows:

- Goods that come down on the conveyor belt are detected by a photocell. Then a pneumatic piston will push the goods over to a packaging station. The piston has a spring return and it is controlled by a sensor so that we know when it is extended. (Assume that it returns without coming into conflict with a new item on the belt.)
- When 100 items have been pushed off the belt, the belt should stop. The operator packs the 100 items and then starts the belt again.
- There is also a built-in stop function as well as an alarm function that is activated if more than 10 seconds elapse before the next item arrives at the photocell.

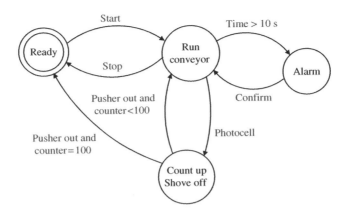

Figure 4.20   State diagram for a packaging facility

In the diagram above, we are using pseudocode, that is, ordinary words and sentences, to indicate transitions and states. In order to further reduce work in the programming that will come later, it can be sensible to use valid state names and individual codes in *Structured Text*. This is done in the next example.

Also note that the transition conditions are clearly marked *thus* in the diagram.

Example 4.23   Mixing Process

In Figure 4.8, we drew a flowchart for the mixing process, and in Figure 4.16, we drew a sequence diagram for the same process. Figure 4.21 shows a state diagram for the process. We see that the flow in the sequences is clearly marked by arrows showing the transitions between the states.

We have used other formulations here in the flow diagram, both in names of states and in conditions for transition (tests and choices). This has been done deliberately in order to come a step closer to a program for controlling this process. Furthermore, flow diagrams are more often used in an earlier phase, where it is natural to use more pseudocode.

The transitions (marked *thus*) and the state names that are used in the diagram below can likely be implemented directly in most systems because they are valid names under the IEC 61131-3 standard.[14]

4.6.2.1   State Tables

Instead of using a state diagram, one can structure the system in tabular form by setting up a *state table*. The same information that appears in the diagram can then be presented in the table. A common structure for such tables is to write down a now state in the column farthest to the left and a possible next state as the top row in the table. The transitions then indicated at the dividing lines between the current now state and the possible next state. A table based on the state diagram in Figure 4.20 is shown in Table 4.4 below.

---

[14] Names (for variables and objects) will in the following begin with a character and not contain any spaces. Underlining is permissible as it is used here in Mix_Drain, for instance.

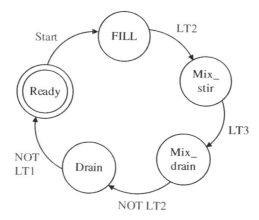

Figure 4.21 State diagram for the mixing process on page

Table 4.4 Example of state table

Next state/ Now state	Ready	Run belt	Alarm	Push off
Ready		*Start*		
Run belt	*Stop*		*Time > 10 s*	*Photocell*
Alarm		*Acknowledge*		
Push off	*Piston out and* *counter = 100*	*Piston out and* *counter <100*		

4.6.2.2 Macro-diagram

As mentioned previously, state diagrams can advantageously be used as aids in structuring large program applications. In this case, the individual states can describe (consist of) major operations that in turn are controlled by their own program units in the PLC.

Then the individual states in the diagram are a sort of *macro-step*. See Figure 4.22. When the transition is satisfied, another program is called up. One can also make up a state diagram that illustrates what will happen within each individual.

4.6.3 Example: Batch Process

In Figure 4.18, we drew a sequence diagram for a batch process. Now, we will draw a state diagram for the system where there has been added a new extra stop button, Stop2, and the following additional condition is specified:

- When the facility has started 10 times, or if Stop1 is pressed, the sequence will complete before the facility stops.
- If Stop2 is pressed, the facility will shut down immediately.

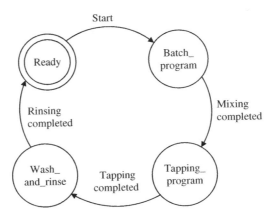

Figure 4.22 State diagram at a macro level

The first extra specification also implies that the diagram must contain alternative branches so that there are two possible paths to continue after the tank is empty. If Stop1 has been activated, or if 10 sequences have been completed, the program goes to its "Ready" state. If not, the "Fill_A" state is activated again. See Figure 4.23.

Notice also the handling of the immediate stop when Stop2 is activated. This is solved here by inserting Stop2 into *all* transitions through to the close of the sequence.

The PLC will then activate and deactivate states in order and, with correct implementation of the diagram in the form of code, this will take place without any of the outputs being changed at all until the Ready state is activated again.

4.6.4 Example: Level Process

A PLC will be used for controlling the fluid level in the tank. The tank is provided with a varying quantity of liquid (control of the fluid stream into the tank is not part of the task). Two sump pumps, P1 and P2, will prevent the tank from getting full. The pumps are controlled with the aid of signals from three level monitors, B1, B2, and B3, which give a logical high signal when they are covered by fluid. See Figure 4.24.[15]

The system will function as follows:

- When the level rises above B2, one of the pumps will start and then stop again when the level drops below B1.
- The pumps will start alternately so that P1 and P2 start one at a time. The changeover in which pump will start will not take place until the level has fallen below B1 and then has come up to B2 again.
- If the level rises above B3, both pumps will run until the level is below B1 again.
- If B3 is on for more than three minutes, a warning lamp will light.

---

[15] The example is created by Assistant Professor Inge Vivås, Bergen University College.

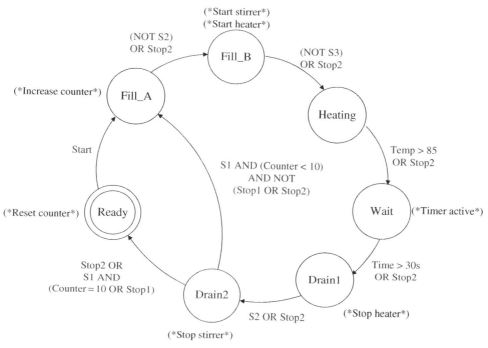

Figure 4.23 State diagram for the batch process. Actions that are to be performed in the steps are written as (*comments*). The transitions are written in ST code

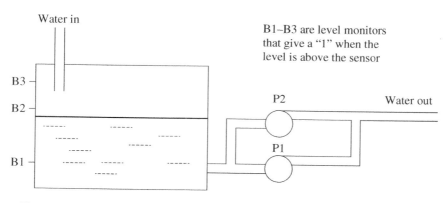

Figure 4.24 Fluid tank with pumps (Reproduced with permission from Inge Vivås)

The facility also has a start button, a stop button, and a reset button that deactivates the alarm.

Figure 4.25 shows a state diagram made to correspond to the system description above. In order to make the transition to program code as simple as possible, the state names used here are permissible state names under the standard. For the same reason, descriptive code has also been used for the transitions between states.

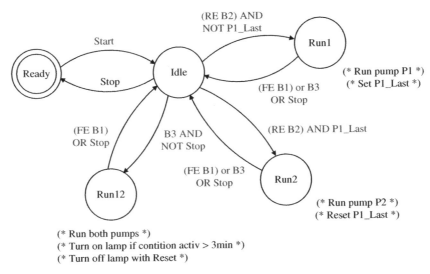

Figure 4.25   State diagram for the level process

As in the previous example, the actions and instructions which are to be performed in the individual states are given in the form of comments.

P1_Last is a Boolean variable which is inserted into the code to keep track of which pump was activated last. When the facility starts up, this variable is FALSE. When the level then exceeds B2, pump P1 will start (because the transition RE B2 AND NOT P1_Last from the Idle state becomes TRUE). The variable P1_Last then takes the value TRUE so that the next time the level rises above B2, pump P2 will start.

About the Transitions

RE stands for "rising edge" and indicates that the conditions where RE B2 is present can only be satisfied if the signal B2 changes state from 0 to 1. FE stands for "falling edge" and is used here to detect when the signal B1 changes state from 1 to 0.

An alternative to writing RE and FE to indicate such flank detection is to use arrows such as ↑B2 and ↓B1.

The transition from the Idle state to the Run12 state perhaps seems a little strange. Here, "NOT Stop" is included as part of the condition. This is included to ensure that the two transitions from the same state want be TRUE simultaneously. Here is the scenario:

- Assume that the level rises above B3. Then the Run12 state is activated.
- If Stop is pressed, the Run12 state is deactivated and the Idle state is activated again.
- If B3 continues to give a signal, however, Around12 will be activated *again* <u>simultaneously</u> as the Ready state is activated. We avoid this by using "*B3 AND NOT Stop*" as a transition to Run12.

One always gets such problems when the diagram has *alternative branches*, that is, when there are several possible ways out of one of the same state. Every possible way has its own transition, and it is an absolute requirement that only one of these transitions can be satisfied (becomes a logical TRUE) at any time. Said in a more elegant way, the transitions must be *mutually exclusive*. If such transitions are not mutually exclusive, it can happen that two or more alternative paths become activated simultaneously and then the program will not function satisfactorily.

The Idle state has many connections, and the requirement for mutual exclusivity naturally applies to all transitions out of Idle. If we study this transition, we will see that the requirement is fulfilled: The use of RE in B2 in the two other transitions leads automatically to there not being any conflict with the Stop transition. (This holds true as long as the level does not reaches B2 *precisely* in the same scan when Stop is activated. In order to be sure, we can include NOT Stop in these transitions.)

The same two transitions also exclude one another when "P1_Last" is included in one of them and "NOT P1_Last" in the other.

An alternative structure that gets rid of the problem is to include specific connectors to the transition condition Stop out of all three states Run1, Run2, and Run12 and direct to the Ready state. However, this will make an unnecessarily messy structure.

On the Choice of States

The choice of states is primarily made here based upon the physical phases of the processes. It seems natural to include three states for running the pumps and a state where none of the pumps operate (the Idle state). No actual program engineering evaluation has been made here.

If we were to do that, it is tempting to include a state for activation of the warning lamp. This would have to originate from the Run12 state. By doing that, we would get somewhat simpler coding of the actions associated with Run12 and we can, by implementation in SFC, use a built-in timer. Figure 4.26 shows a section of the diagram where this change has been made.

(*Note*: The correct syntax for referring to a built-in timer object is used here.)

4.6.5 Example: Packing Facility for Apples

Figure 4.27 sketch of a facility for packing apples in crates.

• When Start is pressed, the conveyor belt 1, which carries the crates, begins to move. The belt runs until a capacitive sensor gives a signal that indicates that an empty crate has come up to the packing station. Then conveyor belt 2 starts.

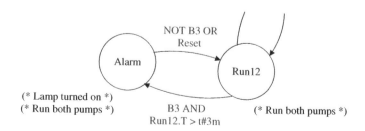

Figure 4.26 Alternative extra state

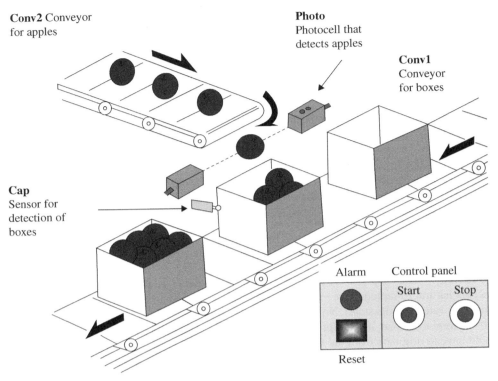

Figure 4.27   Production line—packing of apples (Reproduced with permission from MikroElektronika)

- Belt 2 transports the apples that are to be packed in the crates. A photocell detects each individual apple on the belt. When 10 apples have passed the photocell and thus fallen into the crate, belt 2 stops and belt 1 starts again.
- This will be repeated until the stop button is activated. Then the facility will finish the ongoing packing operation and then shut down.
- If more than five seconds elapse between each apple when belt 2 is active, or more than 10 seconds elapse before the crate arrives at the packing station when belt 1 is running, the operator will be warned and an alarm light will light. The belts will <u>not</u> stop. The alarm resets automatically if a crate or an apple passes the appropriate sensor. It can also be reset with a button.
- If the alarm is active, the facility will shut down immediately if Stop is pressed.

The stop button can obviously be activated at any time, so when we code, we must store the event of Stop being pressed. Since an ongoing packing operation must be completed before the facility shuts down, we check whether Stop has been activated because a crate has been fully packed.

Selection of States

Many people believe that it is difficult to determine which states, and how many states, it is natural to include in a state diagram (or flow diagram). Unfortunately, there is no shortcut or unambiguous way of deciding that.

Since the setup of the diagram has consequences only when the code is to be implemented, it becomes easier when you have had more experience with programming. Then the choices that you make will also be a result of what you yourself prefer as a program developer.

In this concrete example, there are physically only two states: Belt1 is running and Belt2 is running. In addition, one always has an initial state, which in this case is the "ready-to-start" state. In the following, we will first draw up a state diagram based on these three states and then design a diagram with several more states.

The practical differences between the two alternative diagrams, as we said, will not be obvious until we start to make a program based on the state diagram.

In general, it is true that fewer states yield a simpler, but perhaps less comprehensible structure, and more code for programming of actions and events. It is precisely in this decision process that experience and personal preferences[16] come into the picture.

As in the previous examples, the circles are states, transitions are given in italics ***thus***, and actions that are to be performed in the states are given in parentheses (* thus *).

Figure 4.28 shows a diagram designed from what we can classify as the *physical phases* in the process. The diagram is small and simple but still easy to understand. A disadvantage is that relatively many instructions must be performed in the Run_B1 and Run_B2 states.

If we use special conditions for activation of the alarm as shown in Figure 4.29, the coding of the actions will become simpler, and we can use built-in time objects when we come to implement the diagram in SFC. In this diagram, the activation of the alarm is entered as two

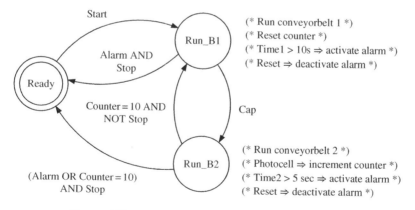

Figure 4.28   State diagram, apple packing, alternative 1

---

[16] Personally, I prefer many states and therefore less and simpler coding of actions and instructions. If we use SFC to build code, the sequential function chart will be larger, but usually more comprehensible and easier to read. Since the action code is also simpler and shorter, there will be room for most of it right in the functional chart, which also improves the overview.

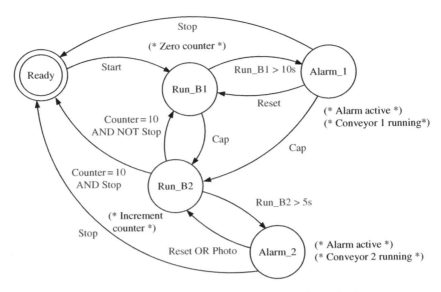

Figure 4.29   State diagram, apple packing, alternative 2

special states, Alarm_1 and Alarm_2. The same alarm is active in both states, but I have used two different alarm states to be able to return to the proper state after the alarm has been reset.

In the diagram below, we see that the complexity is greater, but there are fewer and simpler actions that are to be performed in each state.

Incrementing the counter is still integrated in the Run_B2 state. It can also be performed in a separate state, but then I think we would have unnecessary complexity in the diagram.

4.7   Summary

A state diagram is a useful aid on the path to a completed program, no matter which language you were planning to program in and, practically speaking, no matter what type of process the PLC will control. A state diagram is also easy to convert into program code, not just in SFC, but also in code written in LD, FBD, or ST (this last by using CASE sentences and, possibly, enumerated data types). In the chapters that cover programming languages, you will find some of these examples again from this chapter, and you can study the equivalents between charts and diagrams and completed code.

So when is it advisable to use the various types of diagrams?

Well, it is partly a matter of taste and it also depends a great deal upon the degree of complexity of the process and the program and, as previously mentioned, whether or not it is a sequential system. Both the flowchart and the state diagram can advantageously be used during planning and as a methodical approach to completed program code.

Flowcharts are best suited to sequential systems. The structure and symbols mimic largely the SFC graphical programming language, and the transition to that language is therefore easy. At any rate, it is probably most common to use flowcharts at an early planning phase and then use general words and expressions to describe events and conditions.

State diagrams can be used for both sequential systems and complex systems that do not have a sequential structure, so that the next state can be one of many. The level process in Section 4.6.4 is a typical example of a system where the flow is more combinatorial than sequential. In order to obtain the best possible yield from the state diagram, it is recommended to put in a little extra work to use "legal" variable and state names along with the most correct code possible in the transitions.

In larger systems, the state diagram can be used at the macro level in order to illustrate how program units fit together and are called up.

Sequence diagrams count more as a curiosity. For small simple systems, they can be useful since, when used correctly, they will give us the conditions for activating actions directly without focusing on process states. The disadvantage is that it quickly becomes complicated and time-consuming to draw up such diagrams when larger processes and controls are involved and/or when the sequential structures have alternative branching.

4.8 Test Problems

Problem 4.1
Given a logical circuit as shown in Figure 4.30.
(a) Set up the logical function F.
(b) Draw a connection using only contacts. (For the original F)
(c) Set up a functional table for the function.

Problem 4.2
Given a logical circuit as shown in Figure 4.31.
(a) Set up the logical function Y.
(b) Set up a functional table for the function.

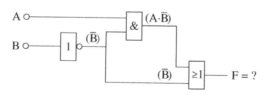

Figure 4.30

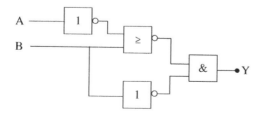

Figure 4.31

Problem 4.3
(a) Convert the following binary numbers to both decimal and hexadecimal numbers:

    1. 110011   2. 10111001.101   3. 01011011.0101

(b) Convert the following decimal numbers to both binary numbers and hexadecimal numbers:

    1. 47   2. 135   3. 423

Problem 4.4
(a) Simplify the following functional expression (all signals are Boolean):

$$\text{Valve} = \overline{\left(LT + \overline{Start}\right) \cdot \left(\overline{Empty} + Alarm + \overline{LT}\right) \cdot \left(\overline{LT + Empty}\right)}$$

(b) Simplify the logical function $F = \left(A + \overline{B}\right)\left(A + C\overline{D}\right)$. Use De Morgan's rule to find $\overline{F}$.

(c) Simplify the logical function $F = \overline{A}B\left(C + D\right) + B\left(\overline{A}\overline{C} + \overline{B}D + C\overline{D}\right)$

Problem 4.5
(a) The control unit for a traffic light is to activate the alarm ($F = 1$) if there is a green light in both directions simultaneously ($G1 = G2 = 1$) or if there is a red light in both directions simultaneously ($R1 = R2 = 1$). Write the logical expression for F and draw up a block diagram (logical circuit).

(b) The logical circuit in a passenger car activates a warning light F if the ignition is on ($I = 1$) and the driver's ($D = 1$) or a passenger's ($P = 1$) seat belt is not fastened and a pressure sensor indicates that a seat is occupied ($S = 1$). Find a logical expression for F and draw the logical circuit.

Problem 4.6
A pump is used to fill a tank. Whether or not the pump (P) runs depends upon the state of four discrete signals:

    A sensor (L) that gives a signal when the level in the tank gets above a lower limit, a sensor (H) that gives a signal when the level gets above an upper limit, a drain valve (V) from the tank that is closed or open, and an alarm state (A).

    The following functional table shows when the pump should operate ($P = 1$):

L	H	V	A	P
0	0	0	0	1
0	0	0	1	0
0	0	1	0	1
0	0	1	1	0
0	1	0	0	0
0	1	0	1	0
0	1	1	0	0
0	1	1	1	0
1	0	0	0	0

L	H	V	A	P
1	0	0	1	0
1	0	1	0	1
1	0	1	1	0
1	1	0	0	0
1	1	0	1	0
1	1	1	0	0
1	1	1	1	0

Problem: Determine the minimized logical functional expression (the algorithm) for the pump.

Problem 4.7

A fluid tank is equipped with three level sensors L1, L2, and L3 that indicate low level, high level, and full tank. The level sensors give a logical high signal when the liquid comes across the sensors.

There are two drains from the tank, each of which is controlled by its own pump, P1 and P2. If the level in the tank comes across the low level, pump 1 should run (P1 = 1). If the level in the tank comes across the high level, pump 2 should run. If the level comes across full, both pumps should run. Filling the tank is not a part of this problem.

(a) Set up a functional table (truth table) that shows the possible combination of states for all signals.
(b) Draw a logical circuit that implements the pump control.

Problem 4.8

A ship's engine must be capable of being stopped and started from both the bridge (S1 and S3) and from the engine room (S2 and S4). The relay control (contactor control) for this operation is shown in the figure below, where contactor K1 connects the main power supply to the engine. Explain how the control functions. Draw the logical diagram (standard digital ports).

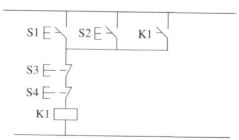

Problem 4.9   Product Sorting

Products of three different lengths on a conveyor belt are to belt measured and sorted. There is just one product at a time on the band. See Figure 4.32. Just as a product has passed FC1, a measuring is performed using two other photocells, FC2 and FC3:

- FC2 is logically low: *short product*
- FC2 and not FC3 is logically high: *medium long product*
- Both FC2 and FC3 logically high: *long product*

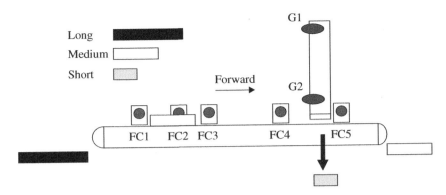

Figure 4.32 Sorting products (Reproduced with permission from Schneider Electric)

The conveyor has two velocities, normal and low, in addition to reverse, controlled by three different signals. When measuring the product length, the belt moves at normal velocity.

Short product: The product is transported forward to photocell FC4. Then the conveyor speed drops to low, and when the product reaches FC5, the conveyor is stopped. The product is then pushed off the conveyor belt by a pneumatic piston.

The end positions of the piston are detected by two sensors, G1 and G2. When the piston has returned to its rear position, the cycle ends.

Medium long product: The product continues forward to photocell FC5, at that marks the end of the cycle. (It is assumed that the product falls off the belt before a new product passes FC1.)

Long product: The conveyor stops for 2 seconds and is then reversed. When the product again passes FC1 (on the return), the conveyor shall continue in the backward direction in a further 5 seconds. It is then assumed that the product has dropped off the conveyor belt and the cycle ends.

Task: Draw a flowchart for the control of the facility.

Problem 4.10   Filling Station

Figure 4.33 shows a system for filling cartons based on weight. Empty boxes come from the left along the conveyor belt and will:

- Stop under the silo
- Be filled to the correct weight
- Be carried away (toward the right)

The scales sense the load on the conveyor belt under the silo and produce two signals:

- **B0** is logically high when the scales are in the ready state (empty box on the belt above the scales)
- **B1** emits pulses when the weight increases—10 pulses per kilogram.

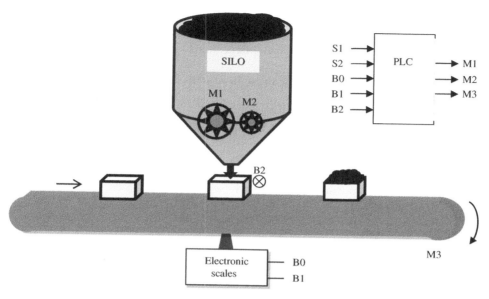

Figure 4.33   Filling station (Reproduced with permission from Inge Vivås)

A photocell **B2** emits a logically high signal when a box is in position beneath the silo. Filling takes place rapidly at first (**M1** high) and then slowly (**M2** high) so that the weight will be as accurate as possible.

A cycle should proceed as follows:

- The facility is started with a button **S1**. Then the belt motor **M3** starts.
- When a box arrives at the filling station (**B2** high), the belt should stop.
- When the scales are ready, that is, when **B0** gives the high signal, the filling should start.
- When 36 kg has been filled into the box, M1 should stop and M2 should start. M2 should run until the weight is precisely 40 kg.
- After a three-second pause, the sequence should be repeated. (Completely until the stop button **S2** is activated. When that happens, the control should make itself ready for the next sequence before the facility shuts down.)

(a) Draw a *flowchart* (Section 4.5.1) that illustrates the sequential flow. You can use oral formulations such as "Wait three seconds" or "Weight stable?"
(b) Make a sequence diagram (Section 4.5.4) that shows the states for all input and output signals in addition to other necessary events such as "ready output" from a counter or a timer (time delay). (See for instance Figure 4.18.)

Problem 4.11   Motor Operation

Two motors M1 and M2, which are controlled by a common set of start/stop buttons, should start every other time the start button is pressed. If Stop is not pressed within 40 seconds, the other motor should start as well. The principle is as follows:

- When the start button is pressed, motor M1 should start. During the course of the next 40 seconds, one of two things can happen:
  1. If Stop is not pressed, M2 automatically starts after 40 seconds. The stop button must be pressed to stop both motors.
  2. If the stop button is pressed before these 40 seconds have elapsed, M1 stops (and M2 naturally does not start).

- The next time the start button is pressed, M2 should start. During the course of the next 40 seconds, one of two things can happen:
  1. If the stop button is not pressed, M1 starts automatically after 40 seconds. The stop button must be pressed in order to stop both.
  2. If the stop button is pressed before these 40 seconds have elapsed, M2 stops (and M1 naturally does not start).

The next time Start is pressed, M1 starts again and the sequence is repeated as described above.

Make a state diagram for the description above. Use reasonable and legal state names and complete transitions in pseudocode.

Part Three
IEC 61131-3

5

Introduction to Programming and IEC 61131-3

As the title indicates, this chapter is an introduction to the IEC 61131-3 standard. This is a general presentation of the standard that is aimed at standardization, shortcomings of traditional proprietary systems, and the advantages of standardization. (The details of the elements of standardization will be discussed in Chapter 6.)

Chapter Contents

- Introduction to the standard:
  Weaknesses of traditional PLSs, advantages of standardization, implementation of the standard
- Brief presentation of the following programming languages:
  Structured text (ST), function block diagram (FBD), LD, instruction lists (IL), sequential function chart (SFC)
- High-level components:
  Configuration, resources, tasks, program organization unit (POU)
- Program processing:
  Programming skills, source code, compiling, machine code, syntactic and semantic errors

---

5.1 Introduction

Many PLC programming standards have been suggested over the years. Suggestions have come from various national and international committees that had the goal of developing a common interface for programmable controllers. In 1979, an international working group was formed that consisted of PLC experts who were tasked to come up with a first draft for a comprehensive PLC standard.

Programmable Logic Controllers: A Practical Approach to IEC 61131-3 Using CODESYS, First Edition. Dag H. Hanssen.
© 2015 John Wiley & Sons, Ltd. Published 2015 by John Wiley & Sons, Ltd.

After the first draft appeared in 1982, it was decided that the standard was too comprehensive to be collected into a single document. The original working group was therefore split up into five different working groups, each of which dealt with its portion of the standard.

The five parts consisted of:

1. General information
2. Hardware and requirements for testing
3. Programming languages
4. User interface
5. Communications

The first standard on programming languages (Part 3) was published in March 1993 and was designated IEC[1] 61131-3.[2] Other additions were published in 2002 and the third, and provisionally last, appeared in 2013.

The standard, which is currently followed to a greater or lesser degree by most of the major PLC manufacturers, includes various programming languages:

1. Structured Text—ST
2. Function Block Diagram—FBD
3. Ladder Diagram—LD
4. Instruction List—IL
5. Sequential Function Chart—SFC

LD, SFC, and FBD are graphical programming languages, while IL and ST are text-based languages. Note that the order in which they are listed above is the same order they are described in the standard. This has no relationship to when the languages first came into use or how much they are used.

The IL programming language will not be described extensively in this book. This decision is based upon an industry evaluation of which language is most efficient in use and which is the most widespread.

I have chosen to begin with the graphical languages LD and FBD, followed by the textual language ST. In addition, SFC will be thoroughly discussed since this language is especially designed for programming sequential controls and for organizing program code in general. This chapter contains a brief presentation of all the languages in the standard, and the four languages mentioned above will be thoroughly treated in their own chapters.

5.1.1 Weaknesses in Traditional PLCs

All PLC manufacturers have used LD as one of the programming languages, but each manufacturer has previously had its own dialect. This means that, for standardization purposes, there have been relatively major differences from one type of PLC to another:

---

[1] IEC stands for International Electrotechnical Commission. This is the world's leading organization for preparation and publication of international standards for all electrical and electronic (and related) technologies.

[2] Previously, the standard was called IEC 1131-3 (without the six-digit identifier). After January 1, 1997, all IEC publications are issued in the 60 000 series. For example, IEC 34-1 is now referred to as IEC 60034-1.

- The use of symbols and programming capabilities varied from one type of PLC to another. This meant that one had to learn a new dialect when one changed brands of PLC.
- It was difficult to structure the programs and to build hierarchical structures. Most PLCs supported a limited number of subroutines, but did not support the use of program *blocks* in LD. If one cannot group the code into blocks with input and output parameters, it is nearly impossible to make good structures that connect various program code blocks.
- The use of only global variables and addresses meant that the programmer had to be careful and screen a part of a program from being influenced by another part. The capability for encapsulation of the individual program parts is important in making a good, legible, and durable code that is also easy to modify later.
- Arithmetic operations were also difficult to implement. Most manufacturers had previously implemented this possibility only by using their own arithmetic blocks.
- Figure 5.1 shows a program code to add two numbers with the Omron C200H PLC. Numbers larger than 9999 (BCD) had to be stored in several addresses in this PLC. In the example, the number stored in addresses IR020 and IR021 are added to the number located in DM0020 and DM0021. The result remains in the addresses DM0030, DM0031, and DM0032. (IR is the input register and DM is the data memory register.)

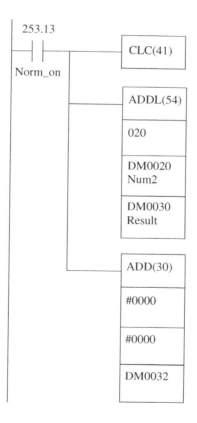

Figure 5.1   Arithmetic operations in LD (Omron C200H)

- Reuse of program code was also difficult when the code could not be stored in separate blocks with input and output parameters. Often, one had a need to utilize the same code again several times. In many traditional LD-based PLSs, reuse is difficult in the best case.
- There were limited possibilities for exercising control of how the execution of the program took place. In most PLCs, the execution of the program was by continual scanning of the program (see Section 1.3.3). How much time the processor took for each such cycle was primarily determined by the size of the program application. However, one frequently found a need to be able to control the updating speed. This made it simpler to structure the code by splitting up the code into several programs that were run at different times and with different cycle times.

5.1.2   Improvements with IEC 61131-3

One of the aims of standardization is for everyone working with PLCs to understand one another better. An example of this would be that someone who is working on a project would be able to communicate better with the programmers of the PLC. It would also be easier to make alterations in the program that someone else has written no matter what PLC it applied to. The threshold for users would be lower and the training time reduced.

The group working with development of the standard studied programming languages from many major manufacturers. Then they set up suggestions for languages that included the most essential features from the individual dialects. In addition to a clear definition of the languages, the standard covers several other aspects such as:

- Addressing
- Execution
- Data formats/data structures
- Use of symbols
- Sequential control
- Connections between languages

Some improvements from the standard:

- It is becoming simpler to build structured programs and collect programs hierarchically. Smaller program parts can be encapsulated into separate program elements that can be coupled in a hierarchical structure. The main program can be split up into separate parts, each of which can have its own execution conditions. Smaller program parts that require faster execution can be placed into their own folders in the program structures. The same is true of program code that is to be executed only if an abnormal condition occurs.
- The possibility of cyclic execution (fixed interval between scans) in which the cycle time can be configured means that the programmer achieves better control. Different program sections can be executed and updated at different times, which also contributes to better structure and simpler control.
- Reuse of program code becomes possible to a greater degree. The standard is not an absolute set of rules. Among other things, it means that code written for a type of PLC cannot be directly imported into a PLC from a different manufacturer, but the code can still be rewritten easily with minor modifications.

- Buying and selling products and services have become simpler since the competence of users has become more generalized. It is been simpler for users who know PLCs from one manufacturer to learn to get around in a programming language from a different manufacturer.

5.1.3   On Implementation of the Standard

It is important to be clear that the IEC 61131-3 standard is not an <u>absolute</u> standard. Manufacturers who want to adopt the standard do not need to follow the standard slavishly. This would have made the standard to comprehensive and detailed and would have limited the possibility for manufacturers to develop software (and hardware) with competitive advantages over other manufacturers.

Instead, the standard defines a comprehensive set of *guidelines*. These are summarized in 76 tables in the document (International Electrotechnical Commission, 2013). Manufacturers determine for themselves to what extent they will follow the guidelines. This also means that there can still be relatively large differences with respect to programming, user interface, graphics, etc. between the various manufacturers' systems even though they have all been certified by the standardizing organization.[3]

As we see, there is a relatively large degree of freedom associated with the right to assert that a system meets the standard. However, there is an unavoidable requirement that the documentation makes clear what is and what is not in line with the standard. This may be done by reference to the individual items in the individual tables.

The documentation for the system must therefore contain a statement of conformity such as "This system conforms to the guidelines in IEC 61131-3 in the following properties." The information in the table must be taken directly from the relevant subparagraphs in (International Electrotechnical Commission, 2013).

Example 5.1

The following table has been taken from the documentation for the programming tool PL7 Pro from Telemecanique (Schneider Electric, 2002 and 2004).

Table number	Characteristic number	Description of characteristics
59	1	Left power rail
59	2	Right power rail
60	1	Horizontal link
60	2	Vertical link
61	1	Open contact
61	3	Closed contact
61	5	Positive transition contact detector
61	7	Negative transition contact detector
62	1	Coil
62	2	Negated coil
62	3	SET (latch) coil
62	4	RESET (unlatch) coil

---

[3] Certification is issued by the international independent organization PLCopen. Many hardware and software producers are members of that organization. The purpose of the organization is increased knowledge and application of IEC 61131-3.

The table refers to subparagraphs concerning graphical elements in the LD programming language. If we compare the paragraphs in the standard, we see that PL7 Pro has implemented all of the properties except for *Transition-sensing coils* described in Table no. 62 on page 142. (*Note*: This documentation is written with reference to the second version of the standard.)

5.2 Brief Presentation of the Languages

5.2.1 ST

As the name indicates, ST is a text-based language. It is, in contrast to ILs (the other text-based language in the standard), a high-level language where many operations and instructions can be performed with a single command line. If we were to compare it to other high-level languages, ST most resembles Pascal or C.

ST has been specially developed to program complex arithmetic functions, manipulate tables, and work with word objects and text. The example below contains ordering of values, conditional instructions, a FOR-loop, and the declaration of a variable. (The example is written with the programming tool CODESYS.)

Example 5.2

```
PROGRAM PLC_PRG
VAR
    Index           : INT := 1;
    Parameter       : ARRAY [0..10] OF REAL;
    Data AT %MW5    : ARRAY [0..10] OF REAL;
END_VAR

IF %MX0.1 THEN
    %MW0 := 0;
    %MX0.2 := %MX20.0;
ELSIF NOT %MX3.0 THEN
    %MW0 := 10;
END_IF;

FOR Index := 1 TO 10 BY 1 DO
    Parameter[Index] := Data[Index];
    Index := Index - 1;
END_FOR;
```

ST will be treated in Chapter 11.

5.2.2 FBD

FBD[4] is a graphical language which, described in a very simplified way, is based on connecting functions and Function-blocks (Figure 5.2). The language includes, among other things, use of

---

[4] Notice that FBD as described in IEC 61131-3 is in accordance with IEC 60617-12.

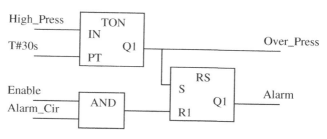

Figure 5.2   Example of code in FBD

standard logical function such as AND, OR, NOT, etc. and function blocks (FBs) such as timers and counters, but self-constructed functions and FBs can also be defined. Many who have little knowledge of digital electronics therefore think that this is a great language to use or at any rate to get started with. It can be practical to use the language to program logical algorithms (Boolean functions) and control functions such as regulator structures and the like. However, the language does not offer anything that cannot be executed in ST, but it gives a better overview (at any rate, for smaller programs).

FBD is covered more thoroughly in Chapter 10.

5.2.3   LD

Ladder Diagram, or just plain LD, is still used to a large degree by many PLC programmers. This is despite the fact that both ST and SFC are more efficient languages in most contexts. The reason that LD is still used so much is that it is simple to understand and that is it is based upon traditional electrical wiring diagrams (relay diagrams). The well-established language has, for a long time, continued to maintain its presence because new engineers and technicians still have to learn to read it, understand it, and apply it. Some people also apply the concept of relay diagram to program code written in LD.

LD basically consists of a set of instructions that execute the most basic types of control functions: logic, time control, and counting, as well as simple mathematical operations. An example of program code is shown in Figure 5.3. The example of code contains standard elements such as contactors (NO and NC), coils, flank-detecting contacts, and a timer.

Most PLC manufacturers nowadays make it possible to perform advanced additional functions in LD, often integrated with other languages such as FBD and ST. For smaller controls, LD can therefore be a fine choice of programming language. The basic functions that are needed in order to implement smaller applications can be learned relatively quickly and the graphical presentation can be understood intuitively.

5.2.4   IL

IL is an assembler-like low-level language. Even though there are disadvantages associated with the use of a low-level language such as IL, the advantage of the language is that it does

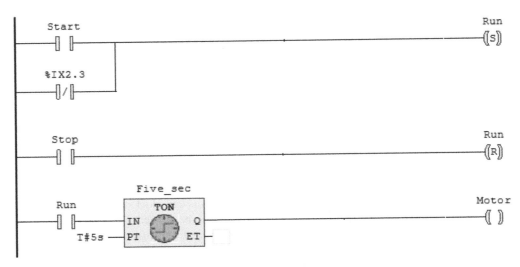

Figure 5.3   Example of program code in LD

not require much computer power. The reason that the language continues to be used is that the language, together with LD, has existed longer than the other languages in the standard.

Many older PLCs can be programmed only with IL/LD. There can therefore be cases where one can use IL, for example, when program code written in IL is taken from an old PLC for modification or analysis. The IL language, however, has limited capabilities and applications because it is hard to learn and not very comprehensible when programming tasks are numerous or complex.[5]

On older PLCs code in IL (or LD) be programmed and transferred to the CPU via a special panel. It was not necessary (or possible), as it is today, to connect a PC for programming and diagnostics. An example of such an older PLC that has a programming panel is the Omron model C20, which is shown in the picture below.

Example of code in IL:

```
LD      run
ST      timer1.IN
LD      counter
GE      5   (* IF counter >= 5, *)
JMPC    next      (* jump to next *)
CAL     timer1(
        PT:=t#10m)
LD      timer1.Q
```

---

[5] Personally, I think that the language is so user-unfriendly and hard to read that it is scarcely worth time to learn it. Perhaps this statement will irritate some people, particularly among the old hands who still prefer IL.

```
ST      motor
next:
   :                          (* etc... *)
```

5.2.5   SFC

SFC is a graphical tool that is ideal for programming sequential controls and implementing state-based control algorithms (Figure 5.4). SFC is actually not a programming language in the traditional sense, but more a graphic approach for structuring program code. It is also brilliantly adapted for this. All of the other languages in the standard can be used together with SFCs, and it is necessary for at least one of them to be able to implement all of the necessary transitions and actions. You will find more about SFC in Chapter 12.

5.3   Program Structure in IEC 61131-3

In this section, we will briefly introduce the basic elements in 61131-3. The basic structures and concepts in the standard will be discussed without going into details about language and language elements.

The standard has been developed in order to be consistent with more advanced logical controllers, as well, where several CPUs are involved, for instance. We will therefore define some concepts that can describe such systems.

The standard specifies a hierarchical approach to programming structure. The sketch in Figure 5.5 illustrates the high-level structural elements defined in the standard and their intrinsic unity. The elements that are defined are found in all PLC systems, even though the manufacturers often use other names and concepts for some of the elements.

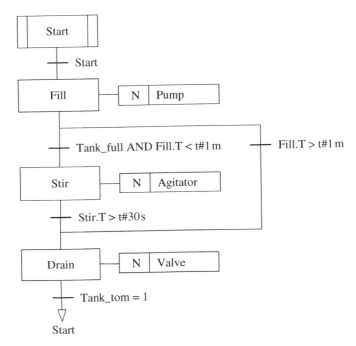

Figure 5.4   Example of SFC

In the succeeding text follows a short definition and description of the individual elements.

Configuration

The top level in the software structure is called a *configuration*, and this is the designation for a programmable control system (defined in *Part 1* of the IEC 61131 standard). Such a control system can, for instance, be a PLC—a controller in a rack with one or more processors. Larger control systems can consist of the network of several configurations. A configuration is therefore also defined as a communications interface with other configurations. A configuration consists of one or more resources (see in the following text). Global variables and directly addressed variables, for instance, I/O, can also be declared at the configuration level. In this case, it will be visible to all resources within the configuration.

Resource

Under each configuration, we find one or more *Resources*. The standard describes a resource as "consisting of a signal processor unit with its user interface and functions for sensor and actuator interfaces." For a PLC, a resource can be a processor (the CPU) but could also be applications in a PLC.

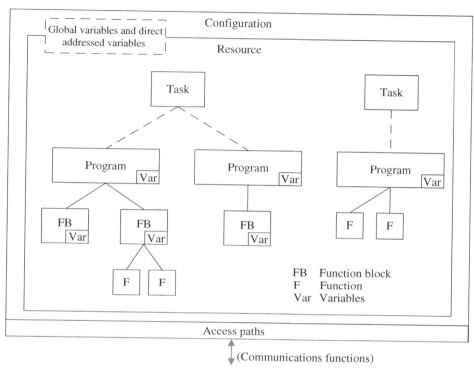

Figure 5.5 Configuration elements and general program structure in IEC 61131-3

Each resource can, in turn, contain one or more programs. The presentation in Figure 5.5 shows one configuration consisting of one resource. Global variables that are declared within the resource are used to process data that is limited to that one CPU, but that should be accessible for all other program units within the resource.

Task

A *task* can be used to control how the program within the resource is executed. Each resource can contain one or more declared tasks. The tasks can, for instance, be configured to perform each individual program organization unit (POU) cyclically, freewheeling, or event controlled. (These concepts was also discussed in Section 1.3.3.)

By associating the program units to various tasks, the POUs can also be performed in their order of importance. This is achieved by assigning a *priority* to the various tasks under the configuration. This parameter defines how the programs that can run simultaneously are prioritized relative to one another. The significance of such a priority, however, is dependent upon implementation and thus depends upon which CPU is handling interrupts. There are two ways that a conflict between two simultaneous programs can be managed:

• The program that has lower priority is interrupted immediately so that execution of the higher-priority program can start.

- The program that has lower priority is not interrupted, but rather continues normally until termination, before the higher-priority tasks are carried out.

Even though not all equipment producers follow the standard, all of them have implemented a method of controlling execution of programs. One practice that has been used, and continues to be used in a number of PLC systems, is to use special types of blocks where run properties for program code are given implicitly (in STEP7 from Siemens, *organization blocks* (*OB*) are used). These can be properties such as cyclic or freewheeling execution or for managing interrupts. With the IEC 61131-3 definition of a task, it is possible to indicate all such program properties *explicitly* and independently of the supplier.

Variable

Variables are used to identify data objects whose content can be altered. This can be data that is associated with inputs and outputs or data in the memory of a PLC. Variables must be *declared* and one must simultaneously indicate what type of information the variable will contain by indicating one of several defined data types, for instance, BOOL, INT, or WORD.

Variables can be declared within individual POUs or in configuration of the resource. In the last case, the variables are *global* (VAR_GLOBAL), and they can be accessed by all the POUs within the same resource or from POUs in another resource.

Programs, Functions, and FBs

One of the concepts that are fundamental for understanding and that will be used a great deal in the rest of the text is the concept of POU. The concept will soon be described more completely, so here we will satisfy ourselves by saying that a POU is an independent program unit. There are four types of POUs defined in the standard:

- *Programs*
- *FBs*
- *Functions (F)*
- *Classes*

Every POU can call up another POU, and the call can be with or without parameters. Normally a program will contain calls of functions and FBs, but it will also be possible (and simple) to call up a program from another program.

NOTE! This book covers only the first three types of POU.

These will be more fully described in Chapters 7 and 8. Here, we shall be satisfied with saying that a resource can contain one or more *programs* which, in turn, can contain several *FBs* and *functions*. These last can be user-defined or predefined and provided together with the PLC as a part of the operating system or included in a *library* that is available in the programming tool.

Most often, the user will build up the program, but these programs can also, as mentioned previously, contain (call) many predefined FBs such as CTU (counter), TON (time delay), or SR (flip-flop) or predefined functions such as COS, SQRT, ADD, MOVE, plus many others.

5.3.1 Example of a Configuration

Here, Figure 5.6 shows an example of a simple configuration that includes one resource and three defined tasks with associated programs and FBs. Note that the programs called by the elements often consist of several separate program units even though these are not shown in this figure (for the sake of comprehensibility).

In the example, it is assumed that the main program is executed freewheeling. Then the scan time can vary from one scan to the next (for instance, be 15 ms in one scan and 25 ms in the next).

Often, it is advantageous to have a cyclic execution of a program, for instance, in data collection or logging or regulating a process like the one shown. A Proportional–Integral–Derivative (PID) control functions best when the cycle time is fixed. This program unit is therefore associated with a task that is configured for cyclic execution. The cycle time does not show in the figure, but can be configured in the task.

If there are many program units, one can also structure according to how critical they are to the operation by associating them with tasks with various *priorities*. Events often happen that must be processed immediately in order to limit loss and damage of equipment or to secure life and health. Examples of such critical operations could be alarm management and routines for emergency stops. Program code that manages such events can then be associated with a task of the *event* type where a certain event is specially monitored.

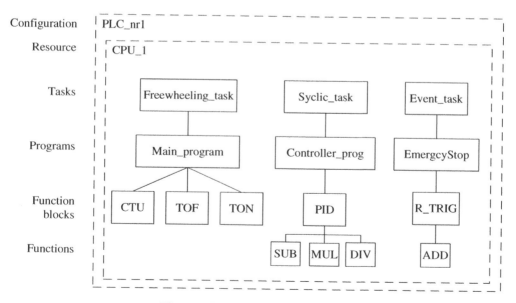

Figure 5.6 Example of configuration

5.4   Program Processing

Most PLC systems have been developed with the goal that persons with little or no previous knowledge of programming should be able to learn how to develop programs. This perhaps is one of the reasons that IEC 61131-3 includes fully five different programming languages.

Particularly, the two graphical languages in the standard, LD and FBD, are considered by many users to be intuitive and easy to understand. This is not just an accident.

LD, which is the first language that was developed for PLCs, is designed on the basis of the relay diagram. Such diagrams are well known to electricians and others with an electrical background and will therefore be a natural first choice for a novice programmer with such a technical background.

FBD has many similarities to the logical circuit diagram. Users with basic knowledge of digital electronics, or knowledge of Boolean algebra and combinatorics, will discover many recognizable elements in this language.

To gain a greater understanding of what a program is, we will hear have a somewhat more general lesson on how program code is implemented and how it is processed in digital hardware (which is indeed what a PLC is, in fact).

5.4.1   Development of Programming Languages

No matter which programming language a user chooses, the PLC will process the program code in the same general way. Before the CPU can understand and perform the instructions in the code, it must be converted into binary form:

- Code in its original form (as the user sees it) is called *source code*.
- The binary form, which is the "native language" of computers and other digital hardware, is called *machine code*.

The very first computers were actually programmed in machine code, where codes in the form of bit patterns were punched into so-called punch cards.

It was naturally enough a terrible job to program in machine code so eventually a language called *Assembler* was developed. Common operations were collected and defined into a set of instructions. Parallel to this, there were developed programs that could interpret assembler instructions and convert them into machine code. This was called *compiling* a code and a program that performed this job was called a *compiler*.

Assembler are what we call low-level language and operate at the register level in the computer. Assembler is not a particularly user-friendly language, but it can give greater understanding of how digital hardware operates and functions. In order to make it simpler to develop a more advanced program, several *high-level* languages have been developed. Examples of high-level languages are Pascal, C++, and Java. For PLCs, the language ST is such a high-level language.

Even though assembler is laborious to program with, and even though many high-level languages have been developed, assembler is still used relatively often. The reason for this is that it is a *resource-efficient* language. In compiling source code written in a high-level language, there is always generated a certain amount of "unnecessary" code as a result of the high-level language using elements and instructions that function for a wide variety of purposes. Compiling source code written in assembler does not generate any unnecessary code (as long as it is well written). This is an advantage in for systems where speed is critical or memory is limited.

The fourth language in the IEC 61131-3 standard, IL, is very reminiscent of assembler. This is because a universal language like IL is often implemented and utilized in program development tools like a sort of bridge between the high-level languages and machine code. This means that it is often possible to convert source code written in another language into IL.

5.4.2   From Source Code to Machine Code

Common to all programming languages is that the source code must be compiled in order to generate a runnable machine code. In the following, we will briefly take up the phases that a program goes through from source code to machine code. Figure 5.7 illustrates the process from the user program (source code) to a runnable program (machine code). This job is usually performed by the development tool.

5.4.2.1   Writing and Editing

All programming tools have one or more *editors*. These are user interfaces where the program writer constructs the program code. This can be a simple editor without graphical symbols and tools, or it can be an editor that is equipped for programming in a graphical language.

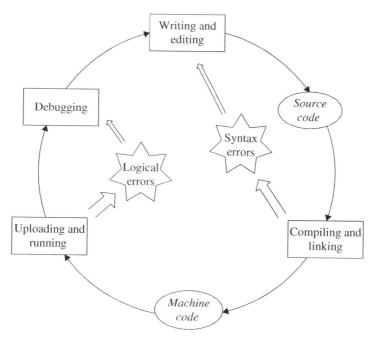

Figure 5.7   The cycle of program development

The former is the case when the programming is done in text-based language like C, JavaScript, or HTML, or the languages IL and ST in the IEC 61131-3 standard.

If the compiler can handle files of the type **.txt**, for instance, one can easily use the Microsoft Windows program Notepad to develop the program code. This is not common with PLCs because they are practically always accompanied by a development tool.

Use of Color

Most editors use color in order to help the user more easily distinguish between comments, variables, and keywords (reserved words). Which colors are used can vary from one development tool to another. CODESYS uses the following by default:

- Reserved words (AND, OR, IF, etc.) are written in uppercase **BLUE**.
- Comments are written in **blue-green**.
- Variables, constants, assignment operators, etc. are written in **black**.
- CODESYS also uses a special color (**dark magenta**) for direct addresses and **olive** for values such as TRUE, FALSE, T#30s, etc., and **red** if these are entered in error. (All the colors can be defined by the user.)

High-level languages such as Visual Basic, Visual C++, or the languages SFC, LD, and FBD in the standard, which have preassigned graphical elements, require editors where the graphical elements are accessible in menus and/or on tool palettes.

Figure 5.9 shows an example of an editor for the Grafcet graphical language, which is a forerunner to SFC. As we see, the editor contains a toolbar with the graphic elements that are accessible for use in programming.

```
PROGRAM Washing_Operation
VAR
      (* Declaring states: *)
      Ready, Filling, Heating, Stirring, Draining : RS;
      (* Inputs and Outputs: *)
      Start              AT %IX2.0 :BOOL;
      Tank_full          AT %IX2.1 :BOOL;
      Tank_empty         AT %IX2.2 :BOOL;
      Temperature        AT %IW0   :WORD;
      Fill_valve         AT %QX0.0 :BOOL;
      Drain_valve        AT %QX0.1 :BOOL;
      Heater             AT %QX0.2 :BOOL;
      Stirrer            AT %QX0.3 :BOOL;
      First_scan           :BOOL    := TRUE;
      Five_min     :TON;   // Timer in TON-modi
      Three_times :CTU;    // Up-Counter
   END_VAR
```

Figure 5.8   Example of editor (From development tool CODESYS v3.5)

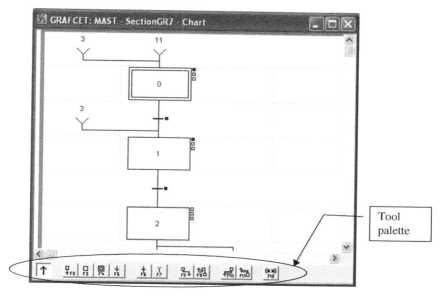

Figure 5.9   Example of editor (From development tool PL7 Pro from Telemecanique)

5.4.2.2   Compiling, Syntax Errors, and Linking

As noted previously, a compiler is the program that converts source code to machine code, which is the code that digital equipment such as a PLC understands and can process.

As mentioned, this compilation is performed by the development tool for PLCs. If the source code contains errors as a result of violation of the rules, it generates error messages in the compiler. Such errors as are discovered by the compiler are called *syntax errors*.[6] Examples of syntax errors are lack of declaration of variables, use of keywords as identifiers, or calling a function or subroutine that does not exist. Common to all syntax errors is that they make it impossible for the CPU to execute the compiled code and is therefore necessary to edit the code in order to remove such errors.

Some development tools, such as CODESYS, are based on the idea that the user performs compiling when he/she wishes to do so by activating and starting the compiler. The compiler goes through all of the code and then generates a sort of report. If the code contains syntax errors, the report generated will contain references to where in the code the error is located (or where it first becomes consequential). This usually happens when the error message contains a reference to the POU that contains the error and what line in the code contains the error.

In some development tools, the compiler runs continuously and automatically whenever the user confirms the statements and instructions that he/she has written. In this way, the user is informed continually of any syntax errors because a marker sits there and blinks at the first error.

Depending upon the design of the development tool, an operation that is called *linking* can also take place in connection with compiling. The compiled source file is then linked to other

---

[6] Syntax: The rules for the formation of grammatical sentences in a language.

necessary files. This can be library files that contain predefined functions and FBs that have been used in the source code or files that have been prepared by the writer.

5.4.2.3 Loading and Running

When the code is free of syntax errors so that it can be compiled, the machine code can be loaded into the PLC for running. Note that many programming contain simulators so that one can test the code without loading it into the PLC.

This is the point at which a new type of error, the *semantic*[7] error (also called logical error) will often turn up. There are two main types of semantic error:

- Those that result in a program crash
- Those that do not result in a program crash but which give the wrong result

An example of the former type is exceeding the watchdog time (for instance, as the result of a loop).

The other type of logical error can obviously be critical even though the program can run without crashing because such errors mean that you are getting an undesired result from the program with reference to the job that the PLC ought to do.

It is quite clear that this latter type is the most common and the one that all programmers take a lot of time to fix. It naturally does not help the situation when the compiler does not have any capability to discover such errors.

Example 5.3   Code that Contains Errors

```
PROGRAM Error_PRG
VAR
    Digital_in AT %IX2.0: BOOL  Syntax error: Missing semicolon
END_VAR

IF Digital_in = TRUE THEN
    %MW0 = 0;                Syntax error: missing colon before =
    %MX0.15 := %MW20;        Syntax error: Word object assigned to
                             Boolean object
ELSIF NOT Digital_in THEN
    %MW0 := 10;
ELSE                         Logical error:
    %MW0 := 20;              This instruction can never be
                             performed.
END_IF
```

5.4.2.4 Debugging

Most of the development tools for PLCs contain a tool for troubleshooting the code. Programmers usually use the word *debugging* instead of troubleshooting and such error-finding tools are called debuggers. Debugging a program involves hunting for and correcting errors.

---

[7] Semantics: Pertaining to the meanings of words and other symbols.

In using a debugger, one can run the program step-by-step, for instance, instruction by instruction, while watching the state of Boolean objects and the contents and other types of variables and objects. Alternatively, one can also insert one or more *breakpoints*. When the program runs, the CPU will stop execution of code when the program indicator comes to such a breakpoint. The purpose of this can be to run quickly through the code when you are sure that it is okay and then to run in a more controlled manner through certain parts of the code. Alternatively breakpoints can be used to study what happens from one program scan to the next. This is practical for studying the content of objects used for counting, among other things. Such a controlled execution of program code, combined with forcing variables to desired values and states make it much easier to find logical errors in the program.

5.5   Test Problems

Problem 5.1
(a) IEC 61131 is divided up into five parts. Which?
(b) What are the five programming languages defined in the IEC 61131-3 standard?
(c) What is the reason for standardizing programming languages for PLCs?
(d) What other aspects besides programming languages are included by IEC 61131-3?
(e) How could we check to what extent a programming tool adheres to the standard?

Problem 5.2
(a) When would it be practical to select SFC, and when should one decide to use ST?
(b) LD is one of the first programming languages for PLCs but is still used a great deal. Why?
(c) What do the concepts of configuration and resource mean as defined in the standard?
(d) Describe the types of tasks that are commonly defined in modern PLCs.
(e) Why would there be a need to assign different *priorities* to different tasks?
(f) What is a POU and what is the relationship between a POU and a task?

Problem 5.3
Explain the following concepts:
(a) Source code
(b) Machine code
(c) Assembler
(d) Compiling
(e) Syntax error
(f) Semantic error

6

IEC 61131-3: Common Language Elements

Chapter Contents

- Use of characters:
  Identifiers, keywords, comments
- Datatypes:
  Numerical and binary datatypes, datatypes for time and duration, generic and user-defined datatypes, arrays and data structures
- Data representation:
  Numerical literals, text strings, time literals
- Variables:
  Single objects, structured objects, local and global variables, initiation, declaration, symbolizing, direct addressing and I/O-addressing

6.1   Introduction

It is one of the goals of the standard that all five languages should be able to integrate, so that, for instance, a POU written in ST can contain a call of a POU written in LD or that a program code with associated variable declarations and comments can be converted from one programming language to another.

In order for it to be possible to implement this, there are many concepts and elements in the standard that follow defined rules that are common to all the languages. This applies to:

- Identifiers
- Keywords
- Comments

Programmable Logic Controllers: A Practical Approach to IEC 61131-3 Using CODESYS, First Edition. Dag H. Hanssen.
© 2015 John Wiley & Sons, Ltd. Published 2015 by John Wiley & Sons, Ltd.

- Literals
- Addressing
- Data types
- Variables

This chapter deals with these common elements.

6.2 Identifiers, Keywords, and Comments

This group of common elements deals with permitted use of characters, either as identifiers, variables, program names, or for comments. For example, some particular combinations of characters are not permitted to be used as identifiers. Such combinations are called *keywords* and are processed as such.

6.2.1 Identifiers

An *identifier* is a fancy word for *name*. Many elements must be given a name before or during the programming. This applies to programs, variables, user-defined functions and functional blocks, and steps and actions (SFC) etc.

    The standard requires that, as a minimum, the first six characters in a name should be tested for uniqueness by the hardware. This means that the system must be able to distinguish between the variable names **Motor1** and **Motor2** (six characters), but not necessarily between the variables **Switch1** and **Switch2** (seven characters).

    However, it is freely up to the manufacturer to implement a higher number and most systems can distinguish names with a length that is much higher than six.[1]

    Other guidelines in the standard applicable to identifiers are:

- Interpretation of identifiers must be independent of character case. For example, the system should interpret Sensor, sensor, and sEnSoR as the same identifier.
- Identifiers may not contain a space.
- They must begin with a letter or an _ (underscore).
- They may not end with an underscore or have two sequential underscores.
- Numerals are permitted, but not first in the identifier.

Example 6.1   Examples of Permitted Identifiers

- AbCDe
- _ABCdE
- AB_CDE
- A_2_3

---

[1] In the programming tool CODESYS (from Software Solutions GmbH) for instance, the length of a permitted name of identifiers is *unlimited*. This applies as well to the meaningful portion of the identifier, that is, the part of the name that is tested for uniqueness.

Example 6.2   Examples of Identifiers That Are <u>Not</u> Permitted

- A_B__C (two adjacent _)
- 1_A_B (numeral first)
- A_B CD (space)
- AbCDe_ (ends with _)

(Note that keywords cannot be used as identifiers.)

Since it varies from one system to another in how many characters are permitted to use in identifiers, it makes sense to be rather modest in the selection of identifiers. Even though most systems will probably support it, it is probably a good idea to avoid identifiers such as **This_ is_a_long_identifier**. It quickly becomes difficult to keep track of such long identifiers and it naturally takes longer to enter them.

6.2.2   Keywords

Keywords are unique combinations of characters that are reserved from being used as identifiers, since they are only to be used as *syntactic elements* in programs. The standard remains open for national standardization organizations to translate keywords and publish a national list in place of the list that is published in International Electrotechnical Commission (2013). It seems doubtful that this is actually taking place. Here are some examples of keywords described in the standard:

- TRUE, FALSE
- IF…THEN…ELSIF…ELSE…END_IF
- AND, OR, NOT, MOD, XOR
- FUNCTION…END_FUNCTION
- VAR…END_VAR

As we see, only uppercase letters are used in the keywords. Normally, the system is not sensitive to the use of upper- or lowercase letters when writing keywords. Generally, the system will automatically correct and display only uppercase letters in the editor and then in a particular color to clearly differentiate the keywords from other words and identifiers. (See Section 5.4.2.1.)

In practice, the complete list of reserved words (that is words that are not permitted to be used as identifiers) is much longer than the list found in International Electrotechnical Commission (2013). The reason for this is that manufacturers offer many predefined functions and functional blocks that are assigned unique identifiers that are reserved against use by programmers.[2]

6.2.3   Comments

Comments can be used everywhere, in all POUs and in any programming language. The purpose of comments is partly to make it easier for the programmer to keep track of his/her

---

[2] For instance, there are a total of 567 different reserved words in PL7 Pro v4.3 (from Telemecanique).

own program code and partly to make it easier for others to read and understand the code. Frequent use of comments is a good habit to get into.

The standard formulates several requirements for how comments are to be implemented. The comments here have been written in *italics* for clarification:

- Comments should be enclosed by (* and *), that is, parentheses and asterisks, both before and after the comment itself:
  (* *This is a lengthy comment, long enough that it may well extend over more than one line of written code* *).
- Comments may be placed anywhere at all in the code, but not in the middle of a variable name or the like.
- Use of nested comments is permitted as long as (* and *) come in pairs, as in this example: (* This (* is *) legal *) but (* this (* is illegal *).
- A comment may contain all characters.
- The standard also defines the alternative[3] character combinations /* and */.
- A one-line comment can be indicated following the character combination // as here[4]:
- *//This is a comment on a single line.*

It is also permitted to use (* and *) for a one-line comment.

Note that the number of characters in a single comment is dependent upon an implementation-dependent parameter.[5] The code example below contains various applications of comments. Since all characters are permitted within comments, there can be several asterisks between (* and *).

Example 6.3   Use of Comments

```
(********* RS FLIP-FLOP *********)
(* Example of function block that
implements a reset-dominant flip-flop *)
(***************************)
FUNCTION_BLOCK RS
    // Declares input variable:
    VAR_INPUT
      Set :    BOOL;
      Reset :  BOOL;
    END_VAR
    //Declares output variable:
    VAR_OUTPUT
      Out : BOOL;
    END_VAR
    Out := NOT Reset AND (Set OR Q1);   (*The FB's program code *)
END_FUNCTION_BLOCK
```

---

[3] This is not implemented in CODESYS.
[4] //is not implemented in CODESYS v2.3.x.
[5] For instance, this is permitted with 256 characters in PL7Pro (v4.3).

6.3   About Variables and Data Types

In traditional PLC systems, only *global*[6] addresses are used, and these often have fixed locations in memory. The disadvantage of this is that the users themselves must be careful that no conflicts occur when they are written to the same addresses from different parts of the program or from different programs. In other words, the user monitors which addresses he/she has used and to what extent they do not overlap with other addresses.

The only advantage with fixed addresses is that the user does not have to declare the variable. With IEC 61131-3, all addresses that will be used must be declared[7] in the form of variables. If you do not specify something else, all variables will be declared as *local* variables within the individual POUs. Then they will be accessible only within the POU where they were declared. Then there will be no conflict with variables declared in a different POU, even though the same variable name has been used. (Section 6.6 deals with variables and declaration.)

Nor is the type of data that an address can contain fixed in traditional PLCs. Since the data type is not declared, the same address or address area can be used for floating-point numbers in one part of program code, for instance, and the four integers in another part of the code. This is possible since the same area in memory is often used for different types of data so that the user must be careful that there is no overlap between addresses that contain different types of data.

Example 6.4   Overlap between Addresses and Types

%MD14	32-bit addresses that contain integers
%MF14	32-bit addresses floating-point numbers

These two objects have different data types but refer to the same address location (same memory area). When using both objects in the program, logical errors in the form of assignment of content will occur because assignment of content to one object will change the other object.

With IEC 61131-3, data types are declared explicitly when the variables are declared. If any conflict arises among various data types, for instance, when a variable that contains data of the floating-point type (REAL) is assigned to a variable that contains data of the whole-number type (INT), this will be considered as a syntax error. The compiler will therefore deliver a message about it (see Section 5.4.2.2).

6.4   Pragmas and Literals

A *pragma instruction* can be used to affect the properties of one or more variables with respect to compilation or precompilation processes. This means that a pragma influences the generation of the code. It can also be used as another type of comment if it does not have a valid prefix that the compiler recognizes.

---

[6] A *global* address is an address that can be read and written to from all POUs in the application.
[7] To declare means to *make a statement*, and this is the word that describes events when a variable is defined by stating variable type, variable name, data type, and possibly an initial value (starting value).

Both syntax and semantics are implementation dependent so that the use of pragmas is entirely up to the manufacturer of the system to define. The only requirement is that it be enclosed in curly brackets of the type { }, both of which are on the same line. A common application in programming is to use them to provide information in the code that is to be displayed on a screen during the run.

Example 6.5

{hello world}
{version 2.5}
{by Dan Lufkin}

CODESYS (v3.5) defines several sets of instructions for pragmas, among others:

- Access instructions for providing reading and writing access to variables in connection with communication with other hardware or software. Possible values are "read," "readwrite," and "none."
- Messaging instructions for sending information to the messaging window during compilation. Possible message types are text, info, warning, and error.

(You will find detailed information on use of these and other types in the CODESYS manual or in online help in the program.)

6.4.1   Literal

In an original grammatical context, the word *literal* means "verbatim" or "literally," but in the digital context, a literal is a "nameless constant.[8]" This somewhat mystical concept refers to two conditions: the word *constant* indicates that it deals with constant values (in contrast to variables where the content can change). *Nameless* refers to the fact that this is a value that is provided directly in the program code instead of being declared beforehand.

In the IEC 61131-3 standard, the concept of literal has a significance that is in line with its digital significance since it deals with how values are assigned. The value format can be numbers, text strings, or time, and there are, naturally enough, rules for how various types of values are entered and how the software will interpret the values. The standard defines three main types of literals:

- *Numerical literals*: Numerical values of the integer and floating-point types
- *Text strings*: Sequences of characters
- *Time literals*: Values such as duration, time of day, or date

When values are assigned to a variable, the format and range of value depends upon the data type of the variable. It is therefore natural to group literals according to data type. That is the way they will be discussed in the following text.

---

[8] The same nomenclature is used in C++ programming and most C++ manuals cover the subject in more depth than we will here.

6.5 Data Types

Depending upon what task the PLC is to perform, there will be a requirement for many different types of data. For example, there may be Boolean (BOOL) variables, perhaps associated with digital I/O, various types of integers (INT, UINT, DINT, etc.), floating-point objects (REAL), or types for management of time (TIME).

While a variable *name* identifies the storage location of a variable and the variable *type* indicates, for instance, whether the variable is global or local, the *data type* indicates what *type* of values (or literals) the variable can have. This is also significant for what operations can be undertaken with the variable in question and how the contents of the variable are stored.

When a variable is declared, the data type must be declared at the same time. The standard naturally defines guidelines for how variables and data types are to be declared and ranges of values for the individual data types. The declaration of a variable, together with its properties (as a data type), is done in a separate declaration field within the individual POU. The declaration is made in the same way, no matter which programming language is being used otherwise in the POU.

The standard defines a set of elementary data types. These will be predefined in PLCs that adhere to the standard. In addition, the standard contains guidelines on how the system can implement user-defined data types.

6.5.1 Numerical and Binary Data Types

Table 6.1 contains all of the basic integer and floating-point types that are defined in International Electrotechnical Commission (2013), while Table 6.2 contains data types in *bit-string format*. It is not certain that the manufacturer has chosen to implement all of these, particularly since some are identical in practice. The tables show, for each data type, information on associated keywords, the number of bits each element accepts, and the resulting possible range of values.

Table 6.1 Integers and floating-point numbers

Format	Data type	Number of bits	Value range	Initial value
Integer (w/sign)[a]	SINT	8	-128 to $+127$	0
	INT	16	$-32\,768$ to $+32\,767$	0
	DINT	32	-2^{31} to $+2^{31}-1$	0
	LINT	64	-2^{63} to $+2^{63}-1$	0
Positive integer	USINT	8	0 to 255	0
(unsigned)[b]	UINT	16	0 to 65 535	0
	UDINT	32	0 to $2^{32}-1$	0
	ULINT	64	0 to $2^{64}-1$	0
Floating-point	REAL	32	$\pm 10^{\pm 38}$	0.0
numbers[c]	LREAL	64	$\pm 10^{\pm 308}$	0.0

D, double; INT, integer; L, long; S, short; U, unsigned.
[a] One of the bits is used as a sign so that the possible range of values is from $-(2^{N-1})$ to $(2^{N-1}-1)$.
[b] Value range: 0 to 2^N-1.
[c] Defined in IEC 60559. See also comments on floating-point numbers in Section 6.5.1.2.

Table 6.2 Bit-string data types

Format	Data type	Number of bits (N)	Value range
Boolean	BOOL	1	0/FALSE
Bit strings	BYTE	8	16#00[a]
	WORD	16	16#0000
	DWORD	32	16#0000_0000
	LWORD	64	16#0000_0000_0000_0000

[a] The prefix 16# indicates that this is a literal in hexadecimal form. See next section.

As we see, a distinction is made between integer types with and without a sign. In many contexts, such as counter values, there is no requirement for negative numbers, and it is therefore an advantage to be able to use separate types for these. Then the system will give an error message or warning for a negative result, and at the same time, the positive value range will be larger for the same number of bits in memory. The purpose of similar types with different lengths (number of bits) is also a question of resources. There is no reason for using more bits than are necessary to store the values in question. If a variable is going to be used for counting the number of bottles in a crate, for instance, it is sufficient to use the data type USINT.

The standard also defines a group of data types that are called *bit strings*. See Table 6.2. In this group, we find a very fundamental data type, namely, BOOL. This type is used for variables associated with digital inputs and outputs as well as status and memory flags.

The other bit-string formats BYTE, WORD, DWORD, and LWORD correspond in many ways to data types for positive integers, SINT, INT, DINT, and LINT. The reason for defining these bit-string data types is because they can be used to store binary information. This can be advantageous during communications with external units and instruments for storing and setting various status bits (flags).

Another application is management of multiple Boolean objects in an efficient way, where each individual bit can represent a digital output or a signal to a stepping motor. In the next chapter, we will see that there are many functions that are defined in the standard in order to be able to manipulate the content of bit-string variables.

The data type WORD is also used for declaration of variables associated with digital inputs and outputs. Many conventional PLCs also use the types BYTE, WORD, and so forth, and an address with the length of 16 bits is also traditionally often designated as a *word*. The example below shows an illustration of the content in a word.

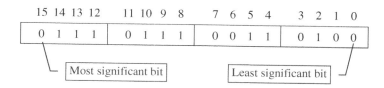

For integers with signs (data type SINT), the most significant bit (MSB) is used for the sign (0 = positive and 1 = negative).

6.5.1.1 Numerical Literals

Numerical literals can also be classified into the main types *integers* and *floating-point* numbers. The integers group thus also includes the bit-string types BYTE, WORD, DWORD, and LWORD. The standard defines several formats for assigning and representing integer values, but it is not certain that all manufacturers have implemented all types. An integer value can be entered directly in the form of a decimal number, for instance, 235. If desirable, the user can also enter (and display) integer numbers in *binary*, *octal*, or *hexadecimal* form.

In order to distinguish these formats from one another, the base number is given, followed by the character # before the value in question. If the value is not preceded by a base number and #, the value is automatically interpreted as a decimal number.

Example 6.6   Integer Literal

Decimal	Binary	Octal	Hexadecimal
0	2#00000000	8#000	16#00
37	2#0010_0101	8#45	16#25
−14	−2#00001110 (or 2#11110010)	−8#16 (or 8#362)	−16#0E (or 16#F2)
12_534	2#00110000_11110110	8#030366	16#30f6

How large a number can be entered and stored depends upon the number of bits that are available (8, 16, 32, or 64). For instance, for the numbers 0.37 and −14 (decimal), it is sufficient with eight-bit data types (such as SINT), while the number 12 534 (decimal) requires a minimum of a 16-bit data type.

As the example shows, there is a guideline for the use of the *underline character*[9] for dividing up long numbers in order to improve legibility. This is particularly useful for entering and representation of binary numbers. And, as with the definition of identifiers, no distinction is made here between uppercase and lowercase letters.

For negative numbers, the table also shows the *complementary* numbers (in parentheses). Even though it is possible to enter the numbers preceded by a sign, they are stored in the *two's complement* format in the PLC. This is the way that negative numbers are handled. Two's complement implies that all bits in the binary representation of the value are inverted and then the number is added to 1 (binary).

Example 6.7

Integer −14 is equal to −00001110 in binary.
The two's complement of this number then becomes $11110001 + 1 = 11110010$.

Negative numbers in octal and hexadecimal form can also be expressed using the two's complement form.[10]

---

[9] This is not possible in CODESYS.
[10] If one selects binary or hexadecimal display in the development tool CODESYS, the complementary values will be displayed on the screen.

6.5.1.2   Floating-Point Numbers

The word *floating point* originates from the way these numbers are represented in the PLC (or in a computer). The number is stored in two parts, the *mantissa* and the *exponent*, according to the following formula:

Floating-point number = Mantissa $\cdot$ 10^{Exponent}

Example 6.8

512.0 can also be written as $5.12 \cdot 10^2$.
12 532 can be written as $1.2532 \cdot 10^4$.
0.125 can be written as $1.25 \cdot 10^{-1}$.

What is "floating" here is the decimal point in the mantissa because this is moved after the number has been entered. Often the letter E is used instead of the base number 10 for representing the number. For example, 12 532 can look like 1.2532E+4, and 0.00001234 is written as 1.234E-5. How large or small the floating-point numbers have to be before this display format is used depends upon the implementation.

Example 6.9

Possible ways of writing to represent a floating-point number:

1.234
3.14
314e-2
−0.6e7

The accuracy and range of floating points depends upon how many bits are used to represent the mantissa and how many are used to represent the exponent. According to Lewis (1995), the range of values for a 32-bit floating-point number (REAL) is from 10^{-38} to 10^{38} for positive numbers and correspondingly for negative numbers (-10^{38} to -10^{-38}). This means that 6 bits are used for storage of the exponent, one bit for the sign and the remainder for the mantissa. Accuracy for a 32-bit floating-point number is given in Lewis (1995) as 2^{-23} or approximately 0.0000001.

  Nevertheless, the use of floating-point numbers is more accurate than simply operating with integers. Floating point is also used for intermediate storage and for the results of arithmetic calculations.

6.5.2   Data Types for Time and Duration

The standard defines some distinct data types that are not ordinary data types in the basic programming languages. These data types are especially designed for control of time and duration (Table 6.3).

  In industrial control systems, there is often a requirement for monitoring the duration of events and actions, for instance, at what time of day or on which day of the week actions should be performed. With these specially designed data types such as TIME, these events can be programmed in a more structured way.

Table 6.3   Time and duration

Data type	Description	Initial value
TIME	Duration	T#0s
LTIME[a]	Duration	LTIME#0s
DATE	Calendar date	_[b]
LDATE[c]	Calendar date	LDATE#1970-01-01
TIME_OF_DAY or *TOD*	Time of day	TOD#00:00:00
DATE_AND_TIME or *DT*	Date and time of day	–

[a] The data type LTIME is a 64-bit integer with sign. The resolution is in nanoseconds.
[b] This is implementation dependent since it depends upon a defined start date. This also applies to DT.
[c] Not implemented in CODESYS.

The similar data types DATE, TOD, and DT are used for many different purposes. It may be to activate and terminate actions according to time of day or to particular dates. This is useful for programming building automation such as air-conditioning and lighting.

Another example of use of these data types is for reporting purposes. There may be requirements for storing the date and time when an alarm was activated or when an operational stoppage took place. If power fails, there may be various actions that should be performed when power is restored, depending upon how long it was out.

6.5.2.1   Time Literals

The standard permits many ways of entering and displaying time and duration. All time literals must have a prefix that indicates the type, followed by the character #. The actual time follows this. The following are used for specification of time and duration:

- **d** for days
- **h** for hours
- **m** for minutes
- **s** for seconds
- **ms** for milliseconds

Time literals must be entered in the proper order: days, hours, minutes, seconds, milliseconds. The guidelines permit both uppercase and lowercase letters, negative values, use of underscore and decimal point, and both short and long forms of prefixes. Below are some examples of correct literals for variables of the type TIME.

Example 6.10

- T#25s
- T#-25s (negative time)
- T#12.4ms
- t#12h
- T#12h23m42s
- t#12h_23m_42s_67ms

- TIME#45m
- time#4m_20s

Note that it is possible, if the manufacturer so permits, that the most significant part of the time literal can include overflow. For instance, a time can be entered as T#29h25m. This would be the equivalent of T#1d_5h_25m.

6.5.2.2 Real-Time Literals

Entering and display of literals for data types DATE, TOD, and DT must also follow a particular order. For the data type DATE, the literal should follow the form:

DATE or D	#	Year	-	Month no.	-	Day no.

Literal for the data type TIME_OF_DAY (TOD):

TIME_OF_DAY or TOD	#	Hours	:	Minutes	:	Seconds

(Note that hours, minutes, and seconds are separated by a **colon**, while year, month, and day are separated by a *hyphen*.)

Literal for the data type DATE_AND_TIME (DT):

DATE_AND_TIME or DT	#	DATE-literal	-	TOD-literal

Example 6.11   Some Real-Time Literals

- DATE#2007-05-31
- D#1968-11-25
- time_of_day#08:45:00
- TOD#17:30:45
- DATE_AND_TIME#1814-05-17-13:45:00
- dt#2007-08-01-12:30:00

For example, the last literal indicates *12:30, August 1, 2007.*

6.5.3   *Text Strings*

The last of the elementary data types is *text strings* represented by the keywords CHAR, WCHAR, STRING, and WSTRING.[11] All these data types are used to manage letters and other characters. The difference between CHAR and WCHAR and between STRING and WSTRING depends only upon the way the content is interpreted and stored. CHAR and STRING are text in *ASCII* format, while WCHAR and WSTRING are text in *Unicode* format.

This last is an expansion from the first version of the standard and was introduced in order to be able to handle a greater variety of characters. This is useful if one needs to enter special

---

[11] WSTRING is supported in CODESYS version 3.5 but not in version 2.3. CHAR and WCHAR are not implemented in any version of CODESYS.

Table 6.4 Data types for text

Description	Data type	Number of bytes per character	Initial value
A single character	*CHAR*	8	'$00'
	WCHAR	16	"$0000"
Text strings of variable length	*STRING*	8	''
	WSTRING	16	""

characters that are not found in ASCII and for handling many languages other than English. The reason that the Unicode character set contains more characters is that each character occupies two bytes of data or 16 bits, while each character in ASCII occupies only one byte (Table 6.4).

To help the compiler help you catch possible errors in the code, there is a difference in entering the literals in the two formats, so that ' ' is used around CHAR and STRING types and " " around WCHAR and WSTRING. Example:

aString	:= 'This enters a STRING'
aWString	:= "This enters a WSTRING"

The first 127 characters in ASCII and Unicode are otherwise the same, so that if you do not have any special requirement, it is recommended that you use the data type STRING for text variables.

When declaring a variable of the STRING type, the programmer, if desired, can also enter the length of the variable, that is, the maximum number of characters that the variable can contain. If no length is stated, a default length will be used. The maximum permitted length of text strings depends upon the implementation.[12]

Typical applications of this data type are found in dialogues with the operator's panel and HMI or for sending data to printers. In the standard, there are several defined functions for management of text strings such as finding the length of the string, inserting characters in a string, and deleting characters from a string.

In addition to ordinary letters and characters, the standard defines some special combinations that can be used to format text for display or printout. These special combinations, which are not themselves displayed on the screen or printout, consist of a dollar sign ($) followed by the letters L, N, P, R, or T. See Table 6.5.

6.5.4 Generic Data Types

This is actually not a specific data type, but rather a general indicator for *classes* of data types. Generic data types are used by manufacturers for specification of input and output variables in functions and functional blocks. The standard does not specify any guidelines for use of generic data types in <u>user-defined</u> POUs, so it is completely up to the manufacturer whether or not this is ever implemented.

Nevertheless, the reason for using general data type classes is, for example, to create a function that is more general with respect to what data types are accepted when using the function.

---

[12] In CODESYS, the default length is 80 characters. The maximum length is currently unlimited.

Table 6.5 Formatting coder for printout and display

Formatting code	Significance for printout
$L	Line feed + carriage return (new paragraph)
$N	New line
$P	New page
$R	Return key
$T	Tab key

Notes:
- Lowercase letters are also permitted, for instance, $p.
- If one actually wants to use a $ in the text, this must be entered with two $'s.
  Example: "Unit price is $$32."

Example 6.12

The standard function DIV (/) can be used to divide two members of any data type (as long as both numbers have the same data type). That is to say that the numbers can be one of any of the following data types: REAL, LREAL, INT, UINT, SINT, USINT, DINT, UDINT, LINT, and ULINT. As one would think, it is very tiresome to have to specify all the data types that can be used in every one of the functions or functional blocks. Instead, we could enter a generic data type that describes the classes of permitted data types. The class that the data types in question belong to is called ANY_NUM. The graphical representation of function DIV in the standard (International Electrotechnical Commission, 2013) is therefore as follows:

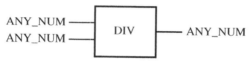

Here is a hierarchical overview of all of the generic data types:
(*Note*: DERIVED deals with *user-defined* data types. See next section.)

```
ANY
  └ -ANY_DERIVED
  └ -ANY_ELEMENTARY
      └ - ANY_MAGNITUDE
      │   └ - ANY_NUM
      │   │     └ - ANY_REAL
      │   │     │      (REAL, LREAL)
      │   │     └ - ANY_INT
      │   │            ANY_UNSIGNED
      │   │              (USINT,UINT, UDINT, ULINT)
      │   │            ANY_SIGNED
      │   │              (SINT, INT, DINT, LINT)
      │   └ -ANY_DURATION
      │        (TIME, LTIME)
      ├ - ANY_BIT
      │     (BOOL, BYTE, WORD, DWORD, LWORD)
      └ - ANY_CHARS
      │   └ - ANY_STRING
      │   │      (STRING, WSTRING)
      │   └ -ANY_CHAR
      │        (CHAR, WCHAR)
      └ - ANY_DATE
           (DATE, DATE_AND_TIME, LDT, TIME_OF_DAY, LTOD)
```

6.5.5 User-Defined Data Types

In addition to the elementary data types and any special data types defined by the manufacturer, it is possible to define one's own data types. These are called derived data types since they are derived from (that is, based upon) the elementary data types.

The purpose of user-defined data types is to be able to obtain a more structured code, particularly in those cases where it is natural to group several I/Os of various data types by defining a new class of I/O composed of elementary data types as members. See Section 6.5.5.4.

Derived data types are defined by means of the keywords TYPE and END_TYPE. It is possible that a development tool will permit only definitions of one type within each set of the keywords TYPE and END_TYPE.

The defined types will be accessible to the entire project (globally). In this way, global and local variables can be declared based upon the new data type.

Sometimes, there is a requirement to be able to process sets of several variables or values in a structured way (ARRAY and STRUCT) or simply to define some additional different properties for the selected data type, for instance, to limit the value range.

After we have obtained a little experience in programming, the use of the elementary data types will be, well, elementary. Structured data types (STRUCT) are a little more complicated and are seen traditionally as not useful in the PLC programming. Nevertheless, they offer an important contribution that improves the capability of producing well-structured program code.

Example 6.13

Assume that the PLC is to be used for monitoring and controlling a cold-storage site. The storage consists of several different freezer rooms, but each freezer room is equipped completely identically, with a freezer unit that is to be controlled and temperature and pressure that are to be monitored.

Instead of declaring one variable for each individual I/O in each freezer room, one can first make a self-defined structured data type called, for instance, Freezer, where all I/Os associated with a room are members of the new data type. Then one can declare a variable of the *type* Freezer in each of the freezer rooms in the storage site.

6.5.5.1 Value Limitation

As mentioned earlier, it is possible to define new data types based upon an elementary type but with a limited range of values.[13] This can be done as follows:

```
TYPE
    HoleNumber : INT (-800..200);
END_TYPE
```

Here, a new data type called *HoleNumber* is defined on the basis of the elementary data type INT, but with a limited value range from −800 through 200. (You can also limit the value range directly when a variable is declared. See Section 6.6.2.1.)

---

[13] The standard suggests that entry of a value range should apply only to integer and binary data types.

6.5.5.2   Enumeration

Enumeration is a user-defined data type that is based upon user-defined text constants. The constants are referred to as *enumeration values*. In enumeration, the program developer enters a list of permitted text strings that a variable can assume. Defining an enumerated data type follows the same syntax as statement of a value range:

```
TYPE
    Color : (Green, Yellow, Red);
END_TYPE
```

Here, the data type **Color** is defined, which can take on one of three possible values: "Green," "Yellow," or "Red." A variable can then be declared based upon the new data type Color. Unless otherwise specified, the variable will then initially have the first value in the list, in this case the value "Green."

Note also that the specified permitted values are compatible with the use of integers. This implies that instead of operating with the values directly, one can use numbers to identify them. In the example above, the value "Green" is automatically assigned the value 0, since nothing else is specified, and "Yellow" takes the integer 1 and "Red" takes the integer 2. This means that it is possible to use variables with an enumerated data type in control structures that loop. If desired, other numerical values can be assigned to the enumerated values:

```
TYPE
    Card:   (Jack := 11, Queen := 12, King := 13, Ace := 14);
END_TYPE
```

6.5.5.3   Arrays

A common derived data type is *Arrays*. This is not actually a user-defined data type since arrays can also be defined directly in the declaration field in a POU or in the list of global variables. However, similar to limitation of a value range, one can define a data type and use it in declaring a variable.

The individual elements in the array can be often elementary data type or a user-defined data type. It is possible to define one-, two-, and three-dimensional arrays. The standard suggests the following syntax[14]:

```
TYPE
    Tab_1dim : ARRAY [lower..upper] OF DATATYPE;
    Tab_2dim : ARRAY [lower1..upper1, lower2..upper2] OF
               DATATYPE;
END_TYPE
```

The only requirement placed upon the lower and upper boundaries is that they are integers that lie within the value range of DINT. A lower boundary can well be 437, for instance, as long as

---

[14] CODESYS does not permit definition of several data types in a block. Each individual type that is defined must be enclosed by TYPE .. END_TYPE.

the upper boundary is higher. In other words, the numbers that are used for the elements are not important but the array's dimension is.

Note that it is also possible to insert initial values in arrays during type declaration, but since initial values are not discussed until Section 6.6.2.1, I have omitted that here.

Example 6.14   Defining Array Data Types

```
TYPE   One_dim:     ARRAY [0..9] OF USINT;                END_TYPE
TYPE   Two_dim:     ARRAY [1..2, 1..5] OF INT;            END_TYPE
TYPE   Three_dim:   ARRAY [0..3, 0..3, 0..3] OF REAL;  END_TYPE
```

Here, three data types are declared based upon array structure: a one-dimensional array with 10 elements, a two-dimensional array with $2 * 5 = 10$ elements, and a three-dimensional array with $4 * 4 * 4 = 64$ elements.

As mentioned previously, it is not necessary to define individual data types in order to use arrays. We will see this in Section 6.9, where variables are declared based directly upon an array structure.

6.5.5.4   Data Structures

Up until now, we have seen a series of elementary data types and how such data types can be organized in array form. Sometimes, there is a requirement for more complex data structures, where several different data types appear as subelements within a comprehensive data type. These subelements can be any one of the aforementioned data types, including enumerated types and arrays.

Structured data types are declared within the keywords TYPE, STRUCT and END_STRUCT, END_TYPE with the following syntax:

```
TYPE Name_of_datatype:
STRUCT
    <Declaration of datatype 1>;
    <Declaration of datatype 2>;
    ...
    <Declaration of datatype n>
END_STRUCT
END_TYPE
```

Example 6.15   Declaration of a Data Structure

```
TYPE    ANALOG_SIGNAL:
    STRUCT
        Raw_value    : WORD;
        Scaled_value : REAL;
```

```
        Min_raw       : INT (-32767..0);
        Max_raw       : UINT (0..32768)
    END_STRUCT
END_TYPE
```

In the example below is a declaration of a data type called **Productdata** that has three subelements of different types. One of the three types is a user-defined enumerated data type called Camera.

Example 6.16

```
TYPE
    Camera  : (OK, LabelError, Leakage);  (* Enumerated datatype *)
END_TYPE
TYPE  Productdata :  (* Structured datatype *)
    STRUCT
        PictureResult : Camera;     (*Sub-element*)
        Weight : REAL;              (* ------"------ *)
        ID      : UINT (0..10000);  (* ------"------ *)
    END_STRUCT
END_TYPE
```

Variables can now be declared based upon the structured data type **Productdata**. You can read how to do this in Section 6.9.2.

This will close the section on literals, elementary data types, and declaration of programmer-defined data types. In other places in the book, this knowledge will be used in all programming examples. Data types are very fundamental in all programming for management of data storage and data representation, and now, we will see how we can specify data types by declaration of variables.

6.6   Variables

Referring to data objects that are accessible in hardware memory is fundamental in all forms of programming. There can be memory areas associated with inputs and outputs or for storage of internal values and states. By entering variables, the programmer is offered an efficient and elegant way of referring to data objects whose content can change.

In the foregoing, we have acquired knowledge about various *data types*. In this section, we will see how variables are *declared*, that is, how they are given names (*identifiers*) and associated with data types. For many who have worked with programming older kinds of PLCs, the introduction of variables will represent something new. We shall therefore start by having a brief look at conventional addressing and conversion to variables by means of symbols.

6.6.1 Conventional Addressing

There is a fundamental difference between addressing in elder PLCs and declaring and using variables in PLCs that follow the standard. In conventional systems, only addresses that are *global* and have *fixed locations* in memory are used.

Global means that the addresses are accessible from all parts of the program and from all programs in the PLC. Fixed location means that the user specifies what portion of the memory the addressed object uses. The memory can be located in the CPU, can be in the form of a separate memory card (e.g., a flash memory), or could be built into an input or output module.

Those who have experience with PLCs from different manufacturers know that the absence of a standard has meant differences in addressing syntax between different types of PLCs. As an example of conventional addressing syntax, we will look at an older Omron model.

6.6.1.1 Addressing in the Omron C200H

The C200H has a memory region that is divided up into nine registers. A register is defined here as a 16-bit storage space, and each register has its address. Like many other producers, Omron uses the concept of *word* for a 16-bit storage space:

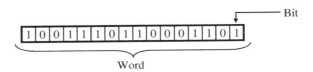

Within the word, each individual bit can be used in addressing Boolean objects. That is, an individual word object can contain the state (on/off) of 16 discrete actuators such as motors, pumps, valves, etc. Alternatively, we can consider the entire word as a binary number.

Each of the nine registers into which the Omron C200H memory is divided has its range of uses or functions. One of the register areas is called the IR area (IR is an acronym for internal relay), and is an area in the memory that is connected to the input and output modules that may be located in the rack. That area consists of 236 words, no matter how many modules are actually installed and configured.

The first two registers in the IR area can be illustrated thus:

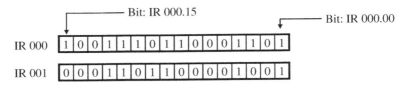

The prefix to the address, for example, IR, is used to differentiate the register areas from one another. The particular storage location is indicated by an integer. The illustration above shows how individual bits within the register can be addressed.

Table 6.6 shows how the registers in C200H are organized.

Table 6.6   Addressing and organization of memory in Omron C200H

Register area	Acronym	Ranges of words and bits	Function
Internal relay	IR	Word: 000 to 235 Bits: 000.00 to 235.15	Addresses for physical inputs and outputs
Special relay	SR	Word: 236 to 255 Bits: 236.00 to 255.07	Contains system clocks, flags, and system information
Auxiliary relay	AR	Word. AR 00 to AR 27 Bits: AR 00.00 to AR 27.15	Contains flags and bits for special functions
Data memory	DM	R/W: DM 0000 to DM 0999 Read: DM 1000 to DM 1999	Used for internal storage of data and for numerical processing and other manipulation of data
Holding relay	HR	Word: HR 00 to HR 99 Bits: HR 00.00 to HR 99.15	Used for data storage and any monitoring of functions in the PLC
Timer/counter	TC	Bits: TC 000 to TC 511	For managing time delays and counters
Link relay	LR	Word: LR 00 to LR 63 Bits: LR 00.00 to LR 63.15	Accessible as working bits and for intermediate storage
Temporary relay	TR	Bits: TR 00 to TR 07	Used for intermediate storage of branch points in LD
Program memory	UM	UM depends upon which memory units the PLC uses	Contains the program being executed by the CPU

6.6.1.2   Symbolization and Conversion to Variables

To facilitate the work of the program developer and to improve the legibility of the code, PLC manufacturers began using *symbolization* as an equivalent to direct addressing. Editors included in the development tools were arranged so that the user could assign unique symbolic names to all addresses that were in use. With a structured and well-reasoned use of symbols, for example, the use of descriptive names such as **Startswitch** and **Pump_no2** meant that symbolization was a significant improvement compared to direct addressing.

Standard IEC 61131-3 introduced variables as a replacement for symbols and hardware addresses as a natural next step in development. The use of variables is also consistent with general high-level computer programming. The transition is actually not very great. For example, association of variables to input and outputs continually takes place by entering an address that is assigned during configuration to the input or output in question. The biggest difference is in the use of data types and in that variables are initially local within the POU in which they are declared, so that no conflicts can arise with variables with the same name being used in another POU.

For many, however, there will be a transition in the beginning to declare variables instead of working with fixed addresses and symbolic names. No matter, this is a temporary transition because the development tools have a dedicated editor for this and the editor will correct declarations of variables on the fly as the programmer works.

6.6.2   *Declaration of Variables with IEC 61131-3*

Before (or during) programming, it is necessary to enter elements for storage of data by specifying what type of data it applies to (integer, floating point, text, etc.) and giving names to these elements with logical, reasonable identifiers. This is called *declaration* of variables and is done at the beginning of all POUs (see definition of POU in Section 5.3). What the declaration editor looks like depends upon the implementation. It can be in tabular form, or, as here, in a text-based form:

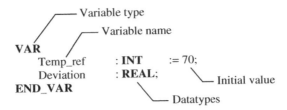

We see that the declaration of variables begins with indicating the type of variable by using the correct keyword. For instance, there are *local* variables, *global* variables, and *input* and *output* variables. Normally, a local variable is declared by using the keyword VAR. When the type is entered, the variable can be given a name by writing in a valid identifier (Section 6.2.1) followed by a data type. If desired, the variable can be given an initial value. Declaration is terminated by closing the group name to the variable type, as is the case here with END_VAR.

Here, we see that we finally can specify how variables are connected together with all the other data types that are defined in Section 6.5.1. In the following example, several local variables of different data types are declared. Note the variable **Light** that is defined on the basis of the self-defined data type **Color** (see Section 6.5.5.2, Enumeration).

Example 6.17   Variables of Different Standard Data Types

```
VAR
    Start            : BOOL      := TRUE;
    Alarm            : BOOL;
    MV               : REAL      := 48.5;
    Temp_ref         : INT       := 70;
    Denomination     : STRING    := 'Degrees';
    Light            : Color     := Yellow;
    Time1            : TOD;
    Time2            : TIME      := time#70m_30s;
    Date1            : DATE      := DATE#2007-06-18;
END_VAR
```

It is also possible to declare several variables of the same data type in succession, as is shown in the next example, where we declare three variables that are all of type INT.

Example 6.18   Declaration of Several Variables of the Same Data Type

```
VAR
    Value_1, Value_2, Value_3  : INT;
END_VAR
```

The compiler helps reduce the use of erroneous data types by checking data types when the variables are used. If, for instance, an attempt is made to assign a value of the REAL type to a variable of the BOOL type, the compiler will give an error message.

6.6.2.1 Initial Values and Value Ranges

Example 6.17 also shows how variables of different data types can be assigned initial values (or starting values). These values overwrite the default values that the individual data types are originally assigned. These default values are, for instance, **0** for integer data type, **FALSE** or 0 for data type BOOL, and '', an empty string for data type STRING.

The entry of initial values naturally takes place under the definition of *literal* as described in Section 6.5.

Range of Values

In Section 6.5.5.1, we saw that it was possible to define data types on the basis of elementary (integer) types but with a limited range of values. It is actually not necessary to first define a new data type in order to be able to use the new type in declaration of a variable. Such a value limitation can be imposed directly during the declaration of variables:

```
VAR
    Hole_Num  :  INT   (-800..200);
    Pos_num   :  UINT  (0..10000);
END_VAR
```

The difference compared to the definition of a new data type is that this value limitation will be valid only locally in the POU in question where the variable is declared. Note that if the variable takes on a value that lies outside the specified range of values, it will result in an error message (e.g., setting a flag).

6.6.2.2 Constants and Retention

Sometimes, there is a requirement to enter and store values that should not be changed by the program code. This is achieved by using the qualifier CONSTANT after entering the VAR keyword:

Example 6.19

```
VAR CONSTANT
    Setpoint : INT := 75;
END_VAR
```

It seems a little odd to mix the two keywords VAR and CONSTANT together, but this is the way it is defined in the standard.

Constants are used to retain parameters and setting such as duration, number, time of day, etc. It is easier and more structured if such values can be declared as a group instead of entering them directly into the program code. Both local and global variables can be declared as constants, that is, the keyword CONSTANT can also be used as an attribute of the variable type VAR_GLOBAL.

RETAIN

Another important qualifier is RETAIN. This is used on variables that should retain their value during an out-of-control situation such as power failure or, for that matter, during a controlled shutdown such as a reboot of the PLC. When the PLC is in RUN again, the values that the variables had before the stop will be used as processing progresses.

Example 6.20

```
VAR RETAIN
    Stored_value    : WORD;
END_VAR
```

RETAIN can also be used for the types VAR_GLOBAL and VAR_OUTPUT.

Note: Many manufacturers implement this as the default value that the variables should take in the event of a power failure.

6.6.3   Local Versus Global Variables

One of the most notable properties of variables in IEC 61131-3 is that variables can be declared locally within the POU in question. This means that the same identifier can be used again as a name for a variable in another POU as long as the variable is declared as local within its own POU. In addition to it being useful in practice to be able to use the same identifier in several places, this also reduces the risk of undesired overwriting of data.

The variables that are declared in the foregoing examples are all local. This is characterized by the group types that are used in the declarations: VAR – END_VAR. Sometimes, it is desirable and necessary to use global variables, variables that are accessible from several POUs within the resource or for several resources (PLCs).

Global variables are not declared within a POU as local variables are, but rather are declared at a higher *configuration level*. The format for declaration is like that for local variables, it is only that another group type is used:

```
VAR_GLOBAL
    ItemCount    : UINT;
    AlarmLight   : BOOL;
END_VAR
```

Two global variables are declared in this example: one variable of the data type UINT called **ItemCount** and a variable of the Boolean data type called **AlarmLight**. These two global variables are now declared, but they cannot be used without further programming. In order to have access to a global variable from a POU, the standard says that the POU where the variable will be used must contain a form of declaration for the same global variable. This is done by using the group type VAR_EXTERNAL:

```
VAR_EXTERNAL
    ItemCount    : UINT;
    AlarmLight   : BOOL;
END_VAR
```

It can seem unnecessary to have to declare the same variable several times, but the reason for this is to keep the programmer from accidentally using a local identifier when he/she has forgotten that the name had already been used as the name for a global variable.[15]

It is not certain that this was a deliberate reference to the existing global variable and that the user had intended to assign a completely different data type and value to the variable. If the compiler had accepted the use of this identifier without it having been declared again, it could happen that the programmer had overlooked this inconsistency.

6.6.4   Input and Output Variables

This has nothing to do with a PLC's physical inputs and outputs, but rather with the variables that are used for reading or transmission of parameters to and from a POU. Three types are defined: VAR_INPUT, VAR_OUTPUT, and VAR_IN_OUT.

You can use these variables when you program a POU that will be called from another POU. If a variable in the POU that is called is declared as VAR_INPUT, the call from the other POU can contain data that will be used in execution of the POU that was called. By declaring a variable as VAR_OUTPUT, the POU that is called can return values back to the POU that made the call.

Example 6.21 shows the variable declarations to the functional block CTU (Count Up) in CODESYS. This FB performs counting of positive flanks, that is, 0–1 transitions in a signal/ variable. (The program code for the counter is not included here, but a symbol for the functional block is shown for the sake of illustration.)

Example 6.21   Variable Declaration for Functional Block CTU

```
FUNCTIONBLOCK CTU
(* CV increases by 1 each time CU has a rising flank. *)
  (* Q becomes TRUE when CV reaches the value of PV. *)
VAR_INPUT    (* Declares input variable: *)
   CU     : BOOL;  (* Count Up *)
   RESET : BOOL;  (* Sets counter value CV to 0 *)
   PV     : WORD;  (* Desired quantity *)
END_VAR
VAR_OUTPUT   (* Declares output variable: *)
   Q      : BOOL;  (* Output ready *)
   CV     : WORD;  (* Current value *)
END_VAR
VAR        (* Declares a local variable: *)
   M : BOOL;
END_VAR
   :
   :  (* Program code for the function block *)
   :
END_FUNCTION_BLOCK
```

---

[15] It is permitted to give a local variable the same name that one has used already for a global variable. In such a case, the local variable will be used in the POU in which it was declared.

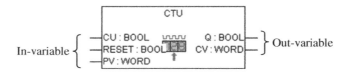

As we see, the declaration contains variables of both types VAR_INPUT and VAR_OUTPUT. A call of this FB must therefore contain three variables (arguments); these will be coupled to the variables CU, RESET, and PV. The state Q and current value CV will be returned to the POU that the call came from.

In addition to these two variable types, there is a type of variable that functions as both an input variable and an output variable simultaneously. This type of variable is declared within the POU by the keyword VAR_IN_OUT. In using this type, the called POU will not only receive values from external variables, as with the use of VAR_IN, but will also receive the actual memory location. In other words, the called POU can change the value of the variables that were used in the call.

6.6.5   Other Variable Types

In addition to the more usual keywords for variable declaration that we have already described, the standard defines three more. Two of these are described briefly here, while the third (VAR_CONFIG) will be discussed in connection with variables and I/O addressing.

VAR_TEMP   Variables that are declared under this keyword will be (re-)initialized with each call to the POU in which it is declared. This means that the variables are deleted from memory every time the POU finishes executing and are set up anew, with type-specific initial values, the next time the POU is called up. This means that such variables cannot be used to determine a value between each call.[16]

VAR_ACCESS   This keyword is used only specifically, depending upon hardware. The purpose is to enable direct access to variables from other hardware.

6.7   Direct Addressing

Even though the standard introduces variables, the standard still permits use of direct addressing, that is, reference to specific memory regions. This can take place in one of two ways: either by using addresses directly in the program or by assigning symbolic names to the addresses in the declaration field. In other words, conventional addressing is still possible.

6.7.1   Addressing Structure

The structure for how a data element is addressed is shown in Table 6.7. As we see in the table, all addresses start with a percent sign (%), followed by a *location prefix* (a letter). The location

---

[16] This is the desired behavior for functions that should yield the same response to every call and there VAR_TEMP is equivalent to VAR. VAR_TEMP is valid for programs and functional blocks.

Table 6.7 Addressing structure for direct representation of data elements

%	1st prefix	2nd prefix	Specific location	Meaning	
	I			Input	
	Q			Output	
	M			Memory	
		None or X		Boolean	: 1 bit
		B		Byte	: 8 bit
		W		Single word	: 16 bit
		D		Double word	: 32 bit
		L		Long word	: 64 bit
			u, v, w, x, y	Hierarchically arranged location Possible meanings: u - rack, v – module, w – channel, x – word, y – bit	

prefix indicates whether the memory region is associated with inputs (I), outputs (Q), or an internal memory (M).

Next follows a *size prefix* that indicates the length of the storage location that the address refers to. This is indicated by X, B, W, D, or L for 1, 8, 16, 32, or 64 bits, respectively. This has nothing to do with data types directly, in the sense that the prefix only indicates the *size* of the storage area and not which type of data it is possible to store there.

Example 6.22 Memory Addresses

Address	Meaning
%MX0.0	Bit 0 (LSB) in memory location 0
%M0.0	---------------”------------------
%MB8	Memory byte 8
%MW12	Memory word 12
%MD45	Double word at memory location 45
%ML14	Quadruple word at memory location 14

Using direct memory addresses can be a little risky. Aside from the legibility of the code becoming significantly worse than with the use of variables or symbolic addresses, there is the risk of referring to memory locations that *overlap* one another.

For example, there is the Boolean address %M4.15 for the MSB in the address %MW4, and the address %MW50 contains the two-byte addresses %MB100 and %MB101.

Figure 6.1 illustrates this concept. Here, there are represented two memory locations, word no. 10 (%MW10) and word no. 11 (%MW11). Each location is 16 bits in range, where each individual bit can be addressed.

This overlapping of references to memory regions means that there will be addresses that cannot be used in programming. If you use direct addressing, it is therefore smart to have a

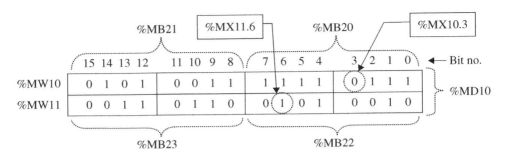

Figure 6.1   Illustration of overlapping between bit, byte, word, and double word

consistent system for the use of memory: For example, you can decide that memory locations 0 through 4 are used for Boolean objects (this gives $5*16=80$ accessible objects) and that locations 5–19 will be used for bytes, 20–29 for memory words, and so forth.

If several double and long (quadruple) word addresses are to be used, it is important to skip over some memory locations so that overlap does not occur. For example, you can avoid using double-word addresses sequentially. That is, you would not simultaneously use the addresses %MD0, %MD1, and %MD2, but rather skip every other location and, for instance, use %MD0, %MD2, and %MD4. The reason for this is that the double-word %MD4 includes the word addresses %MW4 and %MW5, and the double-word %MD5 includes the words %MW5 and %MW6. Word address %MW5 is therefore contained in both of the sequential double-word addresses and will therefore be overwritten by both of the subsequent double addresses. (Similarly, neither can the address %MW5 be used.) Figure 6.2 illustrates this.

6.7.2   I/O-Addressing

If the address refers to data elements in input or output memory, it is also necessary to specify which input or output it applies to. This is done by adding some numbers after the prefixes. The numbers can, for example, indicate module number and channel number. The actual structure of this location reference is *implementation dependent*, but it is a requirement that it have a hierarchical structure. This means that the number farthest to the left indicates the highest level in the address structure with successively lower levels continuing toward the right.

Example 6.23   Direct Addressing of I/O

%IX1.5	Digital input. The numbers can represent channel 5 in module 1
%Q2.4.12	Digital output, for example, in rack 2, module 4, channel 12
%IW12	Input word no. 12, for example, an analog input
%IW3.2	Analog input, for example, channel 2 in module 3
%QW5.2.4.7	Output word. Network address 5, rack 2, module 4, channel 7

Note: These are only *possible* interpretations or meanings of the numbers.

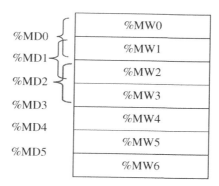

Figure 6.2 Illustration—address overlapping

6.8 Variable versus I/O-Addresses

Direct addressing can naturally be used together with variables by having an identifier connected to a particular data element. This can also be done for internal memory locations, but it is most practical and absolutely necessary to associate variables with the inputs and outputs of the PLC. Such a connection between fixed addresses and identifiers can be obtained by using the keyword **AT** in the declaration.

Example 6.24   Coupling of Variable Names to Addresses

Here, we see that the Boolean input address %IX2.4 is assigned to the variable name Dig_in, while the Boolean output address %QX3.5 is assigned to the variable Dig_out. A_in and A_out are variables associated with an analog input and an analog output, respectively.

```
VAR
    Dig_in    AT %IX2.4    : BOOL        := TRUE;
    Dig_out   AT %QX3.5    : BOOL;
    A_in      AT %IW3.2    : WORD;
    A_out     AT %QW4.1    : WORD;
END_VAR
```

Notice that it is permitted to assign an object with a "shorter" data type to an object of a "longer" data type. The basis for this is that memory locations are only storage locations and as long as the memory location has room (enough bits) to store the object, everything will go well.

On the contrary, the assignment of an object that has a data type that requires more space than the assigned memory location can provide is naturally not permitted. This will therefore trigger a syntax error in the compiler.

6.8.1   Unspecified I/O-Addresses

Sometimes, one would like to declare variables that are to be assigned to I/O without specifying their exact addresses. When you are programming a FB or a program that is to be reused in another context or if you are programming in accordance with the requirements of the client, you will not know the exact address that the variables should be assigned to. This information is not available until all I/O modules have been installed and configured.

In such cases, you can undertake a partial assignment by specifying how the variables are to be mapped to an I/O, without stating the actual address. When you or others at a later time are going to use the program, the address can be specified at the configuration level by use of the keyword **VAR_CONFIG**.

Example 6.25

The following declaration shows how one assigns incomplete I/O addresses in CODESYS by use of **AT** and **%I*** or **%Q***. (*Note*: Even though the example shows declaration in a program, it is more useful for function blocks for reasons that we will come back to the next chapter.)

```
PROGRAM Whichio
VAR
    Input    AT    %I*    : BOOL;
    Output   AT    %Q*    : WORD;
END_VAR
```

When you have installed all the I/O modules and configured them, then you can finish the application in CODESYS by adding a new Global Variable List (GVL), where you specify the exact addresses (note the reference to the current POU (Whichio) where the variables will be declared and used):

```
VAR_CONFIG
    Whichio.Input    AT    %IX2.3    : BOOL;
    Whichio.Output   AT    %QW3.1    : WORD;
END_VAR
```

6.9   Declaration of Multielement Variables

Declaration of multielement variables is done in a similar way to declaration of simple variables. As mentioned previously, arrays can be declared directly with declaration of variables. It is not necessary to define a data type for arrays, even though this is possible. Example 6.26 shows both forms: direct declaration and declaration based upon predefined data types. The variables **younameit** and **sowhat** are declared on the basis of predeclared array data types, while the variables **Oddnum** and **Values** are declared directly as arrays.

Example 6.26   Declaration of Multielement Variables[17]

```
TYPE
Two_dim  :   ARRAY [1..2, 1..5] OF INT := [10, 20, 30, 40,
             6(50)];
END_TYPE
```

---

[17] Note that in CODESYS version 2.3.x, the initial values are not enclosed in parentheses.

```
TYPE
    Three_dim   : ARRAY [0..3, 2..5, 1..4] OF REAL;
END_TYPE
VAR
    Oddnum      : ARRAY [0..9] OF SINT := [1, 3, 5, 7, 11, 13,
                  17, 19, 23, 29];
    Values      : ARRAY [1..3, 1..4] OF INT;
    younameit   : Two_dim;
    sowhat      : Three_dim := [10(3.14)];
    whoops      : ARRAY [1..2, 1..2, 1..2] OF BOOL := [0, 0, 1,
                  0, 1, 1, 0, 1];
END_VAR
```

6.9.1 Arrays

The example above shows how arrays can be initialized (be given an initial content). This can be done either by defining data types or, more commonly, by declaration of a variable. The advantage of the latter method is that several variables can use the same data type but have different initial values. Because initial values must be entered, all of the elements in the array will be given default values for the data type in question. This is the case with the variable **Values** in the example.

It is also possible to partially assign initial values. The variable **sowhat** (data type Three_dim) is declared with initial values for only the first 10 elements. The remaining 54 elements are automatically set to 0. The syntax that is used for giving specific values to the first 10 elements in the variable **sowhat** is in line with what the standard recommends that manufacturers implement in order to give several successive elements the same value:

NumberOfElements(value)

Refer again to Example 6.26, where six elements in the data type Two_dim are set equal to 50. Such a repetition factor can also be used to initiate more complex numerical sequences. For example, 3(2,5,7) is the same as 2, 5, 7, 2, 5, 7, 2, 5, 7.

6.9.1.1 Indexing and Addressing

Arrays are well suited to read, transfer, store, and use large quantities of data in a structured simple way. In the program code, one can read from and write to individual elements in arrays by indicating the index of the element in question.

For a variable called My_table, declared as a one-dimensional array, this syntax is:

My_table[i] where **i** gives the element number.

Example 6.27

Table 6.8 shows the syntax for assigning new values to all the elements in the arrays Oddnum, younameit, and whoops that were declared in Example 6.26.

(*Note*: The array elements can naturally be assigned variables instead of values.)

Note that for multidimensional arrays, that is, arrays that have more than one set of array boundaries, the indices are specified in a significant order, where the array boundaries farthest

Table 6.8 Syntax for assigning new values to arrays

Variable	Initial values		
Oddnum	Oddnum[0] := 3; Oddnum[3] := 7; Oddnum[6] := 13; Oddnum[9] := 17;	Oddnum[1] := 1; Oddnum[4] := 19; Oddnum[7] := 29;	Oddnum[2] := 7; Oddnum[5] := 5; Oddnum[8] := 11;

younameit	younameit[1,1] := 10;
	younameit[1,3] := 30;
	younameit[1,5] := 50;
	younameit[2,2] := 70;
	younameit[2,4] := 90;
		younameit[1,2] := 20;
		younameit[1,4] := 40;
		younameit[2,1] := 60;
		younameit[2,3] := 80;
		younameit[2,5] := 100;	

whoops	whoops[1,1,1] := 1;
	whoops[1,2,2] := 1;
	whoops[2,2,1] := 0;
		whoops[1,1,2] := 1;
		whoops[2,1,1] := 0;
		whoops[2,2,2] := 0;
			whoops[1,2,1] := 0;
			whoops[2,1,2] := 1;

to the left have the highest significance. In other words, the first index varies slowest and the last index varies fastest when we move through the array.

Indirect Addressing

Many traditional PLC systems operate with indirect addressing for efficient management of large quantities of data.[18] In indirect addressing, the actual address location depends upon the value of the variable (index). Using arrays covers this in a similar way by indexing the array elements indirectly, such as here:

Example 6.28

num1 := 3;
num2 := 8;
num3 := 122;
younameit[num1, num2] := num3;

Here, the element younameit[3,8] is set equal to 122.

Example 6.29

Values[2,3] := 5*younameit[1,4] − Oddnum[6] + 300;
     This shows an arithmetic expression in the ST programming language where the array element Values[2,3] gets the value 5*40 − 13 + 300 = 487.

6.9.2   Data Structures

Data structures are powerful data types because the program code can be built up in a highly structured way by declaration of carefully structured data types. The syntax for declaring variables based on structured data types is the same as for variables based on the elementary

---

[18] PL7Pro from Telemecanique utilizes indirect addressing with the following syntax: Address %MW50[%MW10] indicates an address location with address %MW50 + the value of the index address %MW10.

data types. In Example 6.16, we declared the structured data type Productdata. For simplicity's sake, I will go over the declaration of the data type again:

```
TYPE
    Camera    : (OK, LabelError, Leakage);
END_TYPE
TYPE Productdata :      (* Name of the structured datatype *)
    STRUCT
        PictureResult : Camera;           (* Sub-element *)
        Weight        : REAL;             (* ------"------- *)
        ID            : UINT (0..10000); (* ------"------- *)
    END_STRUCT
END_TYPE
```

Such a variable can be declared in a POU based upon the new data type:

Example 6.30   Declaration of Variables of User-Defined Type

```
VAR
    M, N      : UINT;
    Product   : ARRAY[1..100] OF Productdata;
END_VAR
```

Here, a variable is being declared as a one-dimensional array of type Productdata. Each element in the array will therefore consist of three subelements: PictureResult, Weight, and ID. The content of the five first array elements can be, for example[19]:

```
⊟···Product
    ⊟···Product[1]
        ├···.PictureResult = OK
        ├···.Weight = 245
        └···.ID = 10401
    ⊟···Product[2]
        ├···.PictureResult = LableError
        ├···.Weight = 252
        └···.ID = 10402
    ⊟···Product[3]
        ├···.PictureResult = OK
        ├···.Weight = 256
        └···.ID = 10403
    ⊟···Product[4]
        ├···.PictureResult = OK
        ├···.Weight = 248
        └···.ID = 10404
    ⊟···Product[5]
        ├···.PictureResult = Leakage
        ├···.Weight = 189
        └···.ID = 10405
```

---

[19] The example was tested in CODESYS v2.3.x, and the figure shows a screenshot during execution of the code.

6.9.2.1 Accessing

It is fully possible to access subelements in a data structure. In this way, one can read values and write in new values. The syntax is as follows:

Structurename.subelement

If, for example, one wishes to assign an ID number to element no. 5 in Product, this can be done by writing **Product[5].ID := 23512;**
   Below, you can study an example of addressing of subelements. The explanation of the program code will be reviewed later in the book.

Example 6.30 (contd.)   Accessing of Structure Components

```
FOR m:=1 TO 100 DO
    IF Product[m].PictureResult = OK THEN
        IF (Product[m].Weight > 240.0) AND (Product[m].Weight <
          260.0) THEN
            OK_Product[m] := Product[m].ID;
        END_IF
    END_IF
END_FOR
```

This way of managing arrays and structures is very much like the way used in the C++ programming language. In fact, one can consider STRUCT as a forerunner to the concept of class and object-oriented programming in C++.

6.10   Test Problems

Problem 6.1
(a)   Explain the significance of the following addresses:
   1. %IX1.15
   2. %IW5.2
   3. %QX5.9
   4. %MX5
   5. %MD5
   6. %MX12.4
   7. %MB4

(b)   Which of the following symbolic names are not permitted under the standard IEC 61131-3? (Explain why not.)
   1. Scan_no.1
   2. 1_run

3. Next
4. Temperature_heatpump_condenser_outlet
5. M_1
6. Level no5

Problem 6.2
Write a few words on what each of the variable declarations below signifies:

(a) VAR

```
      Lol                     : BOOL;
      Wow        AT %IX2.3    : BOOL;
      Omg        AT %QX3.5    : BOOL      := TRUE;
      Wtf        AT %MW12     : INT;
      Hmm                     : REAL      := 2e2;
      One, Two                : UINT      (-30..150);
      Yo_una_me_it            : ARRAY [1..5] OF INT := 1,2,3,4,5;
   END_VAR
```

(b) VAR_GLOBAL

```
      T_ref   : USINT     := 70;
      Save    : STRING    := 'Degrees';
      Tan     : TOD;
      What    : TIME      := t#70m_30s;
   END_VAR
```

(c) VAR_RETAIN

```
      Rememberme      : DWORD;
      Andme   AT %IW4 : WORD;
   END_VAR
```

Problem 6.3
(a) What do we call words like the ones in upper case in the problem above?
(b) What is the difference between *variable type* and *data type*?
(c) What is a *generic* data type?
(d) What is *direct addressing* and what is meant by a *location prefix*?
(e) A data type (My_Type) is defined as follows:

```
TYPE My_Type :        (A, B, C, D, E, F);
END_TYPE
```

What do we call such a data type and what could be the reason for using such a data type?

Problem 6.4

Show how you would declare the following variables (remember to use permissible variable names):

(a) A variable associated with digital input 22.5.
(b) A variable associated with the digital output 16.2 and which initially is set TRUE.
(c) A variable associated with analog input 4.3.
(d) A floating-point variable with an initial value equal to 250 000 000.
(e) A variable used for storing positive values up to 200.
(f) A constant that will contain the text "Operating error no. 5: Pump failure."
(g) A constant containing the duration 2 days, 8 hours, and 30 minutes.

7

Functions

Chapter Contents

- On functions: Functions versus operators. Calling functions
- Standard functions:
  - Assignment (MOVE) and Boolean operations (AND, OR, etc.)
  - Arithmetic functions (ADD, SUM, MUL, etc.)
  - Comparison (GE, GT, EQ, etc.)
  - Numerical functions (SQRT, SIN, COS, etc.)
  - Selection (MAX, MIN, etc.)
  - Bit-string operations (SHR, SHL, etc.)
  - Conversion between data types
  - Text string functions (LEN, INSERT, FIND, etc.)
- Defining new functions
- Implementation and use of EN/ENO

7.1 Introduction

As described in Chapter 5, the standard defines four types of program organization units (POU). These are:

- Function
- Function block (FB)
- Program
- Class[1]

---

[1] Class is not implemented in CODESYS, and this type is therefore not reviewed in this book. A short description of the concept, though, is presented at the end of the chapter.

Programmable Logic Controllers: A Practical Approach to IEC 61131-3 Using CODESYS, First Edition. Dag H. Hanssen.
© 2015 John Wiley & Sons, Ltd. Published 2015 by John Wiley & Sons, Ltd.

As the name implies, a POU is a structural (and well-defined) part of the program application. As a program developer, you will have an application that minimally consists of one POU of the type Program. This program will in turn most likely contain (call) one or more functions (for calculation, conversion, comparison, etc.) and one or more FBs (as counters, time delays, etc.).

All development tools for PLCs contain many predefined functions and FBs that the programmer can use in applications. IEC 61131-3 defines a large number of functions and FBs, but the producers usually offer many more in addition. It is also possible to make your own.

In this chapter, we will study the generalities of building, structuring, declaring, and calling a POU. In addition, we will review the functions that are defined in the standard.

7.2   On Functions

A function is defined as a POU that yields the same result every time it is called (executed). This implies that a function does not have any memory. The result from a function call is most often one single value, but it can also be a matrix or a structure of many values if the input argument is of such a data type. Examples of standard functions are SIN (sine), COS (cosine), SQRT (square root), ADD (add), and SHL (shift left).

Many of the functions that are defined in the standard belong to the group of *operators* in the Structured Text (ST) programming language and using the function is therefore called performing operations on an *operand*. Example:

```
A  := SQRT(B).
```

Here, SQRT is an *operator* and B is an *operand*. The answer is stored in A. Many of the standard functions also have their own operator symbols that are used in ST instead of the function names. This includes + (ADD), * (MUL), and ≥ (GE).

Operators and other standard functions will normally be implicitly recognized by the development tool. If the tool does not recognize a particular function, this may mean that it belongs to a library that must be associated with the project.

The structure of a function is the same as that of programs and FBs: At the top, there is a declaration field, and below, there follows a program code field (implementation field). The declaration field, naturally enough, will contain declarations of all variables that are used in the code.[2] This takes place in the same way no matter which programming language is used in the program code field.

Example 7.1 shows the use of functions in both the text-based language ST and the graphical language FBD. The functions that are used in the example are the arithmetic function MUL (multiply); the comparison function GE (Greater than or Equal to ≥); the bit-string functions AND, OR, and NOT; and the type-conversion function WORD_TO_BOOL.

The example also shows declaration and call of an instance of the FB RS. (You can see the declaration of the FB RS in Example 6.3.) FBs will be more fully discussed in Chapter 8.

---

[2] For a POU of the type Program or FB, it can also contain a declaration of the presence of other POUs that will be called up in the code.

Example 7.1   Use of Functions in ST and FBD

```
PROGRAM SomeFunctions
VAR // Declaring variables and an instance of the FB RS.
  On, Off, Light  : BOOL;
  A, B            : WORD;
  OneFB           : RS;
END_VAR
```

(***** Program code in ST: *****)

(* Instruction that uses several standard functions: *)
On := WORD_TO_BOOL(A OR NOT B) AND ((A*B) ≥ 5);

(* Call of function block oneFB: *)
OneFB(Set := On , Reset1 := Off, Q1 => Light);

(* *)

(***** Program code in FBD: *****)

The example shows that the use of functions does not have to be declared. This is an indirect result of their not having any memory. This does not apply to FBs, so here an instance of the FB RS is declared (more about this later in the chapter).

Layout and design of the graphical representations of the functions can vary from one tool to another, but some requirements are imposed by the standard. Some of these require that the blocks should be square or rectangular, signal flow should be from left to right, the function name or symbol should appear within the block, and the ° should be used as an inversion symbol.

7.3   Standard Functions

Table 7.1 shows standard functions that are common to all programming languages. These functions can also be implemented as *operators* in ST. For functions where the standard does not specify such operator symbols, the symbols are given in parentheses following the function names.

The practical difference between using operators and function names is that the use of function names requires that operands[3] must be given as *arguments* in parentheses following the name. Some functions perform operations *between* operands, but others perform operations *on* one or more operands, for instance, LOG(A) and MAX(A,B,C).

---

[3] An operand can be a constant, a variable, an address, or even a function call such as SIN(A).

Table 7.1   Standard functions—an overview

Function type	Function name	Comments
Arithmetic	ADD (+), MUL (*), SUB (−), DIV (/), MOD, EXPT (**), MOVE (:=)	MOVE is used for assignment in LD and FBD
Numerical	ABS, SQRT LN, LOG, EXP SIN, COS, TAN, ASIN, ACOS, ATAN	General Logarithmic Trigonometric
Bit-string operations	SHL, SHR, ROR, ROL AND (&), OR, XOR, NOT	Bit shift operations Boolean operations
Selection	SEL, MUX, MAX, MIN, LIMIT	
Comparison	GT (>), GE (≥), EQ (=), LE (<), LT (≤), NE (≠)	
Type conversion	Syntax: **Type1_TO_Type2** Examples: INT_TO_REAL, INT_TO_WORD, BOOL_TO_STRING REAL_TO_INT, STRING_TO_TIME, DT_TO_STRING + many others	Which conversions are supported depends upon implementation
Text-string operations	LEN, LEFT, RIGHT, MID, CONCAT, INSERT, DELETE, REPLACE, FIND	

In the following, we will discuss many of these standard functions. Even though we have not yet studied programming languages, we will show the use of functions by means of examples written in one or more of the programming languages. In the following chapters about programming languages, it is assumed that this material is known beforehand, even though some of it will be explained again.

7.3.1   Assignment

One of the simplest instructions we can perform is to set the content of one variable equal to the content of another variable.

Suppose that you wish to activate a pump connected to the digital output %Q2.3 when a sensor connected to the digital input %I1.8 gives a logical high value.

In ST, it is done thus:

```
%Q2.3 := %I1.8;
```

With symbols and variables:

```
Pump := Sensor
```

The corresponding instruction in LD would look about like this:

This is called *assignment*, and such instructions are used to transfer the content on one operand to another. The operands do not need to be of the BOOL data type; they may be any data type, including structured and array. The general syntax is as follows:

OP1 : = OP2	The order is *from* OP2 *to* OP1.

The operator := belongs to the group of arithmetic functions, and the function name is MOVE. In the graphic languages FBD and LD, the function is represented by a single graphic block with one input and one output[4]:

$$OP2 \longrightarrow \boxed{\text{MOVE}} \longrightarrow OP1$$

7.4 Boolean Operations

This group covers use of the operators AND, OR, XOR, and NOT.

Above, we assigned a Boolean address to another Boolean address. If the output address is to have the value TRUE when the input address has the value FALSE, we would have had to program the following (in LD and ST, respectively):

(LD)

```
%Q2.3:=NOT %I1.8;
```
(ST)

By using the functions AND, OR, XOR, and NOT, we can implement all common Boolean operations. Note that the operators can also be used for bit strings such as BYTE and WORD.

The functions are expandable with respect to the numbers of operands and inputs:

```
%Q2.0 := Var1 OR Var2 OR (%I1.0 AND %I1.1 AND NOT %MX5.2);
```

A graphic representation in FBD/LD will generally look like the following (the function NOT can have only one input value):

Where *** is NOT, AND, OR or XOR

---

[4] In structured text, it is possible to assign several to the same value in one operation: OP1: = OP2: = OP3 := OP4: = ...

Table 7.2   Boolean operations

Function	LD	ST
AND (&)	%I1.0 %I1.1 %Q2.0	%Q2.0 := %I1.0 AND %I1.1;
OR	%I1.1 / %M1 — %Q2.3	%Q2.3 := %I1.1 OR %M1 ;
XOR	%I1.1 %M 1 / %M1 %I1.1 — %Q2.3	%Q2.3 := %I1.1 XOR %M1 ;

Table 7.3   Standard arithmetic functions

Function name	Operator	Function and ST expression	
ADD	+	Addition:	Out := IN1 + IN2 + ...+ INn
SUB	-	Subtraction:	Out := IN1 – IN2
MUL	*	Multiplication:	Out := IN1*IN2*...*INn
DIV	/	Division:	Out := IN1 / IN2
MOD		Modulo:	Out := IN1 MOD IN2
EXPT	**	Potentiation:	Out := IN1**IN2 (= $IN1^{IN2}$)
MOVE	:=	Assignment:	Out := IN

7.5 Arithmetic Functions

This group of operators and functions is used to perform arithmetic operations *between* two operands. Table 7.3 shows an overview.

The graphic representation that is used with these functions in FBD or LD is generally the same for all these functions. They differ only in the function name or the operator symbol in the box.

```
IN1 ──┌─────┐
      │ *** │── OUT      *** Name or symbol
IN2 ──└─────┘
```

IN1 and IN2 can be numbers or variables of the types ANY_NUM or ANY_BIT (see Section 6.5.4). The functions ADD and SUB also apply with the data type TIME. The symbol above shows only two inputs, but the functions ADD and MUL can be used for an arbitrary number of inputs, while the function MOVE has only one input.

Example 7.2

```
Answer := 43 + Var1*((14 MOD 4) - Var2) + Var3/4.7; (* ST-code: *)
```

(* Same expression in FBD code: *)

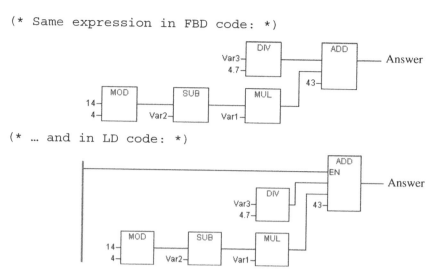

(* ... and in LD code: *)

As we see, the LD code and the FBD code are nearly identical here. The only difference is that the code in LD must be triggered (activated) via an Enable input, since LD is based on the use of a "conductor rail" on the left side (see Section 7.13 EN/ENO). (MOD stands for *modulo*, which is an operation that yields the *remainder* from division. Here, the operation to be performed is 14 MOD 4. 14 divided by 4 equals 3 with 2 remainder. The result is thus 2.)

Division with integers is an important subject in all programming. It will therefore be treated separately later in the book. See Section 10.5.

7.5.1 Overflow

Be aware of the risk of *overflow* when you are working with arithmetic and numerical instructions. If the result is stored in operand of data type INT, for example, the result must lie within the limits of −32768 and +32768. If the result lies outside these limits, you have overflow. The values that are stored in the result can have any value at all, and this is naturally undesirable. The programmer must take care that the resulting values are asserted to a maximum (or possibly minimum) if overflow has occurred. If the danger of overflow is present, you should naturally evaluate the use of other data types or alternative code in a different way.

Some PLCs have system addresses that monitor for overflow, among other things.

Example 7.3

Overflow in the TS X3721 PLC from Telemecanique can be detected and managed by checking the state of the Boolean system address (flag) %S18[5]:

```
Answer := Num1 + Num2;
IF %S18 AND Answer < 0 THEN
  Answer := -32768;
ELSIF %S18 AND Answer > 0 THEN
  Answer := 32767;
END_IF;
```

---

[5] System address %S18 is also used with division by 0 and square root of a negative number.

Table 7.4   Functions and operators for comparison

Name	Operator	Description
EQ	=	Out := IN1=IN2=IN3=IN4= ...= INn
GT	>	Out := (IN1>IN2) & (IN2>IN3) & ... & (INn-1>INn)
GE	≥	Out := (IN1≥IN2) & (IN2≥IN3) & ... & (INn-1≥INn)
LT	<	Out := (IN1<IN2) & (IN2<IN3) & ... & (INn-1<INn)
LE	≤	Out := (IN1≤IN2) & (IN2≤IN3) & ... & (INn-1≤INn)
NE	≠	Out := IN1≠IN2

7.6   Comparison

The comparison operators are used to compare the values of two or more operands. The syntax in ST is as follows (*operator* is one of those listed in Table 7.4):

```
Out := OP1 operator OP2 operator OP3 operator ... operator OPn;
```

The graphic representation that is used with these functions in FBD or LD is, generally, the same for all these functions. They differ only in the function name or the operator symbol in the box.

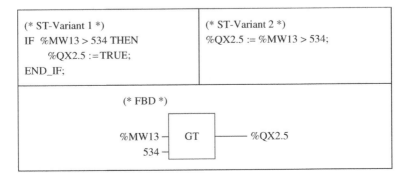

The inputs (operands) IN1 and IN2 can be numbers or variables of a data type that belongs to the class ANY_ELEMENTARY. When using functions on bit strings of differing lengths, the length of the shortest string is increased by filling with zeros from the right.

From the descriptions in the tables, we can understand that the order of the operands is important, just as it is in connection with the inputs to the graphic blocks. For example, if you want the output signal to be TRUE when Num1 is greater than Num2, you must place Num1 at the top of the block GT.

Example 7.4

The codes in ST below show two different possible codes for the same instruction, which is to set a Boolean output to TRUE if the result of a comparison is true. The same instruction is also shown in FBD code.

We see that variant 2 of the ST code is directly comparable with the use of the function in a graphic language. This is a compact way of testing the output of a comparison that is worthwhile noting because it saves a little coding in ST.

Below, there is an example of comparison with more than two operands.

Example 7.5 Comparison of Several Operands Simultaneously

Structured text	Graphic language
Out := (Var1≥Var2) AND (Var2≤Var3);	

7.7 Numerical Operations

We have previously examined a group of functions and operators that are used for arithmetic calculations. The functions that are presented here are also used for calculations, but what is special about these is that they perform operations on a single operand, rather than between operands. The syntax in ST is as follows:

```
OP1: = Function (OP2)
```

Here is a possible graphical representation in FBD/LD. *Name* is the name of the function.

Table 7.5 Numerical functions

Function name	Data type	Description
ABS	ANY_NUM	Absolute value
SQRT	ANY_REAL	Square root
LN	----"----	Natural logarithm
LOG	----"----	Base-10 logarithm
EXP	----"----	Natural exponential (e^x)
SIN	----"----	Sine (radians)
ASIN	----"----	Arc sine (inverse sine)
COS	----"----	Cosine (radians)
ACOS	----"----	Arc cosine (inverse cosine)
TAN	----"----	Tangent (radians)
ATAN	----"----	Arc tangent (inverse tangent)

Numerical expressions are most often used in combination with numerical operations, Boolean instructions, and arithmetic operations, in addition to comparison operations. There is no limit to the number of operators and operands that can be used.

Furthermore, an arithmetic sign can be placed in front of an operand or an operation on a single operand without needing to use parentheses.

Example 7.6

```
(* ST-code: *)
Answer := num1*4 - SQRT(num2) + ABS(num1)*3.14*(23.5 - num3)
          + 12*COS(-num2);
(* FBD code: *)
```

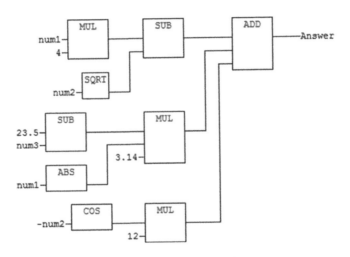

7.7.1 *Priority of Execution*

When the compiler executes numerical expressions, this must take place in accordance with a particular order of priorities. This is as follows (highest priority first):

1. Parentheses
2. Operations performed on an operand, for instance, SIN(x) or ABS(Y)
3. Negation (−) and complement (NOT)
4. *, / , MOD
5. +, −
6. <, >, ≤, ≥
7. =, ≠
8. AND
9. XOR
10. OR

In order to control the order in which the operations are to be performed, one must therefore use parentheses. If you are in doubt, it is much better to use many parentheses than to risk an erroneous result from a calculation. At any rate, there is no limitation on the number of parentheses.

Example 7.7

This expression will be calculated in the order shown by the numbers.

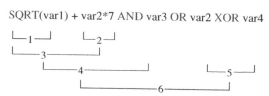

7.8 Selection

This is a special group of functions with the common feature that one of the inputs is assigned to the output. The difference among the selection functions is what criterion is used to select among the inputs. See table 7.6.

7.9 Type Conversion

By far, the largest group of functions is those that perform conversion between different data types. To begin with, one can convert between all of the elementary data types (ANY_ELEMENTARY), even though in practice there is seldom or never a requirement for some of these conversions.

Conversions are most often used in numerical calculations where different data types occur in the expressions. The reason for this is that analog input values often are stored in addresses of the WORD type and if these are going to be used in numerical expressions with a high requirement for accuracy, there is a need for conversion to floating-point numbers.

Note that you generally should not convert from a *larger* to a *smaller* data type, for instance, from WORD to BYTE or from DINT to INT. In the worst case, this results in an error, and in the best case, you run the risk of losing information.

Syntax for the conversion functions in structured text is as follows:

```
Out := datatype1_TO_datatype2(In);
```

In the graphic languages FBD and LD, the symbol will be a single block with one input and one output:

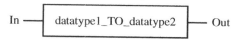

Table 7.6 Functions for selection

Name	Graphic symbol	Explanation and example

SEL	SEL
	BOOL—G
	ANY—IN0 —ANY
	ANY—IN1
		Use it to select which inputs that shall be assigned to the output:
		  G = False (0) gives Out := IN1
		  G = True (1) gives Out := IN2
		Example:
		`        Out := SEL(1, A, B)`
		`        (*Gives Out = B *)`

MUX	MUX
	ANY_INT—K
	ANY—IN0 —ANY
	: :
	ANY—INn
		Multiplexing resembles SEL, except that MUX is used to select one out of many inputs. Which input is selected is determined by the integer value of K (0, 1, 2, 3,...)
		Example:
		`        Out := MUX(0, A, B, C, D)`
		`        (*Gives Out = A *)`

MAX
 	
MIN
	***
	—IN1 —
	—IN2 —
	:
	—INn
		*** - MAX or MIN
		These functions are used to select which of the inputs has the largest or smallest value
		Example:
		`        Out := MAX(5, 14, 8)`
		`        (*Gives Out = 14 *)`

LIMIT	LIMIT —Min — —IN —Max	LIMIT is a limiter of values. The user provides a lower limit (Min) and an upper limit (Max). If the value of (IN) exceeds the upper limit, the value Max is returned. If the value of (IN) is below the lower limit, the value Min is returned. Example: `    MV_out := LIMIT(0, MV, 32767)`
	Permitted data types are ANY_ELEMENTARY	

We are not going to provide examples of all possible conversions because this would be a too lengthy task. Instead, we will show a selection of examples (in ST).

Example 7.8   From Boolean to Other Data Types

```
B    := BOOL_TO_INT(TRUE);        (* Result:    1 *)
O    := BOOL_TO_STRING(TRUE);     (* Result:    'TRUE' *)
RI   := BOOL_TO_TIME(TRUE);       (* Result:    T#1ms *)
N    := BOOL_TO_TOD(TRUE);        (* Result:    TOD#00:00:00.001 *)
G    := BOOL_TO_DATE(FALSE);      (* Result:    D#1970-01-01 *)
```

Example 7.9   From Floating-Point to Other Data Types

These functions round off value up or down to the nearest integer before they are converted to the desired format. This does not apply to conversion to STRING, BOOL, or another floating-point format. (Note that in conversion to text strings, there can be a limit to how many characters the system can handle.)

```
J   := REAL_TO_INT(7.5);          (* Result:      J = 8 *)
A   := REAL_TO_INT(7.4);          (* Result:      A = 7 *)
C   := REAL_TO_INT(-7.5);         (* Result:      C = -8 *)
K   := REAL_TO_STRING(35.27)      (* Result:      K = '35.27' *)
```

There are also two other functions that can be used for conversion from floating point to integer. These are the functions TRUNC[6] and TRUNC_INT:

- TRUNC converts from REAL to DINT.
- TRUNC_INT converts from REAL to INT.

These functions differ from the other ones in that the result is always rounded down to the nearest integer. Example:

```
B  := TRUNC_INT(-23.6)      (* Result: B = -23 *)
B  := REAL_TO_INT(-23.6)    (* Result: B = -24 *)
```

7.10   Bit-String Functions

These are a group of classic functions that are used for everything from control of stepping motors to monitoring of states. Most people will connect these functions with *shift registers*. The standard defines 4 functions that all are based on shifting bit strings a desired number of bits toward the left or toward the right. These are the functions SHL, SHR, ROL, and ROR.

The structure of the input arguments is equivalent for all four.

(Even though these functions can be used for all data types belonging to the generic ANY_BIT, there is, of course, little meaning to using them on Boolean objects.)

---

[6]*Note*: Only the TRUNC function is implemented in CODESYS 2.3. This corresponds to TRUNC_INT in version 3.x.

Table 7.7 Bit-string functions

Function name	Description
SHL	*Shift left* Execution of the function implies that the content in a bit string is shifted N places to the left, with the vacancies being filled by zeros
SHR	*Shift right* Execution of the function implies that the content in a bit string is shifted N places to the left, with the vacancies being filled by zeros from the left. If N is greater than the number of bits in IN, the result is an empty bit string. (The same is true for the function SHL)
ROL	*Rotate left* The content of a bit string is shifted N places to the left when the function is executed. Bits that fall out on the left side are filled in again on the right side
ROR	*Rotate right* The content of a bit string is shifted N places to the right when the function is executed. Bits that fall out on the left side are filled in again on the left side

Example 7.10

```
PROGRAM Shift
VAR
  bait  : BYTE := 2#10110100;          (* = B4 Hex *)
  ord   : WORD := 2#0000000010110100;  (* = B4 Hex *)
  bait_shl, bait_shr, bait_rol, bait_ror :  BYTE;
  ord_shl, ord_shr, ord_rol, ord_ror :      WORD;
  n     : INT := 2;
END_VAR

bait_shl  := SHL(bait, n);
ord_shl   := SHL(ord, n);
bait_shr  := SHR(bait, n);
ord_shr   := SHR(ord, n);
bait_rol  := ROL(bait, n);
ord_rol   := ROL(ord, n);
bait_ror  := ROR(bait, n);
ord_ror   := ROR(ord, n);
END_PROGRAM
```

```
Result from run:
 bait_shl = 2#11010000
 ord_shl = 2#0000001011010000

 bait_shr = 2#00101101
 ord_shr = 2#0000000000101101

 bait_rol = 2#11010010
 ord_rol = 2#0000001011010000

 bait_ror = 2#00101101
 ord_ror = 2#0000000000101101
```

7.11   Text-String Functions

Several of the functional groups that we have presented so far can also be used on text strings, that is, the data types CHAR/WCHAR and STRING/WSTRING. This applies to selection functions, functions for type conversion, and functions for comparison. The groups of functions that are reviewed here are specially designed for use on text strings. These are the functions LEN, LEFT, RIGHT, MID, CONCAT, INSERT, DELETE, REPLACE, and FIND.

Table 7.8 contains possible graphic symbols and explanation and examples of the use of the functions. Because of lack of space in the table, some abbreviations are used: STR, STR1, and STR2 have data type ANY_STRING, and N and M are ANY_INT.

Table 7.8 Standard text-string functions

Name	Graphic symbol and example	Explanation and example in ST

LEN	'GoLFC!' — LEN [STR N] — Out	Returns the length of a text string (number of characters in the string)
		Example:
		`Out := LEN('GoLFC!')`
		`(*Gives Out = 6 *)`

LEFT
 	
RIGHT
	'GoLFC!' — *** [STR STR] — Out
	2 — N
	
	*** LEFT or RIGHT
		Returns a desired number of char (N), starting from the left or right
		Examples:
		`Out := LEFT('GoLFC!', 2)`
		`(*Gives Out = 'Go' *)`
		`Out := RIGHT('GoLFC!', 4)`
		`(* Gives Out = 'LFC!' *)`

MID	'GoLFC!' — MID [STR STR] — Out
	2 — N
	3 — M
		Returns a desired number of characters, N, starting with character number M from the left
		Example:
		`Out := MID('GoLFC!', 2, 3)`
		`(*Gives Out = 'oL' *)`

CONCAT	'Go' — CONCAT [STR1 STR] — Out
	'LFC!' — STR2
	: — :
		The function performs a concatenation of several text strings
		Example:
		`Out := CONCAT('Go', 'LFC!')`
		`(*Gives Out = 'GoLFC!' *)`

INSERT	'Go!' — INSERT [STR1 STR] — Out
	'LFC' — STR2
	3 — N
		The function is used to insert a text string (STR2) into another text string (STR1) in the position following character number N
		Example:
		`Out := INSERT('Go!', 'LFC', 3)`
		`(*Gives Out = 'GoLFC!' *)`

DELETE	'GoLFC!' — DELETE [STR STR] — Out
	2 — N
	3 — M
		The functions used to delete And characters from a string, beginning with character number M from the left
		Example:
		`Out := DELETE('GoLFC!', 2, 3)`
		`(*Gives Out = 'GFC!' *)`

REPLACE	'GoManU' — REPLACE [STR1 STR] — Out
	'LFC!' — STR2
	4 — N
	3 — M
		The function replaces N characters from the string STR1 with the string STR2, beginning with character number M from the left
		Example:
		`Out := REPLACE('GoManU', 'LFC!', 4, 3)`
		`(*Gives Out = 'GoLFC!' *)`

FIND	'GoLFC!' — FIND [STR1 N] — Out
	'LFC' — STR2
		Returns the starting position for a partial string STR2 in the string STR1. If STR2 is not found in STR1, the value 0 is returned
		Example:
		`Out := FIND('GoLFC!', 'LFC');`
		`(*Gives Out = 3 *)`

7.12   Defining New Functions

When making programs for automated processing, you normally get by with the predefined functions and operators provided by the manufacturer, but occasionally, there is a need to define your own functions.

Defining a new function begins with a declaration where the function is assigned an identifier (given a name) and a data type. Following that, the input variables are declared. These are used for conversion of arguments when the function is called.

Example 7.11   Defining a Function that Calculates the Absolute Value

```
(*** Defining the function: ***)
FUNCTION My_func: INT    (*Declaration part*)
  VAR_INPUT
    Num : INT;
  END_VAR

  IF Numb < 0 THEN        (*Implementation part*)
    My_func := -Num;
  ELSE
    My_func := Num;
  END_IF
END_FUNCTION
```

We see that the declaration begins with keyword FUNCTION, followed by the function name and data type. The data type must be consistent with the format of the *result* of the function call, since the function name also acts as a variable where the result of the instructions is stored.

VAR_INPUT is used to declare variables that will receive values transferred in the function call (often called *arguments*). Here, we have only one such variable or operand, namely, the variable Num.

In the code portion of the function, we have here a control structure of the type IF-THEN-ELSE-END_IF. There we check whether the value in the argument is negative. In that case, the value is inverted and returned as the result (My_func := -Num). The definition of the function closes with END_FUNCTION.[7]

In this example, we use only the variable type VAR_INPUT in the function, but it is also permitted to use the variable types VAR_OUT and VAR_IN_OUT. Internal variables, or variables that are used only within the function itself, can also be declared by using the keyword VAR.

---

[7] In some development tools, the start and termination of a POU is implicit. That is, keywords such as FUNCTION, END_FUNCTION, PROGRAM, and FUNCTION_BLOCK do not need to be written in. Start and termination of a POU is also unambiguous since each POU is declared as a separate object. In CODESYS, the keyword to start a POU is generated automatically, while the keyword for termination of a POU is implicit and should not be written, although it is not displayed in the editor.

The code below shows how we can use (call) our new function in the program. Here, we show how the code for the call looks in both ST and FBD.

In a graphic language such as FBD, the function will automatically appear as a rectangular box with a line for each of the input variables on the left side and (usually) a line on the right side. Since our function has only one argument and gives only one value as a result, there is only one line on each side. Similarly, in ST, there will be only one operand (the variable Value).

```
PROGRAM PLC_PRG
VAR
    Value       : INT;
    Abs_value   : INT;
END_VAR


(*Function call in ST: *)          (*Function call in FBD: *)
Abs_value:= My_func(Value);


END_PROGRAM
```

7.13 EN/ENO

The syntax for activating the code in the LD programming language is based on the idea that all instructions must be activated by being connected to a "power rail" that graphically is a vertical line at the left of the instructions. This power rail is constantly "TRUE". This implies that the graphics symbols we wish to use in LD must have an Enable input that can be connected to this power rail. We saw this previously in example 7.2.

Functions that are made for use in LD have such an Enable input called EN. In addition, they have an Enable output called ENO that usually has the same state as EN.

The way this works depends, in part, on implementation but can be as follows:

- Only when EN has the state TRUE (1) the function is called and executed.
- Nothing happens when EN is FALSE (0).
- How ENO works depends partly upon how the manufacturer has chosen to implement the function. If an error occurs during execution of the function, ENO should be reset to FALSE. If not, then one of the following can be implemented:
  1. ENO is like EN at any time. Then the purpose of ENO is just to continue EN to the EN input of the next functions.
  2. ENO is set TRUE or FALSE depending upon the result of the execution.

In order to illustrate the principle, we will expand the function we defined in Example 7.11 by adding EN/ENO so that it can be used in the LD language. (Since the code in this example is so simple, ENO is used here only for continuing EN.)

Example 7.12   Function with EN/ENO

```
FUNCTION My_func    : INT
VAR_INPUT
    EN   : BOOL         := TRUE;
    Num  : INT;
END_VAR
VAR_OUTPUT
    ENO  : BOOL;
END_VAR

IF EN THEN
    IF Num < 0 THEN
        My_func := -Num;
    ELSE
        My_func := Num;
    END_IF
END_IF

ENO := EN;
```

7.14   Test Problems

Problem 7.1
(a) What three types of POU are defined by the standard?
(b) Explain the difference between a function and a function block.
(c) Write the declaration for a Boolean function named Ohoy that has 2 in-variables, A and B, both of the data type REAL.
(d) Which text-string functions are defined in the standard?
(e) Show examples of use of the standard functions CONCAT and REPLACE.
(f) What will be the result from the following function calls if they are executed in the same order as they are listed (all variables are of data type String:
  1. MyString := INSERT('Tomorrow is today', 'yesterday', 11)
  2. A := LEN(MyString);
  3. B := FIND(MyString, 'r');
  4. C := LEFT(MyString, 4);
  5. D := RIGHT(MyString, 5);

Problem 7.2
(a) Which function can be used to limit a numerical variable til values between, for instance, -200 and 200?
(b) Suppose that you want to assign a variable called Input, of data type word, to one of the analog inputs %IW4, %IW5, or %IW6, depending on whether the value of a variable x is 0, 1, or 2.
  1. Which function can be used to accomplish this?
  2. Write the function call in a textual form.

Problem 7.3

Suppose that %MW0 = 0101 1101 0111 0110 and that %MW1 = 0011 1011 1111 1001. What will be the result of performing the following instructions (give the answers in both binary and decimal form)?

1. %MW10 := %MW0 AND %MW1;
2. %MW11 := %MW0 OR %MW1;
3. %MW12 := %MW0 XOR %MW1;
4. %MW13 := %MW0 + %MW1;

8

Function Blocks

Chapter Contents

- On function blocks:
  Declaring and calling. Defining your own function blocks
- Standard function blocks:
  - Flank detection (R_TRIG and F_TRIG)
  - Bistable (RS and SR)
  - Timers (time delays) and various modes (TON, TOF, and TP)
  - Counters (CTU, CTD, and CTUD).
- Nonstandard implementation-dependent function blocks
- Program organization:
  Programs and program calls. Execution control with EN/ENO

8.1 Introduction

In contrast to functions, *function blocks*(FBs) can have internal memory. This means that the result of a call to a FB can depend not only upon the arguments (input values) but also on the values of the FB's own internal variables. In other words, repeated calls of a FB with identical arguments do not necessarily give the same output values.

When a function is called from a POU, the function returns a response in the form of a return value (or an array of values). This is not what happens with a call of a FB. Instead, the result of running a FB is stored in its own output variable. FBs can thus have more than one output.

Programmable Logic Controllers: A Practical Approach to IEC 61131-3 Using CODESYS, First Edition. Dag H. Hanssen.
© 2015 John Wiley & Sons, Ltd. Published 2015 by John Wiley & Sons, Ltd.

8.1.1   The Standard's FBs

IEC 61131-3 defines a set of FBs that, together with the standard's functions, cover the basic operations one associates with PLCs. These FBs are:

- Flank detection: **R_TRIG** and **F_TRIG**
- Bistable (flip-flop): **SR** and **RS**
- Timer (time delay): **TON, TOF, TP**
- Counter: **CTU, CTD, CTUD**

Here, we will study all of these FBs and explain how they work. You will find examples of the FBs in the chapters on programming languages.

8.2   Declaring and Calling FBs

In order to be able to use a FB in a POU, an *instance* of the FB must be declared in the POU. Instances are named multiple uses of a FB type. This sounds somewhat cryptic, but the point is that since a FB has memory and properties that are associated to it by use, one must declare a new instance of every FB that one uses even if their are of the same type.

Suppose that in your program you have to use two RS flip-flops to start (Set) and to stop (Reset) two pumps; P1 and P2. In addition, we will use two timers to provide a delay in starting the pumps of two and five minutes, respectively. In order to be able to start and stop each pump independently, you must declare an instance of each SR flip-flop and on instance of each timer. Declaration is made with the same syntax with which you declare variables, except that you indicate the *type of* FB instead of data type:

```
PROGRAM Call_of_FBs
VAR
        Start, Stop        : BOOL;
        Run_P1, Run_P2     : RS;// Declares two instances of a RS
        Two_min, Five_min  : TON;// and two instances of a Timer
        P1, P2             : BOOL;
END_VAR
(* Program code: *)
```

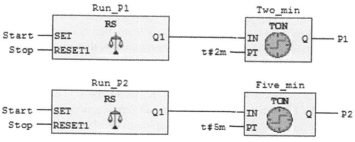

```
END_PROGRAM
```

(In CODESYS, the types of any FBs are not marked in blue as are other keywords.)

When you declare such instances, you can name them anyway you want, so long as it is a permitted name. Personally, I like to name timers according to the length of time delay (such as *five_min*) and counters according to the value that they will count up to (e.g., *Fifty*). Regarding the other two categories of FBs, you will normally use many more of them in a program. For these, I therefore recommend simple, but at the same time fairly descriptive, names:

- RS1, RS2, etc. for bistable of the type RS
- SR1, SR2, etc. for bistable of the type SR
- RE1, RE2, etc. for positive flank triggers (R_TRIG)
- FE1, FE2, etc. for negative flank triggers (F_TRIG)

(RE and FE are acronyms for rising edge and falling edge, respectively.)

Once an instance has been declared, the FBs are made accessible for use in the code field in the POU. (It is also possible to declare an instance of a FB globally.) At any rate, the instance can now be used in a POU via a *call*.

The code above, programmed in CODESYS, shows use of our FB instances in FBD. Notice that the name of the instance will be at the upper edge of the symbol.

In Structured Text, we call instances of FBs by writing the name of the instance together with arguments. A call of Run_P1 can appear as follows:

Run_P1 (Set := Start, Reset1 := Stop, Q1 => P1);

Note that it is possible to use FBs without all inputs associated with variables. In the code on the previous page, the ET outputs are not associated to anything. In CODESYS, they then disappear from the symbols in the code. Any inputs that are not associated will use their initial values in the execution of the block.

In the following, we will study the way all of the FBs *work* in the standard. We will study the *use* of the FBs later when we review programming languages.

8.3 FBs for Flank Detection

In many applications, we would like to perform an instruction only once, for example, precisely *when* a condition is met. For a PLC, this is not natural. It wants to check conditions repeatedly (every scan) and perform an instruction every time as soon as the condition is satisfied. The time between every time the condition is checked is what is called the scan time, as we saw in Section 1.3.3. This can be 20 ms, for example. Therefore, if a condition is met, the associated instructions will be performed at every scan, that is to say, every 20 ms.

Finding out exactly when a Boolean condition is satisfied is the same as detecting when the Boolean condition changes state from FALSE to TRUE (0 to 1) or vice versa, from TRUE to FALSE. This is called *flank detection.*

The standard defines to FBs for flank detection, R_TRIG and F_TRIG. These FBs operate in the same way as the flank triggers P and N in LD (see Section 9.3.3). Both blocks have one input and one output, both Boolean. The graphic symbols for the blocks are shown in Figure 8.1.

R_TRIG is used to detect a rising edge on the Boolean input variable or the Boolean expression associated with the input. When that happens, the output Q becomes TRUE and then remains TRUE for a time equal to the scan time, that is, until the next time the block is evaluated.

Figure 8.1   Function blocks for flank detection

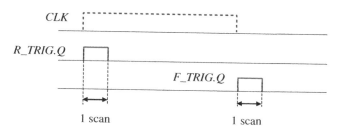

Figure 8.2   Diagram for the input and output signals of the block

F_TRIG is used to detect a falling edge on a Boolean variable or a Boolean expression. In the PLC scan where the input signal becomes FALSE, the output Q becomes TRUE. It then remains TRUE until the next scan (next execution of the block) (see Figure 8.2).

8.4   Bistable Elements

The Bistable[1] elements SR and RS or memories, as they may also be called, are equivalent with the retention elements S and R in LD (see Section 9.3.2).

Figure 8.3 shows a possible graphic representation of the blocks as they can appear in the graphical languages LD and FBD.[2] All variables must be of the type BOOL. The working principles are as follows:

A logical high signal on the Set input (Var1 = TRUE) causes output Q1 to be set TRUE. It then *remains* TRUE even though the signal on the Set input becomes FALSE. The output can only be FALSE again when it receives a TRUE value on the Reset input.

The reason that these are also called memories is precisely that the output retains its value even though the state at the Set input becomes FALSE.

The difference between SR and RS first becomes noticeable when *both* Set and Reset are TRUE:

- SR is Set dominant. This means that Set has a higher priority than Reset and the output goes TRUE even if Reset is also TRUE.
- RS is Reset dominant, which means that the output goes FALSE when Reset goes TRUE, whether or not Set is also TRUE.

---

[1] The word *bistable* refers to that the output from the blocks has two stable states, TRUE and FALSE.
[2] This standard does not place any requirements on graphical layout. The manufacturers can therefore determine what designs they prefer to use for graphic representations of FBs.

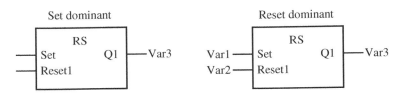

Figure 8.3   Bistable elements

(Note that a 1 is attached to the dominant input variable as a reminder to the user for which of the two blocks is being used.) The Boolean quantities associated with the Set and Reset inputs do not need to be simple Boolean variables, but may also be Boolean expressions.

8.5   Timers

A common element in traditional electrical installations is the *time clock* in its various variants. These are found in both mechanical and electronic implementations. There is also a time clock in the PLC, but there it is present as software. These are called a *timer*. The purpose of using a timer, briefly stated, is to be able to change the state of the Boolean address *at a desired time* after some criterion has been met. The symbol for a timer is shown in Figure 8.4.

Inputs and Outputs

• Input variable **IN**: When the signal at IN changes state (rising edge for TON and TP, falling edge for TOF), the timer will start.
• Timer output **Q**: The state of output Q does not depend upon the input only but also upon the mode selected (TON, TOF, or TP) (see the following text).
• Input variable **PT**: Here, a variable of data type TIME is associated. This may be a time given directly in a standard time format (for instance, t#2m30s). PT is a predetermined time that indicates the desired delay.
• Output variable **ET**: A variable of type TIME that contains the current value in the timer, that is, the time that has elapsed since the timer was activated. When the content of ET equals the content of PT, the timer's output Q changes state.

The standard defines three different *modes* for control of the state of output Q:

• **TON**: The output Q gets TRUE a user-specified time (content of PT) after the condition at the input is satisfied (TRUE signal on IN). In order for the output to change state, the input must be TRUE for at least as long as the predefined time.
• **TOF**: The output gets TRUE immediately when the condition at the input is satisfied and thus when IN becomes TRUE. After the input becomes FALSE again, the output will becomes FALSE after a user-specified time, provided that the input has not gone TRUE again in the meantime (ET resets when IN gets TRUE).

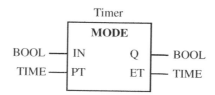

Figure 8.4   Standard Timer

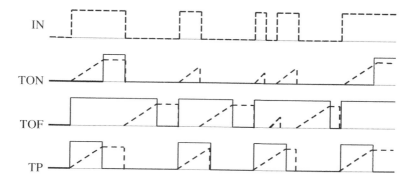

Figure 8.5   Illustration of the difference between the various modes of timer

- **TP**: The output Q goes logically high when input IN goes high and stays TRUE for the user-specified time PT, whether or not IN becomes FALSE in the meantime. (ET resets only when both the input and the output are logically low.)

Figure 8.5 shows a sequence diagram that illustrates the three modes. The solid lines show the state of output Q for a timer in each of the three modes. The dotted lines at the top of the figure show the state of the input IN.

The figure also shows the values in ET (marked ----), which contains the current value in the timer. The output status changes when ET is equal to PT.

8.6   Counters

Counters are FBs that have some similarities in principle with timers. They have an input variable containing the desired number of pulses that are to be counted, an output variable that contains the counters' present value, and a Boolean output the changes state from FALSE to TRUE when the desired count is reached.

The standard defines three types of counters for *counting up*, *counting down*, and *up/down counting*: CTU, CTD, and CTUD. It is unclear why three different FBs are defined for counting when the CTUD block covers all requirements for counting. It probably has some connection with tradition. At any rate, in the following, we will study the symbols and characteristic parameters for all three types.

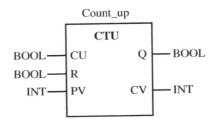

Figure 8.6   Graphic symbol for an up-counter

Table 8.1   Characteristic parameters for an up-counter

CU	Count Up	These are pulses (rising edges) of the input to be counted
PV	Preset Value	Integer that contains a desired preset value
CV	Current Value	Integer type of value whose content increases with one unit for each rising edge at CU
R	Reset (input)	Counter reset so that CV=0 when R becomes TRUE
Q	Done (output)	Is set to TRUE when counting is done (CV=PV)

8.6.1   Up-Counter

The up-counter's parameters and variables are shown in Table 8.1.

8.6.2   Down-Counter

The symbol and operation of a down-counter (Figure 8.7) is very much like that of an up-counter except for two things: on rising edges at the counter input, which is now designated CD, the counter counts downward from a preset value (PV). When CV equals 0, the counter is finished, and Q goes logically high. The reset input for CTU has been replaced here by a load input (LD). When LD is TRUE, CV is set to equal PV.

The down-counter's parameters and variables are shown in Table 8.2.

8.6.3   Up/Down-Counter

The third and last FB for counting is called CTUD and implements a combination of CTU and CTD. The block's input and output variables are the same as those in CTU or CTD (Figure 8.8).

Operation

- *Counting:* The inputs CU and CD are scanned in turn. With a rising edge at CU, the current value (CV) increases by 1. With a rising edge at CD, the value CV decreases by 1.
- *Reset:* When input R is set to TRUE, the CV is set to 0.
- *Load:* When input LD is set to TRUE, CV is set to PV.
- QU returns TRUE when CV >= PV.
- QD returns TRUE when CV = 0.

See Section 9.6 for examples of use of counters in graphic languages.

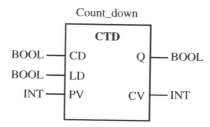

Figure 8.7   Graphic symbol for a down-counter

Table 8.2   Characteristic parameters for a down-counter

CD	Count down	It is the number of pulses at this input that is to be counted
PV	Preset value	Integer that contains a desired preset value
CV	Current value	Integer type of value whose content decreases by 1 for each rising edge at CD
LD	Load	Counter reset so that CV=PV when LD becomes TRUE
Q	Output	Is set to TRUE when counter is done (CV=0)

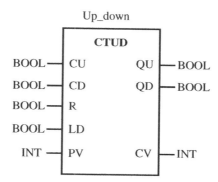

Figure 8.8   Graphic symbol for an up/down-counter

8.7   Defining New FBs

Example **8.1** shows a definition for the standard's FB RS. The declaration and code for a FB is enclosed by the keywords FUNCTION_BLOCK and END_FUNCTION_BLOCK.

This particular block has two input variables and one output variable, all type BOOL. This FB does not have any local variables.

Example 8.1   Defining FB RS

```
FUNCTION_BLOCK RS
(* Example of a function block that implements a Reset-
   dominant flip-flop. *)
VAR_INPUT    //Input variables
```

```
  Set        : BOOL;
  Reset1     : BOOL;
END_VAR
VAR_OUTPUT   //Output variable
  Q1         : BOOL;
END_VAR
(* Function block program code (in FBD): *)
```

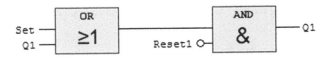

```
END_FUNCTION_BLOCK
```

When a FB is used in the graphic languages, a graphic symbol is generated automatically, based upon the name of the block, the number of inputs (VAR_INPUT), and the number of outputs (VAR_OUTPUT).

8.7.1 Encapsulation of Code

An important point about FBs is that they are very useful for encapsulating code. If you write code for others, for instance, for a client, and have developed a special code that you perhaps would use again in several programs and which you do not want to distribute to others, you can store this code in the form of a FB.

You can then use the FB in a program, where it will do precisely the same job as though the code in the block had been part of the program code. The major difference is that no one can see the code that is stored in the FB, and you have thereby protected this section of the code.

In the beginning of the chapter, we studied a little program where we controlled two pumps with the help of a pair of RS flip-flops and two timers. Let us now fix that code so that it is a FB rather than a program:

Example 8.2

```
FUNCTION_BLOCK Pump_Control
VAR_INPUT
    In1, In2        : BOOL;
END_VAR
VAR_OUTPUT
    Out1, Out2            : BOOL;
END_VAR
VAR
    Run_P1, Run_P2 : RS;
    Two_min, Five_min    : TON;
END_VAR
```

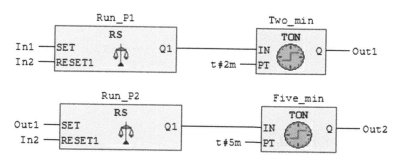

END_FUNCTION_BLOCK

If you compare this code with the code in Section 8.2, you will see that they are identical. The difference is in the declaration field, the fact that this is a POU of the FB type instead of a POU of the program type.

In the program, we can use as many FBs as we care to, of any type, and when we use them, we will not see the code that lies within the FB; we only have to know what it does and how we put it to work in the program. Since you can use a FB several times, and perhaps for various purposes, you should use more general variable names in the declaration. Here, I have used In1 and In2 on the input variables and Out1 and Out2 on the output variables.

Now, if we make a program, we can declare an instance of our new FB (Pump_control) and use it in a code. As mentioned, it will automatically generate a symbol in graphic language, like this:

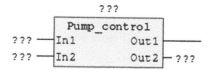

Example 8.3   Calling Our FB

Here, we see the use of our new FB in a program. Like all other FB, we must declare an instance of our FB in the declaration field where we give the instance a name. The instance can then be used in the code field, where we can associate other variables (or expressions) to the inputs and outputs of the instance.

The goal of concealing the part of the code that lies in the FB has been achieved, in addition to the advantage that it is simple to reuse the code in several programs or several times in the same program.

```
PROGRAM Calling_Pump_control
VAR
    Start      AT %IX2.3    : BOOL;
    Stop       AT %IX2.4    : BOOL;
    P1         AT %QX5.0    : BOOL;
    P2         AT %QX5.1    : BOOL;
    PumpCtrl                : Pump_control;
END_VAR
```

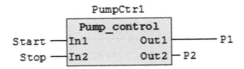

END_PROGRAM

8.7.2   Other Nonstandardized FBs

As mentioned earlier, the development tool that you use will offer many more functions and FBs then are defined in the standard. In addition, users and third-party suppliers develop new FBs that they often make available on the Internet. Before you get started programming your own FB for a particular purpose, it can therefore be a good idea to look around a little in the programming tool library or search on the Net.

In CODESYS, you have access to the standard's FBs by downloading the library *standard. lib* to your application, but you can download many more libraries. Some involve installation of software, but others can simply be downloaded. I would particularly like to recommend library OSCAT, which is a heavy package with over 800 library modules. OSCAT is an acronym for **O**pen **S**ource **C**ommunity for **A**utomation **T**echnology and has support for many other development tools besides CODESYS, including PCWorx and Step7. Not only will you find thousands of useful functions and FBs, the code is also open source.

Among the libraries that are included with the installation of CODESYS, I would like to mention *Util.lib*, where you will find a PID to use in process regulation. The code for the block is not accessible for review, but you will see variable declarations and comments so that you can understand how the block can be used (Figure 8.9):

```
FUNCTION_BLOCK PID
VAR_INPUT
  ACTUAL      :REAL;   (* Actual value (PV - process variable) *)
  SET_POINT   :REAL;   (* Desired value, set point *)
  KP          :REAL;   (* Proportionality const. (P) *)
  TN          :REAL;   (* Integral time (I) in sec *)
  TV          :REAL;   (* Derivative time (D) in sec*)
  Y_MANUAL    :REAL;   (* Y is set to this value as long as
                          MANUAL=TRUE *)
  Y_OFFSET    :REAL;   (* Offset for manipulated variable *)
  Y_MIN       :REAL;   (* Minimum value for manipulated variable *)
  Y_MAX       :REAL;   (* Maximum value for manipulated variable *)
  MANUAL      :BOOL;   (* TRUE: manual: Y is not influenced by
                          controller,
                          FALSE: controller determines Y *)
  RESET       :BOOL;   (*Set Y output to Y_OFFSET and reset
                          integral part *)
END_VAR
```

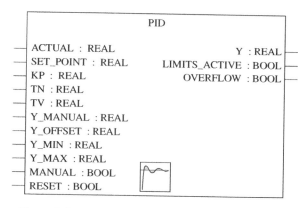

Figure 8.9   Graphic symbol for the PID function block

```
VAR_OUTPUT
  Y                   :REAL;   (* Manipulating variable *)
  LIMITS_ACTIVE       :BOOL;   (* TRUE if value exceed Y_MIN, Y_MAX *)
  OVERFLOW            :BOOL;   (* Overflow in integral part *)
END_VAR
VAR
  CLOCK               :TON;
  I                   :INTEGRAL;  (* Integral and Derivative are
                                     FBs in Util.lib *)
  D                   :DERIVATIVE;
  TMDIFF              :DWORD;
  ERROR               :REAL;
  INIT                :BOOL:=TRUE;
  Y_ADDOFFSET         :REAL;
END_VAR
```

8.8   Programs

The third type of POU in the standard—a program—is defined as:

> ... a logical assembly of all the programming language elements and constructs necessary for the intended signal processing required for the control of a machine or process by a PLC system.

Said a little differently (but perhaps not better): A program consists of addresses, variables, constants, functions, FBs, and control structures combined in a logical way so that it constitutes a runnable code that solves a control problem.

As we see, it is difficult, and perhaps meaningless, to define what a program is. The following chapters on programming languages will, we hope, provide a good understanding of what a program is and how program code is constructed with various programming languages. To begin with, we will be satisfied with the guidelines that the standard specifies. Declaration and use of the program is identical with that specified for FBs, except for the following:

- A program is bounded by the keywords PROGRAM and END_PROGRAM.
- A program is at a higher structural level than FBs, as shown in Figures 5.5 and 5.6. This means that a program can contain instances of FBs, but an FB cannot contain programs.
- A program can, in addition to containing functions and instances of FBs, also call other programs.

8.8.1 Program Calls

A program can call other programs. You can structure your application better by splitting up the code into several POUs of the program and FB types, where each POU handles its share of the control. This is important in larger applications and makes it simpler to maintain and structure the code. Another advantage is that you can reuse snippets of code by importing programs and FBs that you have previously developed for other projects.

When a program is called, any changes in values and variables will be retained for the next time the program is called. This is different from calling up a FB, where only the variables in the current *instance* of the FB are changed. As we have seen, you can declare several instances of the same FB in a program. The values that are changed affect only the current instance and are therefore only significant in the next call of the same instance.

Example **8.4** shows how the code in a program can call other programs in the application. What conditions are used in calling the individual programs will naturally depend upon the project in question. If it is a sequential structure, for example, the next program can be called when the previous program has carried out its part. In this example, it has been done simply by having the programs called as a result of the value in the integer variable value.

Example 8.4   Calling Programs

In this example, the code in the application is divided into four different programs. A main program, called main, calls the other three programs. We see that the individual programs can be written in different languages (Program1, LD; Program2, SFC; and Program3, FBD).

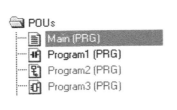

```
IF Value = 1 THEN
  Program1();
END_IF;
IF Value = 2 THEN
  Program2();
END_IF;
IF Value = 3 THEN
  Program3();
END_IF;
```

The program that calls the other programs is coded in ST.

A corresponding code written in FBD or LD can be implemented in CODESYS thus (see next page on EN/ENO):

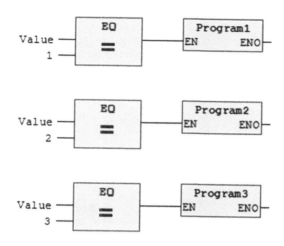

8.8.2 Execution Control

There is often a requirement to use the result from an instruction, a network in LD, or a POU to control other POUs. This can easily be solved by sending the result from the instruction or network to a global variable that is then used to control the execution of other POUs. It is also possible to do this directly by the use of Enable (**EN**) and Enable Out (**ENO**) as we studied in Section 7.13.

If these variables are used in a function, FB, or program, the execution of the POU takes place in accordance with the following rules:

1. If the value to input EN is FALSE (0), none of the instructions that are defined in the POU are executed, and the output ENO is set to 0.
2. If the value to EN is TRUE (1), the defined instructions are executed, and the output ENO is set to 1 as soon as the execution of the instructions is completed successfully (with no errors).
3. For FBs, all outputs (VAR_OUTPUT) will retain their values from the previous call if EN is set to 0.

The third item says that an FB will be "frozen" if EN is FALSE. All the outputs from the block will then maintain their values, no matter what the state of the other inputs is. As soon as the FALSE state terminates, that is, when EN is set to TRUE, normal operation will be resumed.

This EN/ENO functionality is utilized in the example on the previous page. In CODESYS when you want to insert a call of a program or an FB in the graphic languages LD and FBD, you select "Insert Empty Box with EN/ENO." Then click on the question mark inside the box that appears and write the name of the program or the FB that you wish to call up. (You can also click on the question mark and press F2 to call *Input Assistant,* where you can select the proper program or FB from a menu.)

8.9   Test Problems

Problem 8.1
Given the following program:

```
PROGRAM NoWhat
VAR
    Button AT %IX23.5    :BOOL;
    A, B, C              :BOOL;
    RE1, RE2, RE3        :R_TRIG;
END_VAR
```

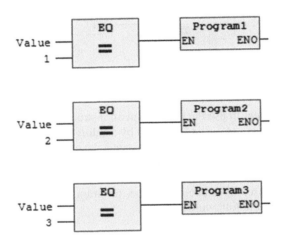

At input %IX23.5, a pushbutton is connected. When the button is pressed, a logically high signal appears on the input.

Tasks:

1. Make a truth table that shows the state of the variables A, B, and C for *the first 8 pushes on the button.* Assume that the button is released between each push and that the initial value for A, B, and C are 0.
2. Is there any meaningful "information" which you can interpret from the pattern of 1's and 0's in your table?

Part Four

Programming

9

Ladder Diagram (LD)*

9.1 Introduction

Programming with LD has traditionally been the most widely used programming language for PLCs. Another concept that is used for code written in LD is *relay diagram*. Even though other, and in many instances more efficient, programming languages have gradually appeared, LD continues to be widely used. There are many reasons for this:

---

* Regarding examples and implementation of code in this chapter: Most of the examples are carried out in software with CODESYS from Smart Software Solutions. If this differs from the standard, there will be a comment. There can be differences that appear as extra functionality, beyond the standard, that is implemented in the development tool in question, or subparagraphs in the standard that are not implemented in the tool. The larger examples are complete with declaration of variables in addition to the code itself.

Programmable Logic Controllers: A Practical Approach to IEC 61131-3 Using CODESYS, First Edition. Dag H. Hanssen.
© 2015 John Wiley & Sons, Ltd. Published 2015 by John Wiley & Sons, Ltd.

- It has been around for a long time.
- The language is graphic.
- It is relatively easy to grasp.

Previous editions of LD had a basic set of instructions sufficient to be able to perform most of the fundamental types of control functions such as logic, time control, and counting, along with simple mathematical operations. Most of the PLC manufacturers currently provide PLCs and programming tools that make it possible to perform advanced additional functions in LD, often integrated with other languages such as FBD and ST.

The basic functions that are needed in order to implement smaller control systems can be learned relatively quickly, and the graphic presentation can be understood intuitively. For beginners in programming, and when smaller applications are to be developed, LD is therefore a fine choice of programming language.

9.2   Program Structure

Figure 9.1 shows a sketch in principle of how code in LD is structured. Both sides of the code are bounded by vertical lines that we can call power rails. The rail on the left always has the state TRUE. You can consider that to be a voltage (+24V) connected to the rail.

The rail at the right has no defined logical state under the standard. It can therefore be considered as implicit, and not all producers implement a vertical right line in the development tool.

Generally, a code in an LD is based upon the following principles:

- If a *condition* or a combination of conditions is satisfied, then one or more *actions* (events, instructions) will be performed.

We can call a set of conditions with associated actions a rung.[1] A program will thus consist of one or more such concatenated rungs that are being executed sequentially by the PLC. Here is an example of an LD code:

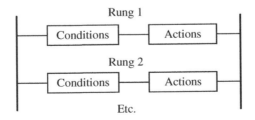

Figure 9.1   The structure in a LD

---

[1] In some implementations, the rungs are called *networks*.

9.2.1 Contacts and Conditions

What constitutes the conditions in Figure 9.2 will most often be a contact or a combination of contacts like those in rung 2 in the figure previously. A *contact* is a graphic element (⊣ ⊢) that is associated with a Boolean variable or a Boolean address.

Even though there is naturally no current going through these logical rungs, we can understand them better if we consider a contact to be like an ordinary light switch:

If it is closed, current goes through the contact. If it is open, the flow is interrupted.

There are several types of contact symbols. The two basic variants are *normally open* (NO) and *normally closed* (NC).

The symbols for the two types associated with the variable Var_A are shown in Figure 9.3.

Detailed Explanation of Operation

Suppose that a normally open contact is associated with address %IX2.5. Because the contact is of the normally open type, this means that the contact is open when the state of address %IX2.5 is FALSE and closed when %IX2.5 has the state TRUE.

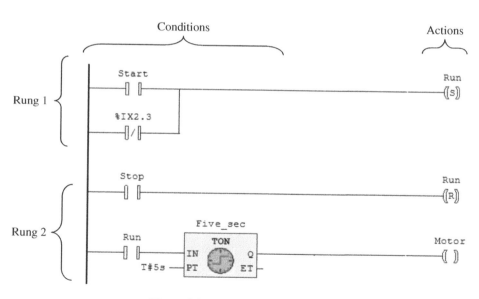

Figure 9.2   Example of code in LD

Normally open contact (NO)   Normally closed contact (NC)

Figure 9.3   Standard contact symbols

In other words: A sensor that is connected to the digital input that has this address will "go hot" through the contact when the sensor gives a logically high signal.

A normally closed contact functions just opposite of this; the contact is closed (conducts current) when the state of the sensor is FALSE, and the contact is open when sensor state is logically TRUE.

9.2.2 Coils and Actions

An *action* or *instruction* in LD can be various things. For example, they can perform an arithmetic calculation, jump to another place in the program code, or change the state of Boolean addresses.

This last event comes in under the group of Boolean instructions, and the graphic symbol that is used for this is called a *coil* (see Figure 9.4).

Coils are placed at the right of conditions, which are placed at the left in the code. As mentioned earlier, we can analyze the rungs by thinking how they conduct current and which contacts are on or off. The job of a coil is to transfer the result (the Boolean state) from a condition on the left side of the coil to the Boolean variable or address that is associated with the coil.

In the same way that contacts can be associated with Boolean input addresses, a coil can be associated with an address to a physical output where it is connected to actuators such as magnetic valves, lights, alarms, relays, and so on.

Symbols for Coils

The inverse coil functions exactly opposite to an ordinary coil: If the condition on the left side has the state TRUE, the variable associated with the inverse coil has the state FALSE.

Example 9.1   The First Program

Assume the following: A sensor gives a high signal when the fluid level in the tank reaches a certain level. The sensor is connected to an input with address %IX1.8. When the fluid level reaches the sensor, a pump should start so that the fluid is emptied out of the tank. The pump is connected to a relay output with the address %QX2.3. The program for this in LD can look like the one shown in Figure 9.5.

Figure 9.4   Standard coil symbols

Figure 9.5   A simple program

The open contact here constitutes the condition and the coil constitutes the action or instruction that is to be carried out when the condition is satisfied. We can read the program in this way:

- When the state of address %IX1.8 is TRUE, the state of %QX2.3 should also be TRUE. Therefore, when the sensor gives a logically high signal, the pump should operate (assuming that the pump in the electrical layout is connected so that it runs when the relay is closed).
- When the state of address %IX1.8 is FALSE, the state of %Q2.3 should also be FALSE. Therefore, when the sensor gives a logically low signal, the pump should not operate.

9.2.3 Graphical Elements: An Overview

Since the PLC program obvious is not a physical hookup of switches, but rather logical functions, there is no physical situation that limits the functions that are possible to be programmed. This means that different and more complex functions than those used in relay controls can be programmed in a PLC.

In the two previous chapters, we presented a series of standard functions and function blocks. All of the function blocks can be implemented in LD as well as several of the standard functions.

Some of the function blocks are so central in programming that the standard defines specific graphic symbols in LD for them. This applies to the bistable function blocks SR and RS and the edge-detection function blocks R_TRIG and F_TRIG:

- SR and RS are implemented in LD as a Set coil –(S)– and a Reset coil –(R)–.
- R_TRIG and F_TRIG are implemented in LD as –|P|– and –|N|– contacts that detect rising and falling edges, respectively.

All of the graphic LD elements defined in the standard are collected in Table 9.1.

9.3 Boolean Operations

The previous chapter presented an overview of all of the functions in the standard. In structured text, these are represented with their individual operators and special graphic symbols are used in FBD. One group of standard functions are the Boolean operations AND, OR, XOR, and NOT. In LD, such operations can be implemented by combining test elements (contacts).

9.3.1 AND/OR-Conditions

In many situations, there are more complex conditions that must be satisfied before an instruction is performed. AND-conditions and OR-conditions and combinations of these are very common. If one is clear about what logical conditions must be met for these events to take place, it is easy to implement them in a PLC program.

Table 9.1   Symbols that are used in LD

Designation		Symbol	Function
Test element	Normally open contact	┤├	The contact closes when the associated Boolean object becomes TRUE
	Normally closed contact	┤/├	The contact closes when the associated Boolean object becomes FALSE
	Flank-detecting contacts	┤P├	Rising edge: The contact is closed only in the scan (see Section 1.3.3) during which the associated Boolean object changes state from 0 to 1
		┤N├	Falling edge: The contact is closed in the scan where the associated Boolean object changes state from 1 to 0
Connections	Horizontal	──	To connect elements in series
	Vertical	│	To connect elements in parallel
Action element	Direct coil	─( )─	The associated Boolean object is set to the same state as the state of the left side of the coil
	Inverse coil	─(/)─	The associated Boolean object gets the inverse of the state of the left side of the coil
	On-coil	─(S)─	The associated Boolean object is set to TRUE when the state of the left side of the coil is TRUE
	Off-coil	─(R)─	The associated Boolean object is set to FALSE when the state of the left side of the coil is TRUE
	Conditional jump to another rung	→ Label	Enables jump to another named rung in the program (the POU) When a jump is activated: 1. The active rung is interrupted 2. The named rung is activated
	Return to call	< **RETURN** >	If a function or function block is programmed in LD, this is used to return to the POU that called up the function or block[a]

[a]RETURN is implicit at the end of the function or function block.

Example 9.2   AND-Condition

Figure 9.6   Implementation of AND-condition

We can read the program code earlier (Figure 9.6) thus:

> The pump will run if Sensor_A = TRUE and Sensor_B = FALSE and
> Switch = TRUE.

We can express it thus in logical form:

$$\text{Pump} = (\text{Sensor}\_A) \cdot \left(\overline{\text{Sensor}\_B}\right) \cdot (\text{Switch})$$

Example 9.3   OR-Condition

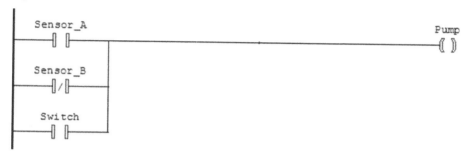

Figure 9.7   Implementation of an OR-condition

We can read the program (Figure 9.7) thus:

The pump will run if Sensor_A gives a high signal **OR** Sensor_B gives a *low* signal **OR**
Switch is switched on.

The program therefore implements the following functional expression:

$$\text{Pump} = (\text{Sensor}\_A) + \left(\overline{\text{Sensor}\_B}\right) + (\text{Switch})$$

Example 9.4   Exclusive OR

Now, it is obvious that any logical function can be implemented in a PLC where all possible
combinations of AND-conditions and OR-conditions can be utilized. For example, here,
Figure 9.8 shows how a 2-input Exclusive OR can be implemented.

Function table			Functional expression
A	**B**	**G**	$G = A \oplus B = \overline{A}B + A\overline{B}$
0	0	0	
0	1	1	
1	0	1	
1	1	0	

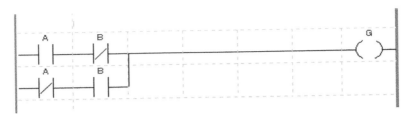

Figure 9.8   Implementation of an Exclusive OR

Of course, the logical expressions can become complicated. In general, one must be sure to include enough of the conditions that are necessary in order for the process to be controlled to behave as one wish. Many inexperienced programmers, however, have a tendency to use unnecessarily complex conditions. It can therefore be sensible to begin by using the techniques and methods for reducing the Boolean expressions, such as those introduced in Chapter 4.

9.3.2   Set/Reset Coils

A function that frequently comes up in an electrical facility is to start an electric motor with the help of a pulse switch (push button). Such a switch completes a control circuit, but only while the button is being held in, and then the current is interrupted when the button is released. This means that the signal from the pulse switch that is used as a condition for starting the motor is present only while the button is being held down. However, the motor should continue to run even though the signal from the push button disappears. How can we do that?

Electrically, this can be designed with the help of a contactor that will stay connected, after the control current turns it on, for as long as the operating current does not disappear. As soon as the operating current cuts off, the contactor will disconnect and can only be turned on again when the pulse switch is pressed in again. Here, we will look at ways to solve this problem in a PLC.

The value of the variables and addresses associated with the coil objects that we have used up till now will always be the direct result of the conditions that set them high or low. This means that if the result of the condition changes state, the variable associated with the coil object also changes state. Such programs are said to be purely combinatorial since they do not take into account any aspect of time such as *when* an event occurs, for instance.

Example 9.5

Let us assume that we have a pulse switch that is used to start a motor and another pulse switch that is used to stop the same motor. We want to make a kind of retention function that keeps the motor from stopping when we release the start button. Assume that both the start button and the stop button are both physically of the NO type. One possible solution is shown in Figure 9.9.

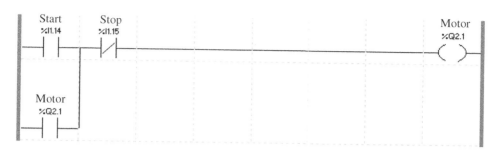

Figure 9.9   Possible implementation of a retention function

We have thus connected the start switch to address %I1.14 and associated this with a normally open contact. The stop switch is connected to the digital input %I1.15. Here, we use the symbol for a normally closed contact so that %I1.15 will be TRUE when the stop switch is *not* pressed. The condition for the motor to start is therefore that the start button is activated but the stop button is deactivated. When this condition is satisfied, this state of address %Q2.1 is set TRUE, which is something that again means that a relay in the PLC's output block is closed so that the motor receives operating voltage.

When the start button is released, the motor will continue to run because the output address %Q2.1 is associated to a contact in *parallel* with the start button. Thus, the condition continues to be satisfied and will be until the stop button is operated.

(Perhaps that was a rather detailed program explanation....)

This is only one example where retention functions are needed. We often have the requirement that the program stores an action when a certain combination of values or states is present. The standard therefore defines two special coil symbols that can be used for this purpose (i.e., to implement memory[2]). With these coils, a Boolean value can be set high (S) and held high until it is reset (R).

—(S)— Set coil—Sets the associated Boolean address (high state).

—(R)— Reset coil—Resets the associated Boolean address (low state).

These coils are otherwise used in the same way as other coils. A contact, or several contacts in combination, are used to structure conditions that must be satisfied for a Boolean quantity (a digital output, for instance) to be set high. After that, the output in question will remain high even though the condition that set it high is no longer present. Now, we can control the motor in Example 9.5 with the following short code (Figure 9.10).

Note that the sequence of the LD rungs can be significant for how the code functions. We will study this further in Section 9.4.2.

---

[2] Such coils are often called *Latched Coils*.

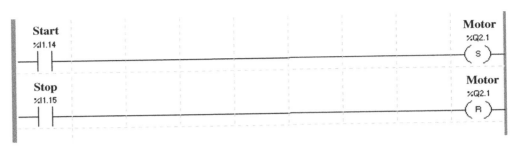

Figure 9.10   Implementation of a retention function with the use of Set and Reset

Example 9.6

A pump is to start when a switch is turned from the Off-position to the Run-position. The pump is stopped by pressing a special stop button. In order for the pump to be able to start again after the stop button is released, the start switch must first be turned to the Off-position before the pump can be started again by twisting the switch to Run. The following program implements this:

```
PROGRAM Rising
VAR
      Pump    AT %QX2.5      :BOOL;
      Run     AT %IX1.7      :BOOL;
      Stop    AT %IX1.8      :BOOL;
      RE1                    :R_TRIG;
      (*Here we declare an instance of the FB R_TRIG *)
END_VAR
```

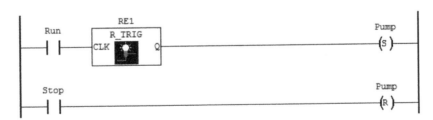

```
END PROGRAM
```

Figure 9.11   Use of the function block R_TRIG and the Set/Reset coils

Note the declaration: Use of function blocks, no matter what type, requires that *instances* of the block be declared together with the POU's variable. This was discussed extensively in Chapter 8. In this example, an instance of the standard function block R_TRIG is declared. The instance is here given the arbitrary name RE1. Legal names follow the general rules for identifiers (see Section 6.2.1).

Use of function blocks require the declaration of an instance for each and every one that is used. This applies even if the blocks are of the same type. A new instance must be declared for each use.

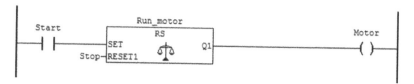

Figure 9.12   Use of a type SR/RS function block in LD

Suppose that we want to manage the Stop button in the example earlier in the same way as the Start button so that it is still possible to start the motor again by turning the Start switch, even if someone continues to hold down the Stop button. Then, we must still declare another instance of the R_TRIG block:

```
PROGRAM Rising2
VAR
    Pump    AT %QX2.5    :BOOL;
    Run     AT %IX1.7    :BOOL;
    Stop    AT %IX1.8    :BOOL;
    RE1                  :R_TRIG;
    RE2                  :R_TRIG;
END_VAR
```

Even though the standard defines S- and R-coils in LD, you can use the function blocks SR and RS instead of these coils or in addition to them. As we will see later in the chapter, there can be an advantage in using these function blocks since the LD code becomes easier to read.

For example, the code in Figure 9.10 can also be implemented as shown in Figure 9.12. Note that the block RS is *Reset dominant*, something that implies that it if both Start and Stop buttons are held in, the motor will stop.

9.3.3   Edge Detecting Contacts

We have seen that the special coils Set and Reset in LD are used as an alternative to the function blocks SR and RS to implement memory. Similarly, there is also defined an alternative to the function blocks R_TRIG and F_TRIG for edge detection. These are implemented like special contacts. (*Note*: not in CODESYS v2.3.x)

$$ \dashv P \vdash \text{ and } \dashv N \vdash $$

The contacts "close" and are held closed *only* during the program scan when the associated Boolean variable changes state. The type P contact detects a change in state from 0 to 1 (rising edge), while the N contact detects a transition from 1 to 0 (falling edge). In other words, the symbols can be used to set Boolean values TRUE/FALSE precisely when the condition is satisfied. An illustration of the operation of the flank contacts compared to an ordinary contact of the type NO is shown in Figure 9.13.

9.3.4 Example: Control of a Mixing Process

This process was presented in Section 4.5.2, but we repeat the description here.

We will, believe it or not, use a PLC to control the process (Figure 9.14).

The mixing process is to function as follows: Assume that the tank is empty at the starting time. When the start button (**Start**) is operated, magnetic valve **MV1** opens so that water flows into the tank.

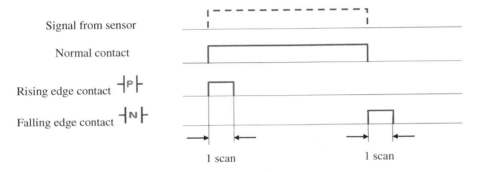

Figure 9.13   Operation of the flank-detecting contacts

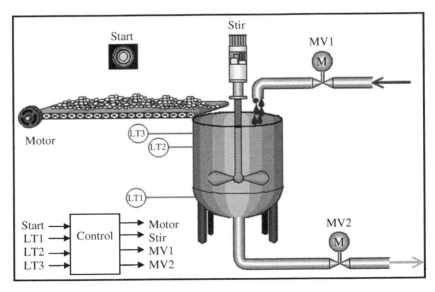

Figure 9.14   Mixing process

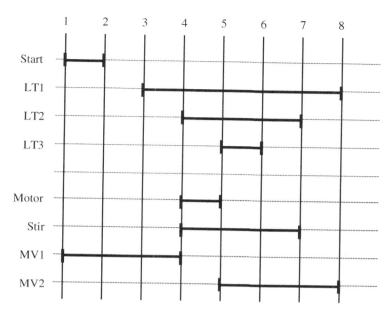

Figure 9.15   Sequence diagram for the mixing process

When the level in the tank reaches level transmitter **LT2**, the water supply is shut off and the **motor** for the conveyor belt starts at the same time that the agitator (**stir**) starts.

When the level comes up to transmitter **LT3**, the motor will stop and the magnetic valve **MV2** on the outlet is opened (the agitator will continue to run). When the level comes below **LT2**, the agitator is also stopped.

The sequence can now be started anew by activating the start button.

In Section 4.5.4, we drew up a sequence diagram for the mixing process. This is reproduced in Figure 9.15.

With such a diagram in hand, it is simple to set up function expressions for each of the outputs and write the program code in LD or another language.

The trick to getting a program code that is unambiguous, that is, where the function expressions do not conflict with one another, is to use memory (Set/Reset) and flank contacts. For example, we see that output MV1 will go logically high when the start button is pressed (Start becomes logical 1). In other words, we want to set output MV1 logically high when the Start signal changes state from 0 to 1. In LD code, this becomes:

The function expression for this code can be described thus:

$$\text{Set MV1} = \uparrow \text{Start}$$

The up arrow there symbolizes a positive flank. With this code, valve MV1 will stay open until we reset the signal. From the diagram, we see that this will happen when LT2 goes logically high:

$$\text{Reset MV1} = \uparrow \text{LT2}$$

The function expressions for setting and resetting the other outputs similarly become:

Set motor = ↑LT2	Reset motor = ↑LT3
Set stir = ↑LT2	Reset stir = ↓LT2
Set MV2 = ↑LT3	Reset MV2 = ↓LT1

A complete code in LD for the process, including declaration of variables is shown below

```
PROGRAM Mixing process
VAR
    Start   AT %IX1.0:
      BOOL;
    LT1   AT %IX1.1:
      BOOL;
    LT2   AT %IX1.2:
      BOOL;
    LT3   AT %IX1.3:
      BOOL;
    Motor AT %QX2.0:
      BOOL;
    Stir   AT %QX2.1:
      BOOL;
    MV1   AT %QX2.2:
      BOOL;
    MV2   AT %QX2.3:
      BOOL;
END_VAR
```

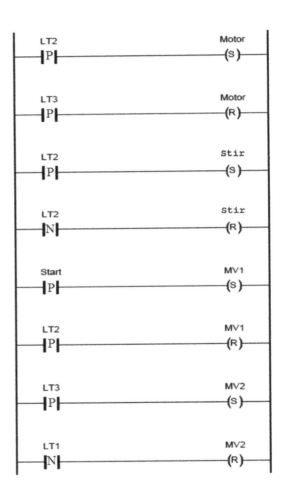

Use of edge detecting contacts in the program code is also significant for the duration of the state of the signal. Since the sequence in this example will start *when* the start button is activated, it is of no significance *how long* the operator holds the start button in. In order for the sequence for this process to start anew, the start button must be activated again so that the PLC registers a new positive flank.

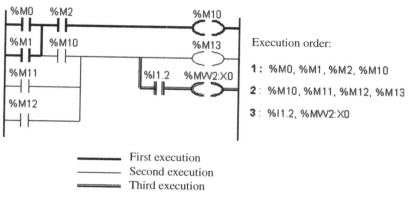

First execution
Second execution
Third execution

Figure 9.16   Evaluation order of a rung

9.4   Rules for Execution

A program written in LD will be executed rung by rung from top to bottom.

Each individual rung in the code is also evaluated from top to bottom, row by row, and in each row from left to right (see Figure 9.16). In accordance with these rules, the PLC will:

- Evaluate the logical state of each contact in accordance with the instantaneous values of variables or states to the inputs for the I/O modules.
- Update the Boolean objects associated with the coils.
- Go to another rung in the same program (jump or return).

9.4.1   One Output: Several Conditions

A typical mistake that many beginners in LD programming make, especially when they are trying to make a program without planning it through first, is to insert code rungs that are in conflict with each other. The problem often occurs as a result of *coils associated with the same address or variables used at several places in the code.* Here, we will study a simple example that illustrates such a conflict.

Suppose that we have two switches that change between being on and off each time a button is pressed. If at least one of them is turned on, a motor should start:

So, if one of the input %IX1.1 or %IX1.2 gets the state TRUE, the output %QX2.0 becomes TRUE and the motor will start. This looks so simple that it's impossible that it won't work, right? Actually, this rung will not function satisfactorily the way we have designed it here.

Why? Well, because we have a conflict between the rungs since we have used the same address (%QX2.0) on two coils in the program.

Splitting the conditions for control of the state of an output or variable in this way is a programming technique that should **never** be used, even if the program behaves as desired! What problems that can arise are not always easy to determine because it depends upon the logical expressions and the states of the variables that appear in the expression.

This is a result of the way the PLC scans (executes) the program: from left to right and from top to bottom. Furthermore, the physical outputs will not be updated until the entire program code has been executed (see Section 1.3.2).

Assume that switches 1 and 2 above the output point in the rung are off. Then the PLC will also set the output logically low. Let's look at two possible scenarios:

1. We turn on switch 1 so that address %IX1.1 gets the state TRUE.
   When the program is executed, the network is analyzed as follows:
   • %IX1.1 is TRUE therefore %QX2.0 becomes TRUE.
   • %IX1.2 is FALSE therefore %QX2.0 will be set FALSE.
   In other words: When the PLC updates the outputs, the output will remain low, even though the desired function was that the output should be set high when one or both of the inputs is high.
2. Now we turn on switch 2 so that address %I1.2 becomes TRUE. Then the following occurs:
   • %I1.1 is FALSE therefore %Q2.0 becomes FALSE.
   • %I1.2 is TRUE therefore %Q2.0 will be set TRUE.

We see that no matter whether switch 1 is off or on, the motor will react only to the state of switch 2. How can we fix a simple program that does the job satisfactorily?

Okay, we *collect the conditions* for control of the output.

9.4.2   The Importance of the Order of Execution

In Section 1.3.2, we learned how a PLC operates with respect to its basic working rules: Read input data, perform program code, and update outputs. Here, we will study an example to see what significance this has for the way our program codes work.

We can hope that then we will see the difference between the values and states of the PLC's physical inputs and outputs and the contents of the addresses or variables that are associated with those same inputs and outputs. This is an extremely important point that many (including instructors and teachers) can struggle to understand.

Two light switches (NO) are connected, each to a discrete input whose address is assigned the variables SW1 and SW2. The following code is implemented[3] in a PLC that is in Run mode:

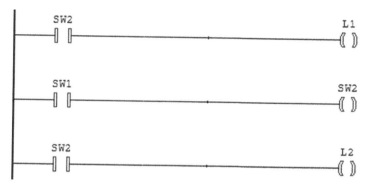

1 What do you think will happen to the lights when switch 1 is turned on and switch 2 is off?
  • Switch 2 is turned off. *Variable* SW2 will then have the state FALSE. So, there is no condition satisfied for the state of variable L1 to become TRUE.
  • Switch 1 is turned on. Therefore, the state of *variable* SW2 is changed to TRUE (because of rung number two).
  • Since the state of SW2 now is TRUE, the state of L2 will also become TRUE.
  Therefore, Light no. 2 will light but not Light no. 1.
2 What do you think will happen to the lights when switch 2 is turned on and switch 1 is off?
  • Switch 2 is turned on, and the variable SW2 will have the state TRUE. Therefore, the condition for setting variable L1 to TRUE is satisfied.
  • Switch 1 is turned off so that the state of the variable SW2 is changed to FALSE and the state of L2 will be set to FALSE.
  Therefore, Light no. 1will light but not Light no. 2.

9.4.3   Labels and Jumps

If desired, *labels* can be used to identify rungs in the code. These are used when you need to jump from one rung to another in the program. Labels are located up on the left corner of the rung, right next to the power rail.

With jumps, the symbol →**Label** is used, where Label is an arbitrary name (so long as it follows the rule for valid identifiers).

A jump can be unconditional or conditional. In unconditional jumps, the jump is directly connected to the rail on the left side, possibly to a contact where you write TRUE instead of the variable name.

In conditional hops, you program a condition as an argument. This condition can be a Boolean variable or a combination of Boolean variables and comparisons.

Each label can be used only once within the same POU. If you want to return after the rung you jumped to have been performed, you can insert ←RETURN→ at the right of the rung.

---

[3]*Note*: It is not certain that the compiler will permit assignment of a variable that is associated with an input address, as is done in the second line of code. CODESYS does not permit it.

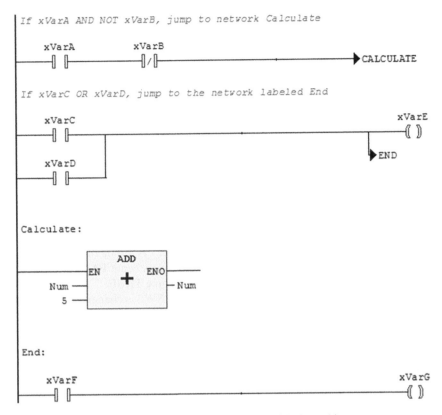

Figure 9.17   Example of commenting, labels, and jumps

It is also possible to associate comments to every individual rung.[4]

An example of use of labels and comments is shown in Figure 9.17. Here, rung 3 has received the label "calculate" and rung 4 the label "end." A jump has been placed in both the first and the second rungs, in addition to comments.

If the condition in the first rung is satisfied, rung 3 is called. Rung 2 is jumped over and is never executed.

If the condition in rung 1 is not satisfied, rung 2 is performed as usual. If either variable xVarC or xVarD is TRUE, xVarE is set TRUE, and in addition, the program jumps to rung 4. In this case, rung 3 is not executed.

9.5   Use of Standard Functions in LD

In the program example earlier, the function ADD is used (here to increment the content in the integer variable Num by 5 each time the rung is executed).

---

[4] If you cannot enter comments in CODESYS, you can activate this feature on the menu under "Tools→Options→FBD, LD, and IL editor."

So even though LD is a language that originally was designed for programming logical (Boolean) conditions for control of discrete outputs, it is fully capable of writing program algorithms that involve other data types.

For example, there is often a need to compare values of an analog signal with a particular value in order to perform actions based upon the result of the comparison. An example of this is to turn off a heating element when a temperature reaches a desired value. In order to perform this and other tests in LD, one can use functions that are defined in the standard.

The concepts EN and ENO were introduced in Section 7.13. EN is an acronym for Enable and is an extra input argument in the standard's defined functions and function blocks. When the state of this input is TRUE, the function is performed. It is this EN input that makes it possible to integrate functions in LD (Figure 9.18).

Even though functions can be integrated into the LD code, there are other (and probably better) ways to solve problems that require use of arithmetic functions, functions for comparison, text-strings, etc. It is a matter of utilizing the strength that lies in the seamless interaction among POUs. If there is a requirement to perform a number of calculations, these can be written in a separate POU that is programmed in Structured Text.

There are several ways to integrate functions in LD. Some manufacturers have chosen to use graphic blocks with the same symbols as function block diagram (FBD). Execution of these blocks is then controlled by means of a conditional activation of the EN input. Another possible implementation is by means of a combination of graphic blocks and *text-based* blocks where it is possible to write the code in Structured Text. Both variants are illustrated in Figures 9.19 and 9.20.

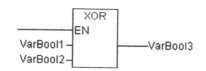

Figure 9.18   A function with EN input

Figure 9.19   Use of EN blocks with FBD symbol

Figure 9.20   Integration of functions by use of a text-based block

9.6 Development and Use of FBs in LD

Using FBs in LD is simple and is done in the same way no matter what type of function block is involved. An instance of the block must be declared in the declaration field in the POU. This is usually quickly accomplished in most development tools or takes place automatically when the block is added to the code. It is not always necessary to assign fixed connections to all inputs and outputs of the function block since FB inputs and outputs can be addressed indirectly.

Example 9.7   Motor Control

Let us use a timer in the example of motor control that was shown in Figure 9.10. Assume that the control is to satisfy the following problem: We start and stop the motor with pulse switches, and we want to have 5 seconds delay before the motor is switched on. One possible implementation of the program is shown in Figure 9.21.

```
PROGRAM MotorControl
VAR
    Start       AT %IX0.0     :BOOL;
    Stop        AT %IX0.1     :BOOL;
    Motor       AT %QX0.0     :BOOL;
    Run                       :BOOL;
    Five_sec                  :TON;
END_VAR
```

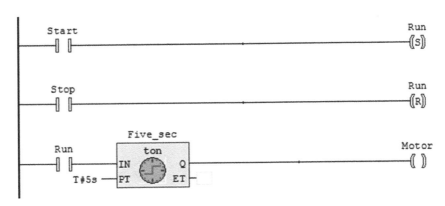

Figure 9.21   Program example with use of timer

The timer can be used for many purposes. In Figure 9.22 in the following text, you will see how you can make your own function block that generates a pulse train, where the user determines the duration of the high and low periods.[5]

---

[5] In CODESYS, you will find an FB already prepared for this in the accompanying library Util.Lib.

Example 9.8 Function Block that Generates a Pulse Train

Since this is a function block, we must declare the different classes of variable. Input and output variables will constitute "connections" when the block is used in another POU. Any internal variables are used to implement the block's function and operation and will not be visible to anyone using the function block later. Also, notice the following two things:

- The two input variables of the type TIME below are both given an initial value of 1 second. When the block is used, it will function (with the output 1 second on and 1 second off) even though the user has not stated any time for these inputs.
- The object reference of the timer outputs (TimerName.Q), which is a Boolean variable, is associated with contact symbols.

```
FUNCTION_BLOCK        Pulse
VAR_INPUT
    StartPulseTrain  :BOOL;
    TimeOn           :TIME      := t#1s;
    TimeOff          :TIME      := t#1s;
END_VAR
VAR_OUTPUT
    PulseTrain       :BOOL;
END_VAR
VAR
    Timer1           :TON;
    Timer2           :TON;
END_VAR
```

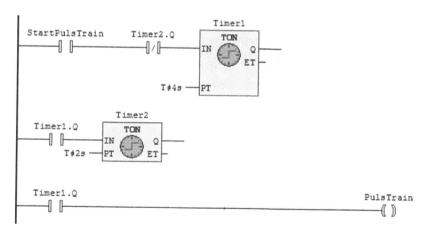

Figure 9.22 Self-developed FB

Finally, let us see how we can put our new function block to work.

Example 9.9   Using Our Own Function Block

Assume that we want to set an alarm when 30 items have passed a photocell on a conveyor belt. The alarm is a light that is to blink 2 seconds on and 1 second off. When a Reset button is activated, the alarm and the counter are set to zero. One possible program code that implements this could be as follows:

```
PROGRAM ItemCounting
VAR
      Photocell        AT %IX1.0    :BOOL;
      Reset            AT %IX1.1    :BOOL;
      Band             AT %QX2.0    :BOOL;
      Alarm            AT %QX2.1    :BOOL;
      Counter          :CTU;
      Blinker          :Pulse;
END_VAR
```

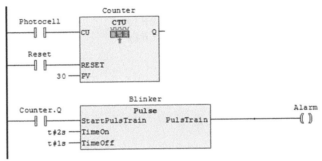

```
END_PROGRAM
```

Note the declaration of "Blinker." As soon as you have programmed an FB, it will be available for use in another POU. You can, as with the function blocks of the standard, declare as many instances as you want of one and the same FB, as long as each instance has a unique name. Here, I have only one instance of our new FB "Pulse," and I have chosen to call it "Blinker."

The graphic design of the block is generated automatically, and the number of inputs and outputs is a direct result of the variables that we have declared under VAR_INPUT and VAR_OUTPUT in the declaration of the FB.

9.7   Structured Programming in LD

In Chapter 4, we discussed sequential processes and various methods for structuring problems. If a process is sequential or mainly combinatoric, this can have significance for the selection of programming languages. Even though sequential control is perhaps easiest to program in sequential function chart (SFC), there is no obstacle to the use of LD, FBD, or even ST. Since LD is the language that has traditionally been used most often, it is very common to use this language for specifically sequential systems as well.

In Section 9.3.4, we studied an example of a mixing process. This process had a sequential nature, but we solved it in LD in a simple way by diligent use of flank contacts and Set and Reset coils. The sequence diagram that we already have prepared will naturally be helpful in the example.

It can be a challenge in sequential controls, particularly when the complexity and scope become larger, in that conflicts can arise that are associated with conditions that are ambiguous. This means that there can occur cases of the same condition that at times in the sequence cause a different event than that which was caused at a different time in the sequence. In other words, it can be necessary to take into account what phase of the sequence we find ourselves in. As we shall see, this is not significant if the program code is implemented with SFC. The same philosophy that lies behind SFC can be used in constructing program codes in one of the standard's other languages.

The technique is to use a Boolean variable (a flag) or a memory (bistable flip-flop) of the type RS for each of the states in the sequential process. When the conditions for the program to go from one state to the next are satisfied, the previous state is reset simultaneously.

After the code for activating and deactivating states has been written, the state variables (or outputs from RS flip-flops if they have been used for states) are used as conditions to control actions and instructions that are to be performed.

In order to demonstrate the method, we will again use the mixing process that we previously studied in Section 9.3.4. We drew a flowchart for this process in Section 4.5.2. There, we used ordinary language to describe the states. If we now are to write a code based on the flowchart, we must use identifiers that are permitted and that will be accepted by the software. Examples of such identifiers can be Fill, Stir, Warm_up, and so on. The same is true of transitional conditions that also can be specified more concretely. It is recommended that these be written in pseudocode or as logical expressions.

In order to make the transition to code simpler, it is therefore advisable to design the flowchart in an implementation-friendly language, while at the same time trying to use state names that describe what is to happen in the states in question. Figure 9.23 shows a more implementation-friendly flowchart.

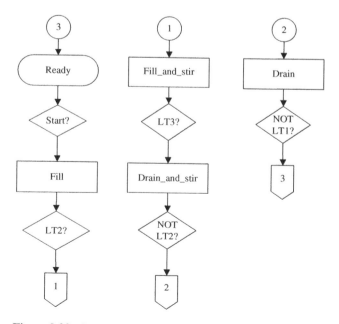

Figure 9.23   Program-friendly flowchart for the mixing process

Looking at the flowchart, we can easily identify states[6] in the process as the rectangular blocks in the flowchart, in addition to the initial state "Ready."

We start by declaring all states and the other variables. If this had been a physical process, we would naturally have associated addresses to the I/O variables.

```
VAR
  Ready, Fill, Fill_and_Stir, Drain_and_Stir, Drain    : BOOL;
  Start, LT1, LT2, LT3, MV1, MV2, Motor, Stirrer       : BOOL;
  RE1, RE2, RE3   : R_TRIG;
  FE1, FE2        : F_TRIG;
END_VAR
```

The program code for activation and deactivation of the states of the process is shown in Figure 9.24. (The code is written in CODESYS v2.3.x, which does not have flank contacts in the library. That is the reason for using the function blocks R_Trig and F_Trig.)

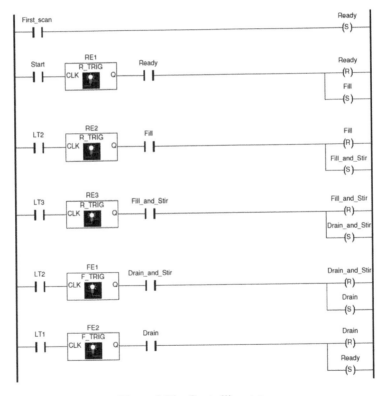

Figure 9.24   Controlling states

---

[6] The word "states" is actually somewhat misleading. In process engineering, a state is a phase in the sequence such as "Fill," "Stir," "Warm," and so on. In developing controls, it is often insufficient to define states only on the basis of the main phases in the sequence. It is often more practical to introduce more states in order to simplify the work of the program code.

In the code, we see that the flags for states are set and reset successively downward. In order for the code to be unambiguous, the same flags are also used for a portion of the conditions for activating and deactivating the states. For example, the state "Fill" is activated only when the previous state (Ready) is active.

When starting the program, it is necessary to get the program to activate the state Ready. This can be solved by giving Ready the initial value TRUE. Alternatively, we can do as we have done here, namely, use a special system flag that is available in all (?) PLCs. Individual manufacturers have defined a function for this, but others have made the flag accessible via a fixed system address. A common designation for this flag is *First Scan* because the flag has the state TRUE only during the course of the first scan.

If you do not have access to such a flag, you can straight away declare a Boolean object that you initially set to TRUE. Right at the end of the program code, you set the object to FALSE in this way:

When the code for activation and deactivation of the states is written, the code for control of outputs is built up by the use of state flags as conditions (Figure 9.25):

Figure 9.25 Program code based on the state flags

The sequence in this example was simple and had few states. Use of this methodology in this example also resulted in more code than we ended up with in Section 9.3.4. Nevertheless, this method of proceeding is absolutely preferable, particularly for sequential processes. Not only does a methodical approach make it simpler to develop the code, there is a major benefit in code that is guaranteed to be unambiguous and, one hopes, free of errors if you master this technique.

A better alternative to using coils of the Set and Reset type is to use flip-flops. This does not result in less coding, but the clarity of the code improves considerably.[7]

As always, it is wise to be consistent during programming. In the following examples, I have used only Reset-dominant memories. The conditions for changing state are implemented on Set inputs. The output of the RS block for the next state is always used on Reset inputs. In this way, the current state is deactivated at the same instant that the next state is activated.

9.7.1 Flowchart versus RS-Based LD Code

In order to clarify the transition from the flowchart to an LD code that is structured around RS flip-flops, we can study a section of the flowchart in Figure 9.23. Here, we see the RS flip-flop that represents the state **Fill** along with the conditions for Set and Reset of the state. The rules for coding of a state are:

- Previous states, together with the transition conditions, constitute the conditions for Set inputs to the RS flip-flop. If there are several previous states, we get conditions in parallel at the Set input.
- The next state, and only that, constitutes the conditions for Reset of the state. If there are several next states, we get conditions in parallel at the Reset input (Figure 9.26).

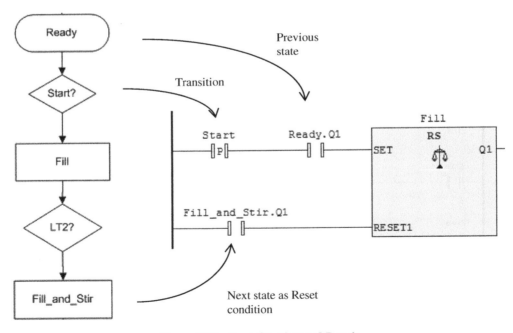

Figure 9.26 From flowchart to LD code

---

[7] Thanks to Assistant Professor Tormod Drengstig at the University of Stavanger ☺.

Example 9.10   Mixing Process, Continued

Figure 9.27 below shows an alternative code to the code in Figure 9.24. We see that the clarity of the state structure is improved. Also, notice the declaration and the use of the Boolean variable First_scan. (The variable is set FALSE at the end of the code.)

This code was developed with CODESYS v3.4, which *does have* flank contacts (-|P|- and -|N|-).

```
Program MixingProcess
Var
  First_scan  :BOOL       :=TRUE;
  Ready, Full, Fill_and_stir, Drain_and_Stir, Drain   :RS;
  Start, LT1, LT2, LT3, Motor, Stirrer, MV1, MV2      :BOOL;
END_VAR
```

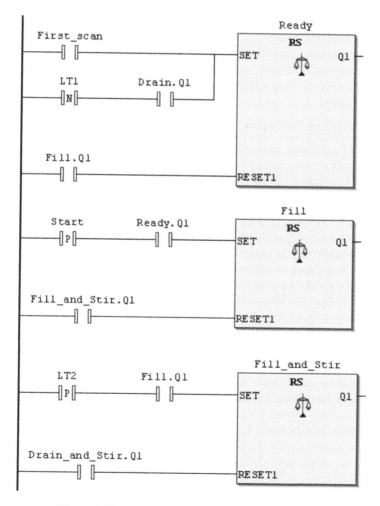

Figure 9.27   Use of memories in state-based LD code

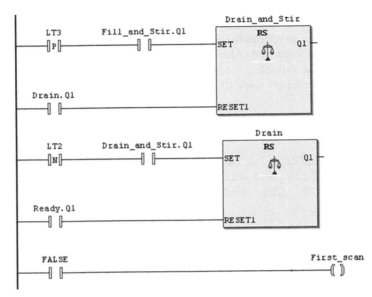

Figure 9.27 (Continued)

Example 9.11   Washing Operation

In Example 4.19, we drew a flowchart for a washing operation on a juice tank at a bottling plant. The flowchart was partially laid out with the idea of implementation by having the states be given permissible names and the conditions being written in syntax that was almost code.

The code for this washing operation will need to contain function blocks for counting and timing, in addition to a comparator for testing values of the temperature.

If this had been an actual process, it would have been necessary to be able to shut off the washing operation whenever desired.

Value declaration and code, written in CODESYS, are shown in Figure 9.28. (I have chosen to include addresses for the input and output signals in the I/O-list as one would have to do if the program were to be implemented in a physical PLC.)

```
PROGRAM Washing_Operation
VAR

  (*Declares the states: *)
  Ready, Filling, Heating, Stirring, Draining    : RS;

  (*Inputs and outputs: *)
  Start               AT %IX2.0        : BOOL;
  Tank_full           AT %IX2.1        : BOOL;
  Tank_empty          AT %IX2.2        : BOOL;
  Temperature         AT %IW0          : WORD;
  Fill_valve          AT %QX0.0        : BOOL;
```

```
Drain_valve       AT %QX0.1       : BOOL;
Heater            AT %QX0.2       : BOOL;
Stirrer           AT %QX0.3       : BOOL;

(*Other objects: *)
First_scan        : BOOL          := TRUE;
Five_min          : TON;          // Timer in TON-mode
Three_times       : CTU;          //Counter
END_VAR
```

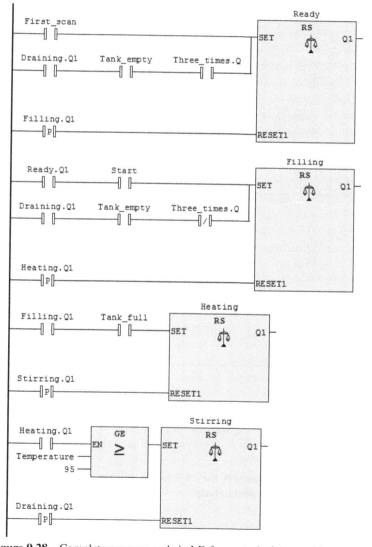

Figure 9.28 Complete program code in LD for control of the washing process

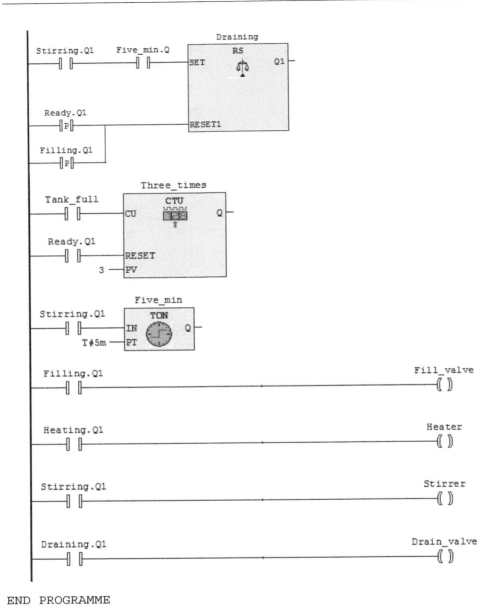

END PROGRAMME

Figure 9.28   (Continued)

Note the use of rising edge contacts for all Reset conditions. The reason for this will be discussed in connection with the next example.

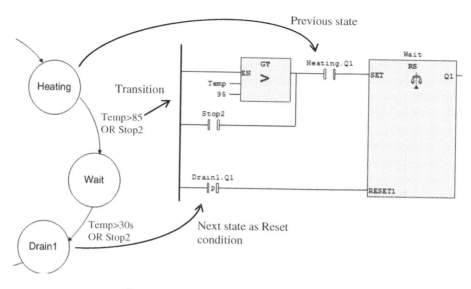

Figure 9.29   From state diagram to LD code

9.7.2   State Diagrams versus RS-Based LD Code

In order to clarify the transition from a state diagram to an LD code, we will study a section of the flowchart from the Batch example in Section 4.6.3. See Figure 9.29. Here, we see the RS flip-flop that represents the state **Wait** with the conditions for Set and Reset of the state. The methodology is the same as the one we learned in the previous section.

   The only difference relative to the flowchart is that here the states are represented by circles, and the transitions are written in pseudocode next to the arrows.

Example 9.12   Batch Process from Section 4.6.3

A complete code for this process is shown later. Note how the timer and counter are activated by the states and how the output from the timer and counter are used as contacts as a part of the conditions (Figure 9.30).

```
VAR
    First_scan  :BOOL  :=TRUE;
    Start, S1, S2, S3, Stop1, Stop2      :BOOL;
    Stirrer, Heater, ValveA, ValveB, ValveC  :BOOL;
    Ready, Fill_A, Fill_B, Heating, Wait, Drain1, Drain2,    :RS;
    Temp         :REAL;
    Counter      :CTU
    Wait_30s     :TON;
END_VAR
```

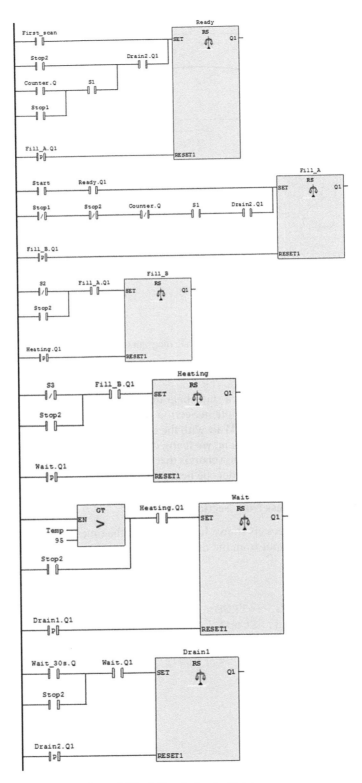

Figure 9.30 LD code for the Batch process

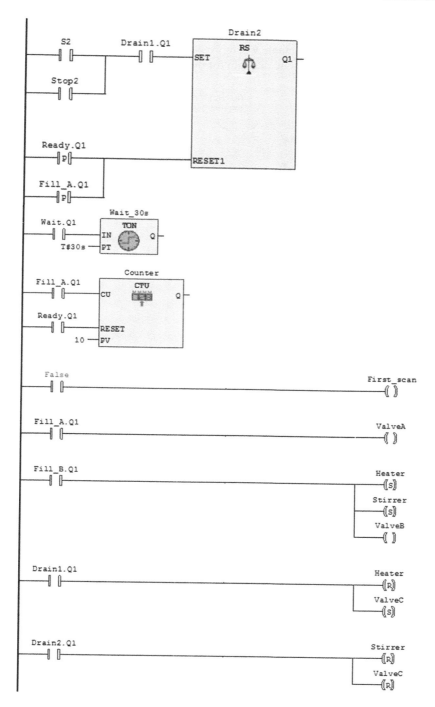

Figure 9.30   (Continued)

Example 9.13   Level Process

In Section 4.6.4, we studied an example where we wanted to control the water level in a tank with the help of two pumps. The state diagram for the process is reproduced here:

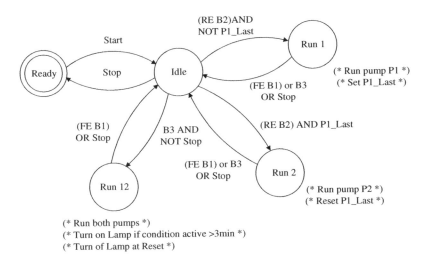

(* Run both pumps *)
(* Turn on Lamp if condition active >3min *)
(* Turn of Lamp at Reset *)

In the diagram, we see that there is one state that is central, namely, the Idle state.

The program will return to this state from all other states. This means that the RS block for the Idle state will have many conditions on the Set input.

This happens also at another moment in this example. If we do not use positive flank contacts (-|P|-) in the Reset conditions, we will get a problem related to setting and resetting the states. This happens particularly in this example because we have many states that returns back to the same previous state.

Without using positive flank contacts we will not be able to set the state Run1 since the Idle state is reset by Run1 at the same time that Run1 is reset by Idle....

Even though it may not always be necessary, it is recommended that you get in the habit of using flanks to reset conditions so that you are certain to avoid problems (Figure 9.31).

```
PROGRAM LevelProcess
VAR
    Ready, Idle, RunP1, RunP2, RunP12    :RS;
    B1, B2, B3, P1, P2, Start_stop, Reset, Light    :BOOL;
    First_scan, P1_Last :BOOL;
    Gone_3m :TON;
END_VAR
```

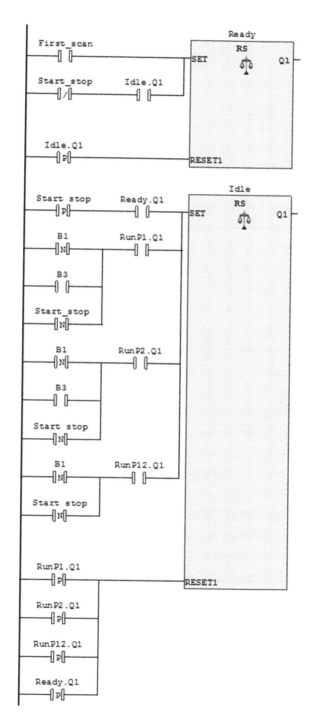

Figure 9.31   LD code for the level process

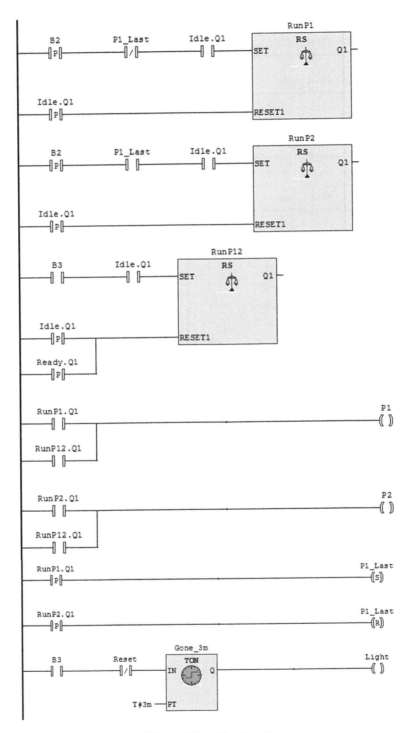

Figure 9.31   (Continued)

9.8 Summary

In this chapter, we have discussed all the standard symbols in LD and also have seen how the most frequently used function blocks are applied in this language. Even though all the examples we have reviewed have been implemented in CODESYS, I would like to believe that the equivalence with other software is generally great enough so that you will be able to implement the codes in other tools without any major problems.

Particularly the methodology for structured programming used here is applicable anywhere. The technique of splitting the desired behavior of a process up into parts and illustrating this with the help of a flowchart or state diagram is very much worthwhile learning. Not only does it save time, it is also easier than starting to program without a graphical representation, even for an experienced programmer. By spending a little time on illustrating the program flow, the coding itself becomes much easier, and the time spent on debugging is reduced considerably. The method is also universal and applicable almost everywhere.

We have not seen how we solve big programming challenges. Sometimes, it can be reasonable to split up the problem into several parts in order to avoid a large program. If it is a big process (with respect to complexity) that is to be controlled, it may be wise to use macro-steps. For example, there we will have an overall sequence and several subsequences, one for each macro-step. What you can do is to start by programming the macro-sequence. This can be done in a similar way as the examples earlier, except that the output from the state must then activate other POUs that contain code for the subsequences.

All modern tools have the capability of implementing such a structural breakdown.

Finally, I would like to present a small cookbook for construction of structured programs in LD. Perhaps it is not applicable to all possible problems, but I do believe that it can be followed in most cases. (Note that Steps 3–6 cannot be done successively, but must rather be carried out separately as you insert the RS flip-flops.)

1. Think the process through step-by-step and identify possible states. This job is usually simpler and faster if the process has a marked sequential structure. Most often, the states will be based on physical events that take place, but sometimes it can be wise to introduce states in order for the coding technique to be simpler. Are there branches in the sequence? An alternative branch exists if there are several possible routes to proceed from the state. Each transition should have its own unique condition, and these must be *mutually exclusive*.
2. Use simple descriptions of the states and preferably use reasonable logical names that you know will be accepted by the programming tool. The more detailed you make this job, the easier it will be to write the code later. The same applies to conditions to activate the states. You can use words, pseudocode, or actual ST code. Then draw a state diagram (or a flowchart) (see Sections 4.5 and 4.6). Remember to define a Ready state that is activated when the system starts.
3. Translate the diagram or chart to LD code. Use reset-dominant memory (RS flip-flops) for each of the states. The Ready state is activated by using a *First-scan* flag.
4. Then program the conditions to activate (set) the various states. These conditions should always contain the output address from the previous state in series with other conditions. This is an absolute rule because it takes care of removing possible conflicts where several states could otherwise be set by similar conditions.
5. Program the conditions to deactivate the states. These conditions will always consist of the address of the next state(s). *Use positive flank contacts.*

6. Program any timers and counters. These can profitably be placed after the code for program-
    ming the states. As an input to these timers and counters, you use the RS output addresses
    for the states that are time dependent or where counting is to take place. Use the output
    addresses from timers and counters together with other conditions for activating states.
7. Finally, you program the actions. Often these are objects associated with physical output
    addresses in the PLC. Again, you use the outputs from the states flip-flops as conditions.
    Make a rung for each action or output.

9.9   Test Problems

Problem 9.1
Write down the Boolean expressions for the LD program codes shown below.

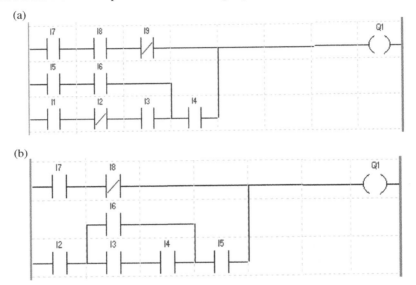

Problem 9.2
The figure below shows a sketch of a fluid tank that contains lubricating oil. As the oil is used,
the level will naturally fall. When it falls below the low-level sensor, a pump will start. The
pump should run until the high level sensor is reached. Then the pump stops. This should be
repeated to "infinity." Make a program in LD.

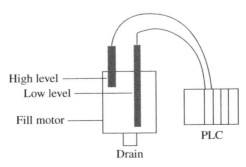

Problem 9.3   Push Button
You are to use a spring-loaded push button to start a fan when the button is pushed for the first time. You are to push the button once again to stop the fan. Write the program code in LD that solves the problem. Use:

%IX1.0	Start_stop (push button)
%QX2.0	Fan

Problem 9.4   Filling Station
Write a program in LD for the filling station that was described in Problem 4.9. You can make the program directly from the description or you can start with the sequence diagram if you drew one for that problem.

Problem 9.5   Filling Station: State-Based LD Code
Make a new code for the same process, but this time start with a flowchart for the process. The code should be state based, that is, built up with sequential code where you use RS flip-flops.

Problem 9.6   Product Sorting
Write a program in LD for the product-sorting facility from Problem 4.9. The code should be based on the flowchart you made in that problem.

Problem 9.7   Apple Packing
Write a program in LD for the apple-packing facility from the example in Section 4.6.4. The code should be based on the state diagram in Figure 4.29.

Problem 9.8   Motor Operation
Write a LD code for controlling the motors in Problem 4.10. The code should be based on the state diagram you made in that problem. The program should include all declarations.

Problem 9.9
We are going to design a control for a garage door in LD. The garage door should function as follows:

- There is a single button (**Button**) inside the garage and a single button on a remote control. Both buttons are connected to the same control unit.
- When one of the buttons is pressed, the door should move up (**D_up**) or down (**D_down**), depending upon whether it is open or closed or which operation it is in the course of performing.
- If one of the buttons is pressed while the door is in motion, the door should stop. Another press on the button should make the door begin to move in the opposite direction.
- Limit switches (**L_up** and **L_down**) should be used to stop the door when fully up fully down.
- A photocell (**Photo**) is installed so that it looks across the bottom of the door opening. If the beam is broken while the door is in motion and closing, the door should stop and then move up.
- A garage light (**Light**) should turn on when the door operates and stay on for 5 minutes after the door has opened or closed
  - (a) Draw a *state diagram or flowchart* from the description earlier. Try to use the fewest possible states....
  - (b) Write a program in LD based on the state diagram. The states should be programmed using RS blocks.

10

Function Block Diagram (FBD)

Chapter Contents

- Program structure and concepts
- Order of execution:
  Rules for execution, feedback. Labels and jumps. Loops
- Declaration and use of functions and function blocks
- Integer division
- Sequential programming with FBD

10.1 Introduction

The second of the graphic languages that are defined in IEC 61131-3 is Function Block Diagram (FBD) (Figure 10.1). The definitions and the graphic symbols are in conformity with the IEC 60617-12[1] standard.

As we said, the FBD language is graphic and follows the same guidelines that are specified for LD with respect to graphics and structure. We reviewed all of the functions and function blocks (FBs) that are defined in the standard in Chapters 7 and 8. They were shown there with their graphic symbols. For some of the blocks and functions, we also showed examples of their use in the graphic languages LD and FBD.

All of the defined blocks, as well as the manufacturers' blocks and user-defined blocks, can be used in FBD. That is precisely the concept of this language: It is based on connections among functions and FBs. Since this includes use of standard logical functions such as AND, OR, NOT, and so on in a graphic form, many people who have some knowledge of digital electronics finds that FBD is an easy language to use.

---

[1] Graphical symbols for diagrams—Part 12: Binary Logic Elements.

Programmable Logic Controllers: A Practical Approach to IEC 61131-3 Using CODESYS, First Edition. Dag H. Hanssen.
© 2015 John Wiley & Sons, Ltd. Published 2015 by John Wiley & Sons, Ltd.

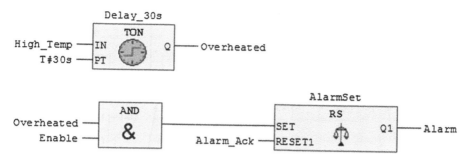

Figure 10.1 Example of code in FBD

10.2 Program Structure

The structure of FBDs is consistent with the structure of LDs with respect to graphic symbols, signal flow, order of execution, and structuring of the code. It is therefore recommended that the reader review the description of LD in Chapter 9 before this chapter on FBD.

LD code is bounded by a power rail on both sides, where the rail on the left has the state TRUE (logical high). This is related to the graphic element contacts, which open and close depending upon the state of the Boolean algebra and in this way provide connections to the power rail on the left side. Such contacts are not used in FBD, and neither are rails. Instead, variables are used directly as input arguments to the functions and FBs. You can also use literals on input connections. An example is shown in Figure 10.2.

Like the rungs in LD, FBD code is also divided into *networks*, placed vertically above one another. Each individual network contains code such as:

• A logical or arithmetic expression
• Calls of other POUs (programs or functions or FBs)
• Jumps or return conditions

Together, the networks create a program that is executed sequentially by the Programmable Logic Controller (PLC).

Since it is not necessary to connect all elements or subnetworks to the left or the right side in the editor, a program in FBD can consist of many networks with separate subnetworks.

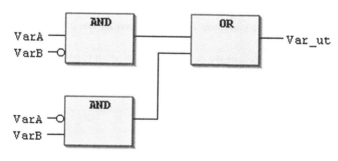

Figure 10.2 Implementation of an XOR with AND and OR

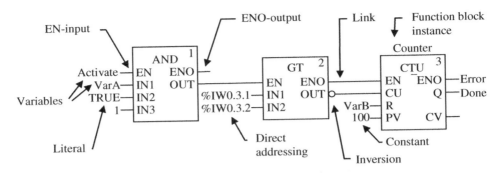

Figure 10.3 Summary of concepts

10.2.1 Concepts

Here, we are actually not presenting anything new. The concepts used here have all been discussed and explained previously, but a little repetition probably does no harm (see Figure 10.3).

EN is an abbreviation for Enable and is an input that activates or deactivates the processing of a function or FB. ENO is set logically high when the instructions in the block are carried out by the program. ENO will thus be 0 when EN is 0. (Note that even when EN and ENO are implemented, there is no compulsion to use them. You can read more about this subject, among others, in Section 7.13 or in Section 8.8.2.)

Inversion can be used on all Boolean inputs and outputs.

The connection called *link* in the figure below is nothing other than a connecting line, which, graphically and programmatically, connects all the functions and all the FBs. Note that the standard does not allow pairing of outputs from FBs. If such connections are needed, they must take place via graphic functions such as AND or OR.

10.3 Execution Order and Loops

The standard does not deal with how the processor handles the use of recursive references, that is, where the output from one block is used as an input to a block placed earlier in the program. This depends upon the implementation. It can therefore be wise to check the manual for what execution priority is provided in the tool that you are using. Nevertheless, it is reasonable to assume that the networks are executed from left to right and top to bottom.

The standard defines two different ways to implement such feedback connections:

- Either explicitly by means of a physical connection from the output to an input:

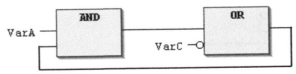

- Or implicitly by means of using the output objects or variables as inputs to other elements. (FB outputs can be used directly, e.g., TON.Q.)

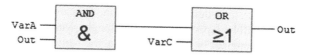

In order for the execution order to be unambiguous, not all manufacturers permit the *explicit* method of creating loops.

10.3.1   Labels and Jumps

As is the case in LD, any of the networks can be associated with a label for use in jumps. (See Section 9.4.3.)

An example of a jump with return is shown in Figure 10.4. The example also shows a network number on the left side of the networks—this is a numbering that is generated automatically in CODESYS. (This numbering cannot be influenced or referred to by the user.) The program functions so that if the condition in network 1 is satisfied so that the jump to **Fill** is activated, network 2 will never be executed.

Example 10.1   Jump and Return in FBD

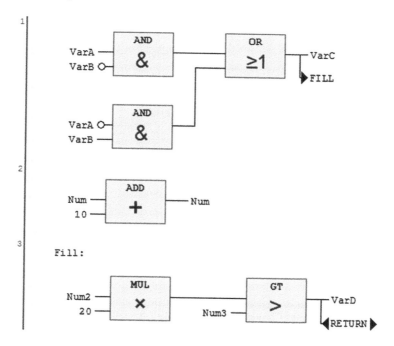

Figure 10.4   Example of jump to a label (Fill) with return

10.4   User-Defined Functions and FBs

As we have seen previously, you can program your own functions and FBs. Since this is a graphic language, we must base the code on using the existing functions and FBs.[2]

We have also seen that when user-defined functions and FBs are used in a graphic language such as LD and FBD, they will be represented by a rectangle, where the name of the function or FB appears within the rectangle. For FBs, in addition, the name of the declared instance of the FB appears above the rectangle.

Which (and how many) connection points are available on the input side and output side is a direct result of which (and how many) input and output variables were defined in the structure of the code for the function or FB.

Example 10.2 shows the code for a user-defined *function* and a program code where the function is called up; both parts developed in FBD. As we studied in Chapter 7, a *data type* is always given when a function is declared. This is because the name of the function acts as a variable and the response or result from a function call is returned to this name.

In this example, the arithmetic sign of an integer is being tested. If the number is negative, the inverted value of the number is transferred to the function name. If the number is positive, the number is returned. In other words, the function returns the absolute value of the number.[3]

Example 10.2   User-Defined Function

```
FUNCTION Absolute   :INT
VAR_INPUT
   Num     :INT;
END_VAR
```

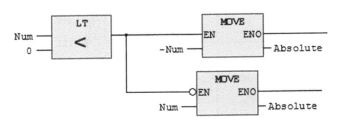

```
END_FUNCTION

PROGRAM Call_Func
VAR
   Value, Abs_value : INT;
END_VAR
(* In CODESYS the function appears like this: *)
```

---

[2] We can therefore use the designations "derived functions" and "derived function blocks."
[3] Naturally, there is already an existing function for this in the standard. It is called ABS and handles all numeric types (ANY_NUM).

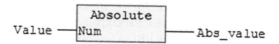

```
END_PROGRAM
```

In order to clarify what determines the appearance of a function or FB in the graphic language, we will look at an example where only the declaration of an FB is included. (*Note*: See also Section 8.7.)

Example 10.3   User-Defined Function Block

```
FUNCTION_BLOCK        Roots      (*Defining of function block *)
VAR_INPUT
   A, B, C    : REAL;
END_VAR
VAR_OUTPUT
   Nroots     : USINT;
   X1, X2     : REAL;
END_VAR
VAR
   D          : REAL;
END_VAR
```

We see that we have given this FB the name Roots and that three input variables, all of the type REAL, have been declared. Also, there have been declared three output variables, one of type USINT and two of the type REAL.

When we go to use this FB in another POU, whether developed in LD or in FBD, the graphic symbol will automatically have three inputs and three outputs, and the name of the variable that was used in the declaration of the FB will appear within the rectangle. When we insert this FB in an FBD program in CODESYS, it will look like this in the program editor:

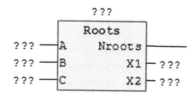

In other words, CODESYS is asking for a name for this instance of the FB, in addition to what variables, or values, are to be used in the various inputs and outputs. The input and output variables in the FB must all be the same data type. (You can naturally add conversion functions if one or more of the variables is of a different data type.)

Finally, we will look at a program code in FBD where we use an instance of this block. The instance is given the name Calc_Roots, and variables are declared that again are associated with inputs and outputs. Note that the output **Nroots** is not associated with any variable. We have previously seen that it is not obligatory to use all inputs and outputs on FBs, such as the elapsed time (ET) output on a timer.

Note that if an *input* is not associated with a value or a variable, the initial value for the data type in question will be used, which is perhaps a different initial value than was assigned during the declaration of the input variables in the FB.

Example 10.4   Application of the Function Block Roots

```
PROGRAM SquareRoot
VAR
   VarA, VarB, VarC    : REAL;
   Root1, Root2        : REAL;
   Calc_Roots          : Roots;    (* Declares an instance of Roots *)
END_VAR
```

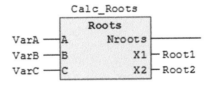

```
END_PROGRAM
```

10.5   Integer Division

When you are going to perform arithmetic calculations, it is important to know about the problems with division of integers. This is a subject that is essential in all programming[4]: What is the result when one integer is divided by another?

Well, if the division "goes through," that is, if there is no remainder, then there is no problem. If the division does not go through, the answer is *truncated*, that is to say, the remainder after the division is deleted. This is the result of how computers handle integer data types as integers (INT). When two integer types are divided, the result is stored temporarily as an integer type, and the answer is truncated *even though in the program you stored the answer in a variable of the REAL type (i.e., floating point).*

---

[4] It is perhaps most natural to use ST for arithmetic calculations, but I would still like to discuss the topic here.

Example 10.5 Integer Divisions

13/10	(=1.3)	=1
99/10	(=9.9)	=9
17/5	(=3.4)	=3
534/200	(=2.67)	=2
534/10	(=53.4)	=53
1/2	(=0.5)	=0

Note that truncation is not the same as ordinary rounding off. In rounding off, the answer to the fourth division above would be rounded up to 3.

You can also note that when we divide a long integral by 10, in practice this is the same as deleting the last digit in the number. (This fact is utilized in Example 10.7.)

If one of the numbers in the division, either the dividend or the divisor, is (or is interpreted as) a floating-point quantity, the PLC will perform the calculation as a floating-point division, and the answer will *not* be truncated. Example 10.6 below illustrates this. (The figure shows a snapshot of the program during execution.)

Example 10.6 A Little Program in FBD

```
PROGRAM
VAR
  ResultA, ResultB : REAL;
END_VAR
```

Both the dividend and the divisor are integers:

One of them are interpreted as floating-point number:

```
END_PROGRAM
```

So, with division where integer variables are involved, at least one of the numbers must be converted to a floating-point number before the division takes place if you want to avoid truncation. As we saw in Section 7.9, there are functions for this, such as INT_TO_REAL.

The next example shows how we deliberately can utilize the fact that the remainder from the division is deleted and how we can use the function MOD in order to calculate the part that gets truncated away. The example also illustrates the use of a jump for making a loop.

Example 10.7   Integer Calculation

We will now write the code for a function that, when it is called up with a long integer (LINT) as an argument, finds and returns the quantity of a particular digit in the number.

(For example, the number 2323622457 contains two threes and four twos.)

The function must therefore have at least two inputs: the number to be searched and which digit is to be searched for.

The problem here is solved by programming a loop where the last digit in the number, at each transit of the loop, is investigated by checking the remainder from a modulus division (Number **mod** 10). At the end of the loop, this last digit is truncated away by dividing the number by 10 (Number DIV 10). The loop is repeated until all the digits have been truncated away and we are left with 0.

```
FUNCTION CntDig :USINT
VAR_INPUT
        Num             :LINT;
        Digit           :USINT;
END_VAR
VAR
        NewNum          :LINT;
        Remainder       :USINT;
END_VAR
```

Assigning Num to the locale variable NewNum as the function is called:

Pulls out the last digit using modulo division by 10

Loop_Start:

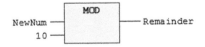

If Remainder equals Digit, the function-variable (CntDig) is incremented by 1

Removes the last digit in the number (NewNum) by dividing the number by 10:

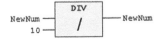

The operation is repeated until NewNum equals 0. Then the function returns.

```
END_FUNCTION
```

Now, the function can be called from a program (or from another type of POU):

```
PROGRAM   Find_Digits
VAR
   MyNum          :  LINT;
   MyDigit        :  USINT;
   NrOfDigits     :  UINT;
END_VAR
```

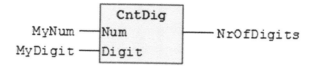

```
END_PROGRAM
```

Finally, we can look at an example from running the program in CODESYS:

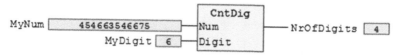

10.6   Sequential Programming with FBD

Even though the similarity of making a sequential program in FBD compared to LD is obvious,[5] we will nonetheless look at an example. In order to directly compare with the LD code, we will take the same problem as in Example 9.11.

(The variable declarations will be identical, so that will not be repeated here.)

Example 10.8   FBD Code for the Washing Operation

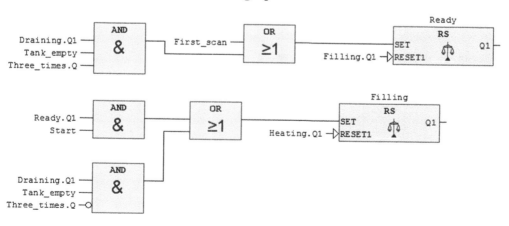

---

[5] The code below is actually generated in CODESYS from the existing LD program. In version 3.x, you will find an option for this on the menu line below FBD/IL/LD→View.

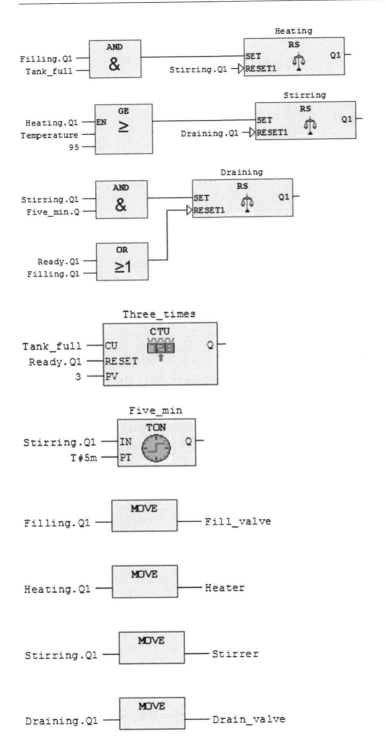

We easily see the connection between contacts in series and in parallel and the use of AND and OR. Personally, I prefer LD over FBD code for such sequential programs because I find them easier to read. (However, perhaps this is only familiarity.)

At any rate, SFC is much to be preferred for sequential programs.

Note the (implementation-dependent) capability that CODEYS offers for indicating detection of rising and falling edges directly to the inputs to the blocks in FBD. We can naturally insert blocks of the type R_TRIG and F_TRIG in the code instead, but this naturally takes up more space and makes the program messier.

In the FBD editor in CODESYS, you can instead right-click on an input (just before the block) and select "Edge Detection." Then you insert a edge detection of the type R-TRIG, symbolized med ▷. Repeat the operation to get a falling edge detection F_TRIG, symbolized by ◁. If the operation is repeated one more time, the flank detector is deleted.

Note also that it's not necessary to use the function MOVE in CODESYS to assign one variable to another; you can use a simple link (connection); thus

$$\texttt{Filling.Q1} \relbar\joinrel\relbar \texttt{Fill\_valve}$$

10.7   Test Problems

Problem 10.1

The signals from the three switches X, Y, and Z are inputs to a control that is to turn on a light in the following cases:

- None of the switches are on.
- Switch X is on and the other two are off.
- Y and Z are on but X is off.
- All three are on.

(a) Set up a logical expression that describes when the light is to be on.
(b) Make a **Program** (PRG) in FBD that implements the logic above. Test the program and verify that it meets the requirements.
(c) Implement the same logic, but now as a **Function** (FUN). (You can copy the code from a) over to a new function.) Then make a program (PRG) called **Calling** from which you call the function. The program should contain two calls of the function so that you can control two different lights.

Note: Avoid using specific variable names in functions and FBs so that these can be used again. Instead, use descriptive names or generic names such as IN1, IN2 etc. Such names should not be related to the process where the FB is used temporarily this time.

Problem 10.2

Here, we are going to make a function that converts between two quantities that are linearly proportional to each other. We often meet such problems in connection with analog signals, and we studied this type of conversion in Chapter 3.

We have learned that when an analog sensor is connected to an analog module, the PLC will represent the signal from the sensor, which can be in volts or milliamps, with an integer (Word) between 0 and 32767 (WAGO PLCs).

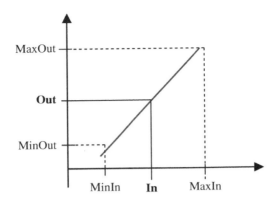

Figure 10.5   Illustration of the function's operation

This value represents a physical value such as temperature (°C), flow (l/min), or pressure (bar).

Calculating what an integer, for instance, 8734, corresponds to in °C can be a little troublesome. It can therefore be a good idea to have a function that performs this conversion. Such a function can also be used to convert from 0–32767 to a percent (0–100) which is certainly a more useful quantity.

The problem is therefore to construct a function, called **Scale**, which converts an integer value to a physical measurement quantity. We will make the function as general as possible so that it can be used again no matter what physical quantity it applies to or which PLC values are to be converted from or to. This means using input variables to provide upper and lower boundaries for both the integer representation and the physical corresponding values.

The problem is illustrated in Figure 10.5. In and Out do not necessarily represent physical inputs and outputs, but rather what is entered as arguments in the function and what is the results from the function.

(a) Find a mathematical expression for the value Out as a function of all of the other variables (MinIn, MaxIn, MinOut, MaxOut, and In).
(b) Program a function (FUN) in FBD that you call **Scale**, based upon your expressions from problem a). Think through what is to be declared as VAR_INPUT and what data types are suitable for use with the different variables. The function name itself should be used as an output variable so the function must be declared with a suitable data type as well.

Hint: Think "opposites" and start with the last mathematical operation that is to be performed. Then work toward the left until all of the mathematical expressions have been implemented.

Problem 10.3

We will now test the function from our previous problem. In order to have some numbers to use, you can pretend that you have a pressure transmitter that gives an analog signal between **1 and 5 V** that represents a pressure between **0 and 2.5 bar.** (If you are using a PLC, you can use a voltage source to simulate this signal.)

(a) Determine the proper Max and Min values for the signal/variable input to the function and the Max and Min values for the output signal. If you do this in practice, you must take into account the signal range to your analog input module. This can be, for instance, 0–10 V. You must also know how your PLC represents the electrical measurement range. (For example, a PLC from WAGO represents 0–10 V with integer values between 0 and 32765. What will an input signal of 1 V be represented by? How about an input signal of 5 V?)

(b) Make a program or use the same program (Calling) you used to call up the function from Problem 10.1) and add a call to your new Scale function. The program should set an assumed Alarm high when the pressure exceeds 2 bar.

(c) Add another call of the Scale function that *converts the value you obtained from the previous call* to a percentage between 0 and 100%.

The figure below shows how the function could be represented when it is used (called) in a graphic programming language:

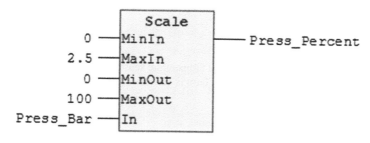

Problem 10.4

(a) Make a **function block** (FB) named **Toggle** that changes the state of a Boolean output each time the state of a Boolean input changes from 0 to 1.
Illustration:

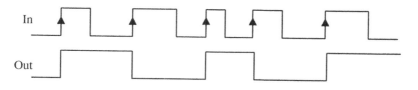

The problem can be solved in several ways, but you <u>can</u> find a use for any of the following functions and function blocks:

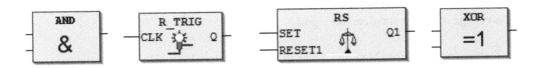

(b) Enter <u>three different calls</u> of the Toggle FB in your calling program.

Problem 10.5

Now, we are going to make code for controlling a cooling fan. Assume that the measurement range for the temperature is 30 to 100°C and that the PLC represents the signal with integer values from 0 to 32767.

The fan can run at three different speeds that are controlled by two digital signals. The motor is therefore connected to two digital outputs on the PLC, **Dig_out1** and **Dig_out2**.

The fan speed is to be controlled as a function of temperature in accordance with Table 10.1.

A **function block** (FB) is to be programmed to control the fan speed.

The function block should have the following variable inputs and variable outputs:

Inputs
1. **Temp**   (Converted) signal from the temperature sensor
2. **Alarm_Ack**   Acknowledgment that the alarm is activated

Outputs output
1. **Dig_out1**   Digital output. Controls the fan speed
2. **Dig_out2**   --------------------"--------------------------
3. **Alarm_out**   Digital output that is set TRUE when the temperature exceeds 90°C. The output remains TRUE until *Alarm_Ack* is activated. It is then set to FALSE, *provided that the temperature has dropped below 90°C*

Table 10.1   Fan speed as a function of temperature

Temperature	Speed	Dig_out2	Dig_out1
$T < 70\,°C$	0–Stop	0	0
$70 \leq T < 80\,°C$	1	0	1
$80 \leq T < 90\,°C$	2	1	0
$T \geq 90\,°C$	3 (max)	1	1

(a) Write the program code for the function block in accordance with the description above. (Remember that you already have the function Scale available from Problem 10.3 that you can use when you call the function block to get a temperature represented in degrees. You can then operate with degrees in the code for the function block.)

(b) Put a call to the function block in your Calling program (you can also use the Scale function there).

(c) In problem (a), could we have made a *function* instead of a *function block*? Justify your answer.

Problem 10.6

A conveyor belt is used for transporting two different products (item A and item B) of different physical sizes (item B is longer than item A). In order to distinguish the items from each other, we can record *how long* the signal from the photocell stays high.

Make the code for a program (or a FB if you wish) that implements this and counts the number of each type.

(You can determine for yourself how long the signal from the photocell must be high in order for the product to be interpreted as type B.)

11

Structured Text (ST)

This chapter introduces one of the two text-based programming languages in the standard. The language has been given the name Structured Text (ST) and has many resemblances to languages such as C and Pascal.

Chapter Contents

- Introduction:
  Composition and program structure, use of color, execution
- Functions versus operators:
- Call of function blocks:
  Flank detection, memories, timers, counters
- Selection and loops:
  IF statements, CASE statements, WHILE-, REPEAT-, and FOR-loops.

11.1 Introduction

Structured Text (ST) is a high-level language that reminds many of the Pascal language. But everyone who has worked in programming, for instance, in C or C++, will recognize much of the syntax and will thereby also easily be able to adapt to ST. The language contains many elements, commands, and instructions that ST uses in common with other high-level programming languages.

ST can, like the other languages in the standard, be used to program entire applications or portions of an application. The standard emphasizes the importance of a seamless integration of the different languages. This is because it is often an advantage to use different languages

Programmable Logic Controllers: A Practical Approach to IEC 61131-3 Using CODESYS, First Edition. Dag H. Hanssen.
© 2015 John Wiley & Sons, Ltd. Published 2015 by John Wiley & Sons, Ltd.

and different program organization units (POUs), so that the strengths of the individual languages are utilized.

The great strength of ST is first and foremost with arithmetic calculations, processing numbers and in handling structured data types. For those who have experience in programming, ST will probably seem like freedom in comparison to the LD. Programming can be done faster, and the program code is much more compressed in comparison to LD.

Finally, some operations are impossible to implement with a graphic programming language.

Nevertheless, it is useful to see how the languages compare. Therefore, during the course of this chapter, we review some of the examples that we studied in the two previous chapters to see how these can be solved with ST.

Figure 11.1 shows an example of code in ST that contains conditional statements (IF sentences) and repetitive loops (WHILE and REPEAT).

Example 11.1

```
WHILE index1 < 100 DO
     index2 := 0;
     Value := Table1[index1];
     REPEAT
          Table2[index2] := Value + Table2[index2];
          IF Table2[index2] > 32767 THEN
               EXIT;
          END_IF
          index2 := index2 + 1;
     UNTIL index2 >25
     END_REPEAT
     index1 := index1 + 1;
END_WHILE
```

Figure 11.1   Example of ST code

11.2   ST in General

As we remarked, some who have experience with other high-level languages will recognize many keywords and instructions as conditional statements and loops. Those which are perhaps initially the most unfamiliar concern the use of standard function blocks (FBs) such as timers and counters.

When working with combinatory controls or sequential controls that are based on logic, its often sufficient to program with logical conditions such as AND, OR, and so on. Managing analog signals requires a little numerical processing and comparison, but as we have seen, this can also be solved in graphic languages by using various functions.

It is also a fact that most of the functions and FBs defined in the standard are programmed in ST by the manufacturers of the development tool. So why not just go ahead and use ST all the way? The answer to this is that you can. Having said that, there are other methods in ST for counting and monitoring time aside from the use of the standard FBs. These FBs have been developed with a view toward graphic languages, and that is where they have their strength.

To go further and look more closely at specific instructions, we will take a look at how programs are built up in ST and what semantics that are defined in the standard.

11.2.1 Program Structure

A program in ST often consists of *conditional statements*, also called *selection statements* such as IF and CASE statements and one or more instructions. In addition, there are *loops* (FOR, WHILE, REPEAT) that are much simpler to implement in ST than in a graphic language.

All instructions terminate with a semicolon (;). It is possible to write an empty statement. In that case, it consists only of a semicolon (and any comments):

```
IF %IX1.3 THEN (* … A conditional statement *)
    (* and some instructions: *)
    bVar := 1;
    iVarA := iVarA + iVarB;
    Result := SQRT (%MD14);
END_IF;
```

Comments

Use of comments in ST naturally follows the rules that are defined in the standard (see Section 6.2.3). No matter which language is being used, the use of comments is a good habit to cultivate. It can sometimes be more difficult to read and understand the code in ST, so use comments relatively often.

Labels

Labels were defined in the previous two chapters. Labels are used in LD and FBD to jump between rungs and networks. Loops can be constructed easily in ST, so there is no need for labels.

Instructions

Instructions are the heart of the program. Instructions can be value assignments, performing calculations, setting and resetting of outputs, and so on. A statement in ST can contain many instructions. All instructions must end with a semicolon (;).

Keyboarding

If you try to write the program code in Figure 11.1, you will discover that you do not get automatic line feeds but instead must produce them yourself by pressing Enter. Furthermore, it can happen that the text on one line does not start in the desired horizontal position.

In Figure 11.1, indentation has been used to improve legibility. Such indentation is done with the TAB key. If you use only spaces, you risk that all of the extra space will disappear when you confirm the statement.

Example 11.2

The code in Figure 11.1 can also be written as shown in Figure 11.2. We see that the legibility is significantly poorer. Note that there is no syntax error in the code, so the program will function as before.

```
WHILE index1 < 100 DO
index2 := 0; Value := Table1[index1];
REPEAT
Table2[index2] := Value + Table2[index2];
IF Table2[index2] > 32767 THEN EXIT; END_IF
index2 := index2 + 1;
UNTIL index2 >25
END_REPEAT
index1 := index1 + 1;
END_WHILE
```

Figure 11.2   Example of untidy code

Execution

When a program written in ST is executed, this takes place instruction by instruction as the control structure, such as loops, for instance, is followed. Boolean and arithmetic expressions which contain several operators are executed in accordance with particular rules governing priority. You can read more about this in Section 7.7.1.

11.3   Standard Functions and Operators

Many of the functions that are defined in the standard belong to the group of *operators* in the ST program language. For many of these standard functions, there are also specific operator symbols that are used in ST instead of the function names. Examples of operators are +, −, ≥, ≤, and /. These correspond to the functions ADD, SUB, GE, LE, and DIV.

Using functions is called *performing operations on an operand*. An example of this is A := SQRT(B). Here, SQRT is the operator and B is the operand. The answer is placed in A. An operand can be a constant, a variable, an address, or even another function call such as SIN(A), for instance. Some of the functions are used as operators *between* operands such as the function MAX(A, B, C).

The difference between operators and other functions is that operators are implicitly recognized by the development tool.

Table 7.1 contains an overview of all of the operators and shows which of them has its own operator symbol in ST. It is possible to use all of the function names in ST, but if there is a defined operator, it is natural to use this.

Operations that are possible to perform with the help of the standard functions can be broken up into the following main groups:

- Boolean operations and operations on bit strings
- Arithmetic and logical operations on integers and/or floating-point numbers
- Numerical and alphanumeric comparisons
- Type conversions
- Operations on text strings

All the Programmable Logic Controller (PLC) manufacturers offer many more functions in addition to the basic ones that are defined in the standard. It will therefore be possible to perform other operations that require the use of implementation-dependent functions. Such operations can be:

- Program operations
- Control operations
- Data exchange operations
- Application-specific and equipment-dependent instructions (communications, process control, etc.)

11.3.1 Assignment

We covered *assignment* in Section 7.3.1. To repeat: the syntax for assignment in ST is as follows:

$$\text{OP1}:=\text{OP2};$$

The direction is *from* OP2 *to* OP1. We also saw that several variables can be set to the same value with the help of the syntax: OP1: = OP2: = OP3 := …

In order to set a Boolean address (or variable) logically high, we can write

$$\%\text{Q2.3}:=\text{TRUE};..$$

Correspondingly, the following instruction will set the variable Var_bool to a logical low state:

$$\text{Var}\_\text{bool}:=\text{FALSE};$$

Most tools also support use of **1** and **0** instead of TRUE and FALSE, so that you can write, for instance, %Q2.3 := 1;

Example 11.3   Various Assignments

```
PROGRAM Assignment
VAR
    Var1, Var2      : REAL;
    Var3            : BOOL;
    Values          : ARRAY [1..32] OF DWORD;
    AWord           : WORD;
    Answer          : UINT;
END_VAR
    Var1 := Var2 := 0.0;
    AWord.15 := TRUE;      (*Bit nr. 15 in AWord is set TRUE *)
    %MW122 := %MW8;
    Var3 := %IX2.2;
    %MD5 := Verdier[9]
    Answer := 44;
END_PROGRAM
```

11.4   Calling FBs

In the previous chapters, we have learned how instances of FBs can be declared and used in the graphical languages. Declaration is identical for all programming languages, so it will not be repeated here.

All FBs have one or more input and output variables. As soon as an instance is declared in a POU, the instance of the input and output variables of the block is also automatically declared. The block is now accessible for use in the code field in the POU.[1]

Use of the instance takes place via calls. In ST, a call is made by giving the name of the instance together with *arguments* (input values).

Example 11.4

$$My\_instance\left(IN1:=\%IX1.4, IN2:=T\#30s\right);$$

No values are returned from calls of FB instances as they are with calls of functions. Instead, the results of the execution of the instance are stored in its output variable. These variables can be referred to in an object-oriented way, no matter what programming language is being used.

Suppose that the FB called in Example 11.4 has an output variable called Q1. Then Q1 can be referred to with the following syntax: **My_instance.Q1**

We can then assign this output to another Boolean variable: bVar := My_instance.Q1;

It is also possible to fetch a result at the same time that an FB is called. This is done with the operator "=>". By using this operator, you can assign output variables against other variables within the parentheses in the call.

---

[1] It is also possible to declare an instance *globally* so that the instance is available to all POUs.

Example 11.5 shows a combination of the instructions in the two previous examples. It is specified here that output Q1 from the FB is assigned to the address %QX2.2.

Example 11.5

$$My\_instance\left(IN1:=\%IX1.4, IN2:=T\#30s, Q1=>\%QX2.2\right);$$

11.4.1   Flank Detection and Memories

Unfortunately, the standard does not define any operators that perform flank detection. If the manufacturer of the development tool has not chosen to implement his own, the FBs R_TRIG and F_TRIG must be used in ST as well. This is somewhat awkward, but you will soon become used to it.

Neither do bistable function blocks, which in LD are represented with Set and Reset coils, have their own defined operators. Luckily, if you assign a value to a variable, the variable will retain this value until a new value is assigned to the variable. In this way, we can implement memory by using IF statements. More on this in Section 11.5.

Another alternative, of course, is to use the FBs RS (or SR) as shown in the next two examples.

Example 11.6

Here, an instance of a RS is declared with the name Memory:

```
VAR
    Memory    : RS;
END_VAR
```

An RS block has, as we know, a Set input and a Reset input (called Reset1) in addition to the output Q1. All of the inputs and output are of the Boolean type.

If our RS instance is to be used to start and stop a motor, perhaps the call could look like the following (the variables Start, Stop, and Motor must naturally also be declared):

$$Memory\left(Set:=Start, Reset1:=Stop, Q1=>Motor\right);$$

As mentioned, no value is *returned* from such a call, as would be the case with calling functions. Instead, the result of the run is stored in the output variable of the instance. This block has only one output variable, Q1. If you have not transferred the state to the output in the call, you can refer to this in another place in the code with the syntax Name_of_instance. Q1, like Motor := Memory.Q1;

Example 11.7

A pump is to start when a switch is turned to the run position. To stop the pump, a separate stop button must be pushed. So that the pump does not start again once the stop button is released, the start switch must first be turned to the off position before it can again be turned to run. (We studied this same example in the LD chapter, Example 9.6.)

In the following, you will see a declaration of variable and program code in ST.

As we see, an instance of an R_TRIG called **RE1** and an instance of the FB RS called **Run_Pump** are declared.

This selection of names can be tricky. For instances of FBs that I do not need to refer to later in the code or that I have not used many of, I personally prefer to use anonymous names such as RS1, RS2, …, RE1, RE2,…, FE1, FE2,…[2]:

```
PROGRAM Rising
VAR
    Pump       AT %QX2.5    : BOOL;
    Start      AT %IX1.7    : BOOL;
    Stop       AT %IX1.8    : BOOL;
    Run                     : BOOL;
    RE1       : R_TRIG;     (* Declares an instance of R_TRIG *)
    Run_Pump : RS;          (* ...and one of the function block RS *)
END_VAR

(* CODE IN ST: *)

RE1(CLK:=Start, Q=>Run);
Run_Pump(Set:=Run, Reset1:=Stop, Q1=>Pump);

END_PROGRAM
```

Here, the assignment operator "=>" is used in both of the FB calls, but if desired, the result of execution of the blocks could be fetched separately. Also, note that it is not necessary to introduce a variable (Run) for temporary storage of the state of the output of the R_TRIG block. We can refer directly to the output as follows:

```
RE1(CLK := Start);
Run_Pump(Set:= RE1.Q, Reset1:= Stop);
Pump := Run_Pump.Q1;
```

(Also, note that here the variable of the physical output Pump is assigned the output of the RS block's output variable in a separate instruction.)

Example 11.8   ST Code for the Mixing Process

In Section 9.3.4, we studied an example for controlling of a mixing process using LD. The control for this process has four input signals (Start, LT1, LT2, and LT3) and four output signals (MV1, MV2, Motor, and Stir). By sequential analysis, we then derived the following algorithms for the control signals:

---

[2] RE is an acronym for "rising edge" and FE is an acronym for "falling edge."

$$\text{Set Motor} = \uparrow \text{LT2} \quad \text{Reset Motor} = \uparrow \text{LT3}$$
$$\text{Set Stir} = \uparrow \text{LT2} \quad \text{Reset Stir} = \downarrow \text{LT2}$$
$$\text{Set MV1} = \uparrow \text{Start} \quad \text{Reset MV2} = \uparrow \text{LT2}$$
$$\text{Set MV2} = \uparrow \text{LT3} \quad \text{Reset MV2} = \downarrow \text{LT1}$$

We see that the control algorithms, as they are presented, will require many instances of FBs for flank detection and flip-flops. This is a result of the slavish method that we used in developing the algorithms in Section 9.3.4. Further analysis of the diagram in Figure 9.15 reveals that all use of flanks for resetting output signals is unnecessary. Furthermore, we see that the Stir signal actually is identical with the LT2 signal. The algorithms can therefore advantageously be modified as follows:

$$\text{Set Motor} = \uparrow \text{LT2} \quad \text{Reset Motor} = \text{LT3}$$
$$\text{Stir} = \text{LT2}$$
$$\text{Set MV1} = \uparrow \text{Start} \quad \text{Reset MV1} = \text{LT2}$$
$$\text{Set MV2} = \uparrow \text{LT3} \quad \text{Reset MV2} = \text{LT1}$$

```
PROGRAM Mixing_process
VAR
    (*Declares input and output variables: *)
    Start   AT %I3.0   : BOOL;
    LT1     AT %I3.1   : BOOL;
    LT2     AT %I3.2   : BOOL;
    LT3     AT %I3.3   : BOOL;
    Motor   AT %Q5.0   : BOOL;
    Stir    AT %Q5.1   : BOOL;
    MV1     AT %Q5.2   : BOOL;
    MV2     AT %Q5.3   : BOOL;

    (*Declares instance of the blocks R_TRIG and RS: *)
    RE_Start, RE_LT2, RE_LT3   : R_TRIG;
    RS1, RS2, RS3              : RS;
END_VAR
    RE_Start(CLK:=Start);          (* Start gone high? *)
    RE_LT2(CLK:=LT2);              (* LT2 gone high? *)
    RE_LT3(CLK:=LT3);              (* LT3 gone high? *)
    RS1(SET:=RE_LT2.Q, RESET1:=LT3, Q1=>Motor); (* Motor *)
    Stir :=LT2;                                  (* Stir *)
    RS2(SET:=RE_Start.Q, RESET1:=LT2, Q1=>MV1); (* Valve MV1 *)
    RS3(SET:=RE_LT3.Q, RESET1:=LT1, Q1=>MV2); (* Valve MV2 *)

END_PROGRAM
```

We see from the code above that it is relatively compact, but it is perhaps more difficult to read compared to the corresponding code in LD or FBD.

11.4.2   Timers

Even though use of a timer in ST is completely equivalent to declaring and calling other types of FBs, timers and counters are used so much that they will get a little extra attention here.

The example below shows LD code and the corresponding ST code for a timer in TON mode, used to provide a delayed connection of an output.

Example 11.9

```
(* Code in LD: *)
```

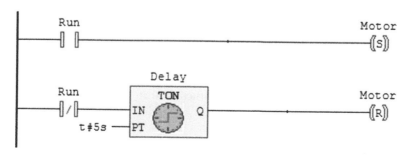

```
(* Code in ST: *)
Three_sec(IN := %IX1.2, PT := T#3s);
%Q2.3 := Three_sec.Q;
```

The next example shows use of TON timers to make an off-delay (TOF).

Example 11.10

```
PROGRAM Off_delay
VAR
    Run, Motor      : BOOL;
    Delay           : TON;
END_VAR
(* Code in ST: *)
    Delay(IN := NOT RUN, PT := T#5s);
    Motor := RUN OR NOT Delay.Q;
END_PROGRAM
```

Corresponding code in LD:

11.4.3   Counters

The example below contains the CTU instance "Count_Items" where the current value increments by 1 each time the condition (%IX2.0 AND Run) is satisfied. When the counter has
counted up to 4400, the output becomes TRUE (Count_Items.Q := TRUE), and this sets the
output %QX4.0 to TRUE.

The counter is reset to 0 by setting the input %IX2.1 logically high.

Example 11.11

```
PROGRAM The4400
VAR
    Count_Items     : CTU;
END_VAR
    Count_Items(CU := %IX2.0 AND Run,
    RESET := %IX2.1, PV := 4400, Q => %QX4.0);
END_PROGRAM;
```

Note that instructions that is too long to fit into one line in the editor will still function
without error. A corresponding code in LD is shown in the following.

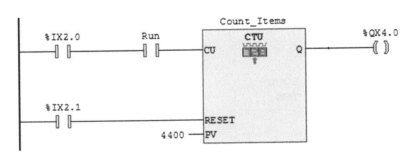

11.5   IF Statements

There is often a need to perform various instructions based upon whether a test gives one
result or another. We call such tests in a program a *selection*. There are two types of selection
statements: the **IF** and the **CASE**. Both of these types are used to select which instructions
will be performed, based upon the outcome of a comparison.

An IF statement in its simplest form means that an instruction, or several instructions, is
performed if the outcome of a logical test is TRUE. If the condition is FALSE, either
no instruction is performed or the next instruction that follows the keyword ELSE is
performed.

A simple IF statement is coded with the following syntax:

```
IF condition THEN (* If the condition is true, the instructions *)
    instruction; (* between THEN and END_IF are executed *)
    instruction;
    :
END_IF;              (* An IF statement always closes with END_IF; *)
```

If other instructions are to be performed if the condition is not satisfied, that is, is FALSE, the keyword ELSE is used:

```
IF condition THEN       (* If the condition is satisfied, *)
    instruction1;       (* instruction1 is executed *)
ELSE                    (* If the condition is not satisfied, *)
    instruction2;       (* instruction2 is executed. *)
END_IF;
```

IF statements can also be nested by using the keyword **ELSIF**. An IF statement in a more general form has the following syntax:

```
IF conditionA THEN      (* If condition A is satisfied, *)
    instruction1;       (* instruction1 is executed *)
ELSIF conditionB THEN   (* If not and condition B is satisfied, *)
    instruction2;       (* instruction2 is executed *)
ELSE                    (* If that one is not satisfied, either *)
    instruction3;       (* instruction2 is executed *)
END_IF;
```

Example 11.12

```
IF PV < 100 THEN
    Kp := 12.5;
ELSIF PV < 200 THEN
    Kp := 17.0;
ELSE
    Kp := 24.7;
END_IF;
```

In the previous example, the basic IF statement principle is utilized in order to get fewer comparisons. Kp will be set to 17.0 if $100 < PV < 200$. If the first condition is not true, this means that the PV is less than 100. In that case, a check is made on whether PV is less than 200. If not, PV is higher than 200, and Kp is set equal to 24.7.

Example 11.13   Calculation of Square Roots

```
Root := B*B -4*A*C;
IF Root < 0.0 THEN
    Nroots := 0;
    X1 := X2 := STRING_TO_REAL('NaN');
ELSIF Root = 0.0 THEN
    Nroots := 1;
    IF A <> 0 THEN
        X1 := X2 := (-B+SQRT(Root)) / (2*A);
    ELSE
        X1 := .X2 := 0;
    END_IF
ELSE
    Nroots := 2;
    X1 := (-B-SQRT(Root)) / (2*A);
    X2 := (-B+SQRT(Root)) / (2*A);
END_IF;
```

The code calculates the roots of a second-order polynomial equation of the form $Ax^2 + Bx + C = 0$. Here, IF-statements are used to check whether the expression under the square root sign in the formula for calculating the roots is negative, zero, or positive. Depending upon the result of the test, you get 0 roots, 1 root (coincident roots), or 2 roots, respectively.

As mentioned in Section 11.4.1, a variable will (naturally enough) maintain its value until it receives a new one. We can then use IF statements to implement a flip-flop. Instead of the RS-based code in Example 11.7, we could have written:

```
RE1(CLK:=Start, Q=>Run);
IF RE1.Q THEN
    Pump := TRUE;
END_IF
IF Stop THEN
    Pump := FALSE;
END_IF
```

11.6   CASE Statements

If there are many comparisons to be made giving differing results, you should consider using CASE statements instead of nested IF statements. CASE is based on testing the value of an integer (INT, SINT, UINT, USINT) or the content of an enumerated data type (see Section 6.5.5.2). Various instructions or statements are performed depending upon the value of the integer or the enumerated variable.

The advantage of using CASE compared to nested IF statements is that more instructions can be associated with one and the same conditional test. The syntax is as follows:

```
CASE Condition OF
     value1:                     Instruction_A;
     value2:                     Instruction_B;
     value3, value4, value6:     Instruction_C;
     value7.. value12:           Instruction_D;
        :
     valueN:                     Instruction_X;
ELSE
     Other_instructions;
END_CASE;
```

- If Condition has the value <value1>, Instruction_A will be executed. If Condition has the value <value2>, Instruction_B will be executed etc. Note that Condition also may be an integer *expression*, that is, it may not be a single variable but rather an arithmetic expression that yields an integer as an answer (see Example 11.15).
- Several instructions can be executed for each outcome of the test variable/expression.
- If Condition does not yield any of the listed values, then nothing is performed or, if using ELSE as before, the instruction that follows ELSE is executed.
- If the same instruction(s) is to be executed for several values of the test variable, these values may be listed, separated by commas.
- If the same instruction(s) is to be executed for several sequential values of the test condition, these values can be listed as Startvalue.Endvalue, that is, with two periods between the values.

If Condition is a variable of the integer type, value1, value2, and so on will also be integer values such as 10, 20, 30, ..., for instance. If Condition is a user-defined enumerated data type, value1, value2, etc. can be text Constance such as Ready, Wait, Run, Fill, and so on. See Example 11.16.

Example 11.14

Here, the content of address %MW1 is tested, and one of three discrete output addresses is set logically high, depending upon the value of %MW1:

```
CASE %MW1 OF
    1:    %QX2.0 := TRUE;
    2:    %QX2.1 := TRUE:
    3..5: %QX2.2 := TRUE;
END_CASE;
```

The next example shows that the test condition can be an integer expression.

Example 11.15

```
CASE A - B OF
    4:Out := TRUE;
    7:IF B>0 THEN Result := %MW5;
      ELSE Result := %MW4;
      END_IF;
END_CASE;
```

The test variable can be of an enumerated data type.

Example 11.16

Assume that a product is to be sorted according to color (by the use of a color sensor). A conveyor belt brings the products down to a sorter, where arrival is registered by a photocell. When a product arrives at the sorter, the color of the product is checked, and the proper piston is activated to shove the item off the belt. The test variable **Color** in the code is a user-defined data type that can have the values Green, Red, or Blue. (RE is an instance of a R_TRIG.)

```
RE(clk := PhotoSwitch, Q => New_item); (* A product is in place *)
IF New_item THEN
    CASE Color OF                          (* Checks color *)
    Green:   Piston1 := TRUE;
             Green_count := Green_count + 1;
    Red :    Piston2 := TRUE;
             Red_count := Red_count + 1;
    Blue :   Piston3 := TRUE;
             Blue_count := Blue_count + 1;

    ELSE
             Error_count := Error_count + 1;
    END_CASE;
END_IF;
```

11.7   ST Code Based upon State Diagrams

In Section 4.6, we studied the use of state diagrams in planning and designing programs. Here, we will see examples of how CASE statements, among others, can be used to efficiently translate state diagrams (or flowcharts) into program code in ST. Relating to state diagrams, we know that:

- Each of the states in the diagram constitutes a *result* of the CASE test.
- Actions that are to be performed in association with the individual states are programmed as instructions within the results in question.
- The possible results are determined by test conditions. As we have learned, these can be of the integer type, where each result has its *number*, or of the *enumerated* data type, where each result gets its own *name*.

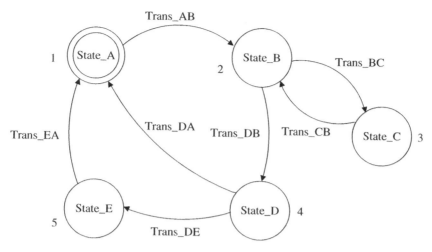

Figure 11.3　A state diagram with general designations

- After the instructions have been carried out in each result, IF statements are used to determine the next result to be executed, that is, the next state that is to be activated.

Figure 11.3 shows a state diagram with general designations of states and transitions. When using an integer type as the test variable in the CASE structure, state names cannot be used directly. Then you call "State_A" 1, "State_B" 2, and so on. A CASE structure for this diagram is seen on the next page.

Since the purpose of this diagram is to show the connection between states and transitions and the CASE structure, no actions are specified to be carried out in the individual states. In the STATE structure on the next page, actions are indicated only as *instructions*. (Note that the integer variable State naturally must be declared.)

```
CASE State OF
  1: Instructions;
     IF Trans_AB THEN
          State:= 2;
     END_IF;
  2: Instructions;
     IF Trans_BC THEN
          State:= 3;
     ELSIF Trans_DB THEN
          State:= 4;
     END_IF;
  3: Instructions;
     IF Trans_CB THEN
          State:= 2;
     END_IF;
```

```
   4:  Instructions;
       IF Trans_DA THEN
             State:= 1;
       ELSIF Trans_DE THEN
             State:= 5;
       END_IF;
   5:  Instructions;
       IF Trans_EA THEN
             State:= 1;
       END_IF;
END_CASE;
```

The reason that CASE statements are so appropriate in this format is that there is only one result that is executed for each value of the test variable. This isolates the instructions that are related to the individual states. Only when that particular result is activated are the instructions performed.

Prioritizing Alternative Paths

It is important to remember the order of priority when there are several possible paths out from the state. Here, the transitions are tested in nested IF statements, where the highest priority transition is tested first, then the next highest, and so on. This is done in both outcomes 2 and 4 of the test in the code earlier.

Actions

As long as the condition requires that a result be active, all of the instructions within that result will be executed at every cycle. If there is an action or an instruction that should be performed only once when the system is in a particular state, this action can be placed within the same IF statement each time the transition conditions are tested. A typical example of such an action is to increment the value of a counter variable each time a particular state is activated or deactivated. (In the sequential function chart (SFC) context, such actions are called pulse actions.)

Test Variables of the Enumerated Data Type

The capability for declaring variables of an enumerated data type is very useful in conjunction with CASE statements and states. It is therefore an advantage if the states in state diagrams and flowcharts are given individual names that follow the standard with respect to legal identifiers. In particular, the test variables can be declared as user-defined enumerated data types with possible values corresponding to the same identifiers. Example **11.21** shows the use of test variables of the enumerated data type.

Timing

There is often a requirement for timed control of states. Examples of this can be a lamp that should light for half a minute, a pump that should run for 5 minutes, a fan that should start in 2 hours, and so on. Implementation of time delays can be done by using the FB timer. It is recommended to insert timers *outside* the CASE structure and preferably use the states as IN conditions. In this way, the timer is activated when the state in question is activated, and then the IN signal goes low when the state is a deactivated.

See the following example of an extract from a code for controlling a traffic light. (The call to the Timer Wait10s is boldface for the sake of clarity.)

Example 11.17   Time Control of States

```
TYPE (* User-defined enumerated datatype (DUT) *)
   Color    : (Green, Yellow, Yell_Red, Red);
END_TYPE
VAR
   State    : Color; (* Variable based on our DUT *)
   Wait10s  : TON; (* Timer instance *)
   G_light, Y_light, R_light : BOOL;
END_VAR

Wait10s(IN := (State = Green), PT := t#10s); (* Notice the IN
   condition! *)

CASE State OF
:
Green:
   G_light := TRUE;
   IF Wait_10s.Q THEN       (* If the transition is true *)
        G_light := FALSE;   (* an instruction is executed *)
        State := Yellow;    (* and the next state is activated*)
   END_IF
:
END_CASE
```

11.7.1   Example: Code for the Level Process

In Section 4.6.4, we drew a state diagram for a level process, where the fluid level in a tank is to be controlled with the help of two pumps. The state diagram is reproduced in the following, followed by a program code in ST based on the diagram:

(* Run both pumps *)
(* Turn on lamp if contition activ > 3min *)
(* Turn off lamp with Reset *)

(* User-defined datatype that defines the possible states: *)

```
TYPE
    States : (Ready, Idle, RunP1, RunP2, RunP12);
END_TYPE
```

```
PROGRAM Level_Process
VAF
```
(* Declares a variable based on our States datatype. The initial value is set equal to Ready: *)

```
    State : States   := Ready;
    B1, B2, B3, P1, P2, Start_stop, P1_Last, Reset, Light   : BOOL;
    RE_B2, RE_Run    : R_TRIG;
    FE_Run           : F_TRIG;
    Gone_3m          : TON;
END_VAR
```

```
    RE_B2(clk := B2);                          (* Calles up all the FBs. *)
    RE_Run(clk:= Start_stop);                  (* Note the IN condition for the Timer *)
    FE_Run(clk:= Start_stop);
    Gone_3m(IN := (State = RunP12) AND NOT Reset, PT := T#3M);
```

```
IF Gone_3m.Q THEN
    Light := TRUE;
END_IF
IF Reset THEN
    Light := FALSE;
END_IF
```

(* The light should go on if the state RunP12 has been active for more than 30 seconds. *)
(* The light should stay on until Reset is pressed. *)

```
CASE State OF
    Ready:  (* Waiting for Start. *)
            IF RE_run.Q THEN
                State := Idle;
            END_IF

    Idle:   (* Program acktive. No Pumps running. *)
            P1 := P2 := FALSE;
            IF FE_Run.Q THEN
                State := Ready;
            ELSIF RE_B2.Q AND NOT P1_Last THEN
                State := RunP1;
            ELSIF RE_B2.Q AND P1_Last THEN
                State := RunP2;
            ELSIF B3 THEN
                State := RunP12;
            END_IF

    RunP1:  (* Run Pump P1 *)
            P1 := TRUE;
            P1_Last := TRUE;
            IF (NOT B1) OR B3 OR FE_Run.Q THEN
                State := Idle;
            END_IF

    RunP2:  (* Run Pump P2 *)
            P2 := TRUE;
            P1_Last := FALSE;
            IF (NOT B1) OR B3 OR FE_Run.Q THEN
                State := Idle;
            END_IF

    RunP12: (* Run both Pumps *)
            P1 := P2 := TRUE;
            IF (NOT B1) OR FE_Run.Q THEN
                State := Idle;
            END_IF
END_CASE
```

11.8   Loops

Sometimes, there is a requirement to perform an action a certain number of times. For this, you can use loops. The standard specifies three types of loops to choose from. There are WHILE loops, FOR loops, and REPEAT loops. All types of selections and loops are processed here in the order stated.

11.8.1   WHILE ... DO... END_WHILE

This instruction performs a repeated action as long as the condition is satisfied. No instructions are performed if the condition is initially FALSE. The syntax is as follows:

```
WHILE condition DO
    Instructions;
END_WHILE;
```

Only the code that lies between WHILE and END_WHILE will be executed. It is therefore strongly recommended that the condition also be updated within the WHILE loop so that the loop does not become endless. In the following example, we use the value Area as a condition. Closing the loop is therefore dependent upon the array radius[k] being correctly set up. If the array does not hold large enough values for the area to be greater than 1000, the loop will never be terminated.

Example 11.18

```
k := 1;
WHILE Area[k] < 1000 DO
    Area[k] := 3.14*radius[k]*radius[k] + 2*3.14*radius[k]*height;
    k := k + 1;
END_WHILE;
```

In the next example, an extra condition is imposed that makes this loop run for a maximum of 200 iterations.

Example 11.19

```
k := 1;
WHILE (Area[k] < 1000) AND (k < 200) DO
    Area[k] := 3.14*radius[k]*radius[k] + 2*3.14*radius[k]*height;
    k := k + 1;
END_WHILE;
```

This is naturally only one possible solution if the array does not have more than 200 iterations. At any rate, the point is to be alert when using loops. Another good solution is to terminate loops by using the instruction EXIT. See Section 11.8.4.

11.8.2   FOR ... END_FOR

This loop is useful when the number of iterations can be determined beforehand. The loop performs the instruction a certain number of times, controlled by an index variable which, if not otherwise specified, increments automatically by 1 in value for each loop. The syntax is as follows:

```
FOR index := initialvalue TO endvalue DO
    Instructions;
END_FOR;
```

When the index variable has a value greater than the end value, no instructions are performed. This is natural since the test of the termination condition takes place at the beginning of the loop.

   To give an incremental value different from 1, you can add the keyword BY, followed by the desired step size.

Example 11.20

```
FOR k := 1 TO 20 BY 2 DO
    Num := Num*2;
END_FOR;
```

Example 11.21

```
FOR x := 1 TO 10 DO
    V2[x] := V1 * 14.8e-4 * x;
END_FOR;
```

These were two examples of simple FOR loops. There is also no barrier to combining several loops or loops with IF statements. In the next example, we combine a FOR loop with IF statements since the instructions within the loop are conditional.

Example 11.22

```
m := 1;
FOR m:=1 TO 100 DO
  IF Product[m].PictureResult = OK THEN
     IF (Product[m].Weight > 240.0) AND (Product[m].Weight < 260.0)
     THEN
        OK_Product[m] := Product[m].ID;
     END_IF;
  END_IF;
END_FOR;
```

Section 11.9 shows a larger example in which FOR loops are central.

11.8.3 REPEAT ... END_REPEAT

This loop behaves like the WHILE statement in the sense that you do not need to know how many times the loop must be performed. A WHILE loop is performed as long as the condition is satisfied, but the instructions in a REPEAT loop are executed *until* a condition is satisfied. This also means that the instructions that are located between REPEAT and UNTIL are executed at least once. The syntax is as follows:

```
REPEAT
    instructions;
UNTIL condition
END_REPEAT;
```

Example 11.23

```
REPEAT
    Values[x] := New_value;
    x := x + 1;
UNTIL New_value > 1000;
END_REPEAT;
```

11.8.4 The EXIT Instruction

This instruction can be used to stop execution of a WHILE, FOR, or REPEAT loop. The risk of creating an endless loop, or a loop that is active too long[3], is greatest when the conditions that control termination of the loop depend upon external parameters. It is best to use a condition that depends upon a variable that is updated within the loop. If the instruction EXIT is performed within a loop, the execution will stop immediately, and the program will continue by performing the instruction that directly follows the loop. Note that if EXIT is placed in an inner loop, this does not stop the execution of any external loops.

The WHILE loop in Example **11.18** is a typical example of a loop that is not guaranteed to terminate. In the code below, EXIT has been added as insurance against the loop being endless:

```
k := 1;
REPEAT
    Area[k] := 3.14*radius[k]*radius[k] + 2*3.14*radius[k]*height;
    k := k + 1;
    IF k >= 200 THEN EXIT;
    END_IF;
UNTIL Area[k] > 1000
END_REPEAT;
```

---

[3] This is very critical because if a loop is active longer than a defined *watchdog time*, then it results in an error where the PLC goes into an error mode and no programs can run.

11.9   Example: Defining and Calling Functions

Lastly, in this chapter, we will take up an example of array processing. The code below defines a sorting function where the input argument is a structured object in the form of a 256-element array of floating-point values. When the function Sort is called, the function will sort all of the elements in the array in decreasing order so that the highest value is stored in element number 0 and the lowest value in element number 255:

```
(*Declaration:*)
FUNCTION Sort  : ARRAY[0..255] OF REAL;
VAR_INPUT
    Tab        : ARRAY[0..255] OF REAL;
END_VAR
VAR
    N          : UINT:= 256;
    j          : UINT;
    k          : UINT;
    Temp       : REAL;
END_VAR

(*Function code: *)
FOR j := 0 TO N - 2 DO
    FOR k := j+1 TO N-1 DO
        IF Tab[j] < Tab[k] THEN    (* The FOR loop runs through all *)
            Temp := Tab[j];        (* the elements. If the next *)
                                   element *)
            Tab[j] := Tab[k];      (* is larger than the previous
                                   one, *)
            Tab[k] := Temp;        (* the elements swap place *)
        END_IF;
    END_FOR;
END_FOR;
Sort := Tab;                       (* The sorted array is returned. *)
END_FUNCTION

(* Program with function call *)
PROGRAM Sorting
VAR
    Unsort_tab    : ARRAY[0..255] OF REAL; (* Original array *)
    Sort_tab      : ARRAY[0..255] OF REAL; (* Sorted array *)
END_VAR
Sort_tab := Sorter(Unsort_tab);       (* Function call *)
END_PROGRAM
```

This closes the chapter on the ST programming language. You will find more examples in Chapter 13.

11.10   Test Problems

Problem 11.1
(a) What is the difference between semantic errors and syntax errors?
(b) Find at least three syntax errors in the code below:

```
PROGRAM Program_1
VAR
    Time1    :TON;
    Count    :INT;
    Start    :BOOL = FALSE;
    Time2    :TON;
Time1(IN := Start, PT := T#1s);
Time2(IN := NOT Start, PT := t#1s);
IF Time2.Q
    start := TRUE;
END_IF
IF Time1.Q THEN
    Count:= Count + 1;
    Start := FALSE
END_IF
END_PROGRAM
```

(c) If the program above had been free of errors, what do you think the result of running the program would have been? Justify the answer.

Problem 11.2
Write code in Structured Text (ST) for a function called "Power" that calculates X^Z and puts the answer in Y. The variables X and Z are of the integer type and Y is a long integer type. Also write the code for a program section that contains a call of the function.

Problem 11.3
A PLC is to be used for monitoring the number of automobiles in a parking garage. The parking garage has three entrances and two exits. Sensors that give a high pulse each time an automobile passes are installed at each of the entrances and exits. There is room for 200 automobiles in the parking garage.

Two lighted signs are installed at each of the entrances. One lights up with a green text "VACANCY," and the other lights up red with the text "FULL" when the parking facility is full. Each of the signs is controlled by a separate digital signal.

(a) Make an I/O list based upon the information given. Choose input and output addresses and suitable symbolic names.
(b) Write a program in Structured Text (ST) for the monitoring program.

Problem 11.4
Make a program in Structured Text that functions like a clock that counts up seconds, minutes, and hours. (Hint: For example, you can set the cycle time of the task equal to 1 second....)

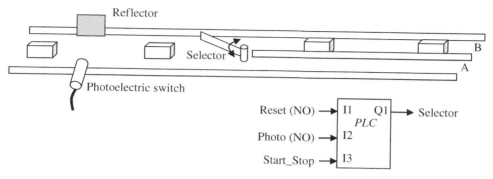

Figure 11.4   Distribution of goods in a packaging facility

Problem 11.5

In a packaging facility, goods that arrive on a conveyor belt are further separated onto one of two tracks. See Figure 11.4. The separation is done by a gate (Selector) that is connected to a single-working pneumatic cylinder with spring return (the cylinder is not shown in the illustration). The gate is normally turned as shown in the illustration, but when it is given a high signal at the output to which the cylinder is connected, the gate swings over so that the goods are sent down track B.

The facility is to distribute goods in groups of 20. That is to say that when 20 items have been sent along track A, the gate swings and 20 items are sent along track B. The counting is done with the aid of a photocell. The process should be repeated continually. A reset button resets the counters to 0. If desired, a two-way (double-throw) switch can be used for Start/Stop.

Write a program in Structured Text that controls the gate in accordance with the above description. The number of groups of 20 that are sent to packing should also be recorded (counted).

Problem 11.6

The power consumption of an (imaginary) motor is to be measured. Both hourly consumption and total consumption are to be calculated. To ensure quality, this is to be done in two ways:

1. Use of a pulse meter: This is a device that measures instantaneous power and sends out pulses. The higher the power, the tighter the pulses. The pulse meter is calibrated so that a rate of 100 pulses per hour corresponds to a constant power consumption of 1 kW.
2. Use of a power meter that measures instantaneous power: The transmitter produces a 4–20 mA signal that corresponds to 0–4600 W. It is assumed that this will be represented by numbers between 0 and 10,000 in the PLC. A problem with this meter is that the value from the transmitter is unstable and jumps around. The program must therefore read the measurement signal at an analog input once per second and average the readings over a 10 second interval so that the mean value can be further used in the energy calculation.

Problem text: Write the program in Structured Text (ST) to calculate energy consumption in kilowatt hours once per hour, in addition to the total energy used. A push button resets all accumulated values when it is activated.

You can choose for yourself whether you want to write a program for each of the two imaginary meters or if the same program contains code for both methods of measurement.

Hint: Be aware of roundoff errors when using integer data types....

Problem 11.7

In this problem, you will ensure that the temperature of the water in the tank stays between two predetermined limits. In the tank, there is a temperature sensor with a transmitter that puts out a 4–20 mA signal, where 4 mA corresponds to 0 °C, while 20 mA corresponds to 90 °C. In the PLC, this is represented by a numerical value in the range 0–32,000. There is a linear relationship between current and temperature.

The system also has a heating element that is turned on when it receives a high signal and turned off when it receives a low signal. You see a sketch of the system below.

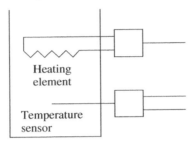

You are now going to control the heating element so that:

- It will be turned on when the temperature drops below a given lower limit. It should be kept on until the temperature reaches the upper limit.
- It will be turned off when the temperature rises above a given upper limit. It should be kept off until the temperature reaches the lower limit.

(a) Program the code for a function block that has three inputs and one output as shown below. The function block should implement the control of the heating element to match the description above. You will use FBD.

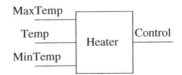

The two inputs **MaxTemp** and **MinTemp** are used to give the upper and lower temperature limits, respectively, while **Temp** is the measured temperature. The Boolean output **Control** will turn the heating element on and off.

(b) Write a program in Structured Text that uses the function block you made in Problem (a). The program should also do the following: In order to check how our temperature control is functioning, the program should store the measured temperature *every half-hour*. The program should record for 24 hours before the record is overwritten by new measurements.

(c) Assume that the system has been in operation for some time and that 24 hours worth of measurement data is stored in an array. Make code that, working from the stored data, finds the number of measurements that correspond to temperatures below MinTemp and the number of measurements that correspond to temperatures above MaxTemp. The program should also find the lowest recorded measurement and calculate the mean value of all the measurements.

12

Sequential Function Chart (SFC)

The chapter discusses the last programming language in the standard: SFC, sequential function chart.

Chapter Contents

- SFC in general:
  Organization, structure and graphics; program structure, graphic symbols, steps, design techniques
- Sequences:
  Diverging and converging with parallel and alternative sequences, mutual exclusion, secure and insecure design
- Transitions:
  Permitted presentation forms, transitions written in different programming languages
- Actions:
  Declaring in LD/SFC/FBD/ST, association with steps, action types (qualifiers)

12.1 Introduction

SFC (Sequential Function Chart) is the last of the languages defined in IEC 61131-3. In 1988, the IEC published the standard IEC 848: "Preparation of function charts for control systems." The standard defined a graphic language for the presentation of sequences in a way that was closely related to a French national standard called *Grafcet*. This language is offered by many European PLC manufacturers. Most of IEC 848 is adopted in SFC in IEC 61131-3. SFC therefore has many similarities with Grafcet (and IEC 848).

Programmable Logic Controllers: A Practical Approach to IEC 61131-3 Using CODESYS, First Edition. Dag H. Hanssen.
© 2015 John Wiley & Sons, Ltd. Published 2015 by John Wiley & Sons, Ltd.

12.1.1 SFC in General

Even though SFC is called a programming language, it is actually not one. It is designed as an aid to making structured programs, particularly in the control of operations that have a sequential nature (Figure 12.1). The language is flexible and can be used at several levels: From the top level, where SFC can be used to describe the main states in a process, to a lower detailed level for code events within the main states.

In other words, SFC can be used to partition (divide up) control-tasks in the same way as top-down design of programs. This was mentioned in Chapter 4 where we discussed flowcharts, among other things. It is a big advantage to be able to use a flowchart or state diagram that has been worked out beforehand as a jumping-off point. For all major programming tasks—at any rate, those of the sequential type—this is a natural way of proceeding. In that way, we get a good overview of the sequence, the states, and the conditions for transitions between the states.

12.2 Structure and Graphics

A sequence in SFC consists of three main elements: *Steps, transitions*, and *actions*:

- *Steps* are most often related to the individual states or phases that are to be controlled.
- *Transitions* contain conditions that must be satisfied in order for the control to proceed from one state to the next.
- *Actions* are associated with the individual steps and define events and instructions that are to be performed in the individual process phases.

  Figure 12.2 shows an example of a function chart in SFC.
  In general, function charts can be described as follows:

- The start of the program consists of a special type of step with double side edges[1] that are called the *initiation step*. This step is activated automatically when the PLC is set to Run

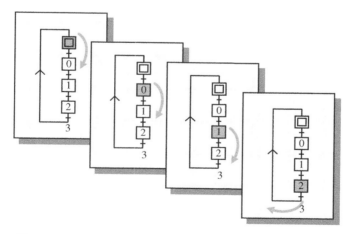

Figure 12.1   Figurative description of a sequence process in SFC

---

[1] The standard allows other graphics forms as well, such as double outer contours around the entire block.

mode. It is also to this step the program usually returns to, either by means of programmed returns or after the program sequence has been completed.
- The other blocks (with single side edges) are *steps*. In Figure 12.2, these blocks are given identifiers such as Stir and Drain. These often represent a particular state or phase in the process that is to be controlled.
- One or more instructions/actions are performed in association with each step. These can be actions associated with outputs or changes in internal variables.
- Small horizontal lines are entered between steps. These mark the transitions. These determine when and where the PLC will continue carrying out the code. When the transition is complete, the step before the transition is deactivated and the step after the transition is activated.
- Branching can be used to create alternative or parallel sequences.
- It is also possible to jump between steps that are not directly associated with each other.

Explanation of the sequence (code)
When the PLC is set in Run mode, the initiation step Ready is activated. When the operator presses the start button (Start=TRUE), the PLC begins the sequence by deactivating the Ready step and activating the Fill step. This step remains active until the tank is full (level sensor Tank_full sends a logically high signal). Then Fill is deactivated and Stir is activated. This step is to remain active for a certain time. This is indicated by the next transition, Stir.T > t#30s. This comparison is satisfied (TRUE) when a *built-in* timer has reached a value of 30 seconds. Then the Stir step is deactivated and the Drain step is activated. When the tank is empty (sensor signal Tank_empty becomes TRUE), Drain is deactivated and the initiation step Ready is activated again. The program is now ready for a new run.

Example 12.1

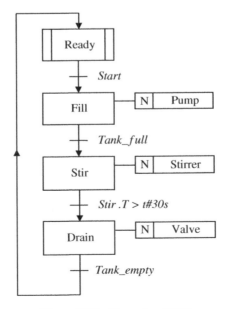

Figure 12.2   Example of SFC

It is this neat and elegant way of programming sequences that should make SFC a clear first choice in many PLC applications:

- Steps that show the phases and states in sequential processes.
- Transitions that define only the conditions that must be satisfied in order for the sequence to continue from one step to a succeeding step in the sequence. Transitions are (often simple) Boolean conditions.
- Actions that couple control of outputs to the individual phases in the process.[2]

12.2.1   Overview: Graphic Symbols

As with the symbols in the other graphical languages, the standard does not impose any requirements for the symbols in SFC to have any particular graphic format, but rather specifies a semigraphic format that utilizes only text characters, as, for instance:

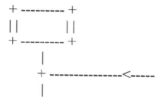

The individual manufacturers naturally enough choose a fully graphic format, but the forms of the symbols in the standard must be followed even though the types of lines and colors may vary. Table 12.1 shows an overview of the symbols in SFC as they *can* look in a fully graphic format.

12.2.2   Alternative Branches

In the example in Figure 12.2, there is only one possible route in the sequence, but a SFC can contain many alternative branches. Let us therefore expand the example by adding the following: If the pump has been running for more than 1 minute without the Tank_ full giving a high signal, the sequence should jump to Drain. See Figure 12.3.

This addition constitutes an alternative sequence, where the sequences first split up (a so-called OR *divergence*), to rejoin again farther down (OR *convergence*). After the divergence (after the Fill step), there follows one transition for each alternative branch.

It is extremely important that these transitions be *mutually exclusive*. This means that the conditions in these transitions must be such that only one of the transitions can be satisfied at any time, thus the word OR. If such transitions are not mutually exclusive, two or more

---

[2] It is not a requirement of the standard that actions be presented in detail in the functional chart, but it is a great advantage for legibility and understanding if this is done if possible.

Table 12.1   Possible graphical symbols in SFC

Steps	Initiation step (one of these)	
	Ordinary step	
Transitions	Between two steps	
Parallel sequences	Parallel branching (AND divergence)	
	Parallel convergence (AND convergence)	
Alternative sequences	OR divergence	
	OR convergence	
Connecting lines	Up and down	And
	Left and right	And
Jumps	Jump to StepX	StepX

alternative branches can be activated simultaneously and that is regarded as an error. In Figure 12.3, the condition *AND NOT Fill.T>t#1m* prevents the two branches from being activated simultaneously.

The alternative branching in this example does not contain any step. This is because the purpose of this particular alternative branch is just to jump over a step. Similarly, alternative branching can be used to create a *loop* that performs one or several steps a desired number of times. (See, for instance, Figure 12.11.)

Note this alternative way of jumping to another step by using the jump symbol ⌙▶ where you enter the name of the step to which you want to jump, in this case, Ready.

Example 12.2

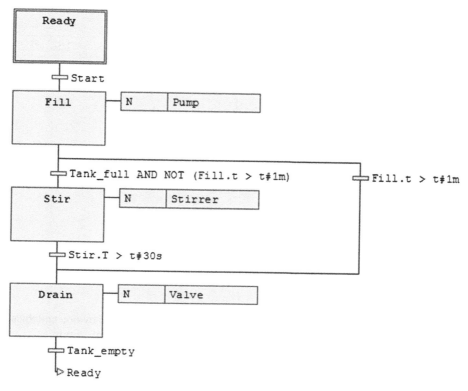

Figure 12.3   SFC with alternative sequences (CODESYS v3.x)

12.2.3   *Parallel Branches*

It is also possible to activate parallel branches in SFC, that is, branches that will be executed in parallel with each other. This branching does not need to contain an equal number of steps, but the branches are *activated simultaneously and are terminated simultaneously*.

    For this reason, there is a <u>common</u> transition condition before the place where the sequences diverge and one common transition condition immediately after the place where the sequences converge.

Example 12.3

Let us alter the SFC diagram in Figure 12.3 by making the following modification: We would now like to have the product mixture (the batch) warmed up after the tank is filled. Furthermore, we want the stirring to take place in *parallel* with filling, heating, and emptying. The result can

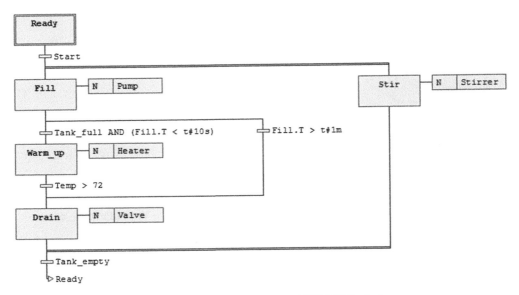

Figure 12.4   Parallel sequence (CODESYS v3.x)

be as shown in Figure 12.4. Note that the parallel sequences are activated by one and the same transition (Start) and that they converge before a common transition (Tank_empty).

Also note that parallel branches are executed independently of each other before they reach the convergence point. In order for parallel sequences to be deactivated, the following conditions must be satisfied:

- All the sequences must have reached their last step. (Both Drain and Stir must be active in Figure 12.4.)
- The transition after the convergence must be satisfied. (Tank_empty must be TRUE in Figure 12.4.)

This means that the transition after the convergence is not evaluated by the PLC before all parallel branches are in their last step.

12.3   Steps

We have seen that each individual step, including the initiation step, is assigned an identifier (a symbolic name). This name must be unique within the POU in question. This means also that the name is local within the POU so that a step in another POU can have the same name.

A step is either active or inactive, but several steps can be active simultaneously.

It is not possible to place two steps consecutively without a transition in between.

One or more actions can be associated with each individual step. These actions can be programmed in any of the languages in the standard.

12.3.1   Step Addresses

Each individual step that is used in the sequence is assigned two variable addresses: **Step_name.X** and **Step_name.T**. These addresses can be used in programming transitions and actions:

- **Step_Name.X** is a Boolean variable that is TRUE when the step is active. When the step is inactive, the state is FALSE. This variable can be used to perform actions when the associated step is activated or deactivated or continually as long as the step is active. The variable can also be used in transitions. Note: I is not possible to manipulate the state of this variable. In that case, it would result in an error message from the compiler.
- **Step_name.T** is a variable of the data type TIME.[3] All steps in SFC, including the initiation step, have built-in timers. As soon as a step is activated, the built-in timer starts and runs until the step is deactivated. In other words, the variable contains the elapsed time for the step in question. When step is deactivated, the timer is reset to t#0s. Neither of these variables can be modified by the user program.

Which identifiers and how many characters are permitted depend upon the implementation, so that it is wise to be conservative. If possible, use descriptive names related to the process or to the system that the program will control.

As mentioned previously, the variables Step_name.X and Step_name.T can be accessed and used in programming actions and transitions, but they *cannot* be manipulated.

The two following examples show permitted and illegal use of the step variables, respectively.

Example 12.4   Examples of Permitted Use of Step Variables

```
IF Stir.X OR (Drain.X AND %IX1.0) THEN
    %QX2.5 := TRUE;
ELSE
    %QX2.5 := FALSE;
END_IF;
WHILE Warm_up.T < t#20s DO
    Calculate;
END_WHILE;
```

Example 12.5   Examples of Illegal Use of Step Variables

```
IF Stir.X OR (Drain.X AND %IX1.0) THEN
    Warm_up.X := 1;       ←Illegal
END_IF;
IF %IX1.12 THEN
    Fill.T := t#45s;      ←Illegal
END_IF;
```

---

[3]You can read about these data types in Section 6.5.2.

12.3.2   SFC in Text Form (for Those Specially Interested...)

The standard also defines the possibility for steps, transitions, and actions to be defined in *text-based* language. This may sound rather strange since the main point of SFC is to structure the program code in a simple graphical way.

Nevertheless, if this capability is implemented, a code in Structured Text (ST) for the sequence in Figure 12.2 can look like this:

```
INITIAL_STEP Ready :
END_STEP;
TRANSITION FROM Ready TO Fill
    := Start;
END_TRANSITION;
STEP Fill :
    Pump(N);
END_STEP;
TRANSITION FROM Fill TO Stir
    := Tank_full;
END_TRANSITION;
STEP Stir :
    Stirrer(N);
END_STEP;
TRANSITION FROM Stir TO Drain
    := Stir.T > t#30s;
END_TRANSITION;
STEP Drain :
    Valve(N);
END_STEP;
TRANSITION FROM Drain TO Ready
    := Tank_empty;
END_TRANSITION;
```

12.4   Transitions

The conditions of the transition determine when the previous step is deactivated and the following step activated. In order for a transition to be tested at all by the PLC, all of the steps directly above the transition must be active.

When the transition is satisfied, the previous step is deactivated first, before the following step is immediately activated.

Two transitions cannot be placed adjacently without a step in between.

Figure 12.5 shows the sequence for the automatic packaging facility that we made a flowchart for in Section 4.5.3. All of the transitions are programmed here in ST, and they must all be either simple Boolean variables or Boolean expressions. The result of testing a transition is therefore either TRUE or FALSE.

A transition condition that should always be satisfied is represented by TRUE.

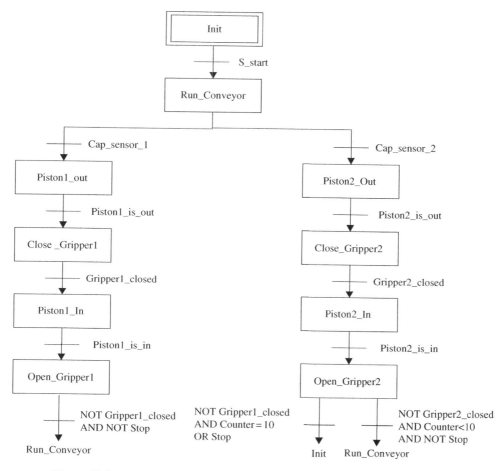

Figure 12.5   Sequence for the packaging facility, with added transition conditions

Even though we have, up till now, chosen to use Structured Text (ST) to describe the transitions, it is permitted to use all of the other languages in IEC 61131-3. Most manufacturers have only implemented ST transitions directly in the diagram. Transitions written in other languages must then be given a name that is called from the diagram (see next section.)

However, the standard defines the possibility that transitions may be programmed in the graphical languages LD and FBD directly between two steps. Figure 12.6 shows an example where FBD code is used to program a transition.

12.4.1   Alternative Definition of Transitions

In the examples we have studied up till now, the transitions have been coded directly within the sequences. To what extent this is possible and to what extent the code in the transitions is directly visible vary, as we mentioned, from one development tool to another. Some manufacturers

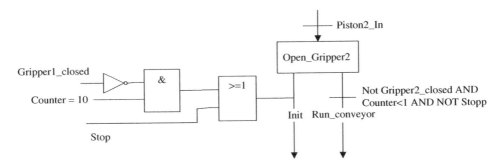

Figure 12.6   Transition programmed in FBD

have implemented only short transition codes written in the sequences, but larger transition codes can be programmed as named separate entities that are called from SFC.

Nevertheless, the code (conditions) for a transition can in some cases be comprehensive. There is not always room or it is not practical to put the code within the sequence diagram itself. The solution is then to name the transition and program it in a separate window/editor. Example: The transition from Step4 to Step5 is given the identifier *Trans_45*. The named transition can be programmed in any of the languages (except for SFC) within the keywords TRANSITION and END_TRANSITION in the following way:

```
TRANSITION Trans_45 FROM Step4 TO Step5:
  :
  Program code;
  :
END_TRANSITION
```

Example 12.6   Defining a Transition in LD

We would now like to identify the transition that was presented in FBD code in Figure 12.6 with a name. We would also like to program the associated conditions in LD. The sequence could now look like this:

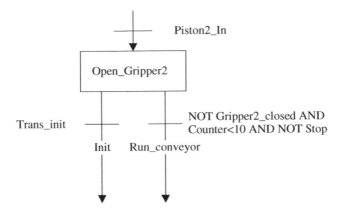

Defining the transition can be done in LD code, for instance, as follows:

```
TRANSITION Trans_init FROM Open_gripper2 TO Init:
```

```
   Gripper1_closed      Counter_is_10
 ──────┤/├──────────────────┤ ├──────────┐
                                           │
        Stop                               │
 ──────┤ ├──────────────────────────────── 
```

```
END_TRANSITION
```

We might think that the requirements in the standard for definition of transitions amount to a little overkill. In most, if not all, development tools, the user is not required to use the defined keywords in programming transitions. The manufacturer has probably chosen to add these keywords implicitly. Furthermore, there will most likely be separate code windows where you can program transitions that cannot be coded in the chart directly. (To see how transitions can be programmed outside the sequence in CODESYS, you can study the example in Section 13.4 on page 404.)

12.5 Actions

One or more *actions* (instructions) can be associated with each separate step. If no actions are associated with a step, the step is either a delay step or a step that functions to converge alternative branches.

There are naturally rules for how actions and instructions are presented in the function chart. In the IEC standard, an individual action is presented as a rectangular box that is associated to the step in question. See Figure 12.7. This direct link to the step makes it easy to see where and how the actions are activated or initiated.

The first field in the rectangle always contains a *qualifier*.

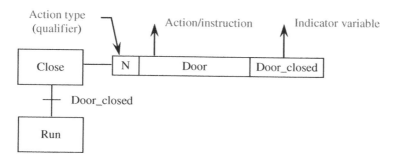

Figure 12.7   Example of action

This is a character, or possibly two characters, that identifies the *type* of action that is to be performed. If the qualifier is a time type, a time is also shown in the TIME format in this field.

The next field contains the action or name of the action that is to be performed. Most often, this is a single action or instruction that typically changes the state of a Boolean variable. In such cases, the action is the name of a Boolean variable.

If there are other types of instructions or more instructions that are to be performed, a user-selected (but permitted) name is given in the action field. This name points to a named program code that contains a set of instructions. In both cases, the qualifier specifies which action is to be executed.

The third and last field can contain an *indicator variable*, if needed.

Such indicator variables are not a requirement in the standard, and it is therefore up to the manufacturer to implement the capability if he wishes to provide it. Usually the indicator variable will be a variable that is changed as the result of the action that is being performed. Often, the indicator variable will be used as a condition in the next transition as in the figure below.

12.5.1   Action Types

To make it easier to control how and when actions are executed, the standard specifies a set of action types. Table 12.2 shows an overview of the defined types.

Table 12.2   SFC action types

Qualifier	Type	Description
N	Non-stored	Action that is performed as long as the associated step is active
S	Set (Stored)	Stored action. Performed until it is reset
R	Reset	Deactivates a stored action
P	Pulse	A pulse action that is performed once each time the step is active. (See Section 12.5.2)
L	Time Limited	Time-limited action. Stops after a given time or when the step is deactivated
D	Time Delayed	Time-delayed action. Starts after a given time if the step is still active
SD	Stored and time Delayed	Stored and time-delayed action. The action is set active after a given time, even though the step deactivates before that. The action continues until it is reset
DS	Time Delayed and Stored	Time-delayed and stored action. If this step is still active after the specified time, the action will start. It will run until it is reset
SL	Stored and time Limited	Stored and time limited. The action starts when the step becomes active and will continue during the given period or until it is reset
P1	Pulse—rising edge	A pulse action that is executed only once when the step is *activated*
P0	Pulse—falling edge	A pulse action that is executed only once when the step is *deactivated*

S—stored; D—delayed.

The first three types in the table, **N**, **S**, and **R**, are the ones most used, along with actions of type **P** (or **P1**, and **P0** if these are implemented). An **N** was given in the example earlier. The letter **N** refers to an action of the **N**on-stored type and indicates an action that is to be performed continually as long as the associated step is active. This choice is also the default.

The other action types, all of which deal with time, are needed only in exceptional cases. One of the reasons for this is that the built-in timers in the steps are sufficient for most cases of time management of the sequence. Furthermore, it is usually a good design technique to create the function chart so that you avoid actions that need to be activated and deactivated, "independent" of the process in the sequence. This increases the programmer's control and thereby reduces the risk of unforeseen events.

12.5.2 Action Control

It is important to be clear that the standard defines that all actions are executed *one extra time* after the action is deactivated. This means that the actions are performed at least twice. This does not apply to actions of type P1 and P0.[4] These are executed only once. Such an extra execution is illustrated in Figure 12.8 for a type N action.

This rather strange requirement for an extra execution is luckily not an absolute requirement, because it sometime creates trouble. (See Example 12.10.)

When it comes to the time-related action types L, D, SD, DS, and SL, use of this will require that the associated delay or duration (of the TIME type) be stated. To what extent this can be done in the qualifier field or elsewhere depends upon the implementation. Figure 12.9 shows how this can look for the action type SD. Here, the time is stated in the

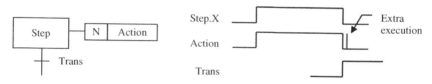

Figure 12.8   All action types, except for P1 and P0, are executed one extra time

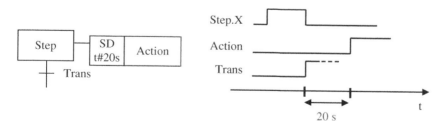

Figure 12.9   Specification of associated time for a time-dependent action

---

[4]Action types P1 and P2 are implemented in CODESYS as "step actions," that is to say that they are not implemented as IEC actions that are associated with steps but are "built-in" to the steps.

qualifier field together with the action type. The figure also shows the functional principle for an action of the SD type.

Note that all action types that are stored must be reset at another place in the sequence by using the qualifier R and giving the same action name. This also applies to action types S, SD, DS, and SL.

The possibilities of activating actions in different ways are also significant for how we build up the sequence, something that the next example shows.

Example 12.7

Take the starting point in the SFC in Figure 12.4. Now, we want the stirring to continue for 2 minutes at the same time that filling and heating is going on. If the step Drain is reached before the time has elapsed, the action is reset. In the previous example, we also put in some insurance by using an alternative sequence. We can now solve this by using action type L for the pump and specifying that the pump operate for a maximum of 1 minute. An operator-controlled stop and a lamp that stays lit as long as the facility runs have also been added (Figure 12.10).

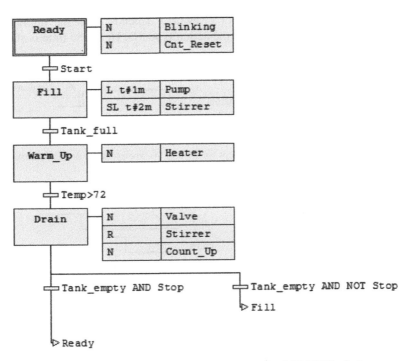

Figure 12.10   Use of different action types (in CODESYS v3.x)

12.5.3 Alternative Declaration and Use of Actions

An action sometimes involves more than setting or resetting Boolean quantities. We often wish to change the value of numerical variables or perform a set of instructions. Such actions can be programmed outside the action charts themselves and identified by means of action names, so that they can be called up from the function chart.

Actions can be programmed in IL, LD, ST, FBD, or even in SFC and will be subobjects for the POU that contains the function chart.

The next two examples show possible ways the manufacturer can choose to implement actions that are more comprehensive.

Example 12.8 The Principle for Actions from SFC

The example below shows calling an action with the name Calculate and the code for the named action (with syntax under the provisions of IEC 61131-3).

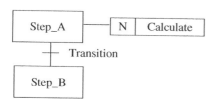

```
ACTION Calculate;
IF Count > 10 THEN
     Light := TRUE;
END_IF;
IF Enable_Inc THEN
     Value := Value + 50;
END_IF
END_ACTION
```

As we see, IEC 61131-3 specifies that the instruction set will be included between the keywords ACTION and END_ACTION. In many programming tools, though, these keywords will be implicit or built into the program objects where the actions are programmed.

Example 12.9

The standard also defines the possibility that actions can be programmed in an extra field in the graphical action blocks that are linked to the steps in SFC. An example of this is shown below:

```
N  Calculate

IF %MW50 > 10 THEN
    Light:= TRUE;
END_IF;
IF %I1.0 THEN
      %MW10 := %MW5 + 50;
ELSE %MW10 := %MW5;
END_IF;
```

When the manufacturer chooses to implement the ability to state actions in this way, the extent to which new program code can be shown in this extra field will probably be limited. A large code field in the functional chart would quickly become incomprehensible.

The standard also defines the possibility of using action objects associated with an SFC in other POUs. This does not apply the other way around, so that all actions that can be called up from an SFC must be programmed locally in the POU.

Example 12.10

Let us expand the tank example in Figure 12.2 with more requirements. This time, the lamp should blink before start and after three runs have been completed. Otherwise, it should shine steadily. With these modifications, the function chart becomes as shown in Figure 12.11. (I have shown the actions on the side in the figure.)

Note: We have a type P action where we increment a counter value. In practice, this will increment the value by two every time the step is activated. The solution is either to use a REAL variable which increments the value by 0.5 or to use a P1 or a P0 action.

12.6   Control of Diagram Execution

Manufacturers who implement SFC as one of the languages also implement some special objects (flags) that can be used as a kind of external control of SFC execution. Such objects are not implemented in the standard, and it is therefore not possible to define them in general. However, it is possible to say something general about them.

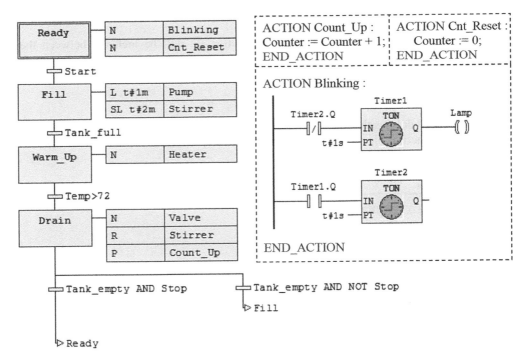

Figure 12.11   SFC sequence with actions that are called up

Table 12.3   Implicit SFC variables defined in CODESYS

Variable	Type	Functional action
SFCInit	BOOL	When the flag is set TRUE, all steps are deactivated and the initiation step is activated. All steps, actions, and other flags are reset. Nothing is processed again until the flag is set back to FALSE
SFCReset	BOOL	Corresponds to SFCInit except that the initiation step is processed (the flag can therefore be reset in the initiation step)
Pause_SFC	BOOL	As long as this variable is TRUE, all execution of the diagram will stop. Execution of actions also pauses so that the state of outputs, for instance, freezes
SFCTrans	BOOL	The flag becomes TRUE as soon as a transition has been performed
SFCCurrentStep	STRING	This variable stores the name of the step as active at any time. If several steps are active (parallel sequences), the name of the step farthest to the right is registered

No matter which of the development tools you use, where SFC is one of the languages, it is probable that the following objects (flags) are defined (although possibly with different names): **SFCInit**, **SFCReset**, and **SFCPause**.

CODESYS defines these flags plus a few others for control of time, error management, and information. Some of these are shown in Table 12.3, but there could be many others, so check the documentation.

You can see examples of use of a couple of these objects in the next chapter.

Note: All flags are implicit and must be activated and *declared* before use.

12.7   Good Design Technique

Good structure and design of the SFC chart is naturally important. One thing is that the program should be comprehensible and logical. Another thing that is even more important is that the program has to be capable of being run and that possible conflicts are eliminated. In particular, improper use of alternative and parallel sequences is something that can quickly create problems. We will try to explain this by means of two examples.

Example 12.11

Figure 12.12 shows a sequence where a classic error has been committed. An alternative sequence diverges *within* a parallel sequence. Since the transitions that activate the branching in an alternative sequence must always be mutually exclusive, Step_C and Step_D can never be active simultaneously. Therefore, the parallel sequence can never be closed and Step_F and the subsequent step will never be reached. A simple way to fix the problem in this example is to introduce a "step" that converges the alternative branches *before* the AND convergence.

In the example above, the design error was catastrophic in the sense that the processing comes to a halt. Faulty design can also, under certain circumstances, function for a while and then suddenly generate a serious error. See the next example.

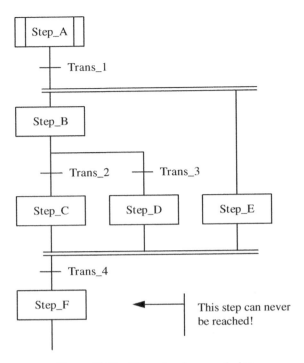

Figure 12.12   Example of wrong design

Example 12.12

In the diagram in Figure 12.13, there is a branching *out of* the parallel sequence, and this can create unforeseen problems. The following can happen here (assume that Step_A is active):

- Trans_1 is satisfied, which will activate Step_B and Step_C.
- Then assume that Trans_2 is satisfied in addition to Trans_4. This means that Step_D and Step_F are activated.
- Now, when Trans_5 and Trans_1 are satisfied, Step_C becomes activated again. Thereby two steps (C and F) in the same branch are active simultaneously, something that is not permitted under the standard.

What consequences this will cause depends upon how the manufacturer has implemented SFC. In the worst case, the PLC will go into an Error mode.

A cookbook
Here, I present a possible procedure for working on designing a sequence in SFC. It is in no way applicable to all possible problems, but perhaps it can be of some help.

1. Think through the sequence(s) and particularly into how many steps the sequence ought to be divided. If you have done proper preliminary work, you will have one or more flow-charts or state diagrams as a starting point. It can often be a good idea to split up the

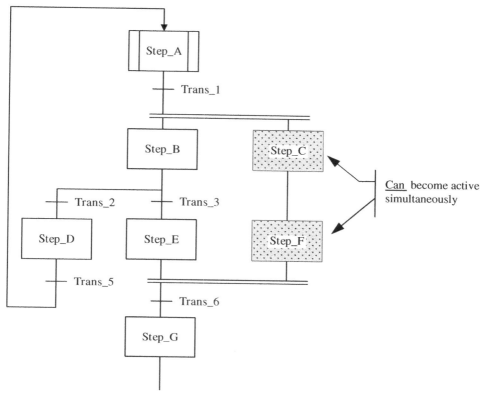

Figure 12.13   Example of risky design

problem into several sequences. When it is a large process that is to be controlled (large with respect to complexity), it is probably a good idea to use macro-steps. Then, for example, you will have an overall sequence with several subsequences, one for each macro-step. It is also possible to call up another sequence via an action.

2. Also evaluate whether alternative or parallel sequences are needed:
    • You need an alternative branch if there are several possible paths through the sequence, and only one of them should be chosen. Then each transition to each branch has its own condition.
    • You need a parallel branch if there are two or more branches to be traversed *simultaneously*. Then there will be a common transition to all the branches.

3. Construct the sequence(s).

4. Program the transitions. These usually consist of simple Boolean tests or time conditions. Remember to use mutually exclusive conditions for alternative sequences.

5. Program the actions. Individual Boolean actions are stated directly in the SFC diagram, but other actions are programmed as objects under the POU and are called up from SFC.

6. There will also probably be a requirement to manage other external events that may take place such as power failure or activation of an emergency stop. Here, implicit SFC variables such as SFCPause and SFCInit can be useful.

In the next chapter, you will find some larger SFC examples.

12.8   Test Problems

Problem 12.1
In a test laboratory for measurement of hull resistance for various types of ship hulls, the hulls are attached to a cable that pulls the ship hull through the water. In order to calculate the average speed, a PLC and two photocells are used. In addition, a start button is used to activate the program. See Figure 12.14. Towing of the boat is done manually and is therefore not a part of the program in the PLC.
   Write a program in SFC that measures the time that the boat takes to pass the distance bounded by the two photocells and calculates the average speed.

Problem 12.2   Product Weighing
See Figure 12.15. Products A and B will be filled and weighed in turn on scales no. 1. At the same time, product C will be filled and weighed on scales no. 2. Filling is controlled by opening and closing of the solenoid valves S1, S2, and S3.
   Assume that there are discrete sensors that give a high signal when a sufficient quantity of each product has come onto the scale. You can call these signals **A_ready**, **B_ready**, and **C_ready**.
   When all the products are weighed, the outlet solenoid valves (SV1 and SV2) on either scale are opened for 15 seconds so that the material empties into the mixer. The mixer should start at the same time.
   After the scales are empty, the mixer will continue to go for 10 seconds. Then the solenoid valve on the mixer (SB) is opened so that the mixer empties. During emptying, the mixer should run for 20 seconds. Then the mixer is considered empty, and the working cycle is completed.
   Make a program in standard SFC for controlling the facility.

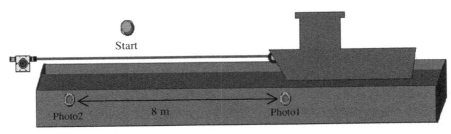

Figure 12.14   Test rig for hull resistance measurement (Reproduced with permission of Schneider Electric)

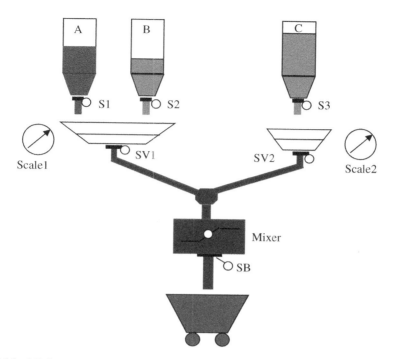

Figure 12.15 Mixing process—Problems 12.2 and 12.3 (Reproduced with permission from TheLearningPit.com)

Problem 12.3   Product Weighing: Modifications
The process in the previous problem now may not start unless an emptying sequence has been performed. Furthermore, should there be a power outage during a run; reconnection of line voltage should be handled as follows:

- A lamp blinks as an indication that emptying must be done.
- Emptying is started with a push button.
- The lamp starts shining steadily, solenoid valves SV1, SV2, and SB open, and the mixer starts and runs for 15 seconds.
- After that, the lamp turns off and the normal process can be started again.

Add the necessary modifications in the program from Problem 12.2 to take care of this. You can either add steps to the sequence from the previous problem or make your own small sequence that runs if a power outage has taken place.

Problem 12.4
The figure below shows a sequence in SFC that has errors and weaknesses. (The actions are not included for the sake of simplicity.) What is wrong with this sequence?

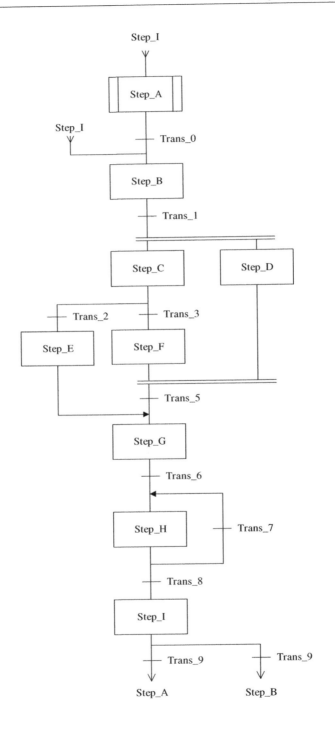

Problem 12.5 Mixing Process

Figure 12.16 shows a sketch of the mixing process at the University of Tromsø, Department of Engineering and Safety. The facility consists of the following: tank with pipe, three fluid pumps, one mixer, one heater, three level indicators calibrated for various fluid levels, and a control panel with signal lights and spring-loaded push buttons. During operation, two products will be filled into one tank. The mixture will then be warmed up during mixing. When a desired temperature is reached, the tank is emptied.

Description of the sequence:

* In the initiation step, the **Ready** light will be lit. The sequence will start when the **Start** button is pressed. Then **Pump1** starts, the Ready light turns off, and the **Run** light lights.
* When **Level1** gives a high signal, Pump1 stops and **Pump2** starts. At the same time, the **Mixer** starts.
* When **Level2** becomes TRUE, Pump2 stops and the **Heater** is turned on.
* When the desired temperature is reached, **Temp** >= 50 °C, the heater is turned off.
* Five seconds after that, the Mixer stops and **Pump3** starts.
* When the tank is **Empty** (becomes logically *low*), the whole sequence is repeated automatically 50 times. Then the Run lamp turns off, and the Ready lamp lights again.

In order to ensure safe operation, some interruption routines must be added. What happens during an interruption depends upon what caused the interruption. There are two possibilities:

1. Operator activates **Stop**: No matter where in the sequence the process is working, the inlet pumps must stop, the heater turns off, the mixer starts, and the emptying pump starts. When the tank is empty, the mixer stops, but the emptying pump continues to run for 5 seconds. After that, the facility can be started again by pressing the start button.
2. Timer interruption shall occur if:
   * More than 30 seconds elapse from the time Pump1 starts until Level1 gives a signal OR
   * More than 20 seconds elapse from when Pump2 starts until Level2 is reached OR
   * More than 1 minute lapses from the time Pump3 starts until the tank is empty OR
   * It takes more than 10 minutes from the time the heater is turned on until the desired temperature is reached.

In all cases, the following should happen:

The active pumps and the heating element must be turned off immediately, and the **Error** signal light must blink. The operator must check the facility and correct any error. When this has been done, the operator confirms it by holding in both Start and Stop for at least 5 seconds. Then the tank should empty automatically so that the facility is ready for starting again.

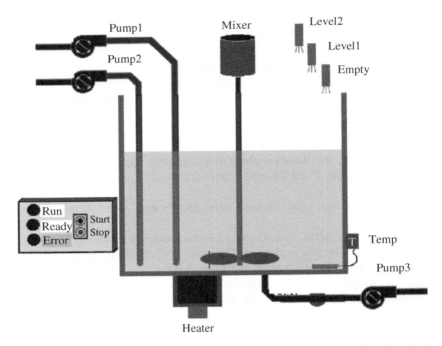

Figure 12.16   Mixing facilities in Problem 12.5 (Reproduced with permission of The LearningPit.com)

Problem 12.6   Batch Process
Make an SFC program for the batch example in Section 4.5.6.

Problem 12.7   Product Sorting
Make an SFC program for the product sorting given in Problem 4.9.

Problem 12.8   Filling Station
Make an SFC program for the filling station given in Problem 4.10.

Problem 12.9   Motor Operation
Make an SFC program for the Motors given in Problem 4.11.

Problem 12.10   Apple Packing
Make an SFC program for running the apple packing facility from Section 4.6.5 and the associated state diagram from Figure 4.27.

13

Examples

As the title indicates, this chapter contains only examples. They are practically oriented (but partly imaginary) program code examples. The examples are programmed entirely in conformity with the standard as described in this book.

Chapter Contents

- Example 1—Function block, ST
- Example 2—SFC
- Example 3—SFC
- Example 4—ST/FBD/SFC

13.1   Example 1: PID Controller Function Block: Structured Text

The output MV(t) from a PID controller can be expressed mathematically as

$$MV(t) = MR + K_P e(t) + \frac{K_P}{T_I} \int_0^t e(t)d\tau + K_P T_D \frac{de(t)}{dt}$$

where

MV(t), manipulating value—MV
MR, manual reset (or bias)
e(t), deviation (between the set point r(t) and the process value y(t))
K_P, controller gain
T_I, integration time in seconds
T_D, derivative time in seconds

Programmable Logic Controllers: A Practical Approach to IEC 61131-3 Using CODESYS, First Edition. Dag H. Hanssen.
© 2015 John Wiley & Sons, Ltd. Published 2015 by John Wiley & Sons, Ltd.

This function is in a continuous form and cannot be directly implemented in a computer or a programmable logic controller (PLC), but with the use of some mathematical approximations for the derivative and the integral, the function can be expressed in a discrete form:

$$\mathrm{MV}(k)=\mathrm{MV}(k-1)+K_{\mathrm{P}}\left[\left(1+\frac{T}{2T_{\mathrm{I}}}+\frac{T_{\mathrm{D}}}{T}\right)e(k)-\left(1-\frac{T}{2T_{\mathrm{I}}}+\frac{2T_{\mathrm{D}}}{T}\right)e(k-1)+\frac{T_{\mathrm{D}}}{T}e(k-2)\right]$$

A new quantity has been introduced here, namely, the sampling time T. In practice, this will be the update time, that is, how often the expression is executed. In a PLC, one will normally insert such a PID block in a task that is updated cyclically, and T will then be the scan time for the task. (*Note*: MV($k-1$) is equal to MR on the first execution.) The letter k indicates the cycle number. MV($k-1$) and $e(k-1)$ are therefore the respective values of the differences between the values of the manipulating value and the deviation from the previous cycle to the current cycle.

Below, you will find a function block written in Structured Text (ST) that implements the PID controller function. In order to calculate the cycle time T, I have used a function from the SysTimeRtc library. The function returns the clock of the PLC in milliseconds.

```
FUNCTION_BLOCK PID
VAR_INPUT
      Man_auto       : BOOL;      // 0 - Manual, 1-Automatic
      PV             : WORD;      // Process value
      SP             : REAL;      // Set point
      MR             : REAL;      // Bias - Manual Reset
      Kp             : REAL;      // Proportional gain
      Td             : REAL;      // Derivative time
      Ti             : REAL;      // Integral time
END_VAR
VAR_OUTPUT
      MV             : WORD;      // Manipulating Value
END_VAR
VAR
      T              : REAL;      // Cycle time
      Dev            : REAL;      // Deviation - Difference SP - PV
      MV1            : REAL;      // MV value in previous cycle
      Dev1           : REAL;      // Difference value in previous cycle
      Dev2           : REAL;      // Difference value two cycles ago
      T1,T2:ULINT;
      A, B           : REAL;      // Factors
END_VAR


T1  := T2;
SysTimeRtcHighResGet(pTimeStamp := T2);
T = ULINT_TO_REAL(T2-T1)/1000; // Determines the cycle time.
```

```
IF T1=0 THEN
    MV := MR; // Start value for MV
END_IF


Dev := SP - WORD_TO_REAL(PV); // Deviation


IF Man_auto = TRUE THEN
    (* Calculates MV: *)
    A := 1 + T/(2*Ti) + Td/T;
    B := 1 - T/(2*Ti) + 2*Td/T;
    MV:= MV1 + Kp*(A*Dev - B *Dev1 + (Td/T)*Dev2);
    (* Updates variables: *)
    MV1  := MV;
    Dev2 := Dev1;
    Dev1 := Dev;
ELSE
    (* MV when controller is in manual mode: *)
    MV := MR;
    MV1 := MV;
END_IF
END_FUNCTION_BLOCK
```

(*Note*: You will find a PID FB in CODESYS UTIL library.)

13.2   Example 2: Sampling: SFC

Samples are to be taken from a conveyor belt that transports goods. See Figure 13.1. Every 10th item will be selected. A sample is taken by stopping the belt while a **Piston** pushes the item off the belt to a testing station. When the system has taken 50 samples, the conveyor belt will stop. The belt motor is started again by giving a high signal (**Motor**) to the contactor K1. The motor is protected by a motor monitor (**MotorProtect**):

* A capacitive sensor (**CapSensor**) detects when an item has come into position to be pushed off the belt.
* If the (**Stop**) button is activated, the belt should stop after the first sample.
* If the emergency stop (**EStop**) (NC) button is pushed or the motor protection turns off, the facility and the program are stopped immediately. They should start up again in the same program state when the start button is activated.

The pneumatic cylinder is single acting, that is, it goes to its plus position when the valve Y1 receives a high signal (24V DC) and returns to its minus position when the signal goes logically low again. The cylinder has built-in sensors that give signals when the piston has traveled completely out (B+) and completely in (B−).

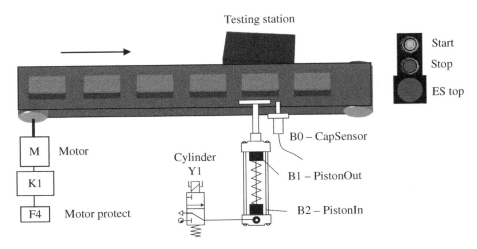

Figure 13.1   Facility for taking samples

13.2.1   List of Variables

Inputs	Outputs	Internal	Comments on internal signals
Start	Motor	NumSamples	Total samples taken
Stop	Cylinder	Count10	Counter to 10
EStop		Count50	Counter to 50
MotorProt		SFCPause	Freezes the sequence
CapSensor			
PistonOut			
PistonIn			

13.2.2   Possible Solution

The solution that follows here is implemented in CODESYS. This means that some implementation-specific considerations must be added:

• Because CODESYS has not implemented the action types P1 and P0 as IEC actions, I have used the built-in Entry and Exit actions.
• A configurable object called SFCPause can be used in all SFC POUs (see Section 12.6). This object may also be explicitly declared as a Boolean object. Since it must be declared within the SFC POU, it must be declared as an input variable so that the value transfer from other POUs can take place.
• When SFCPause is set logically high, the execution of the SFC will stop. When the object is reset, the execution continues from where it stopped. SFCPause is used here to freeze the sequence when the emergency stop is activated or when the motor monitor turns off.

```
VAR_GLOBAL
(* Defines variables that are used in several POUs: *)
    Start        AT %I2.0    : BOOL;
    EStop        AT %I2.1    : BOOL;
    MotorProt    AT %I2.2    : BOOL;
    Motor        AT %Q3.0    : BOOL;
    Cylinder     AT %Q3.1    : BOOL;
END_VAR


PROGRAM Freeze
(* Here, SFCPause is set TRUE if the Motor protection or the
   emergency stop is activated. *)
VAR
    SetPause : SR;
END_VAR
```

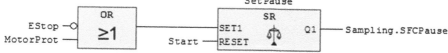

```
END_PROGRAM


PROGRAM Safety
(* When the SFC stops, the actions are not performed. Even
though Emergency stop is physically connected in the
drive circuits to the actuators, the signals to the
actuators are also deactivated in the program when the
sequence freezes. *)

  IF Sampling.SFCPause THEN
    Motor := Cylinder:= FALSE;
  END_IF

END_PROGRAM
```

On the next page is a POU that contains the sequence for sampling. Comments:

• When CapSensor detects a new item on the belt (see the NewItem transition code), it activates the Count step where NumItems is incremented.
• As long as fewer than 10 items have passed, the sequence goes in a loop back to RunBelt.
• When 10 items have passed, the sequence goes to the TakeSamples step, where the belt is stopped, the cylinder piston goes out, and the counter NumSamples is incremented.
• When the piston is completely out, the next step is activated and the piston returns. The path forward depends upon the Stop button and whether or not 50 samples have been taken.

```
PROGRAM Sampling
VAR_INPUT
  SFCPause   : BOOL; (* Object that must be declared
                       explicitly *)
END_VAR
VAR
   Stop        AT %I2.3   : BOOL;
   CapSensor   AT %I2.3   : BOOL;
   PistonOut   AT %I2.3   : BOOL;
   PistonIn    AT %I2.3   : BOOL;
   NumItems               : USINT;
   NumSamples             : USINT;
   RE1                    : R_TRIG;  (* Used in the NewItem
                                        transition *)
END_VAR
```

| ACTION ResetNum50 | ACTION ResetNumItems | ACTION Count_StepEntry |
| NumSamples := 0; | NumItems := 0; | NumItems := NumItems + 1; |

ACTION TakeSample_StepEntry	TRANSITION NewItem
NumSamples:= NumSamples + 1;	RE1(CLK := CapSensor);
	NewItem := RE1.Q;

In the boxes above, you will find the content (in ST code) for the actions and the NewItem transition that are called from the SFC sequence. Even though keywords such as ACTION and TRANSITION are implicitly given in CODESYS, they are included here in order to be a little more consistent with respect to IEC 61131-3. The figure at the right shows how the application is structured in folders in CODESYS. An editor is opened for programming by double-clicking on one of the folders (all of the languages in the standard can be used).

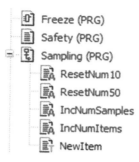

13.3   Example 3: Product Control: SFC

A producer of freeze-dried food is monitoring the final product of food bags for any errors in marking, wrong weight, or leakage (lack of vacuum). This is done by having the bags transported down a conveyor belt to a station where they are weighed and a picture is taken with a Vision camera (industrial camera). At the end of the belt, there are gates for sorting the bags into various categories. See Figure 13.2. Here is a brief description of the facility:

- Photocells are used to detect items on the belt (**BagOnBelt**) and to detect whether the bag is standing in an upright position (**BagUpright**) (the bags must be upright for the camera to be able to read them).
- A load cell is used to check the weight. The cell puts out an analog **Weight** signal. The weight must be between 240 and 260 g.
- The Vision camera is programmed to be able to check whether the label is correctly positioned and that there are no holes in the bags (they must be crumpled because of vacuum). The camera also has its own inputs and outputs. A discrete signal (**TakePicture**) is used to tell the camera that it should take a picture. The program that is in the camera analyzes the picture and sets one or more outputs high, depending upon whether there is an error with the bag or not. The signals from the camera are given logical names **BagOk**, **LabelErr**, and **Leakage**. *Note: The signals change only each time a new picture is taken.*

Three gates are placed, one after the other, at the end of the conveyor belt to send the bags along in the right lane. **Selector1** sends the bags on to lanes (A and B) or (C and D), **Selector2** sends bags down lane A or lane B, and **Selector3** sends bags down lane C or lane D. Wrong weight has a higher priority than leakage, which has a higher priority than a labeling error. Figure 13.1 shows a sketch of the facility.

The gates are turned by single-action pneumatic cylinders with spring return. The gates are normally turned as shown in the illustration, but when the cylinders are given a high signal, the gates swing over.

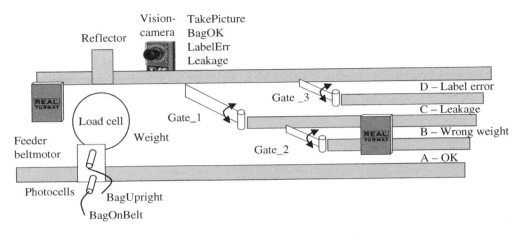

Figure 13.2 Product monitoring and sorting

13.3.1 Functional Description

- On a **Start** signal, the belt starts and a bag is fed out (the signal **Feeder** is set high for 1 second). (*Note*: The feeder is not illustrated in the figure.) After that, if everything is okay, a new bag is fed out onto the belt every 5 seconds. Then there is time enough to sort the previous bag before a new one arrives at the photocells.
- When the bag arrives at the weigh station (signal from the photocells goes high), the belt stops for 1 second so that the bag can be weighed and the camera can take a picture (**TakePicture** is set high). If only the **BagOnBelt** signal is high and the **BagUpright** signal is not, an alarm **BagDown** is set high and the belt remains still until someone lifts up the bag. The operator confirms this by activating Start.
- The gates are set to their proper positions by the return signal from the load cell and the Vision camera. The number of bags in each category is to be counted.
- If Stop is activated, the facility should stop before, or when, the next bag arrives at the photocells. Assume that Stop remains high until a new Start signal starts the facility again and deactivates the Stop button.

13.3.2 List of Variables

Summary of all signals represented by symbolic names:

Inputs	Outputs
Start	Feeder
Stop	Beltmotor
Weight (analog signal)	TakePicture
BagOnBelt	Selector1
BagUpright	Selector2
BagOk	Selector3
LabelErr	
Leakage	

13.3.3 Possible Solution

As always, there are many possible solutions. Here, we present one of them:

A separate sequence takes care of feeding out bags at a suitable tempo. This takes place continually every 5 seconds until Stop is activated or the BagDown alarm goes high. Objects that are used in both sequences (POUs) are declared globally. The main sequence (next page) handles weighing, picture taking, and sorting as follows:

- If a bag has fallen over after the photocells, the belt is stopped and the BagDown alarm goes high. The sequence does not continue until someone has lifted up the bag and pressed Start. Then the alarm is Reset the sequence continues with TakePicture.
- After 1 second, it is assumed that the load cell has stabilized. The program reads in the weight value and sets WeightOk either TRUE or FALSE. (For the sake of simplicity, grams were used for comparison.)
- The gates are positioned and the proper counter is incremented in accordance with the information about weight, leakage, and labeling. Note that WeightErr has the highest priority in sorting. Next to that comes leakage.
- As long as Stop has not been activated, the sequence continues in the Run step.
- There are two steps in the sequence where no actions are performed (Merge1 and Merge2). These steps converge OR branches.
- Most of the actions are direct actions on Boolean objects, but some actions are programmed "outside" the sequence. These are actions for incrementing the number of products and managing picture results.

```
VAR_GLOBAL
    Start      AT %IX2.0   : BOOL;
    Stop       AT %IX2.1   : BOOL;
    Feeder     AT %QX3.0   : BOOL;
    BagDown                : BOOL;
END_VAR


TYPE Camera :   // User-defined enumerated datatype
    (OkBag, LabelError, LeakBag);
END_TYPE


TYPE ProductData :   // Structured datatype based on Camera
STRUCT                  // This is used to store information
    PicResult : Camera; // on each product.
    Weight    : REAL;
    ID        : UINT (0..10000);
END_STRUCT
END_TYPE


PROGRAM Feed_Bags
END_PROGRAM
```

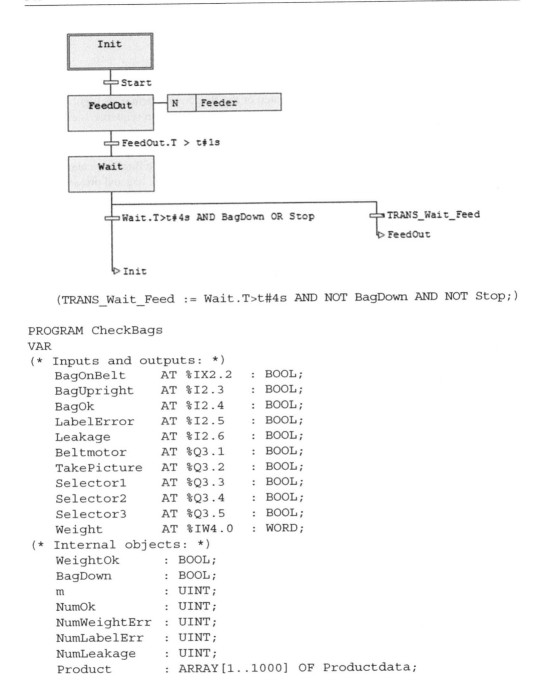

(TRANS_Wait_Feed := Wait.T>t#4s AND NOT BagDown AND NOT Stop;)

```
PROGRAM CheckBags
VAR
(* Inputs and outputs: *)
    BagOnBelt      AT %IX2.2   : BOOL;
    BagUpright     AT %I2.3    : BOOL;
    BagOk          AT %I2.4    : BOOL;
    LabelError     AT %I2.5    : BOOL;
    Leakage        AT %I2.6    : BOOL;
    Beltmotor      AT %Q3.1    : BOOL;
    TakePicture    AT %Q3.2    : BOOL;
    Selector1      AT %Q3.3    : BOOL;
    Selector2      AT %Q3.4    : BOOL;
    Selector3      AT %Q3.5    : BOOL;
    Weight         AT %IW4.0   : WORD;
(* Internal objects: *)
    WeightOk       : BOOL;
    BagDown        : BOOL;
    m              : UINT;
    NumOk          : UINT;
    NumWeightErr   : UINT;
    NumLabelErr    : UINT;
    NumLeakage     : UINT;
    Product        : ARRAY[1..1000] OF Productdata;
END_VAR
```

Finally, we present all the major actions that are called in the steps of the main sequence. Note how information about the individual items (ID, weight, and picture result) are stored for possible later use and history.

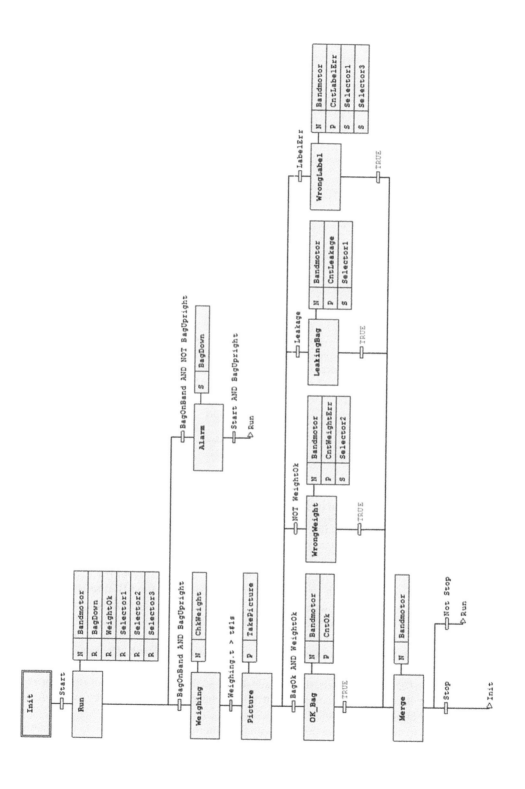

Actions

Aksjoner

- 📋 CheckBags (PRG)
  - 📄 ChkWeight
  - 📄 CntLabelErr
  - 📄 CntLeakage
  - 📄 CntOk
  - 📄 CntWeightErr

```
ACTION ChkWeight
  m := m +1;
  IF (Weight > 240.0) AND (Weight
    < 260.0)
  THEN
     WeightOk := TRUE;
  ELSE
     WeightOk := FALSE;
  END_IF;
  Product[m].Weight := Weight;
  Product[m].Id := m;
END_ACTION
```

```
ACTION CntOk
  NumOk := NumOk + 1;
  Product[m].PicResult:
    = OkBag;
END_ACTION
```

```
ACTION CntWeightErr
  NumWeightErr := NumWeightErr + 1;
  Product[m].PicResult := OkBag;
END_ACTION
```

```
ACTION CntLeakage
  NumLeakage := NumLeakage
    + 1;
  Product[m].PicResult :=
    LeakBag;
END_ACTION
```

```
ACTION CntLabelErr
  NumLabelErr := NumLabelErr + 1;
  Product[m].PicResult :=
    LabelError;
END_ACTION
```

13.4   Example 4: Automatic Feeder: ST/SFC/FBD

Cod spawn are fed in a research facility for marine fisheries. The spawn are separated according to genetic origin and size into 300 tanks (tubs). A PLC-controlled feeding robot is used to feed the spawn according to a fixed time schedule.

The robot is motor driven and moves on a rail that is suspended from the roof above the tanks. The feeding robot feeds out two types of food, food A and food B, through tubes that can be opened and closed by magnetic valves. See Figure 13.3. The type and quantity of food that are fed from the robot depend upon the number of the tank.

In order to know when the robot has arrived at the tank, an inductive sensor is placed on the feeder to detect metal clips that are fastened on the rail above each tank. The tanks are placed so that the robot can follow the rail around the room and in this way come back to its original position (position 0). In other words, the rail is installed so that it forms a sort of ring. The only information that the program receives about where the robot is, derived by counting the number of metal clips that it passes.

The feeding is to take place in accordance with the pattern shown in Table 13.1. The quantity is determined by how long the magnetic valves are held open.

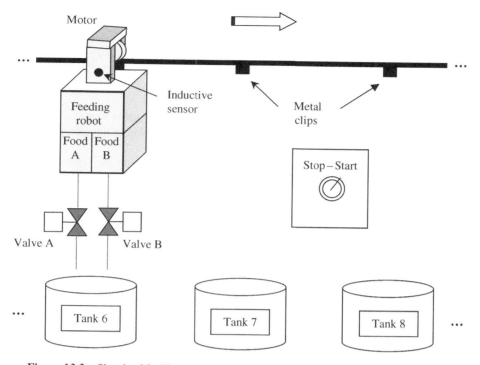

Figure 13.3   Sketch of facility with feeding robot, transport rail, and some of the tanks

Table 13.1   Shows when various tanks are fed, plus quantity, and type of food given

Tank nr.	Frequency	Food type A	Food type B	Quantity
1–100	Every hour	X		3 seconds
101–200	Every 2 hours	X	X	Both 3 seconds
201–250	Every 2 hours		X	6 seconds
251–300	Every 3 hours	X	X	Both 5 seconds

Other requirements and specifications:

- All of the external equipment, plus switches and sensors, are controlled by/give out discrete signals. Handling emergency stops takes place exclusively by means of hardware.
- At the start, assume that the robot is at the beginning of the rail at position 0 (which is marked with a metal clip as the tank positions).
- At the signal to start, the robot is activated and makes its feeding rounds in accordance with Table 13.1. After completing a round, the robot stops and waits in position 0 until it is time for the next round.
- When the switch is set to Stop, the robot should finish feeding the current tank and then go to the starting position.
- The robot moves at a speed that allows it to complete a feeding round at a maximum of about half an hour.

13.4.1 Planning and Structuring

The most important, and often the most difficult part of the job in developing a control for a facility, is to structure the problem. How should one tackle the many requirements and how should you manifest the requirements in the program design? There is no fixed answer, and the capability for making a structured program code is often proportional to experience.

Luckily, this ability is dependent upon wisdom to about the same extent, and we have learned some techniques that we can use to help us on our way. One of these techniques is to structure the problem by constructing a state diagram.

The challenge in this example is to find a good way of managing the feeding. Different tanks must have different quantities of food at different times. In order to accomplish this, we must test both tank number and how much time has elapsed. Figure 13.4 shows a state diagram that illustrates the problem.

The states in the diagram are mainly based upon the operations that the robot is to perform: *run*, *stop*, and *feed*. A separate state (To_Init) has been included where the robot runs straight back to the starting position without undertaking any feeding. This state is activated when the operator presses Stop.

When the robot is on a feeding round, it runs until the sensor detects that it is come to a new tank. When that occurs, the program jumps to a state (Count) where the robot stops and the counter is incremented. In this state, the decision is also made about food type and quantity. The results of these tests, which are based on tank number and time of day, activate 1 out of 3 possible feeding states: Feed_A, Feed_B, or Feed_AB.

On the following pages, we present two equivalent programs for control of the robot. Alternative 1 is written in SFC. Alternative 2 is written in ST and FBD.

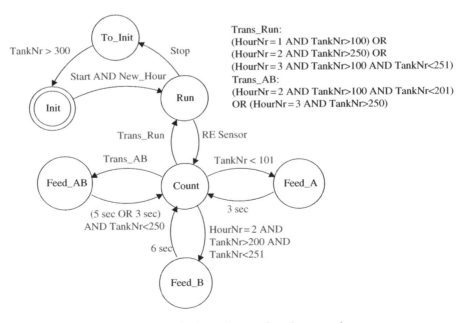

Figure 13.4   State diagram for robot control

13.4.2   Alternative 1: SFC

The feeding robot starts a new feeding round every hour, and feeding is done in accordance
with the specifications in Table 13.1 (and the state diagram). This means that the program
must also keep track of the *time*.

The time control is handled here with the help of a separate SFC sequence. The variables
Start, **Stop**, **HourNr**, and **New_Hour** are therefore declared as global variables.

The two SFCs below are not coded in any program but rather with a separate drawing tool
(MS Visio). This is done in order to obtain a more compressed diagram but also to show the
code for all the actions together in the diagram in their own fields under their action types and
action names. (To what extent this is possible in practice depends upon the implementation.)

```
VAR_GLOBAL
    Start       AT %IX3.0  : BOOL;   // Start switch (double-throw switch)
    Stop        AT %IX3.1  : BOOL;   // Stop switch (double-throw switch)
    Sensor      AT %IX3.2  : BOOL;   // Detects metal clips on the rail.
    Motor       AT %QX4.0  : BOOL;
    ValveA      AT %QX4.1  : BOOL;
    ValveB      AT %QX4.2  : BOOL;
    New_Hour               : BOOL;
    HourNr                 : USINT;
END_VAR


PROGRAM TimingControl // Sets the variable New_Hour and
                      // increments the variable HourNr
```

```
END_PROGRAM
```

```
PROGRAM MainProgram
VAR
    TankNr    : UINT;
END_VAR
```

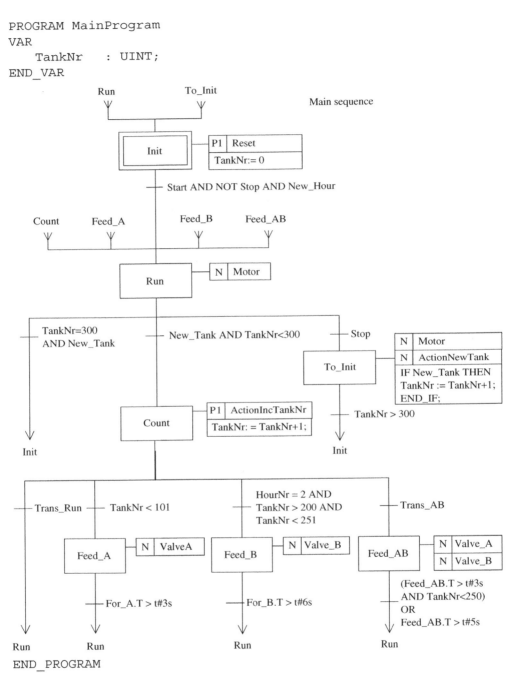

```
END_PROGRAM
```

The variable New_Tank that is used in some of the transitions is an output from an R_TRIG that tests when the signal from the tank sensor goes high. (In the state diagram in Figure 13.4, this is given as "RE Sensor.")

The sequence also contains two transistors that are coded outside the sequence in order to save space. These are the transistors named Trans_Run and Trans_AB:

```
TRANSITION Trans_Run
    (HourNr=1 AND TankNr>100) OR (HourNr=2 AND TankNr>250) OR
    (HourNr=3 AND TankNr>100 AND TankNr<251
END TRANSITION

TRANSITION Trans_AB
    (HourNr=2 AND Tanknr>100 AND TankNr<201) OR
    (HourNr=3 AND TankNr>250)
END TRANSITION
```

13.4.3 Alternative 2: ST/FBD

This program is written with its starting point in the code in alternative 1. The time control is also managed here in a separate POU, but this time it is implemented in FBD. The main program is written in ST, based upon a CASE structure. (The global variables are the same so the declaration is not repeated here.)

```
PROGRAM TimingControl
(* When an hour has passed, the New_Hour variable becomes
TRUE. At the same time, HourNr is incremented. When HourNr is
equal to 4, HourNr is set to 1. In other words, HourNr takes
on the values 1, 2, and 3. *)
VAR
    One_Hour : TON;
    Run      : RS;
END_VAR
```

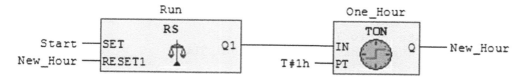

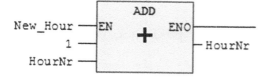

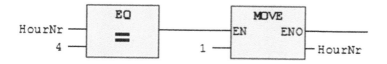

This time, the main program is implemented in ST. Since the process and facility have a
behavior that can be described with a set of distinct states, it is natural to use CASE statements.[1] The test variable is of the enumerated data type where the separately defined possible
values of the variable are states from the state diagram.

```
TYPE      States: (Init, Run, To_Init, Count, Feed_A, Feed_B,
                   Feed_AB);
END_TYPE

PROGRAM MainProgram
VAR
   State      : States := Init; // Declaration of the test
                                 // variable State, based on the
   New_Tank : BOOL;             // user-defined datatype States.
                                 // Initial value is Init.
   RE1, RE2 : R_TRIG;
   Wait_3s, Wait_5s, Wait_6s  : TON;
END_VAR

CASE State OF
Init: // Initial state. Awaiting New_Hour = True
      TankNr := 0;
      Motor := FALSE;
      IF Start AND NOT Stop AND New_Hour THEN
          State := Run;
      END_IF

Run:  // Runs on to the next tank if Stop is not activated
      Motor := TRUE;
      RE1(CLK:= Sensor, Q=> New_Tank);
      IF Stop THEN
          State := To_Init;
      ELSIF (New_Tank AND TankNr<300) THEN
          State := Count;
      ELSIF (New_Tank AND TankNr=300) THEN
          State := Init;
      END_IF

To_Init: // Runs the robot back to start position
      Motor := TRUE;
      RE2(CLK:= Sensor, Q=> New_Tank);
      IF New_Tank THEN
          TankNr := TankNr + 1;
```

[1] See Section 11.6 on page 339.

```
        END_IF
        IF TankNr = 300 THEN
            State := Init;
        END_IF

Count: // The robot has arrived at a new tank. Tests whether
       // feeding should take place
        Motor := FALSE;
        TankNr := TankNr + 1;
        IF Trans_Run() THEN
            State := Run;
        ELSIF TankNr<101 THEN
            State := Feed_A;
        ELSIF (HourNr=2 AND TankNr>200 AND TankNr<251) THEN
            State := Feed_B;
        ELSIF Trans_AB() THEN
            State := Feed_AB;
        END_IF

Feed_A: // Feeds with food type A
        Wait_3s(IN:=ValveA , PT:=T#3S);
        ValveA := TRUE;
        IF Wait_3s.Q THEN
            ValveA := FALSE;
            State := Run;
        END_IF

Feed_B: // Feeds with food type B
        Wait_6s(IN:=ValveB , PT:=T#6S);
        ValveB := TRUE;
        IF Wait_6s.Q THEN
            ValveB := FALSE;
            State := Run;
        END_IF
Feed_AB: // Feeds with food types A and B
        Wait_3s(IN:=ValveA , PT:=T#3S);
        Wait_5s(IN:=ValveA , PT:=T#5S);
        ValveA := ValveB := TRUE;
        IF (Wait_3s.Q AND TankNr<250) OR Wait_5s.Q THEN
            ValveA := ValveB := FALSE;
            State := Run;
        END_IF

END_CASE
END_PROGRAM
```

A closer analysis of the state Count will reveal that two of the test conditions that enter into the IF statements are not specified. This is because these conditions are implemented as separate *functions* that are called from the main program. There are several reasons that this is done in this way:

- First, the conditions are rather large.
- Second, the function names will themselves function as a Boolean variable. Since these are only logical tests, there are no input arguments to the functions. When the conditions being tested in the functions are satisfied, the function name is assigned to the result, that is, a logically high value.
- The third reason for doing it in this way is to show that it is possible.

Here are the function codes:

```
FUNCTION Trans_Run          :  BOOL
IF
    (HourNr =1 AND TankNr>100)  OR
    (HourNr =2 AND TankNr>250)  OR
    (HourNr =3 AND TankNr>100 AND TankNr<251)
THEN
    Trans_Run := TRUE;
END_IF;
END_FUNCTION

FUNCTION Trans_AB : BOOL
IF
    (HourNr =2 AND TankNr>100 AND TankNr<201) OR
    (HourNr =3 AND TankNr>250)
THEN
    Trans_AB := TRUE;
END_IF;
END_FUNCTION
```

Part Five

Implementation

14

CODESYS 2.3

14.1 Introduction

This chapter introduces the CODESYS programming tool, version 2.3 (specifically version 2.3.9.42), developed by Smart Software Solutions GmbH.

There are four reasons why I have chosen to present this particular development tool:

1. CODESYS follows the IEC 61131-3 standard to a very great extent and is therefore well suited for learning programming in accordance with the standard:
   - It supports all five defined languages (+ an extra variant of FBD).
   - All data types are implemented.
   - All of the standard operators, functions, and function blocks (FBs) (plus many more) are implemented.
   - Addressing conforms to the standard.
   - Comments, identifiers, and syntax are also in conformity with the standard.
2. CODESYS is a hardware-independent programming system for PLCs, microcontrollers, and other hardware. By this, we mean that the tool has not been developed by a PLC manufacturer, but rather that there are many (>250) hardware manufacturers who have chosen to use CODESYS as the development tool for their equipment. One example is WAGO,[1] which, in the course of a very short time, has gained a large market share with its controllers and I/O connectors for Ethernet and fieldbuses such as CAN, DeviceNet, and so on.
3. The program contains a simulator so that the program code can be fully tested without the requirement for hardware. It also comes with a graphic visualization tool.

---

[1] WAGO Kontakttechnik GmbH & Co. KG. Check www.wago.com.

Programmable Logic Controllers: A Practical Approach to IEC 61131-3 Using CODESYS, First Edition. Dag H. Hanssen.
© 2015 John Wiley & Sons, Ltd. Published 2015 by John Wiley & Sons, Ltd.

4. Finally, yet importantly, CODESYS can be downloaded *free of charge* from **codesys.com** (you must register first). The program is in its full version and is not time limited, although some additional components are time limited.

CODESYS stands for "controller development system" and offers a simple (?) approach to the powerful IE C-specified programming languages and standardized functions and FBs. In addition, it offers a series of other libraries with ready-made functions for a large number of applications.

Here, we will look at editors, menu selections, usage, and capabilities of CODESYS by studying and implementing a concrete project example. En route we will take up the following subjects (not necessarily in the order given):

• Starting CODESYS and defining a new project
• Configuring a target PLC
• Setting up communications
• Adding libraries
• Defining new program organization units (POUs)
• Various program editors
• Compiling the program and correcting syntax errors
• Defining special data types
• Running the program with the built-in simulator or soft PLC

14.2   Starting the Program

After installation, you will probably find the program on the desktop. Look for the icon ![icon]. If the software is distributed by WAGO, it will be installed under C:\Program Files (x86)\WAGO Software\CODESYS V2.3, and you will find it on the Start menu, probably under Programs\WAGO Software\CODESYS.

Start the program by double-clicking on the icon or the filename CODESYS.exe.

Have a little patience and a program window will open as shown in Figure 14.1. If the program has been run previously on your machine, the last project will open. If you want to define a new project, you must in that case select New on the File menu (or click on the New button in the row at the left of the CODESYS window).

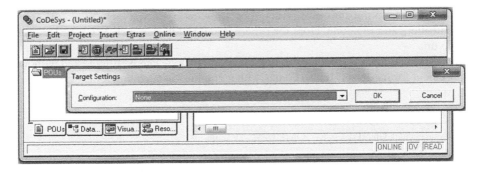

Figure 14.1   Starting a new project

Specify a controller, if any

CODESYS will now ask you if you want to specify which "target" (software PLC, ordinary PLC, or other hardware) you are working with. Search through the list (configuration) until you find the proper hardware. Possibly, you could choose "3S CODESYS SP PLCWinNT" if that is installed. This is a soft PLC you can choose to install together with CODESYS. If you have not made this choice or do not have any hardware, you can select **None**. You will still have the capability of testing your code by using a built-in simulator.

In the window in Figure 14.2 below, I have selected the PLC 750-881 from WAGO, which is a controller with Ethernet connection.

Make a new POU and store the project

You will now get questions about whether you want to define a POU (see Figure 14.3). If you do not want to do that now, you can click on Cancel. You can define as many POUs as you want or need later. If you select OK without changing any of the selections, the software will define a default program POU with the name PLC_PRG.

You can naturally use another name or select a different language.

A little review about POUs:

- A POU can be a function, an FB, or a program.
- A POU can be associated with actions and can call up other POUs.
- Every POU consists of a declaration part and a code part.
- The code is written in one of the IEC standard's programming languages that include IL, ST, SFC, FBD, or LD, in addition to the proprietary CFC.
- Standard FBs such as timers and counters are found in the *standard.lib* library. These are automatically included in the new project.

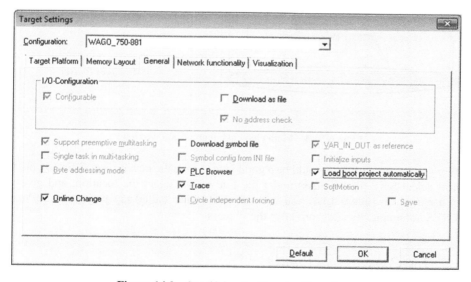

Figure 14.2   Specifying the Target with settings

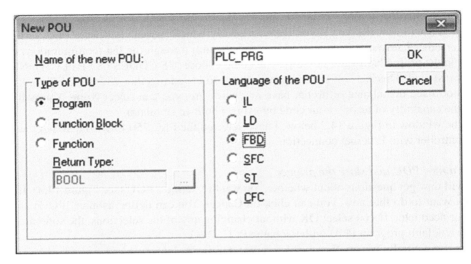

Figure 14.3   Defining a new POU

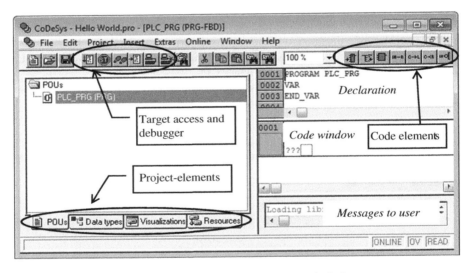

Figure 14.4   Main elements, menus, and windows

Before you go any further, it could be a good idea to save the new project. Click on the Save button or select Save (or Save As) under the File menu, select the location, and give your project a name. (In Figure 14.4, you will see that I have called my project Hello World.) CODESYS automatically adds .pro after the filename.

14.2.1   The Contents of a Project

A project contains all the objects in a PLC program, including the following elements: the POUs, data types, visualizations, and resources. This last includes libraries, targets (PLCs), and the configurations of these.

In the following, we will discuss many of the menu choices (the ones that are not self-explanatory) and explain the essentials of using the software.

14.3   Configuring the (WAGO) PLC

Double-click on "PLC configuration" that you find under Resources (Figure 14.5). See Figure 14.6.

Right-click on K-Bus (this is the bus that handles communications with the modules and that is integrated into the PLCs from WAGO). Select Edit and the configuration window as shown in Figure 14.7 will open.

Now you can add the modules that are connected to your target node (PLC). Click on the + sign on the menu line or right-click and select Add. Look around in the library until you find the module you want. Figure 14.8 shows an example of a completed configuration.

It is important that the modules follow in the same order in which they are mounted from left to right in the PLC rack and that you select the correct module *variant* if there are several

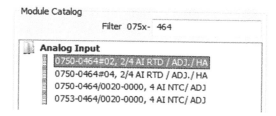

Figure 14.5   Alternative choices for the module 750-565 (an RTD module)

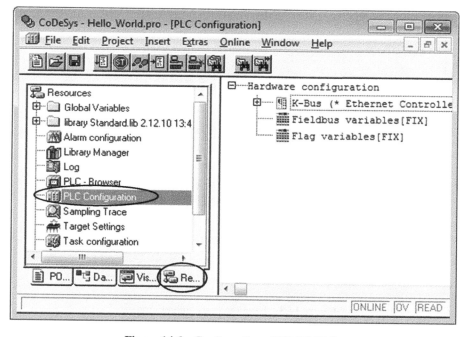

Figure 14.6   Configuration of WAGO PLCs

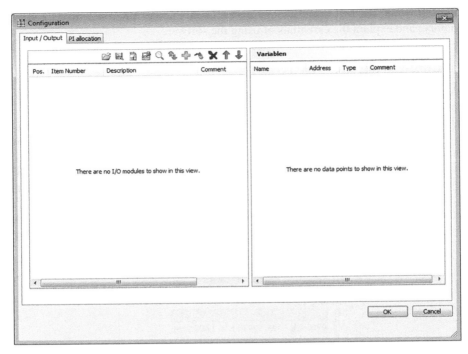

Figure 14.7   The configuration window

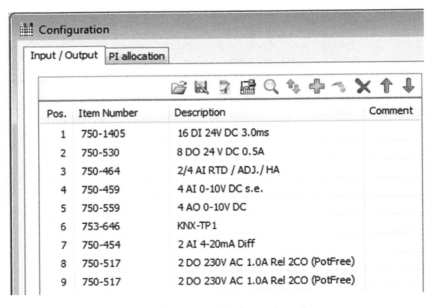

Figure 14.8   Example of a configuration

choices. This last item is important because one variant, for instance, may assume that four bytes are generated in the I/O card, while another variant of the same module perhaps assumes two bytes.

If you choose wrong, you will find that all your addressing is wrong and that you will not be able to get into contact with your I/Os. This is true for the WAGO module 750-464, for instance, which is an RTD module that can be configured as four two-wire inputs or two three-wire inputs.

WAGO offers a special tool for configuring the modules, the WAGO IO-CHECK. The program can also be used to accomplish an entire configuration. This is done most simply by utilizing the scanning functionality in the tool for scanning a connected PLC to find the modules that are connected. IO-CHECK does not find all the modules unambiguously, so a little correction is necessary. When you are satisfied, you can export the configuration to an XML file that can be opened within the CODESYS configuration window.

A screen capture from WAGO IO-CHECK is shown in Figure 14.9.

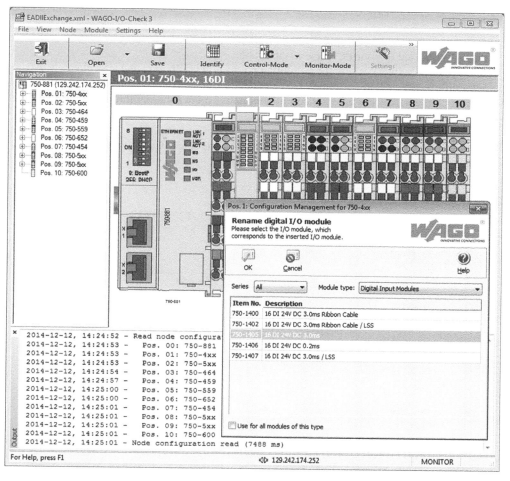

Figure 14.9   Screen capture from WAGO IO-Check

It is also possible to open IO-CHECK directly from the configuration window in CODESYS. You will find a button for this on the tool line. Therefore, you can scan the PLC for modules and correct the list if necessary, either in IO-CHECK or in CODESYS. It can happen that after you have pressed Save and closed IO-CHECK, you find that CODESYS is uncertain about one or more modules. In that case, a small window will appear where you must specify exactly which variant of the module you have mounted in your rack.

Note: In order to be able to scan the PLC, you must first get into contact with it. We will look at this in the next section.

14.4   Communications with the PLC

In order to be able to send program code to the PLC or to scan the PLC for modules, we must first establish communications. Here, you have several choices; you can communicate with a PLC that is:

- Locally connected to your PC via a service cable
- Connected to a network where the communications go via Ethernet and a local gateway (see next section)
- Connected to a network where the communications go via Ethernet through a gateway that is on another PC in the network

Click on Online on the menu line in CODESYS and select Communication Parameters. Then you will get the window shown in Figure 14.10.

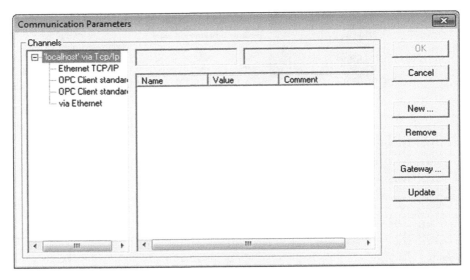

Figure 14.10   Configuring communications parameters

14.4.1   The Gateway Server

On the right side of the window in Figure 14.13, you will find a button marked Gateway. This is a communications server that starts automatically when you start the PC. You will find a symbol for the server down at the lower right in the Windows Taskbar. When you go online with the PLC, you will see that this symbol lights up.

   If you are only going to communicate with a PLC that is connected to the same PC as you were working on, you do not need to do anything more with the gateway. If you need to communicate with a PLC that is connected to another PC, then you must specify a password in the gateway to the PC that the PLC is connected to.

   If you right-click on the symbol, you will see some choices such as Inspection → Settings. Here, you can specify a password, among other things (see Figure 14.11).

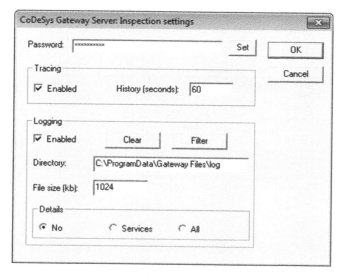

Figure 14.11   Configuration of the gateway server

14.4.2   Local Connection via Service Cable

If this is the first time that CODESYS is being used after installation and you do not have a communications setup that you can reuse, select New. In the window that opens then, you can specify a new channel by giving it a name and selecting a driver.

If you are going to communicate with the PLC via a service cable, select Serial (RS232) as shown in the figure below (I gave my channel the name Local_Com). Then click OK and you will go back to the previous window.

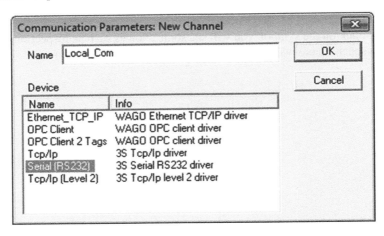

Now you have to specify the correct Com port. You are probably using a USB cable, so in practice this is a virtual Com port. The easiest way to find out which Com number was assigned to the port when you plugged in the cable is to go to the Start menu in Windows and select Devices and Printers. (Mine was assigned COM8.)

Then keep clicking in the Value field on the port until the proper number is shown (Figure 14.12).

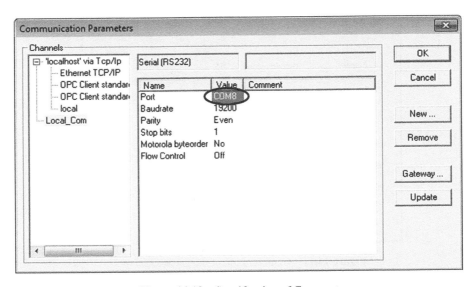

Figure 14.12   Specification of Com port

14.4.3   Via Ethernet

Specification of communication is much like that for the serial port; only now we choose the driver 3S TCP/IP (or possibly the specific WAGO Ethernet TCP/IP):

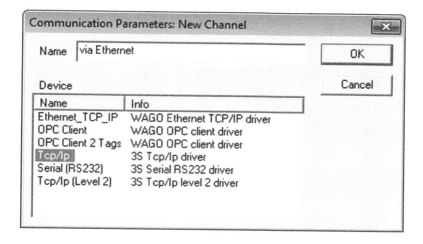

Give the channel a suitable name and press OK. Then specify the PLC's IP address (Figure 14.13).

The IP address can be set statically by the PLC in question, or it can be assigned by the Dynamic Host Configuration Protocol (DHCP). You need to know this anyway. If you are using a PLC from WAGO, you can use the WAGO Ethernet Settings tool which you can get free of charge from WAGO Support.

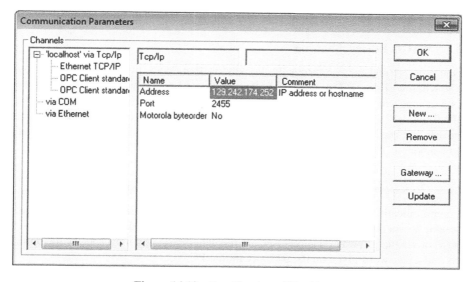

Figure 14.13   Specification of IP address

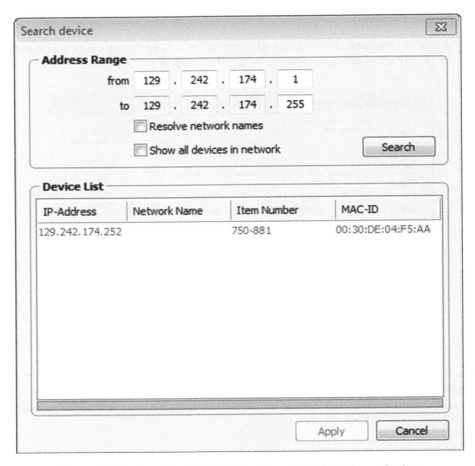

Figure 14.14   Search for the PLC's IP address in WAGO Ethernet Settings

14.4.3.1   WAGO Ethernet Settings

Open the program and select Settings. In the window that opens, then select "Search device." Then the window shown in Figure 14.14 will open. If you know which subnetwork mask your PC has, you can search all connected units on that subnet (possible addresses from 1 to 255).

In the figure below, the program has found my unit and the address it has been assigned in the network. (If there are several PLCs connected, check the MAC address of the unit you wish to connect to.)

14.4.4   Communication with a PLC Connected to a Remote PC

In the communications window, you will see a button marked "Gateway." When clicked, you will be able to specify whether you want to communicate using the local gateway (address localhost) or via the gateway on another PC. In this latter case, you must specify the remote IP address and a password given on the gateway in that PC:

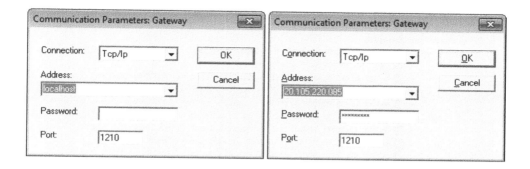

14.4.5 Testing Communications

When you have provided the necessary values in CODESYS, you can test whether you have contact with the PLC by going to the menu Online → Login. If you get contact, you will probably pull up the following window:

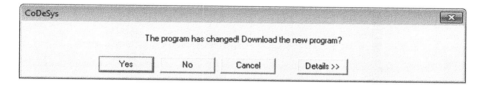

Select Yes and your project (with your configuration plus the default specifications) will be uploaded into the PLC. To test whether you have configured correctly, you can again open the configuration window. Here, you can read the status of the digital inputs and manipulate the status of digital outputs (by clicking in the boxes associated with the individual outputs) (see Figure 14.15).

A red arrow pointing right marks an output and a yellow arrow pointing left marks an input.

14.5 Libraries

When you define a new project, the library **standard.lib** is automatically loaded. You can check this for yourself by double-clicking Library Manager, which you will find under Resources. Then the window shown in Figure 14.16 will open. The standardl.lib library includes, among others, all the POUs of the FB type that are defined in the standard. These are:

Bistable	RS and SR
Counters	CTU, CTD, and CTUD
Timers	TON, TOF, and TP
Triggers	R_TRIG and F_TRIG

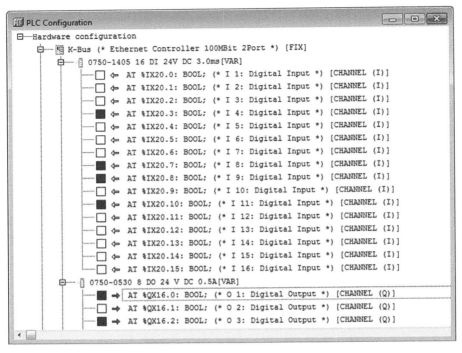

Figure 14.15   Analysis of addresses and tests of (digital) I/O

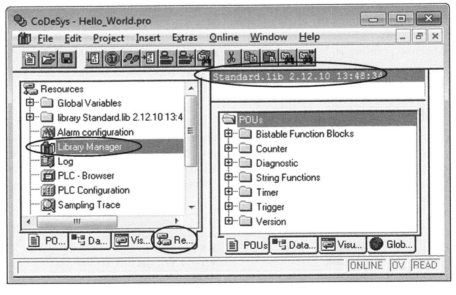

Figure 14.16   Default library in a new project

The library also contains the standard string functions along with a few other FBs that are offered by CODESYS. (Since these are not defined in the standard, they will not be discussed here.) You can call up information about the selected FB by clicking on a particular FB in the contents list.

There is also a series of other libraries that accompany the installation of CODESYS which you can add. To do that, click with the right mouse button in the window where the standard. lib library is displayed and select *Additional Library*. You now will be able to look around in the catalogs for other libraries.

A library that has been mentioned in the book is Util.lib. You will find this under the catalog ...\CODESYS V2.3\Library. In this library, you will find, among other things, controllers such as a PID plus a series of FBs for mathematics and signal processing. An external source for a library that contains hundreds of functions and FBs is OSCAT, which you can download free of charge on the Internet.

If you have programmed some POUs that you think you could use again, it is also possible to save a project as a library by selecting Save as... and specifying type .lib. (If you wish, you can export the project by selecting Export... under Project in the menu and saving the project to a file that you can import into another project by selecting Import....)

14.6   Defining a POU

Click on the POU banner down to the left in the CODESYS window. Then right-click in the window above (where the overview of your POUs is shown). Then select Add Object... and a new window opens (see Figure 14.17).

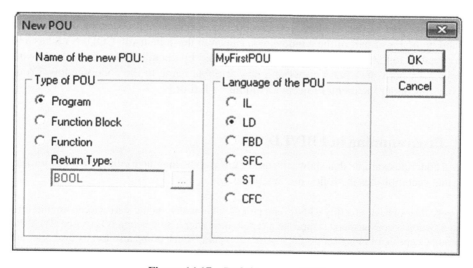

Figure 14.17   Defining a new POU

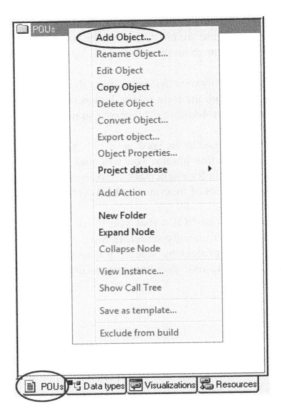

Specify the desired name and type and select the programming language. In the figure, there is defined a POU of the type FB named MyFirstPOU and the language selected is LD. Click OK and the code and declaration window to our new POU will open.

In the upper part of the window, you can declare variables and instances of FBs that you need, and in the lower part of the window, you can enter the code itself. CODESYS has a built-in functionality for "Autodeclaring" which is activated by default. This means that a window for declaration pops up when you write a new variable name in the code window. (You can deactivate this under the menu Project → Options → Editor.)

14.7   Programming in FBD/LD

To take a concrete example that shows the use of the graphic language editors, we will implement a code that accomplishes the following functionality:

Suppose that we have a facility with several pumps, all of which should start at a certain time after a Start button is activated and stopped at a certain time after a Stop button is activated. The delay should be capable of being set differently for each pump. Each pump also has its own Start and Stop buttons.

Here, it is a good idea to make a special FB that handles the input and output connections of a pump and then to make a little program that we use in each instance of the FB for each pump that is to be controlled. We will make this FB in the following in both FBD and LD.

14.7.1   Declaring Variables

We began by coding our FB. We can solve the functionality for this by using an RS flip-flop for starting (Set) and stopping (Reset) and two timers to provide the delayed connection and delayed disconnection. Make a new POU of type FB called PumpControl and select FBD for the language.

When we now go to upload the code, there are several ways to proceed. We can first declare the necessary instances of FBs that we need—two timers and one RS block—or we can utilize the autodeclaration function in CODESYS. For the sake of illustration, we will choose a combination here.

Click in the programming field with the right mouse key and select Box (or key Ctrl+B on the keyboard). CODESYS will now set up an empty box which by default is a two-input AND operation. In order to change this, you can double-click on the word AND (if the word is not already highlighted) and press F2 on the keyboard. Then the Input Assistant will open where you can look around for the desired function or FB (Figure 14.18).

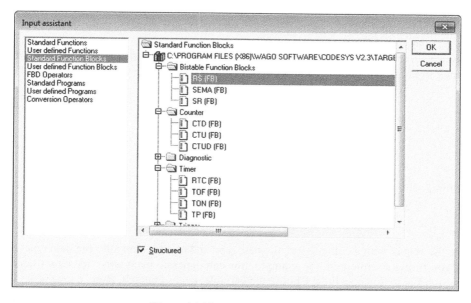

Figure 14.18   Input Assistant (F2)

If you know the name of the FB or the function you want, you can also write it (in this case you can write RS). After you have made your choice, press Enter. Now you will have created the following code:

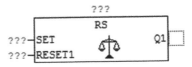

Click on the question marks on the top side of the block and write in the name you want, for example, OnOff, and press Enter. You will then get the following window:

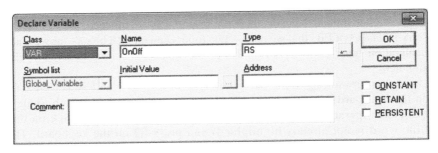

Here, you can just press OK, but note that you are specifying an internal instance of an RS (a standard FB) with the name OnOff. Under "Class," you can instead specify that it is to be declared globally, that is, be accessible to all POUs. The selections VAR_INPUT and VAR_OUTPUT are seldom used in conjunction with declaration of an FB instance, but we will soon use these as well for declaration of other variables.

After you have pressed OK, you will see that you have got a new line in the declaration field between the keywords VAR and END_VAR.

Now we will declare some general variables we need. Click in the declaration field, move the cursor to after VAR_INPUT, and press Enter. Write in the following:

xOn	: BOOL;
xOff	: BOOL;
tOnDelay	: TIME;
tOffDelay	: TIME;

Similarly, after the keyword VAR_OUTPUT, you write

xOut	: BOOL;

Note the syntax with a colon before the data type and a semicolon after the data type. Note that if you forget a semicolon, for example, this can generate many error messages later on. Use the Tab key to tidy up a little. Choose the variable names yourself. Here, a lowercase x has been used to denote a Boolean variable and a lowercase t to show that the data type is TIME. Since there are several input variables, we have also used names there to make it simpler to identify them.

Also declare two timer instances of type TIME as internal objects (under VAR), to which you give the names OnTime and OffTime, in addition to another RS block with the name Run. Your declaration window will now look something like this:

```
0001 FUNCTION_BLOCK PumpControl
0002 VAR_INPUT
0003     xOn          :BOOL;
0004     xOff         :BOOL;
0005     tOnDelay     :TIME;
0006     tOffDelay    :TIME;
0007 END_VAR
0008 VAR_OUTPUT
0009     xOut     :BOOL;
0010 END_VAR
0011 VAR
0012     OnOff    :RS;
0013     Run      :RS;
0014     OnTime   :TON;
0015     OffTime  :TON;
0016 END_VAR
```

14.7.2 Programming with FBD

We will now add more code based on the use of the objects and variables already declared. Note that instead of writing in the variable names in the code, you can press F2 and select them from the list of variables that have already been declared:

- Click on the question marks on the left side of the existing block **OnOff** and enter the variable **xOn** for the SET input and **xOff** for the RESET1 input.
- In the same way, click on the right of the output from the block (to the right of Q1). You will see a little square that indicates that you can insert something there. Right-click and select Box again. Overwrite AND with TON to enter a timer. Give this the already declared name **OnTime**. Replace the question marks on the PT input with the variable **tOnDelay**.
- Insert a new box in the square to the right of the timer. There you specify an RS to which you assign the declared name Run. You will now have the code:

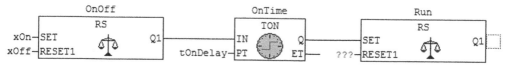

- Now right-click on the little line that marks the RESET1 input in the Run block and insert a new box. That will be the second declared timer, **OffTime**. Connect the PT input to the variable **tOffDelay**.

- Then insert a box by right-clicking the little line before IN on OffTime. Now replace AND with NOT in order to indicate an inverter. As the input to this, we will use the output from the RS block OnOff. CODESYS does not offer the functionality in FBD to insert vertical "wiring," so instead, we must use "object referencing." Therefore, write OnOff followed by a full stop (a dot). A list of the object's inputs and outputs will then pop up. Select Q1.
- Finally, it remains only to indicate what will come out as the result of our code. Click with the right mouse key in the square after the Run block and this time select *Assign* to make an output connection. Replace the question marks with **xOut**. The finished code for your FB should look like this:

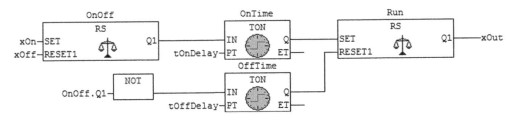

Since this is an FB, we unfortunately cannot test it until we have made a program that calls it up. We will do this in the next section.

Some other things about the use of the FBD editor:

- A good alternative to the NOT function is to use the built-in inversion functionality. All input and output signals on the block can easily be inverted by right-clicking on the line in question and selecting "Negate." That will bring up a little circle on the line to indicate that the signal is being inverted.
- Similarly, there is a built-in Set–Reset functionality that you can also activate by right-clicking. You can then choose that a variable associated with a signal from a block is set high (Set) when the conditions permit it so that it is kept high until it is set low (Reset) some other place in the code.
- You can specify a label at the top of each network. This is used to identify the network if you have the need to jump to a named network in the code.
- You can also comment in the various networks. To insert a comment in the network, you can, for instance, right-click on the gray field at the left of the network (where the network number is) and select "Comment." That will give you an opportunity to write in a comment.

14.7.3   Programming with LD

To demonstrate some of the functionality in the LD editor, we will now implement an FB in LD that functions in a similar way to the program we wrote in the previous section. We could, with a few changes, implement the FBD code directly in LD, but then we would not have thrown much light on the typical LD elements.

Make a POU of the FB type, this time choosing LD as the language. For instance, you can call it PumpControl_LD. In order to avoid writing a declaration for the variables again, you can highlight the declarations from the previous POU (select everything beginning with VAR_INPUT through the last END_VAR) and copy (Ctrl+C). Make the corresponding selection in the new POU (so that you replace the keywords that were there previously), and paste in (Ctrl+V) your copy.

Here, we are going to use Set and Reset coils instead of the RS blocks (just for the fun of it...). So delete therefore the Run-block declaration. Then change the data type of the object OnOff from RS to BOOL. We will now insert the code shown in Figure 14.19.

One possible procedure for inserting the code is as follows:

- Click on the symbol for a Contact in the menu (-I I-). You can either right-click and select "Contact" or use keys Ctrl+K. You will now have produced a contact in your code with question marks above it. Write in the variable name **xOn**.
- Click on the line at the right of contact and select the symbol for a Set coil on the menu (S). On the upper side of this, you can enter the variable **OnOff**.
- Insert a new rung (right-click "Rung After") and insert a similar code as above, but this time with the variable **xOff** on the contact and a Reset coil connected to **OnOff**.
- Insert still another rung with a new contact that is here connected to the variable **OnOff**. Click to the right of the contact and insert the timer OnTime. You will find a button for timers in the menu, or you can right-click and select from the list. Specify **tOnDelay** on the PT input.
- Then insert a Set coil after the Q-output to the timer. Connect it to **xOut**
- Copy the previous rung by first clicking on the gray field to the left of the network and press Crtl+C directly followed by Ctrl+V. You will now have made two identical rung. In the latest rung, change the names to OffTime and tOffDelay. Then right-click on the contact and select "Negate" to get an inverted contact. Right-click on the coil symbol and select Set/Reset to change the coil to a Reset coil.

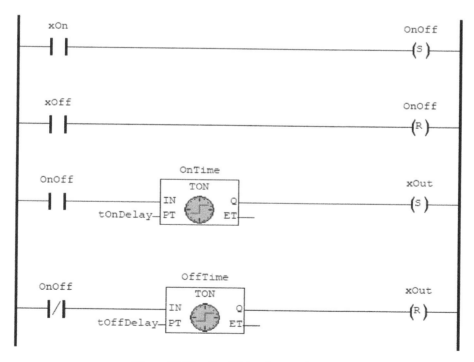

Figure 14.19   Our FB implemented in LD

Now it is finally time to test our FBs. So make a new POU in LD of the type Program, or use MyFirstPOU if you made it previously.

We will now insert an instance of our FBs in the code window. Select "Box with EN" from the menu or right-click the menu. (This implies that the box we are inserting gets an Enable input that will automatically be connected to the power rail in LD so that the code in the block will be executed in any event.)

Now click on AND in the box that comes up and press F2 to open Input Assistant. Click "User-defined Function Blocks" and select one of your FBs:

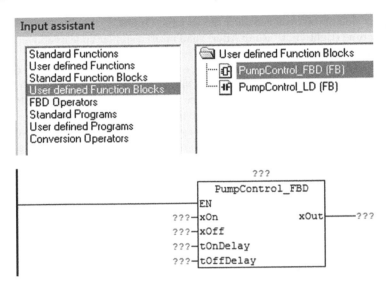

As you would expect, we need to give our instance a name and connect variables to the inputs and outputs. You can therefore declare the necessary objects beforehand in the declaration field. (*Note*: Times can be specified directly in the code so we do not need to detour through any variables for the inputs.)

In the declarations shown in the following, I have included the necessary objects and variables to control two pumps (testing both of my FBs). If you do not have a PLC connected and want to run the code in simulator mode, you drop the addresses.

```
PROGRAM MyFirstPOU
VAR
        Pump1           : PumpControl_FBD;
        Pump2           : PumpControl_LD;
        P1              AT %QX16.0   :BOOL;
        P2              AT %QX16.1   :BOOL;
        Start_P1        AT %IX20.0   :BOOL;
        Start_P2        AT %IX20.1   :BOOL;
        Stop_P1         AT %IX20.2   :BOOL;
        Stop_P2         AT %IX20.3   :BOOL;
END_VAR
```

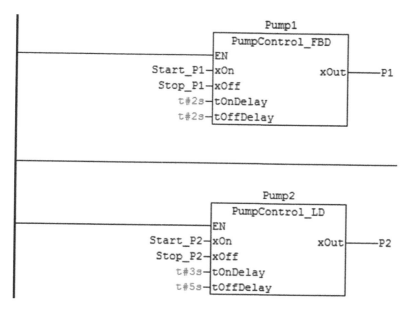

Figure 14.20 Code for calling our FBs

14.8 Configuring Tasks

All the programs that we want to download in a PLC must be connected to a task. If this is not done, the programs will not be compiled by CODESYS or transferred to the PLC. As described in Chapter 5, one can define several tasks of different types and with differing priority. One or more POUs of the program type can therefore be associated with each task. This also means that your project can contain programs that are not necessarily related to each other; you will determine yourself which ones you want to test or run.

Go again to the Resources banner and double-click on "Task configuration." A window will open in which you can define new tasks and associate programs:

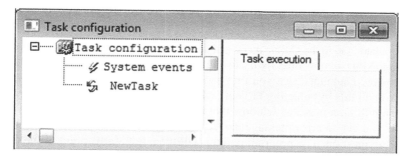

Right-click on "Task configuration" at the top of the window and select "Append task." Then specify the name and indicate the desired type of task (and any priority). In Figure 14.21, I have defined a cyclic task named MyTask with a cycle time of 100 ms,

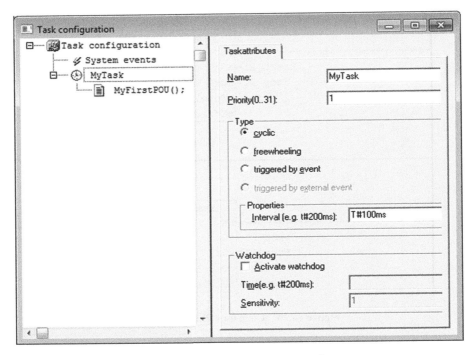

Figure 14.21 Defining a new task

which means that the program that is associated with this task will be executed 10 times per second.)

To associate a program, right-click on the name of the task and select "Append program call." You will now have the opportunity to look around for the program that you want to connect to. You can also write in the name of the program. (Here I have entered our little program, MyFirstPOU.

14.9   Downloading and Testing Programs

If you are not connected to a PLC, you can still test your program because CODESYS contains an integrated simulator. Go to the Online menu and activate this by clicking on "Simulation mode."

Even though you can now directly try to compile and run the program by selecting Online → Login, it is recommended that you first try compiling only the code in order to discover any errors. You do this by selecting Project → Build from the menu line or by pressing F11. You will then pull up a message window that informs you about errors or tells you that all went well. If you get an error message that reports a syntax error, you can double-click on the message in question. The program pointer will then, hopefully, point to the position of the actual error in the code. (Note that it is not certain that the compiler will be able to identify uniquely where the error is located or what is wrong. Sometimes, it only indicates the symptoms from the error.)

Correct any errors and then go to Login. You will then get the following message:

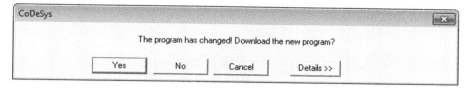

Click on Yes and your desired code will be downloaded to the PLC (or the simulator). Set the PLC (simulator) on Run by pressing F5 or clicking on Online → Run.

Note that you also have access to such frequently used functionalities via a special row of buttons under the menu line:

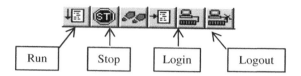

Now we can hope that your program will run and that you can test it by manipulating values. To do that, you can double-click on the desired variable. If this is a Boolean variable, the text < := **True** will appear on the right side of the variable. (Double-clicking on it again will change it to False.) See Figure 14.22.

The variable, however, has not yet changed state. In order for this to take place, you must write the desired value to the PLC by selecting Online → Write Values (Ctrl+F7).

Note that if you are working with a physical PLC, you cannot manipulate variables connected to an input in this way because the PLC will scan your inputs and overwrite your attempt to change the variable. Instead, you can select Online → Force Values (F7). Similarly, you must use "Force Values" if you want to manipulate values for variables (outputs) that are updated from the code.

In this way, you can test your code for various combinations of signal states. If you double-click on an analog variable, you get the capability of writing in a new value. It is also possible to manipulate values in FB instances, as Figure 14.23 shows.

Note that you can open several windows while you are online, so that you can check anything that is taking place in user-programmed FBs that are called up by your program.

14.9.1   Debugging

Debugging is a powerful and extremely useful functionality for testing the code and looking for logical errors. By adding one (or more) so-called breakpoints, the program execution will stop when it reaches a breakpoint. For example, you can run the program one instruction at a time and in this way closely follow what happens when the program is running in order to discover errors and weaknesses in your code.

When you are online, click on the gray field on the left of an instruction or a network. See the figure below where I have done this for network 2 in my program.

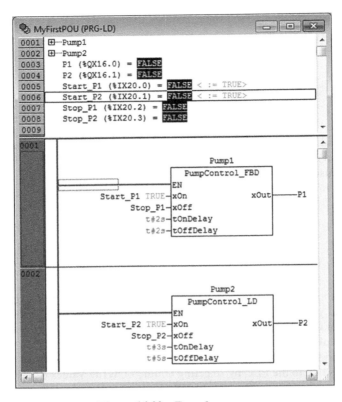

Figure 14.22   Test of program

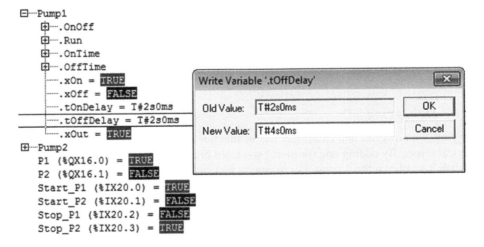

Figure 14.23   Online manipulation of PT values to a timer

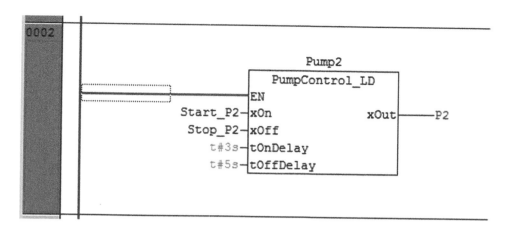

The execution of the program will then halt there and wait for an action from the user. Press F8 (Online → Step In) to run the next instruction or network. If the network contains a call to another POU, this will be opened in the editor so that you can continue to run one instruction at a time in the called POU. When all code lines have been executed there, the program pointer will return to the next network in the main program. Finish debugging and run the program as normal by selecting Run (F5) again.

Step over (F10)
If you do not need to debug the code in a called POU, you can select "Step over" instead. Then the code in the called POU will be executed in its entirety.

Single Cycle (Ctrl+F5)
This selection means that the PLC will perform one single cycle. It can be useful if you want to check whether a counter functions, for instance.

14.10   Global Variables and Special Data Types

To close this chapter, we will take a quick look at how you can declare global variables and define your own special data types.

Under the Resources banner, you will find Global_Variables. Just double-click and a window will open. All the variables you declare there will be global, which is to say they can be used in all POUs. Global variables can also be used for addresses or given as initial values, for instance. Note that if you have a *local* variable in a POU with the same name as a global variable, the local one will be used by the program.

Definition of special data types is useful in some situations. This applies particularly to enumerated data types and structured data types. This latter can be used to declare variables that have submembers (see, e.g., Section 13.3, where we define a structured data type called "ProductData").

You will find a special banner for data types in CODESYS. Right-click the folder "Datatypes" and select "Add object." Write in the desired name and click on OK. The figure below shows the definition of an enumerated data type called States:

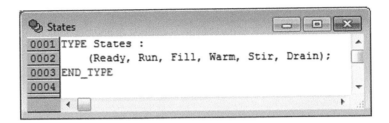

Special data types are used in the same way as the standard types. The declaration below shows an example of a declaration based on the States data type, together with the use of a couple of standard data types. Note that you can also provide an initial value for enumerated types:

```
PROGRAM Hallo
VAR
        Start    AT %IX20.0   :BOOL
        Stop     AT %IX20.1   :BOOL;
        Temp     AT %IW4      :WORD;
        Phase    :States := Ready;
END_VAR
```

15

CODESYS Version 3.5

This chapter introduces very briefly the CODESYS programming tool, version 3.5 (service pack 3), developed by Smart Software Solutions GmbH.

You will find many similarities between the two CODESYS versions but also some differences, especially regarding the integrated development environment (IDE).[1]

Chapter Contents

- Start CODESYS and define a new project
- Add libraries
- Define new POUs
- Declare user-defined datatypes
- Declare variables and instances of standard functions and function blocks
- Compile programs and correct syntax errors
- Configure and use the Gateway Server
- Run, monitor and debug the program with the built-in software PLC

15.1 Starting a New Project

After starting the program, you will get a screen image that looks approximately like the one shown in Figure 15.1. You can select whether you want to:

- Start a new project (File → New Project)
- Open an existing project (File → Open Project)
- Upload code from a PLC connected through the Gateway (File → Source upload)

---

[1] Integrated development environment.

Programmable Logic Controllers: A Practical Approach to IEC 61131-3 Using CODESYS, First Edition. Dag H. Hanssen.
© 2015 John Wiley & Sons, Ltd. Published 2015 by John Wiley & Sons, Ltd.

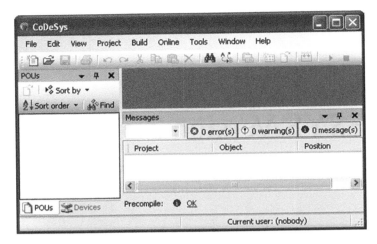

Figure 15.1   Start-up window

When you select New Project, a window like the one shown in Figure 15.2 will open. Assume here that you are going to write a program code for one device. The simplest thing to do then is to select "Standard Project" because this will save you a little configuring. Remember to give the project a reasonable name and to specify where you want it to be saved. Press OK.

The selection of "Standard Project" also means that CODESYS will define the following automatically:

- A POU with the name PLC_PRG the associated application
- A cyclic Task where the POU "PLC_PRG" is called up every 200 ms
- References to the newest available libraries (containing standard and supplier-defined functions and function blocks)

All this can be altered easily with a little configuration. This means that you can define your own POU with your own name, change the cycle time for the task or change the task type to freewheeling or event based.

After you have pressed OK, the program interface will appear roughly as shown in Figure 15.1, but the POU window and the Device window at the left will now contain more information. The selected project name will appear on the CODESYS title line and as the root folder in the POU and Device windows.

15.1.1   Device

Figure 15.3 shows how the folder structure in the Device window can look for our specific project. The Device window in CODESYS is a separate window that, if it is not already being displayed, you can show by selecting View → Devices. In this window, you will specify, among other things, which unit (PLC) is to be used. The Standard Project automatically contains the built-in soft PLC. In the project, this can have the name Device (CODESYS Control Win V3), depending upon which version of CODESYS you are using. If desirable, you can rename the Device name to, for instance, My_PLC.

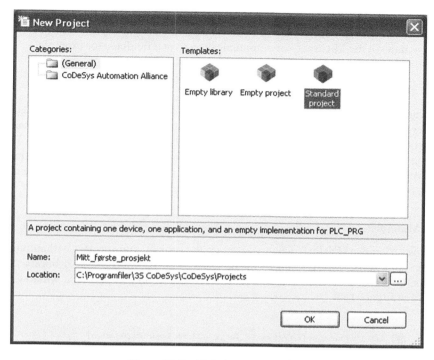

Figure 15.2 Defining a new project

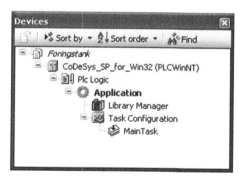

Figure 15.3 Units

Note that the automatically generated POU, PLC_PRG, is deleted from the folder structure. The reason for this is that all code is stored in separately defined program units in the POU window. We will get back to this in Section 15.2.

You can, of course, also specify a different (physical) PLC instead. This can be done by right-clicking on the root folder and selecting **Add Device**. This will open a window that shows all available and compatible PLCs. By available, I mean PLCs that you have installed *Target files* for.

Note: If you first mark the existing Device (here PLCWinNT) and then right-click on Add Device, you will pull up a different list. It shows an overview of *couplers* that you can select if you have units in the PLC rack for communication over a fieldbus, for example.

15.1.2   Application

An application is a collective concept for a concrete set of program codes, task configurations, and library references. It is quite possible to work with several applications simultaneously, because you can select which application is to run on the PLC (or in the simulator). For each application, we can configure how the programs will be executed. For example, some programs can run cyclically, others freewheeling or event based. It is also possible to build up hierarchical structures of several applications and run multiple applications on the same device.

Library Manager

If you chose "Standard Project" when you set up the project, your project will automatically contain an application with references to the latest version of the standard library. You can check this for yourself by double-clicking on the folder. This will pull up a window like the one shown in Figure 15.4.

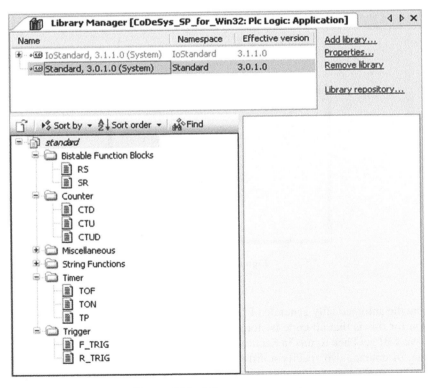

Figure 15.4   Library management

This standard folder has been selected here, and the contents of the folder are shown in the figure, below on the left of the window. Among other things, we recognize the standard function blocks such as RS, CTU, and TON. The standard library also contains functions that are not implemented by separate operators. This applies to string functions such as LEN and CONCAT, among others.

In addition to the standard library, you can choose to use functions and function blocks from many other special libraries. Simply select "Add library" and gorge yourself in a plethora of libraries.

Task Configuration

Here, you can configure the existing tasks or add any new tasks. The purpose of tasks is partly to organize the program, mostly to control how the program is executed in the device. See also Sections 1.3.3 and 5.3 for more information about tasks.

Often your project will consist of only one task. Then you do not need to do anything but check that the cycle time is satisfactory and that the program-type POUs you want to run are assigned to a task. See Figure 15.5. The figure shows that the individual POUs can be added

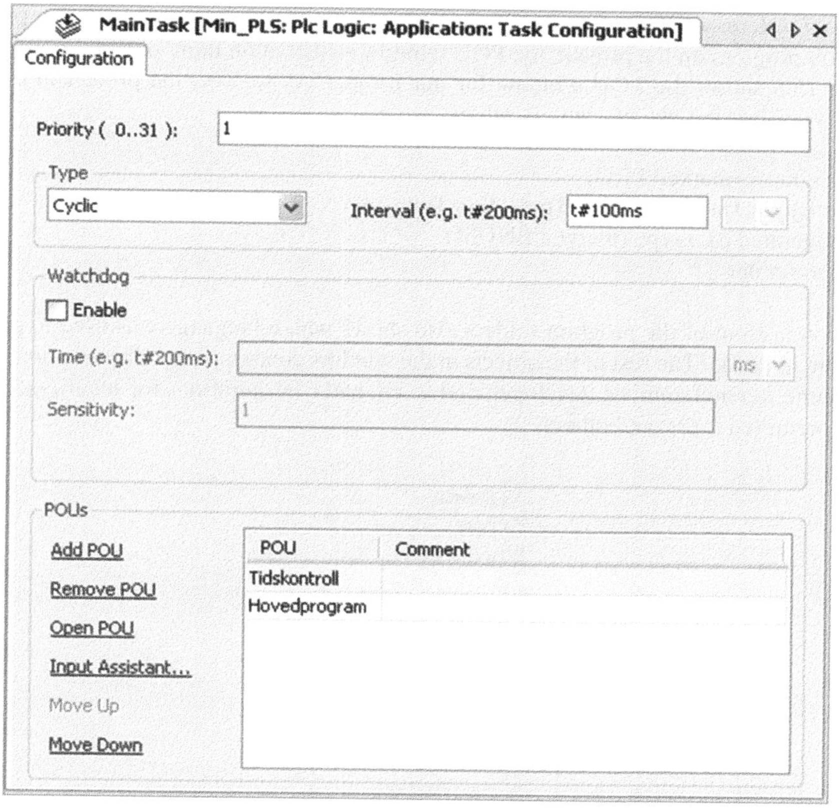

Figure 15.5 Task configuration

to the desired task and that the sequence in which the codes are executed can be predetermined.

15.2   Programming and Programming Units (POUs)

The other window at the left in the user interface has the name POUs. This window will contain all of the POUs that you program, some programs, functions, and function blocks, as well as some objects such as:

- Self-defined data types and structures (DUT—data unit type)
- Global variables
- Visualization objects

You can find out what folder structure the POU window can contain by right-clicking on the root name (your project name) in the window and selecting *Add Object.* See Figure 15.6.

(Selecting Device here has the same effect as in the Device window, namely, adding a new device in the project that will appear in the Device window.)

If you select a new program object (POU), the window will look like the one shown in Figure 15.7. (Here, you can choose the type of POU and the language you wish to program in.) As you progress on the project, the POU window will contain more objects.

Figure 15.8 shows the POU window for our project. As we see, the project in question contains the following objects, among others:

- Two programs (marked PRG)
- Four functions (marked FUN): Trans_0 to Trans_3
- An enumerated data type (marked ENUM)
- Global variables

The icon in front of the program folders also shows which language was used to program the POU in question. The rest of the objects in the window contain project information such as project name, version number, developer, and so on, and configurations for security, compiler version, permitted users, and others.

Figure 15.6   Objects that can be added

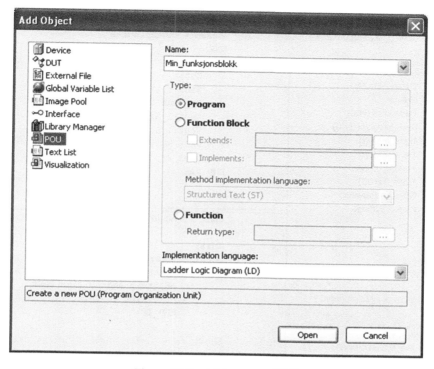

Figure 15.7 Adding a new POU

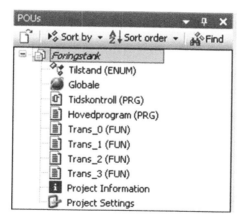

Figure 15.8 The POU window

As you open the programs, variables, or DUT objects, the code will be shown in a program editor on the right side of the screen. You can have as many objects as you wish simultaneously open. They will be arranged under individual banners in the program editor (Figure 15.9).

Figure 15.9   Larger extract from CODESYS that also shows a program editor

No matter which language you use to program the POUs, all of the objects will have a declaration field at the top where you declare the POU by name and type and declare variables. The window below the declaration field contains code in the language selected. If you use a graphical language, you will also have access to a special menu with objects that you can insert into the program code.

15.2.1   Declaration of Variables

Even though it is possible, and recommended, you do not need to declare variables in advance. If CODESYS does not recognize an identifier that you write, a window will come up automatically for declaration of variables (Figure 15.10).[2]

---

[2] This function is called Auto declare and can be configured away if desired.

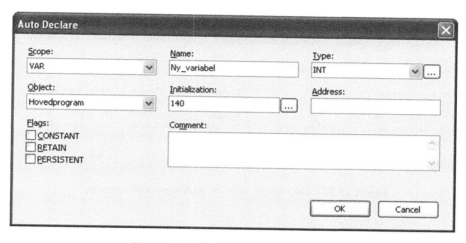

Figure 15.10   Auto-declaration window

The window will already contain the name of the POU and the identifier, but you must specify what type of variable you are declaring. If desired, you can give an initial value, and if it is an I/O type, you can specify an address.

As you declare variables, they will come up in the declaration field in the program editor. You can naturally edit the variable list subsequently if desired. When using "Auto declare," the variables have a tendency to come up every which way in the field, and then it can be a good idea to group them, according to data type, for instance. There can also be a need to write comments in the declaration field.

15.3   Compiling and Running the Project

When you are done programming, or even better, while you are still writing the program code, you must *compile* the project. (*Note*: Remember to configure tasks and be sure that all of your programs are assigned to a task.) In order to compile, you select Build on the menu (Figure 15.11):

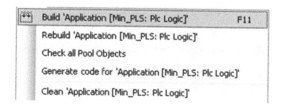

Figure 15.11   Compiling and building menu

If it is not already open, a message window will open. See Figure 15.12. Here, there will be information about the result of compilation. All syntax errors in the program will be shown with information about what is wrong and where in the code this takes place. Usually you will need to interpret this information in order to correct the errors:

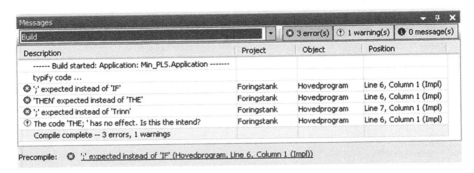

Figure 15.12   The message window with errors and warnings

When everything is right, it may possibly look like this (Figure 15.13):

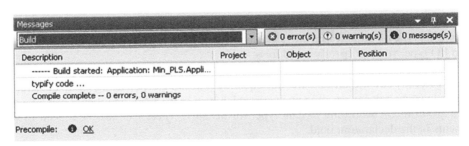

Figure 15.13   A successful build

Now, all that is needed is a little configuration of communications, and then you are ready to download the program to the (software) PLC.

15.3.1   Start Gateway Server and PLS and Set Up Communications

When the computer starts, a couple of CODESYS-related services will also start up automatically. These are the CODESYS Gateway and the CODESYS SP (SP=soft PLC). You will then have the following symbols on the line for task management in Windows (at the bottom right of the screen): and .

If they do not look quite the same as shown here, it is because they are not running (or perhaps because you are using an older version of CODESYS). If they have not started, you can click with the right mouse key on the symbols and start the services.

The next thing you must do is to set up a communications link between CODESYS and the PLC. This must be done even if the PLC is the built-in soft PLC. Perform the following three steps to set up the communications:

1. Open the dialogue window for communications.
2. Scan the network for available PLCs and select the desired Device (PLC).
3. Set the active path.

Open the Dialogue Window for Communications

This opens automatically if you try to connect to the PLC without first having configured the communications. We normally open this by going into the Device window and double-clicking on the PLC unit, for instance, My_PLC (PLCWinNT). Either way, you will pull up the following window (Figure 15.14):

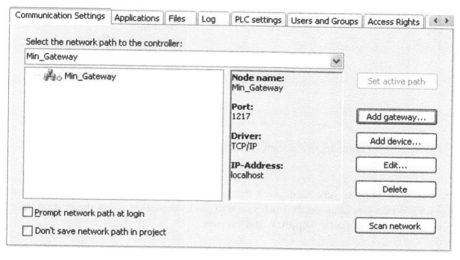

Figure 15.14   The communication settings window

This window shows a Gateway already configured. If you do not have a Gateway already configured, select "Add Gateway." Then specify the name and define the driver type **TCP/IP** and "IP address" **localhost**.

Scan the Network for Available PLCs

Press the **Scan network** button. Hopefully, the PC will then find the connected PLC or soft PLC. *Note*: Make sure that the one you want to use is up and running, either in the form that the service has started (software PLC) or that the physical PLC is connected to the PC and is powered.

It can happen that you will be shown several choices, either because you have several versions of software PLC installed or that your PC is connected to a network where several PCs are running with associated software PLCs. If there is only one soft PLC running, the window can look like this (Figure 15.15):

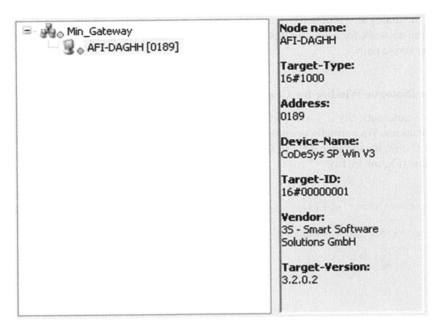

Figure 15.15   Scanning the network and choosing target

Here, the available unit has been given the name of the computer, with a port address in parentheses). When you click on the unit, you will get information about the unit on the right-hand side in the form of name, supplier, and version.

Set the Active Path

You do this by clicking on the unit that has come up under the Gateway and select *Set active path*. The desired connection will now be in **bold**.

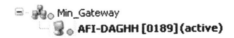

Now, you can (if desired) close the configuration window for the Device, go to the main menu in CODESYS, and log in:

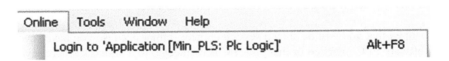

You will probably get the following window:

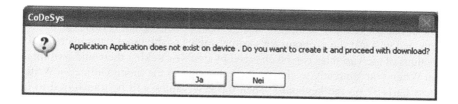

Press **Yes** and the project will be downloaded to the PLC. Finally, all that is left is to set the PLC on RUN to run the program. This is also done with the Online menu.

Though it is not covered here, CODESYS version 3.5 has, as version 2.3, good functionalities for debugging and forcing of variables.

15.4 Test Problems

Problem 15.1

(a) Open CODESYS and start a new project. Select "None" as Target. (We will use a simulator that is built into CODESYS.) Make a new program POU named Roots, and select as T (Structured Text) as the programming language. Store the project somewhere and give it a reasonable name.

(b) Go to the Resources banner → Task Configuration and define a new cyclic Task called Main with cycle time set to 1 second. Connect your POU to the Task and close this window.

Soon we will write the following program code into our POU:

```
Root      : B*B    -4*A*C;
IF Root < 0.0      THEN
    Nroots  :=   0;
    X1 :=   X2    :=   STRING_TO_REAL ('NaN');
    Info    :=   'No real roots';
ELSEIF Root =    0.0   THEN
    Nroots  :=   1;
    Info    :=   'Concurrent roots';
    IF a <> 0 THEN
        X1    :=   X2    :=   (-B+SQRT (Root))  /  (2*A);
    ELSE
        X1    :=   X2    :=   0;
    END_IF
ELSE
    Nroots  :=   2;
    X1 :=   (-B-SQRT (Root))  /    (2*A);
    X2 :=   (-B+SQRT (Root))  /    (2*A);
    INFO    :=   'Two real roots';
END_IF;
```

(c) Declare all the variables you need to for the code above.
(d) Write in the code and compile the project (F11 or Project → Build). Fix any syntax errors.
(e) Go to Online → Simulation mode. Transfer the code to the Simulator (Online → Login). Set the simulator to RUN (Online → Run). Now, your program is running.

   Now, we will test the program for various values of the input parameters A, B, and C. The values of the variables can be changed by double-clicking them and writing in a new value. When you are ready to change the values, go to the menu Online → Write Values or press Ctrl+F7 on the keyboard. Then the new values will be transferred to the PLC simulator.

(f) Change the values online to $A = -2$, $B = 3$, and $C = 2$. What is the result?
(g) Now, change the value of A to $A = 2$. Now, what is the result?
(h) Now, change the value of B to $B = 4$. What do you get now?
(i) What does this program do?
(j) Try to improve the program so that you get an answer when the values of variables are like those in item g.

Problem 15.2

We will now convert the program in Problem 15.1 to a function block.

(a) Make a new POU, this time type Function block. Give the POU the name Find_roots. Use ST as the programming language again.
(b) Copy the program code and variable declaration from the POU in Problem 15.1.
(c) Convert the variable declaration so that A, B, and C now become input variables; X1, X2, and Info become output variables and the rest (Roots and Nroots) as ordinary internal variables.
(d) Make still another new POU, type Program, and call it Calling_Fun. Select FBD as the language. Then go to Task Configuration and add this POU to your Task. (You can now remove the program call that is there from previously, but this is not necessary.)
(e) Declare the following variables in Calling_Fun: X, Y, Z, Root1, Root2, and Text. The last one is type STRING, the others are type REAL.
(f) We will now call up our function block (Find_roots) from the Calling_Fun POU. Go to the code window and click with the right mouse key. This opens an input assistance window where you can browse for POUs and other things. Go to "User-defined Function Blocks." Here, you will find your FB. Select it and press OK.
(g) Give the block a name and write something above the block, Roots, for instance. Again, you will get an input assistance window where you again must find your FB.
(h) Now, connect variables to your block's inputs and outputs. In order to access block's outputs, you need to click on the— on the first output with the right-hand mouse key and select "Assign."
(i) Test the new program with the same values as in Problem 15.1 and check that it works properly.

Bibliography

Else Lervik og Mildrid Ljosland. Gyldendal-Tisip. 2003: Programmering i C++ – En innføring i strukturert og objektorientert programmering. (82-05-30733-4).

Simon Haykin. Wiley, 1989: An Introduction to Analog and Digital Communications.

T.A. Hughes. XXXX: 3. Edition: *Programmable Controllers*.

IEEE 1451.2 (Institute of Electrical and Electronics Engineers). Sep. 1997: *Standard for a Smart Transducer Interface for Sensors and Actuators – Transducer to Microprocessor Communication Protocols and Transducer Electronic Data Sheet (TEDS) Formats*.

International Electrotechnical Commission. 2013: *Programmable Controllers Part 3, Programming Languages (IEC 61131-3), edition 3.0*.

Karl-Heinz John, Michael Tiegelkamp. 2001: IEC 61131-3: Programming Industrial Automation Systems. (3-540-67752-6).

Kurt-Even Kristensen, Petter Brækken. XXXX: EMC – *Del 1: Introduksjon, standardiseringsorganisasjoner, direktiver og normer*.

R. W. Lewis. 1995: Programming Industrial Control Systems Using IEC 1131-3. (0-85296 827-2).

Terje K. Lien. 1995: Digital Styring for Mekatronikk. (82-519-1201-6).

Ouwehand, Drost. XXXX: *Styrings- og automatiseringsteknikk, 1 og 2*.

Frank D. Petruzella. McGraw-Hill, 1998: Programmable Logic Controllers.

Max Rabiee. Goodheart-Willcox Company Inc, 2002: Programmable Logic Controllers.

Schneider Electric. Nov. 2002 and Jan. 2004: *Technical Documentation*.

Jon Stenerson. 2. Edition. Prentice-Hall, 1999: Fundamentals of Programmable Logic Controllers, Sensors and Communications.

Index

Printed and bound by CPI Group (UK) Ltd, Croydon, CR0 4YY

12/01/2025